THE POLITICS OF THE POLICE

The Blue-Coated Worker: A Sociological Study of Police Unionism, Cambridge University Press, 1978

Chief Constables: Bobbies, Bosses or Bureaucrats?, Oxford University Press, 1991

Beyond Law and Order: Criminal Justice Policy and Politics Into the 1990s (ed. with Malcolm Cross), Macmillan, 1991

Accountable Policing: Effectiveness, Empowerment and Equity (ed. with Sarah Spencer), Institute for Public Policy Research, 1993

Policing (ed.) Dartmouth, 1996

The Oxford Handbook of Criminology (ed. with Mike Maguire and Rod Morgan), 2nd edn, 1997

THE POLITICS OF THE POLICE

Third Edition

ROBERT REINER

Professor of Criminology
London School of Economics

OXFORD
UNIVERSITY PRESS

OXFORD
UNIVERSITY PRESS

Great Clarendon Street, Oxford OX2 6DP

Oxford University Press is a department of the University of Oxford.
It furthers the University's objective of excellence in research, scholarship,
and education by publishing worldwide in

Oxford New York

Athens Auckland Bangkok Bogotá Buenos Aires Calcutta
Cape Town Chennai Dar es Salaam Delhi Florence Hong Kong Istanbul
Karachi Kuala Lumpur Madrid Melbourne Mexico City Mumbai
Nairobi Paris São Paulo Shanghai Singapore Taipei Tokyo Toronto Warsaw
with associated companies in Berlin Ibadan

Oxford is a registered trade mark of Oxford University Press
in the UK and in certain other countries

Published in the United States
by Oxford University Press Inc., New York

British Library Cataloguing in Publication Data
Data available

Library of Congress Cataloging in Publication Data
Data available

ISBN 0–19–876543–6

1 3 5 7 9 10 8 6 4 2

Typeset in Adobe Minion
by RefineCatch Limited, Bungay, Suffolk
Printed in Great Britain by
T.J. International Ltd., Padstow, Cornwall

For Toby, Charlotte and Joanna

He who lets himself in for politics, that is, for power and force as means, contracts with diabolical powers and for his action it is not true that good can follow only from good and evil only from evil, but that often the opposite is true. Anyone who fails to see this is, indeed, a political infant.

Max Weber, 'Politics as a Vocation'

If the Lord does not guard the city, the watchman keeps watch in vain.

Psalm 127

What is good? . . . Only to do justice, and to love mercy, and to walk humbly with your God.

Micah, VI, v: 8

The romance of the police force is . . . the whole romance of man. It is based on the fact that morality is the most dark and daring of conspiracies. It reminds us that the whole noiseless and unnoticeable police management by which we are ruled and protected is only a successful knight-errantry.

G. K. Chesterton, *The Defendant*

CONTENTS

PREFACE TO THE THIRD EDITION

The politics of policing, like everything else, has been fundamentally transformed since I wrote the first edition of this book, in the last millennium, in the Orwellian year of 1984. Then the police were subject to a storm of political conflict and controversy. During the 1984–5 miners' strike they were in equal measure reviled by the Left and revered by the Right. Labour politicians like Jack Straw, Paul Boateng, and Peter Hain, together with future Labour politicians like Harriet Harman and Patricia Hewitt (then prominent in the civil liberties movement), campaigned to limit police power and autonomy, and sought to subject the police to primary control by democratically elected local government. This sharp polarization of political perspectives on policing was especially shocking as it came after some decades in the middle of the twentieth century when the British police seemed to stand above politics, as consensual symbols of national pride and solidarity.

By the time I wrote the second edition, in 1992, policing had become less intensely politicized. The love affair between the Conservatives and the police cooled, as ministers began to wonder why there seemed to have been no pay-off in terms of falling crime rates for the special treatment the police had received during the 1980s relative to the rest of the public sector. On the other side, Labour, in its new realist guise under Neil Kinnock and John Smith, sought to recapture lost ground in the politics of law and order by courting the police. The shadow home secretary, Tony Blair, successfully won back public confidence for Labour when he promised to be 'tough on crime and tough on the causes of crime'. For their part, police chiefs had come to realize the urgent need to regain popular support, which had been eroded by a succession of scandals together with increasing public concern about crime and disorder. In the early 1990s there was a growing consensus between political and police elites about the need to reform policing in a community-oriented direction, aiming to ensure efficiency and quality of service.

All this was abruptly changed in 1993, when Conservative Home Secretary Kenneth Clarke launched a package of police reforms, which were continued enthusiastically by his successor, Michael Howard. They were predicated on an explicit narrowing of police priorities to 'catching criminals', and a reconstruction of police organization and management on 'businesslike' lines to ensure the economic achievement of the government's performance targets.

The New Labour government elected in 1997 broadly accepted the changes in police governance of the mid-1990s, even though they were almost the obverse of the model of accountability many of them had campaigned for during the 1980s. However, Labour placed policing in a different context with the Crime Reduction Programme and the Crime and Public Order Act of 1998. These require the police to work in partnership with local government and other social agencies to produce evidence-led analyses of local crime and disorder problems, and develop 'joined-up' strategies for their solution, regularly monitoring their success.

The problems of police discrimination, corruption, and abuse, which were at the heart of political conflict in the 1980s, have not gone away by any means, and the media continue to highlight recurring police scandals in these areas. But they have been relatively submerged by an overriding and consensual concern with security and protection from the risks of crime and disorder. As Jack Straw has rightly pointed out, the fact that Stephen Lawrence's murder has become the emblematic cause célèbre of policing in the late 1990s indicates a sharp contrast with the early 1980s. Then—as now—racial discrimination by the police was a highly contentious issue, but in the urban disorders of the 1980s the key complaint was discriminatory policing of young black men as suspects (which remains a potent concern, as indicated by the controversies around stop and search). However, the demand for effective and equal protection of ethnic minorities against crime, starkly symbolized by Stephen Lawrence's brutal and unsolved murder (still unsolved at the time of writing, after more than seven years), has come to the political forefront. There is a new consensus around the prioritization of crime control and reduction as the priorities for policing, with partisan conflict raging about which party can deliver this most effectively.

What continues to be overlooked is the wider social context of policing. Indeed, this is increasingly bracketed out as the focus narrows on what works in policing—the pursuit of magic-bullet strategies like 'zero tolerance' that hold out the deceptive promise of a technical solution to the problems of crime and disorder. The analysis of the history of policing in this book argues that, while police strategy is important, the successful legitimation of the British police in the nineteenth and early twentieth centuries depended upon the wider social process of increasing social inclusion and the spread of citizenship. The apparent decline in the effectiveness and legitimacy of the police since the late 1960s was only superficially due to failures of police policy and tactics. The key changes were in the wider social context, above all in the shift to neo-liberal, free-market economic policies, with a reversal of the general (if slow and spasmodic) trend to increasing social equality and solidarity that had prevailed since the eighteenth century Enlightenment. Interdependent with the recent transformation of political economy and social structure, there has occurred a cultural revolution, the growth of an increasingly rugged individualism and neo-Social Darwinist celebration of the survival of the fittest. Policing an ever more fragmented and pluralistic post- or late modern world has become an increasingly fraught enterprise.

This book's review of the history, functioning, and governance of the British police suggests that there is a fundamental paradox of policing, encapsulated in the quotes in the frontispiece. Policing is about the basic intransigences of human nature and social organization. As elaborated in the Introduction, policing is the aspect of control in any social relationship or group that is directed at the identification and emergency rectification of conflict and deviation. Its resource in accomplishing this is legitimate force, and its mode of deployment is surveillance with the threat of sanctions. Policing inherently operates with dirty hands. It uses morally dubious means to achieve the overriding imperative of preserving and reproducing social order. In divided and complex societies, however, there is unlikely to be agreement about the borderline between order and oppression. One side's reasonable and necessary force is the other's unjust tyranny. The police have developed in modern societies as the specialist organization charged with the maintenance of order, and entrusted with the capacity to deploy the legitimate force that states monopolize. This 'diabolical power' is a perpetual scandal in liberal democracies which—notwithstanding the inequalities and conflicts generated by complex market societies—purport to represent popular will and the rule of law.

The paradox is that not all that is policing lies in the police, to paraphrase Durkheim on the contract. The police will appear more successful the less they are actually necessary. The sources of order lie outside the ambit of the police, in the political economy and culture of a society. To the extent that these provide most people with meaningful and rewarding lives, conflict, crime, and disorder will be relatively infrequent. Subtle, informal social controls, and policing processes embedded in other institutions, regulate most potential deviance. When these informal control processes are successful, the police will appear highly effective in crime prevention, and deal effectively and legitimately with the crime and disorder that do occur. The police stand as romantic symbols of order and morality, 'knights errant' ever ready to protect against threats.

The last three decades of the twentieth century were characterized by a set of profound transformations. Social and economic inequality and exclusion increased sharply and rapidly, reversing the post-Enlightenment slow march of solidarity and justice. The popular and political reactions to the attendant dramatic rise of crime and disorder are increasingly punitive and harsh. Policing is being pressured to have zero tolerance of the socially marginal and outsiders. The war of all against all that is inherent in laissez-faire economics enjoins people to become ever more ruthlessly assertive defenders of purely individual interest. In short, the three pillars of the good life identified by the prophet Micah, justice, mercy, and humility, have been undermined. With the conditions of civility eroded, 'the watchman keeps watch in vain'. Good policing may help preserve social order: it cannot produce it. Yet increasingly this is what is being demanded of the police.

As in the first two editions of this book, I wish to pay my intellectual debts, but without putting any responsibility on others for arguments or opinions they might not share. As the references indicate, my understanding of policing owes much to numerous scholars and writers who were listed in the prefaces of the previous editions, many of whom have become friends. They include (in alphabetical order) John Alderson, David Bayley, Trevor Bennett, Egon Bittner, Jean-Paul Brodeur, Mike Brogden, David Brown, Maureen Cain, Mike Chatterton, Stan Cohen, David Dixon, David Downes, Richard Ericson, Nigel Fielding, Marian Fitzgerald, David Garland, Steven Greer, Frances Heidensohn, Dick Hobbs, Simon Holdaway, Mike Hough, Barrie Irving, Tony Jefferson, Les Johnston, Tony Judge, Leonard Leigh, Mike Levi, Barry Loveday, Mike Maguire, Peter Manning, Geoffrey Marshall, Rob Mawby,

Doreen McBarnet, Mike McConville, Eugene McLaughlin, Wilbur Miller, Rod Morgan, William Ker Muir Jr., David Nelken, Tim Newburn, Clive Norris, Maurice Punch, Philip Rawlings, Cyril Robinson, Paul Rock, David Rose, Andrew Sanders, Stephen Savage, Andrew Scull, Joanna Shapland, Clifford Shearing, Lawrence Sherman, Jerome Skolnick, David Smith, Nigel South, Richard Sparks, Betsy Stanko, Philip Stenning, Kevin Stenson, John Styles, Ian Taylor, Laurie Taylor, Tank Waddington, Sandra Walklate, Mollie Weatheritt, Jock Young, and Michael Zander. In writing this third edition I have drawn much from a new generation of scholars who began publishing in the 1990s, including Carole Adams, Ben Bowling, Jennifer Brown, Tom Bucke, Adam Crawford, Chris Crowther, Bill Dixon, Carolyn Hoyle, Martin Innes, Ian Loader, Carol Martin, Debbie Michael, Karim Murji, Jim Sheptycki, Graham Smith, Howard Taylor, Neil Walker, and David Wall. Looking at that list I realize with some shock that I have examined or supervised nearly all their Ph.Ds.—police researchers seem to be getting younger all the time. I owe a special debt to my own Ph.D. supervisor, Michael Banton, for getting me started in the study of policing, over thirty years ago. Needless to say, none of the above is responsible for the failings of what follows.

As with all writers my most profound debts are highly personal. My children, Toby and Charlotte, now grappling with their own university work, have stimulated me with fresh ideas throughout all three editions of this book. My wife, Dr Joanna Benjamin, was working on a book of her own while this was completed, so there has been a sharing of absent-mindedness. None the less she has provided constant encouragement, inspiration, and a model of intellectual commitment. My sister Ann and her family have also been an unfailing source of support in good as well as hard times. Finally, our dog, Carina, has taken me for refreshing walks that kept me going.

I owe my original impetus and inspiration for anything I do to my late parents. As the Book of Proverbs (1: 8) enjoins, I will endeavour to hear the moral instruction of my father and not forsake the law of my mother.

INTRODUCTION: POLITICS, POLICE, AND POLICING

WHO ARE THE 'POLICE'? WHAT IS 'POLICING'?

Most research on the police has been concerned primarily with immediate policy matters. Researchers have usually assumed a taken-for-granted notion of the police and their proper functions (Cain 1979). A particular modern conception has tacitly been taken to be inevitable. The police are identified primarily as a body of people patrolling public places in blue uniforms, with a broad mandate of crime control, order maintenance and some negotiable social service functions. In addition, the police organizations contain non-uniformed detectives, concerned primarily with the investigation and processing of criminal offences, as well as backroom administrative staff and managers.

Anyone living in a modern society has this intuitive notion of what the police are. However, to understand the nature and role of policing, especially over a broader span of space and time, requires some conceptual exploration of the taken-for-granted idea of police. Modern societies are characterized by what can be termed 'police fetishism', the ideological assumption that the police are a functional pre-requisite of social order so that without a police force chaos would ensue. In fact, many societies have existed without a formal police force of any kind, and certainly without the present model. The police's contribution to the control of crime and maintenance of order today is debatable, as studies of police effectiveness indicate (see Chapter 4). The problematic nature of this notion of the police is becoming increasingly evident. Contemporary societies are characterized by a process of fragmentation and diffusion of the police function (Shearing and Stenning 1983, 1987; Shearing 1992, 1996; South 1988, 1997a; Johnston 1991, 1992, 1993, 1996, 2000; Hoogenboom 1991; Reiner 1992b: 779–81, 1996; Bayley and Shearing 1996; O'Malley and Palmer 1996; Sheptycki 1997, 1998, 2000; Loader 1997; T. Jones and Newburn 1998; Braithwaite 2000).

It is important to distinguish between the ideas of 'police' and 'policing'. 'Police' refers to a particular kind of social institution, while 'policing' implies a set of processes with specific social functions. 'Police' are not found in every society, and police organizations and personnel can have a variety of shifting forms. 'Policing', however, is arguably a necessity in any social order, which may be carried out by a number of different processes and institutional arrangements. A state-organized specialist 'police' organization of the modern kind is only one example of policing.

SOCIAL CONTROL

The idea of policing is an aspect of the more general concept of social control. Social control is itself a complex and much-debated notion (S. Cohen and Scull 1983; S. Cohen 1985; Zedner 1993; Hudson, 1997; Sumner 1997). In some sociological theories social control is seen broadly as everything that contributes to the reproduction of social order. This makes the concept all-encompassing, virtually coterminous with society. It would include all aspects of the formation of a culture and the socialization of the individuals who are its bearers.

The problem with this broad concept of social control is its amorphousness. It fails to distinguish the specificity of what are ordinarily understood to be control processes. This is that they are essentially reactive, intended to prevent or respond to threats to social order. As Stan Cohen acerbically expressed it, the broader usage is 'a Mickey Mouse concept', and the term should be restricted to refer to 'the organised ways in which society responds to behaviour and people it regards as deviant, problematic, worrying, threatening, troublesome or undesirable' (S. Cohen 1985: 1–2).

In either its broad or its more specific interpretations the idea of social control may be evaluated positively or negatively, according to different political interests and positions. In conservative versions of functionalist sociology (especially during the heyday of Parsonian functionalism in the 1950s), social control was seen as the necessary bulwark of the consensus that underpinned social order. Ensuring adequate control mechanisms in the face of threatening deviance or disintegration was a functional prerequisite of any viable society, although it was especially hard to accomplish in rapidly changing modern societies.

The development of labelling theory and subsequent radical positions within criminology and the sociology of deviance changed the moral evaluation of social control institutions. Far from being seen as a necessary protection against deviance, social control came to be regarded as producing deviance through the effects of labelling and stigmatization (Becker 1963; Lemert 1967). Social control agents were seen as oppressors to be questioned and opposed (Becker 1967). More structuralist or Marxist versions of critical criminology saw these simple reversals of moral blame as merely making social control agents 'fallguys' for the inexorable working of a wider structure of power and privilege (Gouldner 1968; McBarnet 1979). All radical analyses, however, see social control at least in part as the oppressive maintenance of the privileged position of dominant groups. More complex critiques, however, see social control as inextricably intertwining the maintenance of universally beneficial order *and* social dominance and oppression: 'parking tickets' *and* 'class repression' as Marenin (1983) expresses it.

The concept of policing is clearly closely related to that of social control, and is subject to the same variations in usage and interpretation. Indeed a recent dictionary (C. Wilson 1993) definition identified policing as 'the function of maintaining social control in society'. However, as with the broad usage of social control, this wide definition of policing carries the danger of amorphousness. It misses the specificity of the idea of policing as a particular aspect of social control processes. Thus punishment is clearly an aspect of social control, but is usually regarded as something which should be kept separate from policing, even though any police intervention may be experienced as punitive by those who are policed. The police may in fact exercise forms of kerbside punishment, as in the notorious 1991 Rodney King case in Los Angeles, but this is seen as scandalous in terms of a liberal democracy's values of legality (Skolnick and Fyfe 1993; Geller and Toch 1996). Thus policing cannot usefully be analysed as coterminous with social control but must be seen as a specific phase or aspect of it.

THE IDEA OF POLICING

The essential concept of policing is the attempt to maintain security through surveillance and the threat of sanctioning (Spitzer 1987; Shearing 1992). Policing implies the set of activities aimed at preserving the security of a particular social order, or social order in general (Reiner 1999). That order may be regarded as based on a consensus of interests, or a manifest and/or latent conflict of interests between social groups differentially placed in a hierarchy of advantage, or perhaps a complex intertwining of the two (Marenin 1983).

The above formulation emphasized that policing activity is aimed at securing social order. How effective any form of policing is, and its relationship to other elements in the preservation of social order, are moot points. Policing does not encompass all activities directed at achieving social order. It refers to a specific aspect of control processes, excluding punishment, for example, as well as activities aimed at creating the conditions of conformity in the first place (such as socialization, measures to secure family stability, encouragement of religion or other forms of internalized ethical controls).

What is specific to the policing sub-set of control processes is that they involve the creation of systems of surveillance coupled with the threat of sanctions for discovered deviance—either immediately or in terms of the initiation of penal processes or both. The most familiar such system is of course the one denoted by the modern sense of police as discussed above: regular uniform patrol of public space coupled with post hoc investigation of reported or discovered crime or disorder.

THE IDEA OF POLICE

Policing thus defined may be carried out by a diverse array of people and techniques, of which the modern idea of police is only one (Johnston 2000; Sheptycki 2000a). Indeed the term 'police' itself originally carried a broader connotation than 'policing', let alone the narrow institutional meaning it implies today (Rawlings 1995, 1999). This was exemplified by the 'science of police' which was a broad international movement in the eighteenth and early nineteenth centuries, aimed at maintaining and promoting the 'happiness' of populations (Radzinowicz 1948–69; Reiner 1988; Pasquino 1991; McMullan 1996, 1998; Garland 1997; Neocleous 1998; 2000).

Policing may be done by professionals employed by the state in an organization with an omnibus policing mandate—the archetypal modern idea of the police—or by state agencies with primarily other purposes (like the Atomic Energy Authority Police, parks constabularies, the British Transport Police and other 'hybrid' policing bodies; see Johnston 1992: Chap. 6). Police may be professionals employed by specialist private policing firms (contract security) or security personnel hired by an organization whose main business is something else (in-house security; see Shearing and Stenning 1987; South 1988; Johnston 1992; Michael 1997, 1999; T. Jones and Newburn 1998; Button 1998a, b, 1999; Forst and Manning 1999). Patrol may be carried out by bodies without the full status, powers, equipment or training of the core state police (Police Foundation/Policy Studies Institute 1996: chap. 4; Hofstra and Shapland 1997). Policing functions may also be performed by citizens in a voluntary capacity within state police organizations (like the Special Constabulary; see Leon 1989, 1991; M. Gill and Mawby 1990; R. I. Mawby 1991), in association with the state police (like neighbourhood watch schemes; see Bennett 1990; McConville and Shepherd 1992; Laycock and Tilley 1995), or in completely independent bodies (like the Guardian Angels, and the many vigilante bodies which have flourished at many times and places; see Johnston 1996; Abrahams 1998). Policing functions may be carried out by state bodies with other prime functions, like the army in Northern Ireland, or by employees (state or private) as an adjunct of their main job (like concierges, bus conductors or shop assistants, *inter alios* guarding against theft). Policing may be carried out by technology, like CCTV cameras or listening devices (Norris and Armstrong 1999; Sheptycki 2000b). Policing may be designed into the architecture and furniture of streets and buildings, as epitomized by Mike Davis's celebrated example of the bum-proof bench (Davis 1990: 1998). All these policing strategies are proliferating today, even though it is only the state agency with the omnibus mandate of order maintenance that is still popularly understood by the label 'the police'.

THE EVOLUTION OF POLICING

Until modern times policing functions were carried out primarily as a by-product of other social relationships and by citizen 'volunteers' or private employees. It has been shown by anthropological studies that many pre-literate societies have existed without any formalized system of social control or policing. A well-known cross-cultural study of the relationship between legal evolution and societal complexity in a sample of fifty-one pre-industrial societies found that 'elements of legal organisation emerge in a sequence, such that each constitutes a necessary condition for the next' (Schwartz and Miller 1964: 160). Police in the sense of a 'specialized armed force used partially or wholly for norm enforcement' were found in only twenty of the fifty-one societies in the sample (Schwartz and Miller 1964: 161). These were almost all societies that were sufficiently economically developed to have monetary systems, and with a high degree of specialization including full-time priests, teachers, and official functionaries of various kinds. Police, the study found, appear 'only in association with a substantial degree of division of labour' (Schwartz and Miller 1964: 166), and are usually preceded by other elements of a developed legal system like mediation and damages.

It seems uncontentious that specialized policing institutions emerge only in relatively complex societies. They are not, however, a straightforward reflex of a burgeoning division of labour, as the Durkheimian undertones of Schwartz and Miller's analysis imply. While policing may originate in collective and communal processes of social control, specialized police forces develop hand in hand with the development of social inequality and hierarchy. They are means for the emergence and protection of more centralized and dominant state systems.

A valuable review of the anthropological literature concluded that the development of specialized police 'is linked to economic specialization and differential access to resources that occur in the transition from a kinship- to a class-dominated society'. (Robinson and Scaglion 1987: 109). During this transition communal policing forms are converted in incremental stages to state-dominated ones, which begin to function as agents of class control in addition to more general social control (Robinson, Scaglion, and Olivero 1994). The complex and contradictory function of contemporary police, as simultaneously embodying the quest for general and stratified order — 'parking tickets' as well as 'class repression' (Marenin 1983) — is thus inscribed in their birth process.

British police ideology has always rested upon the myth of a fundamental distinction between their model of community-based policing and an alien, 'Continental', state-controlled system. Conventional histories of the British police attempt to trace a direct lineage between ancient tribal forms of collective self-policing and the contemporary Bobby. Such claims have been characterized aptly as 'ideology as history' (Robinson 1979). It is true that many European systems of police did develop more overtly as instruments of state control (B. Chapman 1970; R. I. Mawby 1991; Brodeur 1995). Revisionist histories, however, have emphasized the relationship between modern police development and the shifting structures of class and state in Britain as well as the United States and other common law systems. The supposedly benign 'British' model was in any case for home consumption only. A more militaristic and coercive model was from the outset exported to colonial situations, including Ireland (M. Brogden 1987; S. Palmer 1988; D. Anderson and Killingray 1991, 1992; Brewer *et al.* 1996).

Although contemporary patterns of police vary considerably in detail, they have tended to converge increasingly around fundamentally similar organizational and cultural lines, without the qualitative distinctions of kind implied in traditional British police ideology (Bayley 1985; R. I. Mawby 1991, 1999; Brodeur 1995). This has been facilitated by the emergence of a new international of technocratic police experts who are responsible for the diffusion of fashions in police thinking around the globe, as witnessed by the recent spread of enthusiasm for 'community policing' strategies (Skolnick and Bayley 1988; Friedmann 1992; Stenson 1993; Brodeur 1995, 1998; Manning 1997; P. Waddington 1999*a* 206–226; Herbert 2000).

POLICE: FUNCTION OR FORCE?

It is problematic to define contemporary police mainly in terms of their supposed function (Klockars 1985). As Bittner has emphasized, the police are called upon routinely to perform a bewildering miscellany of tasks, from controlling traffic to controlling terrorism (Bittner 1970, 1974). This has been a commonplace finding of empirical police research from the outset (as shown in Chapter 4 below). The uniting feature of the tasks that come to be seen as police work is not that they are aspects of a particular social function, whether it be crime control, social service, order mainten-ance, or political repression. Rather it is that they all involve 'something that ought not to be happening and about which someone had better do something now!' (Bit-tner 1974: 30). In other words, policing tasks arise in emergencies, usually with an element of at least potential social conflict. The police may invoke their legal powers to handle the situation, but more commonly they resort to a variety of ways and means to keep the peace without initiating legal proceedings. None the less, under-lying all their tactics for peace-keeping is their bottom-line power to wield legal sanctions, ultimately the use of legitimate force. 'A benign bobby . . . still brings to the situation a uniform, a truncheon, and a battery of resource charges . . . which can be employed when appeasement fails and fists start flying' (Punch 1979*b*: 116).

The distinctiveness of the police lies not in their performance of a specific social function but in being the specialist repositories for the state's monopolization of legitimate force in its territory. 'The policeman, and the policeman alone, is equipped, entitled and required to deal with every exigency in which force may have to be used' (Bittner 1974: 35). This should not be construed to imply that all policing is about the use of force. On the contrary, 'good' policing has often been seen as the craft of handling trouble without resort to coercion, usually by skilful verbal tactics (Muir 1977; Bayley and Bittner 1984; Norris 1989; Kemp, Norris, and Fielding, 1992; McKenzie 1996).

Nor are the police the only people who can use legitimate force. This remains the right (and in some circumstances the moral duty) of every citizen. There are many occupations in which the potential for the legitimate use of force may arise with a fair degree of frequency, most obviously in the case of private security officers, although their only legal police powers are those of the private citizen (Button 1999). Legitim-ate force may also regularly need to be wielded by people not exercising a primarily policing role, for example workers in the health or social services handling disturbed patients, or public transport staff who may have to deal with disorder. However, they are not 'equipped, entitled and required to deal with every exigency in which force may have to be used' (Bittner 1974: 35). Indeed, other workers are likely to 'call the cops' at the earliest opportunity in troublesome situations, and use legitimate force themselves only as an immediate emergency measure in the interim.

POLICING AND POLICE: AN INTERIM CONCLUSION

To sum up, 'policing' is an aspect of social control processes which occurs universally in all social situations in which there is at least the potential for conflict, deviance, or disorder. It involves surveillance to discover actual or anticipated breaches, and the threat or mobilization of sanctions to ensure the security of the social order. The order in question may be based on consensus, or conflict and oppression, or an ambiguous amalgam of the two, which is usually the case in modern societies.

While policing may be universal, the 'police' as a specialized body of people given the primary formal responsibility for legitimate force to safeguard security is a feature only of relatively complex societies. The police have developed in particular as a key institution in modern societies as an aspect of the rise of modern state forms. They have been 'domestic missionaries' in the historical endeavours of centralized states to propagate and protect a dominant conception of peace and propriety throughout their territories (Storch 1976).

This is not to say, however, that they have been mere tools of the state, faithfully carrying out tasks determined from above. Whether this is regarded as legitimate or not (Reiner and Leigh 1992), all police forces have been characterized by the discretion exercised by the lowest ranks in the organization, a discretion facilitated above all by the basic nature of police work as dispersed surveillance. The determination of police work in practice is achieved by the interplay of a variety of processes and pressures, among which formal policies determined at the top have historically been of relatively little significance (Grimshaw and Jefferson 1987).

Many of these features of modern police organisations are currently under great challenge, and policing is undergoing profound changes in what many commentators have interpreted as a fundamentally new stage of social development. These issues will be returned to in the Conclusion of this volume, after a detailed consideration of the history, functioning, and accountability of the modern police in Britain.

POLITICS AND POLICING

'The group of words, police, policy, polity, politics, politic, political, politician is a good example of delicate distinctions' (Maitland 1885: 105).

Most police officers stoutly maintain that policing and politics don't mix. Chief constables regularly declaim on the political neutrality of the police service. Sir Robert Mark, commissioner of the Metropolitan Police (the Met) in the early 1970s, wrote (1977: 12): 'We [the police] discharge the communal will, not that of any government minister, mayor or public official, or that of any political party.' During the 1984–5 miners' strike, for example, it was firmly declared by chief officers and ministers alike that the police were not acting at the behest of the government, despite much evidence to the contrary (Reiner 1991: chap. 8). As shown in Chapter 2 below, it was an important part of the legitimation of the British police in the face of initial opposition that they were non-partisan.

This notion of the political neutrality or independence of the police cannot withstand serious consideration. It rests on an untenably narrow conception of 'the political', restricting it to partisan conflict. In a broader sense, all relationships which have a power dimension are political. Policing is inherently and inescapably political in that sense. 'The civil police is a social organization created and sustained by political processes to enforce dominant conceptions of public order' (Skolnick 1972: 41).

As argued above, their specific role in the enforcement of laws and the maintenance of order is as specialists in coercion. The craft of successful policing is to be able to minimize the use of force, but it remains the specialist resource of the police, their distinctive role in the political order. In this sense, the police are at the heart of the state's functioning, and political analysis in general tends to underplay the significance of policing as both source and symbol of the quality of a political civilization.

Some police tasks are avowedly concerned with the control of behaviour which is explicitly political in motivation and intended impact. Examples range from activities defined as 'subversive' (the province of the Special Branch) to the maintenance of order in demonstrations or some industrial disputes. The control of overtly political behaviour is the task of the specifically political police, or 'high policing' (Bunyan 1977; Turk 1982*a*, *b*; Brodeur 1983; P. Gill 1994, 1997*a*, *b*; Mazower 1997; Huggins 1998; Sheptycki 2000*a*). A characteristic of the English police tradition is the attempted unification in the same organization of the 'high policing' function of regulating explicit political dissidence with the 'low policing' task of routine law enforcement and street-level order maintenance. In most other countries there is a greater degree of organizational separation, although the Special Branch developed in the late nineteenth century as a separate, specifically political, unit within the police in Britain (B. Porter, 1987).

What chief constables are most concerned to claim is that the police are not involved in partisan politics, but impartially enforce the law. This narrower claim is also sustainable only in small part, if at all. A distinction must be made between partisanship in intent and in impact. In a society that is divided on class, ethnic, gender, and other dimensions of inequality, the impact of laws, even if they are formulated and enforced impartially and universalistically, will reproduce those social divisions. This is the point encapsulated in Anatole France's celebrated aphorism about 'The majestic equality of the law, which forbids the rich as well as the poor to sleep under bridges, to beg in the streets, and to steal bread' (Le Lys rouge, Paris, 1894). In practice, of course, the inequalities of social power are likely to have an impact on the processes of legislation and administration of justice, so that the law itself may deviate from formal impartiality (Hain 1984; Griffith 1997). For both these reasons the impact of law and its enforcement in an unequal society will be objectively political even in the narrower sense of partisanship, favouring some groups at the expense of others. 'The rich get rich, and the poor get prison' (Reiman 1997)—and they get policing. Policing bears down most heavily on the most marginal and least powerful groups in our society, who are in effect denied the full status of citizenship (P. Waddington, 1999a) and are 'police property' (J. Lee, 1981). The unequal impact of policing is most marked at times of economic or political conflict or crisis (Hall *et al.* 1978; Crowther 2000a, b).

As I shall argue, the British police tradition has to a large measure eschewed overt partisanship. The constitutional structure within which it operates, autonomous of direct control by elected authorities, is intended to preserve this. Moreover, it must be emphasized that, while policing is inherently political and indeed partisan in reproducing social inequalities, at the same time it preserves the minimal conditions of civilized and stable social existence from which all groups benefit, albeit differentially (Marenin 1983).

However, if policing is an inherently political activity, it does not follow that it usually appears as such. Policing may be inescapably political, but it need not be politicized, that is, the centre of overt political controversy over its manner, tactics, or mode of operation and organization. Like riding a bike, policing is the sort of activity that is thought about mainly when the wheel comes off. When things are running smoothly it tends to be a socially invisible, undiscussed routine.

This book is concerned with the de facto politics of policing in terms of its uneven social impact (Chapter 4), the political ideology of police officers and the political role of the police in popular ideology (Chapters 3 and 5), and the politicization of the police, their involvement in overt political conflict (Parts I and III). As Chapter 1 will show, the British police were established in the face of acute political opposition. To gain acceptance, the architects of the British policing tradition constructed an image, organization, and strategy which were intended to win over the various strands of political opposition (W. Miller 1999). Over the first century and a quarter of its existence the police in England and Wales were largely successful in accomplishing their depoliticization, and came to be seen as legitimate by the mass of the population.

It should be noted, however, that there are inherent limits to police legitimation in any society. Since policing is centrally concerned with the resolution of conflicts by using the coercive powers of criminal law, ultimately resting on the capacity to use force, there is in most police actions someone who is being policed against. In this sense the police are inherently dealers in and dispensers of evil and can never command universal love. For policing to be accepted as legitimate, it is not necessary that all groups or individuals in a society agree with the substantive content or direction of specific police operations. It means at minimum only that the broad mass of the population, and possibly even some of those who are policed against, accept the authority, the lawful right, of the police to act as they do, even if disagreeing with or regretting some specific actions. Of course, in conditions of relative social harmony, acceptance of judicious policing may be a lot more wholehearted. But as policing is inherently an activity concerned with the ordering of conflict, 'policing by consent' cannot imply complete and universal approval. To suggest otherwise is dangerous in that it raises expectations which can never be realized (Fielding 1991; P. Waddington 1999*a*). This is the inherent limit to all the fashionable notions of 'community policing', despite this becoming the 'rhetorical giant' (Manning 1997: 11) of police reform talk around the world. As P. Waddington (1999*a*: 223) sums it up trenchantly, '"community policing" is an oxymoron, for if the police could serve the *whole* community there would be little point in having a police at all'.

However, despite the conflicts and travails at the birth of policing, and the still storming political controversies about the causes and impact of the new police, by the 1950s something like the maximal possible degree of consent had been achieved in Britain. This was partly a result of police strategy, but the necessary background context was a wider pacification of social relations and the institutionalization of class conflict. After the 1960s a set of interrelated changes once more politicized the police, and by the 1980s political conflict raged about the direction and control of policing. After 1981 and the influential Scarman Report, a number of initiatives developed within the police seeking to depoliticise and relegitimate the force, notably through 'community' and 'problem-oriented' policing, and 'quality of service' (Waters 1996; Leigh, Read, and Tilley 1996).

These initiatives were, however, always challenged by the contradictory implications of Conservative law and order ideology, as well as the implications of their neo-liberal economic policies for social divisions, crime, and order (Sullivan 1998). Largely as a result of increasing recorded crime, the Conservatives in the 1990s prioritized an explicitly crime-control conception of policing, and sought to achieve results through a managerialist, 'businesslike' remodelling of police organization. Labour has continued this since 1997, albeit with some inflexions of its own, through its Crime Reduction Programme (Home Office 1998; Downes 1998; Maguire 1998*b*, 2000; Walklate and Evans 1998; Walklate 2000; Reiner 2000*b*).

The politics of policing at the end of the twentieth century thus exhibits a number of paradoxes. Despite many years of criticism and loss of legitimacy the police remain pivotal—at least symbolically—to a crucial policy concern of the public: crime. There is now bipartisan consensus around a fundamentally 'law and order' definition of the issue, and of the police role. However, there is fierce partisan conflict over specific strategies and over who can deliver the best results. Policing and crime control have been stripped of their wider political significance in terms of social justice, but are fiercely contested at a pragmatic level.

The competing arguments and strategies will be evaluated in the light of the substantial body of evidence about police culture, operations, and images that is reviewed in Part II. The nub of my conclusion is that all the reform initiatives of recent years have been vitiated by a failure to reject the 'law and order' framework, and to recognize the inherent limitations of policing. They have been fatally damaged by government policies which aggravated unemployment and exclusion, especially among the young and ethnic minorities, creating problems of policing a new and growing underclass (Crowther 2000*a*, *b*). The problems arguably reflect broader structural changes in political economy and culture, often referred to in a broad-brush way as 'globalization', which limit the scope of action of governments. However, the divisive and unsettling consequences of globalization—whatever the possible benefits in terms of economic growth—have led to extensive debate, about whether and how they might be mitigated (Albrow 1996; Martin and Schumann, 1997; Bauman 1998; P. Hirst and Thompson, 1999; Held *et al.* 1999; Panitch and Leys 1999; Giddens and Hutton 2000).

The social, economic, and cultural transformations of the last quarter of the twentieth century multiplied the problems facing the police. In the early 1990s the police stood at a lower ebb in public trust and esteem than at any time since they were established in the nineteenth century. They had been rocked by scandals revealing gross miscarriages of justice. At the same time the police appeared increasingly less able to protect people from criminal victimization, which was rising at record speed. Serious disorder, on a scale without precedent since the Second World War, developed during the 1980s in a variety of contexts, including political and industrial conflict and a miscellany of leisure pursuits from football to 'joyriding', and continued in the 1990s, although more spasmodically. The militarization of the police in response undermined police legitimacy without stemming the rise of disorder.

In the first half of the 1980s, the police were pigs in the middle of sharply polarized political debate. They were the darlings of the Tories and in conflict with Labour-controlled police authorities, to which the national Labour Party threatened to make them more accountable. Gone were the halcyon days of consensus, when the police stood above the party fray as beloved totems of the nation.

By the mid-1990s the configuration had changed. Seeking to be 'tough on crime and tough on the causes of crime', New Labour courted the police assiduously, while the Tories sought to apply tough 'businesslike' market-based rigours to their management and accountability. There was good news and bad news for the police. The good news was the return of a degree of consensus about policing, and about their symbolic importance to a vital objective for any government. This was reflected in a stabilization of public confidence in the police, following its precipitous decline up to the early 1990s (Mirrlees-Black and Budd 1997; Yeo and Budd 2000). The bad news was the new consensus view that the police were failing badly on almost every front, and in need of drastic reform. It was increasingly apparent that the police feel trapped in a time warp. They were intent on reform. However, the impact of reforms on public perceptions of the police is continuously being undercut by scandalous revelations, as well as unrealistic expectations of performance and probity built up in the bygone era when the lid was shut tight on scandals.

In response to all these problems, police and government have pursued a number of reform strategies, and competing ones have been on offer. Police thinking at policy-making levels is a bricolage of different themes originating at different times in response to the crisis of the moment. There remain echoes of the Scarman philosophy emphasizing peace-keeping and consensus, which were reinforced by the 1999 MacPherson report on the Stephen Lawrence case, and point towards 'community' and 'problem-solving' policing. Such Scarmanesque echoes are intertwined with facets of management theory, the 'quality of service' language of consumerism, and bytes of business-speak. However, these softer tones have since the early 1990s been threatened increasingly by a renewed enthusiasm for tough policing, embodied above all in the much-debated notion of 'zero tolerance' (Bowling 1996, 1999c; Dennis 1998; Weatheritt 1998; R. Burke 1998; Innes 1999a, b; Walklate and Evans 1999; Silverman 1999).

This book sets out to analyse how the police got to their present situation, and what research on their working suggests about the prospects of success for the reforms being pursued. The verdict is far from encouraging, largely because the effects of neo-liberal, free-market economic policies have been to increase social divisions, poverty, injustice, relative deprivation—and the anger they give rise to—the bitter fruits of which the police must cope with. To seek to return to the 'Golden Age' of consensus about policing symbolized by the Dixon of Dock Green myth is chimerical at best. The more pragmatic but attainable target is to achieve public recognition for doing a 'dirty work' occupation as professionally, efficiently, and impartially as it can be done in an ever more fragmented and divided society. Whether even that can be achieved must be doubtful in a period of massive social transformation, generating profound dislocation and insecurity.

PART I

HISTORY

1

THE BIRTH OF THE BLUES: THE ESTABLISHMENT OF PROFESSIONAL POLICING IN BRITAIN 1829–56

'I never saw any of them again—except the cops. No way has yet been invented to say good-bye to them.' Philip Marlowe's fatalistic lament, with which Raymond Chandler concludes his classic mystery *The Long Good-Bye*, embodies a basic assumption shared even by those who are critical of the police. Welcome or unwelcome, protectors, pigs or pariahs, the police are an inevitable fact of modern life.

A consideration of the process by which modern professional policing in Britain came into being makes problematic this taken-for-granted notion. The establishment of the police was a protracted and painful process, in the face of bitter resistance and smouldering hostility. In the late eighteenth and early nineteenth centuries the police idea was fiercely contested.

INTERPRETATIONS OF POLICE HISTORY

Traditional accounts of the origins and development of policing in Britain operated within a framework of palpably conservative assumptions. The police were seen as an inevitable and unequivocally beneficent institution, a cornerstone of national pride, which had been developed by English pragmatic genius as a response to fearsome threats to social order and civilized existence. There was initial opposition to the police, but it arose from vested interests, malevolence or blinkered obscurantism, and was rapidly dissipated when the benefits of a benign police institution became apparent to all.

This view of police history as the inevitable march of progress came under challenge in the 1970s, as a new revisionist account of the development of the police became dominant. In this the police were seen as a means (together with associated reforms of criminal procedure, punishment, social policy and political representation) of maintaining the dominance of a ruling class against the interests and opposition of the various sections of the working class, who constituted the majority of the population.

This revisionist interpretation was itself challenged by later work (S. Cohen and Scull 1983). More recent research suggests that both the traditional and the early revisionist accounts embody questionable assumptions (Bailey 1981a; D. Jones 1982, 1983; Emsley 1983; M. Brogden 1987; Styles 1987; S. H. Palmer 1988; Hay and Snyder 1989; Taylor 1997, 1998; Philips and Storch, 1999; Miller 1999). A more complex picture of police development is emerging. (Excellent syntheses can be found in Emsley 1996, 1997; D. Taylor 1997, 1998: chaps. 4, 5; Rawlings 1999). To assist the reader in following the various interpretations, a chronology of the key events in British police history is given in Appendix I.

THE COP-SIDED VIEW OF HISTORY: THE ORTHODOX STORY

The orthodox studies are all more or less informative versions of the same 'ideology as history' (Robinson 1978). There is a spectrum of sobriety and rigour running from jingoistic eulogies intended for a popular audience (Minto 1965), through the early pioneering explorations of the English police tradition (M. Lee 1901; Reith 1938, 1940, 1943, 1948, 1952, 1956), to some awesomely detailed and scholarly work (Radzinowicz 1948, 1956, 1968; Hart 1951, 1955, 1956; Critchley 1978). The orthodox interpretation, even in its straightforward form, still appears in some local force histories, and even the occasional general history (Stead 1985). Although the different orthodox accounts vary in analytical penetration and informative detail, they share certain core assumptions. These can be distilled into the answers to ten questions about the 'new' police. The orthodox view can then be contrasted with the revisionist position on these issues.

(i) What was the source of the need for a new police?

The orthodox view sees the need for police reform as the twin pressures of urban and industrial revolution. These brought new problems of order which were met by the new police. 'The breakdown in law and order marched in step with the progress of the Industrial Revolution' (Critchley 1978: 21).

(ii) What was wrong with the old policing arrangements?

'The eighteenth-century system was one of very severe penalties . . . but very weak and capricious enforcement machinery' (D. Philips 1983: 54). The punitiveness of the criminal code was both inhumane and counter-productive. It made victims reluctant to prosecute, and juries loath to convict. That certainty of punishment was a more effective deterrent than severity was a fundamental axiom of the late-eighteenth-century 'classical' criminology of Beccaria and others (Roshier 1989). It was closely tied in with the arguments for police reform proposed by such writers as Patrick Colquhoun and Jeremy Bentham (the utilitarian philosopher and social reformer).

The key agents of the 'old' policing system, the constables, watchmen and amateur justices, were widely lampooned by eighteenth- and nineteenth-century advocates of police reform, and their criticisms are retailed by the orthodox view. The office of constable had become so onerous that it became common to hire deputies. Penny-pinching led to the use of men who were 'scarcely removed from idiotism' (Critchley 1978: 18). Many magistrates exploited their offices for fees (the so-called 'trading justices'). The London nightwatchmen, the 'Charlies' (instituted in the reign of Charles II), were said to be 'contemptible, dissolute and drunken buffoons who shuf-fled along the darkened streets after sunset with their long staves and dim lanterns, calling out the time and the state of the weather, and thus warned the criminal of their approach' (Critchley 1978: 30). Those members of the old constabulary who were not ineffective were represented as corrupt, milking their offices for rewards and fees. Thief-takers became thief-makers. The prototype of both, Jonathan Wild, had sub-ordinates who 'stole on commission, and surrendered what they had taken to Wild who then returned the goods to their erstwhile owners' (Rock 1977: 215). In short, the old system was said to be uncertain, uncoordinated and haphazard, relying on private and amateur effort, and prone to corruption.

(iii) What were the motives for police reform?

The large and rapidly growing cities were seen as breeding-grounds of crime and disorder, due to their anonymity. The novelist and lawyer Henry Fielding was, as a Middlesex judge in the 1740s and 1750s, an early advocate of police reform and collaborated with his brother John in establishing the Bow Street Runners, a pioneer-ing body of thief-takers. He compared London to 'a vast wood or forest, in which a thief may harbour with as great security as wild beasts do in the deserts of Africa or Arabia', while Horace Walpole wrote of being 'forced to travel, even at noon, as if one were going to battle' (Critchley 1978: 21). Rapid urban and industrial development brought immense social dislocation and disruption in its wake, engendering demoral-ization, crime and social conflict. 'Civilisation works its miracles and civilised man is turned back almost into a savage,' wrote de Tocqueville after visiting Manchester (cited in Hobsbawm 1968: 86).

Patrick Colquhoun, a London stipendiary magistrate who was a major exponent of police reform, attempted in his 1795 *Treatise on the Police of the Metropolis* to quantify the number of criminals and the amount of loss engendered by their crimes, as a contribution to the then burgeoning 'science of police' (Reiner 1988; Pasquino 1991; McMullen 1996, 1998; Garland 1997). In 1810 the government began publishing annual figures of indictable committals for trial in England and Wales, which showed an apparently inexorable increase (Philips 1980: 180). Even at the time, it was debated whether these reflected a 'real' increase in offending, as opposed to such factors as increasing ease of prosecution. But the home secretary, Robert Peel relied heavily on these statistics in the parliamentary debate before the 1829 Metropolitan Police Act was passed.

In addition to the fear of rising crime, the orthodox view recognized the import-ance of public disorder as a motive for police reform. This was a concern about disorder in the double sense of declining moral standards, and the threat of riot. Colquhoun and other police reformers waxed loquacious about moral decay, which was also seen as a source of political conflict (Philips 1980: 177).

The role of politically motivated disorder in the creation of the new police tended to be underplayed by the orthodox view. The notorious Peterloo Massacre (the popular name given to the brutal—there were eleven deaths and hundreds of injuries—suppression by magistrates, cavalry, and yeomanry in 1819 of a large but peaceful demonstration in St Peter's Field, Manchester, in support of parliamentary reform) did not feature in Critchleys book (the standard orthodox reference). It got the briefest of mentions in Reith (1956: 122), and was assimilated to the 'crime industry'. The only political disorders that featured prominently in the orthodox histories were the Gordon Riots, the reactionary anti-Catholic demonstrations that were the immediate stimulus for Pitt's abortive 1785 Police Bill, the first attempt to establish a professional police force. Concentrating on them allowed the problem to be more readily depicted as 'City [of London] gangsterdom' (Reith 1943: 29).

The overall theme of the orthodox histories, then, was that police reform was motivated mainly by fear of crime, but also by moral and mob disorder, all engendered by the problems of rapid transition to an urban industrial society. The early nineteenth century was seen as 'the golden age of gangsterdom'(Midwinter 1968: 14) or 'an epoch of criminality' (M. Lee 1901: 203).

(iv) Who opposed the new police?

Given this picture of the new police as unequivocally necessary to control the evil by-products of industrial growth, the orthodox view was at something of a loss in explaining opposition to the establishment of the police. Not that the weight and power of this opposition could be denied. From the middle of the eighteenth century a growing chorus of voices unsuccessfully urged the creation of a professional police. Instead a series of expedients was introduced, notably the 1792 Middlesex Justices Act, creating twenty-one paid magistrates controlling seven police offices.

After Pitt's 1785 Bill there were several inquiries into the policing of London which considered the establishment of a centralized professional police for the metropolis. In 1798 a Select Committee on Finance, largely influenced by Colquhoun, favoured a new police, but no legislation was introduced. Six parliamentary committees—in 1812, 1816, two in 1817, 1818, and 1822—were set up to consider London's policing arrangements, but recommended against a new police, before Peel was eventually successful in 1829.

The orthodox historians' only explanation of this was to impugn the intelligence or integrity of the opponents of the police. The rock upon which Pitt's 1785 Bill had foundered was the City's opposition to encroachment on their corporate rights, and Peel deftly avoided this problem by excluding the City from his 1829 Act. Much of the resistance to the police legislation from 1785 to 1856 was couched in a rhetoric drawing on the supposed traditional liberties of Englishmen, which was invoked by aristocratic Tories and working-class radicals alike. The frequently quoted passage from the 1822 Committee Report—'It is difficult to reconcile an effective system of police, with that perfect freedom of action and exemption from interference, which are the great privileges and blessings of society in this country'—is dismissed by Critchley as 'thoroughly reactionary'.

Reith saw the opposition in an even more sinister light: 'It was the efforts of gangsterdom alone, and the success of its propaganda, which frustrated for nearly a century every attempt to end the menace of crime and disorder by creating police' (Reith 1943: 12). Altogether the orthodox view had no analysis of the social location and basis of the various currents of thought concerning the police, and denied the opposition any meaning or rationality that was not venal.

(v) How long did opposition to the police last?

After the new police took to the streets, the orthodox histories have to account for the opposition of the masses who were not directly represented in the parliamentary debates. This opposition, although clearly virulent in the early 1830s, was depicted as rapidly evaporating once the worth and virtue of the new police became apparent. At first pamphlets circulated exhorting the populace to 'Join your Brother Londoners in one heart, one hand for the ABOLITION OF THE NEW POLICE', and attacking 'Peel's bloody gang'. During the fighting between the police and a meeting of the National Political Union, a PC Culley was fatally stabbed. The inquest jury returned a verdict of 'justifiable homicide'. This clearly indicated the strength of continuing public opposition to the police, but the conventional view had it that after a parliamentary inquiry, 'public opinion . . . veered in favour of the police' (Critchley 1978: 55). In the orthodox narrative, this was the crucial turning-point. 'The police, though they did not then know it had won their final and conclusive victory over the Ultras. More importantly, they had won an even greater victory in the long term—the seal of "public approval" (Ascoli 1979: 105). Altogether, in the orthodox view, opposition to the police may have been nasty and brutish, but it was blessedly short.

(vi) What was new about the 'new police'?

The orthodox histories argued both that the 'new' police established between 1829 and 1856 was a novel creation in terms of efficiency and integrity, and that it had roots in ancient traditions of communal self-policing.

The 'newness' consisted of the institution of a bureaucratic organization of professionals, rationally administered and directed towards a policy of 'preventive policing', that is, regular patrols to deter crime, suppress disorder and maintain security. Gradually with the spread of the 'new' police throughout the country, following the Metropolitan 'prototype', a more coordinated network of systematic law enforcement came into being, but without a degree of central direction that would be incompatible with traditional liberties, thus striking a balance 'nicely adjusted to the British genius' (Critchley 1978: 101).

The 'newness' of the Metropolitan Police was also emphasised by stressing the high standards of entry and discipline established by Peel and the two commissioners he appointed, Colonel Charles Rowan (of the Light Brigade) and Richard Mayne, a barrister. This meant that few of the old parish constables or watchmen were eligible, and indeed only one-sixth of the original intake of nearly 3000 men remained in the force four years later.

On the other hand, the force's ancient origins in communal self-policing and the continuity of the office of constable (with its common-law powers theoretically unaffected by incorporation into a bureaucratic body) were also stressed. This argument was pioneered by Melville Lee (1901: xxvii): 'Our English police system . . . rests on foundations designed with the full approval of the people, we know not how many hundreds of years before the Norman conquest.' It was echoed by Reith, who saw the police as 'directly traceable to the dawn of European history, and to the customs of the Aryan tribes of the Continent whom their leaders made responsible for securing the observance of tribal laws' (Reith 1943: 14. See also Rolph 1962: 1–10; Critchley 1978: 1–28; Ascoli 1979: 1, 9–16). These arguments all go back only as far as the tenth century, by which time there was already a clear-cut feudal hierarchy into which the vestigial kin structure and communal self-policing traditions had been incorporated for order maintenance by a succession of invaders (Robinson 1979: 49, n.36).

(vii) What was the social impact of the new police?

In the orthodox account, the social impact of the police was the clearly benign one of solving the problem of order and checking the spread of lawlessness. '3000 unarmed policemen, cautiously feeling their way against a hostile public, brought peace and security to London in place of the turmoil and lawlessness of centuries' (Critchley 1978: 55–6). This not only protected individual victims from depredation but stabilized society for future growth within a liberal democratic framework. The reformers' purpose was enunciated most clearly by Colquhoun in his *Treatise on the Police of the Metropolis*: 'Everything that can heighten in any degree the respectability of the office of constable, adds to the security of the state, and the life and property of every individual'. The orthodox analysis suggested that this purpose was concretely achieved by the English police system.

Reith waxed loquacious on the splendid advantages brought about by Peel's creation. 'It is an unquestionable historical fact that the appearance of public orderliness in Britain, and of individual willingness to cooperate in securing and maintaining it, coincides with the successful establishment of the police institution' (Reith 1943: 3). The same sentiments were echoed by most of the orthodox histories (M. Lee 1902: xxv–xxvii; Gorer 1955: 294–8, 305–12; Critchley 1978: xvii; Ascoli 1979: 3–4, 346–9). In the orthodox view the police were not only successful in the more immediate and mundane jobs of crime control and order maintenance; through their efforts they were ultimately to transform the whole national character, and, indeed, world civilization.

(viii) Who gained from the new police?

It was a striking theme of the orthodox analysis that not only did the police benefit society as a whole but, contrary to initial fears, their major impact was on the welfare of the working class and the poor. They were the guardians of the weak against the strong. Melville Lee (1901: xxx) claimed the police were 'designed to stand between the powerful and the weak, to prevent oppression, danger and crime'. Reith took up the argument. The 1839 Royal Commission report on the setting-up of a rural constabulary was said to provide 'a remarkable picture . . . of the sufferings endured by the working classes as the consequences of absence of police' (Reith 1956: 203). Critchley also pursued the theme that the poor had most to gain from the police. 'The wealthy paid gamekeepers to protect their property and slept with arms near at hand, and the middle-class tradesmen formed voluntary protection societies. The poor simply managed as best as they could until the reform of rural police was at last put in hand' (Critchley 1978: 28).

While on the one hand the poor and the working class were singled out by the orthodox histories as beneficiaries of the police, they were also pinpointed as the source of most crime. This followed on from Colquhoun's contemporary analysis linking indigence and crime to the need for police (*Treatise on Indigence*, 1806). Ascoli also stressed the particular contribution of the poor to the eighteenth-century 'crime problem': 'While the upper and middle classes exploited the financial possibilities of privilege and position, the lower orders—with no such advantages—resorted to crime on an unparalleled scale' (Ascoli 1979: 28). Despite this, by 1837 the new police were 'universally accepted' (Ascoli 1979: 111).

The orthodox historians were thus unanimous in claiming the universal benefits of the police, but some emphasized the special gains of the poor and working class. They not only came to be protected from criminal victimization but were prevented from sinking into crime themselves through the promotion of that 'moral improvement of the labouring classes by the exercise of supervision and restraint' which Colquhoun saw as a prime police function (Radzinowicz 1956: 233).

(ix) Who controlled the police?

It was a central claim of the orthodox histories that English police power was only the crystallized power of the people. This was one reason for their eagerness to stress the roots of the police in ancient traditions of communal self-policing. The police were the police not of government but of the community. 'Happily for English liberty there has never existed in this country any police force at the disposal of the central government, powerful enough to coerce the nation at large. Our national police has always been of the people and for the people' (M. Lee 1901: 61). Reith emphasised 'the historic tradition that the police are the public and that the public are the police' (Reith 1956: 287).

Critchley more soberly rejected this idea of 'a mystical fusion between the policeman and the ordinary citizen' (Critchley 1978: xviii). But both he and Ascoli claimed emphatically that the new policing arrangements were democratically accountable: 'The device which is most characteristically English has been to arm the police with prestige rather than power, thus obliging them to rely on popular support' (Critchley 1978: xviii).

The Metropolitan Police were made accountable to the home secretary as their police authority, to the obvious chagrin of the 'arrogant and inefficient' justices and parochial authorities whose status and power was thus undermined (Ascoli 1979: 93–5). The relationship between home secretary and Metropolitan commissioner was rapidly negotiated as one in which the minister 'should deem it imprudent' to interfere in the force's internal working over the head of the commissioner, or in its '*operational* role' (Ascoli 1979: 106–12). The commissioner was 'the servant of the Crown and people, answerable to Parliament, in its capacity of *vox populi* . . . He, and every member of his force, is subject to the same law of which they are the executive arm . . . He is, by definition, as impartial in his field as the judiciary' (Ascoli 1979: 11).[1]

Mayne's victory over the attempt of Samuel Phillips, under-secretary at the Home Office, to intervene more closely in police matters was seen as a triumph over 'bureaucratic arrogance'. That it left the path clear for considerable practical autonomy for the professional police commissioner was no danger. 'Not once did Rowan and Mayne seek to abuse their power nor did they consider themselves anything other than servants of the public, with a statutory duty to preserve the King's Peace (Ascoli 1979: 112).

A measure of central direction over provincial policing arrangements marched on steadily from the 1835 Municipal Corporations Act (which required all boroughs to institute police forces). It was opposed by a continuing strain of rhetoric, denouncing each step as a sinister French, Russian or Venetian (but at any rate distinctly continental) usurpation of the traditional English rights of self-government, what Birmingham MP George Muntz called 'local institutions which had been in existence since the time of King Alfred' (cited in Critchley 1978: 116–7). In the end, the 1856 Act expressed a rough balance between the continuing responsibilities of local government and justices, and a measure of central government supervision. This was exercised through the establishment of a Home Office Inspectorate of Constabulary, which had to certify a force as efficient before it could qualify for a new Exchequer grant of 25 per cent of the cost of pay and clothing.[2] This proved to be a wedge with which the Home Office was able to introduce more central direction, and chief constables to construct a large measure of autonomy from local control. But it incorporated a balance of nominal power such that the orthodox histories could see the pattern of policing arrangements as embodying the principle of democratic accountability.

The final ingredient in popular control of the police was the strategy governing recruitment and training. 'It was a deliberate policy to recruit men "who had not the rank, habits or station of gentlemen" . . . the police was to be a homogeneous and democratic body, in tune with the people, understanding the people, belonging to the people, and drawing its strength from the people' (Critchley 1978: 52, citing Gash 1961: 502).

Thus the orthodox analysis maintained that the 'people' control the police. Partly this was a matter of formal channels of legal and democratic accountability. But fundamentally it derived from selecting the police in a representative way, and imbuing them with a sense that their powers derived from consent not coercion.

(x) What model of historical explanation underlies orthodox police history?

The orthodox histories operated with a model of explanation which is teleological and unilinear. By 'teleological' I mean that the underlying dynamic driving the development of the police was an assumed 'fit' between the 'new police' model and the order maintenance requirements of an industrialized, liberal-democratic society. This urged on the progressive unfolding and realization of the police idea. But police development was not just the product of impersonal forces. The structural problems of industrialism and urbanization constituted merely 'the demand for order'. The supply of appropriate ideas and institutions to provide the requirements for order without eroding traditional liberties came from a battery of 'far-sighted' reformers who were the personalization of national genius. The accomplishments of these perspicacious 'pioneers of policing', the Fieldings, Colquhoun, Peel, Rowan and Mayne, were celebrated in the orthodox histories (Stead 1977). However, the 'correct' ideas of these great men (as well as the 'false' notions of the opposition) were essentially epiphenomenal. At most they oiled (or spoked) the wheels of development and speeded (or retarded) its progress.

The pattern of development was portrayed as 'unilinear', that is, it had one clear direction, and despite temporary spills and setbacks never departed from this trajectory. The irresistible force of industrialisation and its control problems, meeting the immovable object of stubborn English commitment to liberty, could result in only one outcome: the British bobby. Critchley and Radzinowicz emphasized English empirical trial and error, and the absence of tidy logicality, grand philosophical design or 'lofty constitutional principles'. But trial and error was only the specific mechanism by which the path was charted. The implicit explanation of police development was that the model which ultimately emerged (in stages, to be sure) best met the conflicting demands of order and liberty. The implicit explanatory schema was of the mutually conditioning interaction of innovative ideas and social circumstances, a sort of idealist dialectic. The works of Lee, Reith and the other simpler exponents of the orthodox view differed only in having a less complicated and conflict-ridden (that is, less dialectical) model of straightforward idealist determination.

Having outlined the traditional view of police history, I shall turn to a similar analysis of the 'revisionist' critique that became dominant in historical work of the 1970s, contrasting its answers to the same questions. Revisionism was an unequivocal advance, specifying much more concrete and precise social bases of political conflict around the police, and relating policing to a wider context. However it embodied opposite distortions to the orthodox account—a lop-sided rebuttal of cop-sided history.

While the orthodox view has been usefully analysed as 'ideology as history' (Robinson 1979), and revisionism has undeniably exposed orthodoxy's shortfalls as history, this does not dispose of it as ideology. The Reithian Police Principles (Reith 1956: 286–7) may not be or ever have been realized in practice. But they have undeniably been a significant reference point for British police thinking. Moreover, as an aspiration for what a police force should be like they ought not be dismissed too readily. A police force with the Reithian ethic as an institutional ideal to which obeisance is paid is preferable to one which is not committed explicitly to the 'transmuting of crude physical force . . . into the force . . . of public recognition' (Reith 1956: 286).

A LOP-SIDED VIEW OF HISTORY? THE REVISIONIST ACCOUNT

The model I have constructed of the traditional view is clearly an ideal-type. It synthesizes the essential elements of the work of a diverse group of writers, none of whom fits the pure model in every respect. The ideal-type of 'revisionism' I am about to construct is probably even more of a 'one-sided accentuation'.

The essence of revisionism was captured in the quote from Engels that heads Storch's 1975 article, the flagship of the approach.[3] 'Because the English Bourgeois finds himself reproduced in his law, as he does in his God, the policeman's truncheon . . . has for him a wonderfully soothing power. But for the workingman quite otherwise!' How does revisionism answer the same ten questions that the orthodox view addressed?

(i) What was the source of the need for a new police?

Revisionism stressed that industrialization and urbanization occurred within a specifically capitalist framework. Crime and disorder, those consequences of industrialism which the traditionalists identified as the basis of the demand for order, are not hard and unequivocal categories. Each was defined variously by different political viewpoints and social classes. At the root of the new problem of order was the shifting and accentuated pattern of class division and conflict associated with the rise of capitalism, in both town and country.

The rapid growth of large cities involved the development of much greater segregation between classes. The poor areas may have generated more crime and disorder as a consequence of anonymity, demoralization and despair. The upper-class perception of routine crime altered, so that it came to seem symptomatic of a deeper threat to the social order as a whole, stemming from the 'dangerous classes', the rapidly growing urban poor (Silver 1967: 3).

The meaning of collective disorder also changed: 'The market system was more allergic to rioting than any other economic system we know' (Polanyi 1944: 186). Until the early nineteenth century riotous protest was an accepted and mutually understood means by which the politically unrepresented masses communicated grievances to the ruling elite—'bargaining by riot'. But with the spread of industrial capitalism riot came to be regarded not as a form of proto-democracy but as a fundamental threat to the social and political order (Hobsbawm 1959: 116).

Capitalism also required a tighter disciplining of hitherto relatively loosely regulated aspects of social relations. 'A stable public order was a precondition of rational calculation on the part of industrial capitalists' (Spitzer and Scull 1977a: 277).

The development of a formally 'free' labour market meant that the traditional practice of workers retaining some of the produce they handled had to be stopped, and replaced by the 'cash nexus' (Bunyan 1977: 61). Payment in kind was redefined as theft. 'From the outset there was nothing impartial about the police. They were created to preserve for a colonial merchant and an industrial class the collective product of West Indian slavery and London wage labour' (I. MacDonald 1973). This was part of a broader pattern of change whereby a 'moral economy', in which prices and relationships were seen as subject to traditional conceptions of justice, was replaced by a pure market economy, governed only by the impersonal laws of supply and demand (Thompson 1971, 1975, 1992).

The new mechanized conditions of factory production also required that the formally free labour force be subject to even tighter discipline in both work and 'leisure' time to fit the rhythms and regimentation of capitalist organization. This produced 'the criminalisation of traditional street pastimes which were solely recreational' (P. Cohen 1979: 120–1). The police officer became a 'domestic missionary' (Storch 1976), 'the moral entrepreneur of public propriety' (P. Cohen 1979: 128), charged with converting the folkways and mores of savage street-dwellers to respectability and decency.

Revisionists distinguished between fractions of the ruling class in a significant way. It was not just that industrial cities aggravated the control problems of an unchanged ruling class. The ruling class itself altered, with the industrial bourgeoisie gaining in significance relative to the still dominant landed gentry. The bourgeoisie and their property were more exposed to crime and disorder, less embedded in traditional social networks of deference and paternalistic personalized authority, and more reluctant to give their time or life and limb in voluntary police bodies. This points to the revisionist answer to the second question about the new police.

(ii) What was wrong with the old police?

The revisionists challenged the orthodox view that the main problems with the old private-enterprise police arrangements were corruption and inefficiency. There was no issue about the widespread corruption of the old justices and thief-takers (Spitzer and Scull 1977a, b), although this is endemic in detective work and continues today (P. Cohen 1979: 133–4; Hobbs 1988; Newburn 1999).

The main question, however, was about the alleged inefficiency of the old police. Several critics discerned a scent of upper-class snobbery and condescension in the traditional knockabout humour at the expense of the old constables and Charlies (M. Brogden 1982: 53). What was represented by respectable contemporaries as inefficiency or corruption pure and simple may have been fear of the sympathy between the old police and their own communities which made them unreliable as the policing of morality and disorder became politicized (or even in policing routine crime). Above all, the loyalty of a working-class police drawn from the local community could not be depended upon by manufacturers for controlling industrial disputes (Foster 1974: 56–61; Storch 1975: 89, 92–3; Leon 1990, 1991). It has been suggested that similar motives stimulated the later American establishment of state police forces and the 'professionalization' of city forces in the late nineteenth and early twentieth centuries (Robinson 1978).

In any case, the revisionists argued that social order in the eighteenth century was not dependent upon the direct effectiveness of the formal control apparatus. Contrary to the view of contemporary reformers that the eighteenth-century criminal justice and penal systems were an antiquated and irrational mess, a judgement which the orthodox police historians all shared, they effectively maintained the stability of the old hierarchical social order. A combination of rules and rituals emphasized both the majesty and terror of the law, embodied above all in the 'Bloody Code' (the proliferation of new capital offences in the early nineteenth century; analysed by Thompson 1975; Hay 1975*b*; Styles 1977) and the ceremonials of sentencing to death and public execution (see Linebaugh 1991; Gatrell 1994). This was combined with strict adherence to legality (so the system symbolised impartial and formal justice). Despite the proliferation of the death penalty for many new offences, less than half the people condemned to death were executed. This was precisely the nub of the utilitarian reformers' criticism that severe nominal punishments, which were unlikely to be carried out, were counter-productive as deterrents. Hay turned the orthodox argument on its head. The moral bonds built up between superiors and subordinates throughout the social hierarchy by the process of interceding to seek mercy, and the debts incurred when it was granted, cemented a social order of small communities based on personal ties more effectively than an efficient criminal justice system could have done. In the end the rulers gained most from their own mercy. 'The private manipulation of the law by the wealthy and powerful was in truth a ruling-class conspiracy ... [which] made it possible to govern eighteenth-century England without a police force and without a large army' (Hay 1975*b*: 52–6).

The old institutions of suppressing riot were, claimed the revisionists, counter-productive rather than merely ineffective for the restoration of social stability. The traditional means of responding to collective disorder were the army, the militia (raised by compulsory ballot of all inhabitants by the lord lieutenant of a county), and volunteer forces, notably their cavalry component, the yeomanry and special constables (Leon 1990, 1991). The militia was politically unreliable, as those selected often employed deputies, who would be drawn from the same social strata as rioters. The army was like a sledgehammer. It could only alternate 'between no intervention and the most drastic procedures—the latter representing a declaration of internal war with lingering consequences of hate and resentment' (Silver 1967: 12). Moreover, as soldiers were also drawn from the poor they were politically unreliable on occasion (Stevenson 1977: 33–4). The volunteer forces, especially the yeomanry, had been *politically* dependable. But urban bourgeois manufacturers were less ready to answer a call to arms—'the classic confrontation of an agrarian military tradition and a pacific commercial and industrial one' (Silver 1967: 10). Not only were the manufacturers less personally valorous than their hunting and shooting rural counterparts, but they saw that 'the use of social and economic superiors as police exacerbated rather than mollified class violence' (Silver 1967: 10). As the 1839 Royal Commission on the Rural Constabulary put it: 'the animosities created or increased, and rendered permanent by arming master against servant, neighbour against neighbour, by triumph on the one side and failure on the other, were even more deplorable than the outrages actually committed.' This motivated the establishment of a 'bureaucratic police system that ... drew attack and animosity upon itself, and seemed to separate the assertion of 'constitutional' authority from that of social and economic dominance' (Silver 1967: 11–12).

Finally, the new manufacturing and merchant urban bourgeoisie lacked certain protections against crime which the rural gentry enjoyed. They did not have the ecological safeguards of large estates and lack of proximity to the 'dangerous classes' (M. Brogden 1982: 49–50). Nor did they enjoy the services of private retainers and guards. Finally, their capital took the form of movable merchandise and machinery, much more vulnerable to theft or damage.

In short, the revisionist view emphasized not so much the intrinsic ineffectiveness of the old privatized policing as its growing unsuitability for the new class relations of a capitalist society.

(iii) What were the motives for police reform?

The immediate motives for establishing the new police were to the revisionists the same as in the orthodox account, but with the emphasis and prime mover reversed. The basic cause of increasing disorder was capitalist development. This disrupted existing social networks, destroyed moral communities, replaced personal bonds by the cash nexus, and caused immense deprivation and demoralization. We have noted that the official crime statistics which began to be published in the early nineteenth-century registered an upward trend, and this continued until a peak in the 1840s. Between 1805 and 1842 the rate of committals for trial went up four and a half times, and the absolute numbers seven times (Gatrell and Hadden 1972: 372–4). However, the revisionists questioned how much of this was a genuine increase in criminality, and how much was due to changed sensitivities, penal reform, the availability of police, and other factors leading to a greater propensity to prosecute offences. What was certainly true was that many respectable and influential contemporary commentators took the figures as indicating that 'the progress of wickedness is so much more rapid than the increase of the numbers of people' that a new police was needed to deal with it. Police reform was part of a much broader rationalization of the penal code, punishment (the use of prison as the standard mode), criminal procedure and the prosecution process, as well as other aspects of social policy with a control element (Donajgrodski 1977b; D. Philips 1980).

But while the crime panic engendered by the rise of capitalism was recognized by the revisionists as a factor in police reform, it was subordinated to the more general demand for moral and political order, reversing the orthodox priorities. 'The

existence of the modern police force owes little to the exigencies of combatting professional crime and was developed primarily as an instrument of political control and
labour discipline' (P. Q. Hirst 1975: 225).

However, the crucial reason for the creation of the new police was seen as neither
crime control, moral discipline nor riot control *per se*. It was the need for a force
that could stabilize relations between conflicting social classes as far as this was
possible. Therefore the police were charged with an 'omnibus mandate' of regulating all facets of working-class life (Storch 1975: 88; M. Brogden 1982: 53–71). In the
revisionist view, then, the motive for formation of the new police was the maintenance of the order required by the capitalist class, with control of crime, riot, political
dissidence and public morality being separate subsidiary facets of this overall
mission.

(iv) Who opposed the new police?

Opposition to the new police came partly from sections of the upper class. But this
was not irrational obscurantism, as the orthodox histories implied. The source of
ruling-class opposition was a distinct sector of the class, the landed gentry, and was
perfectly rational in basis. The gentry did not need to support a public police out of
rate-payers' money, when their own security was adequately protected by privatized
means. They could rely on 'large numbers of personal servants to guard their plate
and their wives' (Hay 1975: 59). Furthermore, their local political power-bases would
be undermined by a more rationalized and professional police, for they controlled the
magistracy that was the focal point of the old system. This remained a strong strand of
the opposition to each increment of standardization from 1829 to 1856, and
accounted for the form that local police authorities ultimately took. Furthermore, it
was feared that the development of a more rationalized system of crime control would
rupture the delicately constructed relationships of deference and condescension that
were the microscopic basis of order. The gentry could expatiate high-mindedly on the
threat to traditional liberties posed by the importation of French- , Russian- , or
Prussian-influenced policing schemes, and scoff at the evidence of the volume of mere
larceny assembled by Colquhoun and Peel (J. Palmer 1976: 11–16).

But if initial opposition to the police did come from the landed gentry, this evapor-
ated as the threat of Chartism grew. Later upper-class opposition was over the specific
form and control of the police rather than the principle itself (M. Brogden 1982: 56).

The source of deepest opposition to the new police was the working class, both
before and after the inception of professional policing. This was only indirectly
reflected in parliament, for the working class did not have the vote. But in places with
class-conscious working-class majorities, following the 1832 Reform Act's
enfranchisement of the petty bourgeoisie 'who were dependent on working-class
custom', pressure could be put on MPs to achieve a measure of indirect working-class
parliamentary representation (Foster 1974: 52–4). As Foster's study of Oldham shows,
such pressure was used to oppose all thePolice Bills of the period, the Oldham MPs
invoking the standard libertarian rhetoric about 'tyranny', and describing the police

as 'an unconstitutional force so palpably for the express purpose of coercing the people' (Foster 1974: 69–70).

But the prime arenas for working-class opposition to the police were extra-parliamentary. It was expressed in collective disorder and small-scale street conflicts. Storch detailed graphically the numerous anti-police riots that followed the coming of the 'plague of blue locusts' to working-class communities in the north (Storch 1975: 94).

(v) How long did opposition to the police last?

Whereas in the orthodox histories initial working-class opposition to the police disappeared fairly rapidly after the advent of the new police, the revisionists traced a line of intermittent overt hostility (expressing continuous latent conflict) right down to the 1980s urban disorders. Conflict was only attenuated, not ended, once the police became established (Storch 1975: 106–8).

Philip Cohen discerned the same 'ancient tradition of collective self-defence' against police interventions in street life in the London of the early 1900s. During the 1920s, overt physical conflict between the police and the working class as a whole came to be replaced by a perennial hostility between the police and working-class male youth, which continues today (P. Cohen 1979: 120–1. see also White 1986).

M. Brogden documented a similar 'residue of continuing, if spasmodic conflict between the police institution and the lower orders . . . For the . . . participants in the street economy . . . attitudes to the police institution throughout the first century of policing remained essentially unchanged. They were subject to continuing, occasional, and apparently arbitrary "culls"' (M. Brogden 1982: 180–1). He traced a direct line from the nineteenth-century anti-police riots in Liverpool to Toxteth in 1981: 'The composition and objectives of the street combatants of July 1981 replicates the sentiments of those earlier anti-police demonstrations' (M. Brogden 1982: 241–2). While relations between the regularly employed, respectable and organized sections of the working class and the police were not characterized by open conflict to the same degree, approval was tentative and brittle, with many violent and bitter struggles in the first two decades of this century between police and strikers (M. Brogden 1982: 186–9). Brogden's (1991) oral history of inter-war policing on Merseyside revealed such conflicts vividly.

(vi) What was new about the 'new police'?

To the revisionists, the novelty of the 'new' police was neither efficiency nor integrity. The revisionists were more sceptical both about the poor press accorded the 'old' police and about the laurels heaped on their successors. Individual ineffectiveness, indiscipline and corruption remain endemic among modern police officers. The novelty of the 'new' police was that they were a bureaucratically organized force charged with a mandate to 'prevent' crime by regular patrol and surveillance of the whole society (but especially the denizens of the 'dangerous classes'—St James's was to be guarded by watching St Giles). Intermittent and spasmodic law enforcement dependent upon private initiative was replaced by continuous state policing financed by the public purse. Control dependent upon legitimation by particularistic traditions of personal deference was displaced by impersonal authority legitimated by values of legal rationality and universalism. '[T]he bureaucratization of police work placed day-to-day operations of the control system in the hands of faceless agents of the state, men who no longer operated in their own self-interest, but (presumably) in the general interest' (Spitzer and Scull 1977a: 280–1).

With this notion of a sharp break between old and new, the revisionists rebutted the orthodox 'citizen in uniform' mythology of fundamental continuity between the modern constable and antique traditions of tribal self-policing. The police were changed by new legal powers and by becoming a large, disciplined and technologically advanced organization, clearly distinct from the ordinary citizen.

(vii) What was the social impact of the new police?

In the revisionist account the advent of modern professional policing transformed the social order into a 'policed society'. This 'is unique in that central power exercises potentially violent supervision over the population by bureaucratic means widely diffused throughout civil society in small and discretionary operations that are capable of rapid concentration' (Silver 1967: 8). The net result was the penetration of society by the political and moral authority of the dominant strata, the construction of an essentially manipulated (and thus vulnerable) consensus.

The new police constituted part of a move to a more centralized social order, in which the state penetrated the depths of society, spearheaded by the police institution. But for the police to operate as the advance scouts of the state implies an imperative of some integration with the policed. The consent which they have to negotiate is perennially tenuous and liable to be disrupted in times of crisis when the coercive reality of the police again comes to the fore (Silver 1967: 15, 20–4; Storch 1975: 107–8; P. Cohen 1979: 128–36; M. Brogden, 1982: 236–7). In normal times, however, the police paint a surface gloss of serenity on the rotting fabric of capitalism.

(viii) Who gained from the new police?

Revisionism stood on its head the orthodox conception of universal benefits from policing, with special gains to the poor and weak. The beneficiaries of the new police were seen as the bourgeoisie who established them, and the police themselves, who carved out opportunities for social advancement and greater power. The bourgeoisie gained most from the new police, who protected their property, safeguarded their security and stabilized the social order on which their power and position was based (Bunyan 1977: 63–4; M. Brogden 1982: 71).

The petty bourgeoisie, particularly shopkeepers, were also identified as benefiting especially from the new police, who protected them from depredation and economic competition from the lower strata involved in the street economy (M. Brogden 1982: 182–3). This particular view was largely shared by the orthodox historians. The middle classes are seen as beneficiaries of policing in all historical work (D. Jones 1983: 165).

Finally, creation of the new police opened up an avenue of social mobility to those working-class men who were prepared to endure the hostility of their erstwhile fellows. As the police occupation gained some measure of professional stability it began to draw in working men who were attracted by the middle-class image of respectability and a career (P. Cohen 1979: 134–4; Steedman 1984, Part 2). The chief constables (who in the county forces often were ex-army officers) became powerful figures with a considerable measure of autonomy over an important area of local policy (M. Brogden 1982: 70–1; Steedman 1984: 41–55; Wall 1998).

(ix) Who controlled the new police?

The one thing on which revisionists agreed was that 'the people' did *not* control the police. But there was some debate about whether or not the provincial police were controlled by the local elite (or in the case of the Metropolitan Police by the home secretary). As indicated earlier, the home secretary nominally had control over the Metropolitan Police as its police authority. But from early on the commissioners were conceded a large discretion to determine the conduct of the force. The commissioners also successfully fended off control attempts from the existing magistracy. However, the relationship between the Home Office and the commissioner continued (and continues) to be ill-defined, with, for example, a prolonged argument between the home secretary and commissioner in 1886–7 over the issue of the policing of demonstrations in Trafalgar Square (Bailey 1981b: 94–125).

Much discussion among revisionists was centred on the degree of control of police by local elites in the counties (through the magistracy) and in boroughs (through the watch committee). The two positions on these issues reflected wider theoretical differences between an 'instrumentalist' conception of the police as 'tools' of the dominant class and a 'structuralist' account of policing as a function of the political economy.

Foster implied an instrumentalist view in his description of the struggles over control of the police in Lancashire between the working-class movement and the manufacturers in the first three decades of the nineteenth century. When local constables were controlled by the town vestry in Oldham, or by the Police Commission following the 1826 Oldham Police Act, they were exposed to popular pressure. However, the 1839 County Police Act placed control of the police in the hands of the magistracy, and the police became a weapon of the employers. The rules of conduct for the new force laid down that policemen should be 'non-political', that is, insulated from the earlier form of popular control (Foster 1974: 56–61).

The clear import of Foster's account was that the police were under the control of the police authorities, and the question was: who dominated the authority? After 1839 power over the police shifted decisively to the bourgeoisie. Storch also suggested an instrumentalist view when he attributed the 'implantation of a modern police in the industrial districts of Northern England' to 'a new consensus among the propertied classes that it was necessary to create a professional, bureaucratically organised lever of urban discipline' (Storch 1975: 86).

The structuralist account was put most clearly by Spitzer and Scull (1977a, b),

P. Cohen (1979) and M. Brogden (1982). One of the main theses of Brogden's book was that, contrary to the weight of both orthodox and radical received opinion, chief constables achieved a large measure of autonomy very early on after the establishment of the new police. This was true not only of county forces, whose chief constables had overt control over policing, but also of boroughs, where chief constables were supposed to be under the direction of the watch committee. (A similar position was advanced in Jefferson and Grimshaw 1984b.) In the case of Liverpool, Brogden's material indicated that the Head Constable began to show a measure of independence from the Watch Committee as early as 1841 (five years after the force was established), and by the end of the century had achieved 'considerable latitude of decision-making'. However, Liverpool may well have been a special case: it was one of the largest borough forces, and Brogden emphasized the peculiarities of the local political economy. Moreover, it was Brogden's thesis that the organisational autonomy constructed by the chief constable was a relative one. Neither chief constable nor local elite had much freedom of manoeuvre, as both were constrained by the exigencies of the political economy. Thus Brogden referred to the oft-cited instance of the 1890 Watch Committee instruction to Head Constable Captain Nott-Bower to 'proceed against all brothels'. This order has usually been invoked to demonstrate Watch Committee control. Brogden argued that the episode meant the opposite. Not only was it an isolated occurrence, but the chief constable could within a year revert to the old approach because the strict prosecution policy had such damaging effects on trade. But what Brogden illustrated was not so much the autonomy of the chief constable, as that both he and the Watch Committee were just bearers of structural imperatives (M. Brogden 1982: 69).

However, while the revisionists argued about the precise relations of local elite and police chief, and of both to the political economy, they were united in denying the orthodox claim that the new police were subject to popular control.

(x) What model of historical explanation underlies revisionism?

The revisionist account was just as teleological and unilinear as the orthodox history. In the instrumentalist variant, the ruling class was induced to establish the police by the perceived 'fit' between the police and the control requirements of capitalism (as distinct from industrialism *per se*). 'The genius of the British ruling class is that they realised the need to have such a force and set about creating it' (I. MacDonald 1973, cited in Bunyan 1977: 62).

In the structuralist account the link between the exigencies of capitalism and police development was not necessarily mediated by a clear ruling-class perception of this purpose. But there was the same notion of an inexorable drive along only one possible trajectory. The working-class resistance which revisionists admiringly celebrated was none the less doomed to romantic failure. The ideas of the opposition (laudable) or the proponents of police reform (oppressive) were ultimately epiphenomenal. The real dynamic was the unfolding requirements of capital. To the idealist dialectic of the orthodox view was counterposed a materialist dialectic of a similarly deterministic kind.

ORTHODOXY AND REVISIONISM: CRITIQUE AND SYNTHESIS

In many respects revisionism constituted an unequivocal advance in our understanding of the emergence of the new police. Above all, it was located in a broader analysis of the social conflicts and in particular the class and power structure of the eighteenth and nineteenth centuries. This was hardly surprising, for it was largely the work of professional historians sharing a wider concern for social, economic and political history. However, the revisionist view was in many respects merely an inversion of the traditional approach. To the latter's uncritical consensus model it opposed an equally one-sided conflict perspective. Just as the orthodox historians, faced with evidence of hostility and opposition to the police, dismissed this as malevolent or misguided, so too the revisionists, confronted with apparent periods and pockets of working-class consent to policing, regarded this as manipulated, a brittle skin over a bubbling volcano of resentment. To the revisionists, conflict between police and the working class in a capitalist society had structural roots, so periods of social integration could be only an artificially constructed, temporary truce. On the other hand, in the traditionalist analysis a liberal-democratic industrial society was structurally integrated, so social conflict could only be a superficial phenomenon (and was often regarded as manipulated by agitation—a counterpart to the revisionist conception of an artificially constructed ideological consent and creation of false consciousness). I shall critically evaluate the orthodox and revisionist analyses in terms of the ten dimensions on which I compared them, suggesting a more complex picture than the unilinear development of policing implied by both approaches.

I shall start with question (x), the basic model of historical explanation, as the logically prior issue. Both the orthodox and revisionist approaches assumed a 'fit' between the type of police system and the control requirements of an industrial or capitalist society. It was those conditions, not of their own making, which called into being the actions of the men who made their own history by creating a new police force. The ultimate question is whether a complex modern industrial society could exist without some sort of police force, in the minimal sense of a body of people mandated to intervene in situations potentially requiring the exercise of legitimate force. This is an essentially metaphysical issue, dependent upon conceptions of human nature, the 'iron laws' of social interaction and organization (if any), views of morality, justice, and even deeper matters of ultimate ends, meaning and the nature of being—the province of religious belief. Anthropological evidence clearly documents small-scale societies without police, and the police function has complex conditions of emergence (Robinson and Scaglion 1987; Robinson, Scaglion, and Olivero 1994). It seems utopian to suppose that we could do without a police force in any conceivable large-scale and complex industrial social order, whether or not it was capitalist. (Perhaps I am a victim of 'police fetishism', a special case of 'legal fetishism'.

See Collins 1982: 10–14.) But, even if some police force is seen as necessary in the last analysis, it does not follow that alternative lines of development were impossible. Without constructing a 'counter-factual' history of the police, let us consider just one or two possibilities.

Is it conceivable that Peel might not have been able to pilot the 1829 Act so skilfully through parliament? After all, most histories do express surprise that, following so many decades of opposition, the Act was eventually passed as smoothly as it was. It may be granted that the metropolis would eventually have needed a new police. But by the time that eventuality materialized, perhaps the reformed parliament would have taken a different view of making the home secretary the police authority? Perhaps it would have wanted to include a measure of local elected representation for the police authority—no taxation without representation.[4] This would have greatly altered the pattern of present controversies. Or we can contemplate a rather different counter-factual. Is it not conceivable that those contemporaries who pressed for a more militaristic response to the industrial and political disturbances during the post-Napoleonic Wars and Reform Bill crises could have carried the day?[5] Then we might not now speak of England's comparative uniqueness in not having a 'third force' explicitly specialized for suppressing riots, and of its relatively benign tradition in crowd control. Once it is conceded that the path of development was not tightly predetermined, our perspective on all the other questions shifts. Above all, the ideas and arguments of contemporaries assume a new significance as independent sources of influence, not just more or less wise or misguided epiphenomena hastening or hindering, but not diverting, the course of history. Furthermore, while these ideas and arguments are related to class position, and broadly limited by structural constraints generated by the political economy, they are not foreordained by them. Nor are people's strategies necessarily the best for their interests.[6] It is in this light that I shall turn to the other nine questions about the emergence of the police, and try and construct a critical synthesis, which must perforce be tentative in the light of the amount of ongoing research on each topic.

(i) What was the source of the need for a new police?

The police are needed to deal with conflicts, disorders and problems of coordination which are necessarily generated by any complex and materially advanced social order. The orthodox histories (and undoubtedly many police officers themselves) see these as stemming from a perennial and asocial struggle between good and evil (Robinson 1979). To deny the reality of the evil deeds that big city police confront every day would be to invite the opprobrium that practical police officers, who are in the 'tomorrow business', rightly heap on armchair academic utopians. None the less many of the personal or group conflicts they confront are rooted in structural contradictions and problems which are inevitable in any advanced society, capitalist or socialist. The most fundamental difficulty in analysing and dealing with policing in a capitalist society is that the police have the inextricably dual function of handling troubles derived both from the problems of *any* industrial society *and* from its specifically capitalist form (Marenin 1983). Orthodoxy neglects the latter dimension, the implication of the police in conflicts generated by inequality and privilege. But the revisionists push aside the aspects of policing concerned with universal interests in social order, cohesion and protection, falsely implying 'that all social relations can be described in the language of power and domination' (Ignatieff 1983: 101). This rail-roads any actually experienced sense of the morality, justice, necessity or mere secular usefulness of legal rules and the means of their enforcement into a falsely conscious acceptance of dominant ideology. The police cannot be written off either as 'conning bastards' or as all sweetness and light (M. Brogden 1981). Problems of inter-personal offending and political conflict would be engendered by the pressures of industrializa-tion and urbanization whatever the social framework, but in early-nineteenth-century England they took the concrete form of class conflict in capitalism—although intra-class victimization must not be overlooked. However, this sort of overarching perspective only has the propaedeutic function of pointing our attention in a certain direction. To assist our enquiries further we must proceed to the interrogation of the usual suspects.

(ii) What was wrong with the old police?

The orthodox histories depicted the old control institutions as corrupt and inefficient; the revisionists portrayed them as effective in maintaining ruling-class hegemony in the eighteenth century precisely through a lack of technical rationality. What they agreed on was that the old institutions were ineffective in a direct instrumental sense.

More recent research has cast doubt on the received certainties of both sides of the debate, as well as documenting the varied and uneven transition to the 'new' (Storch 1989; Philips and Storch 1999; Emsley 1996: chap. 1; D. Taylor 1997, 1999; W. Miller 1999). Neither the old constables nor the watchmen were as ineffective or corrupt as painted by orthodoxy (Kent 1986; Paley 1989; Weaver 1994; Reynolds 1998). Some of the provincial justices had been assiduous and effective in crime detection (Styles 1982, 1983).

Nor were the existing forms of riot control as ineffective, either technically or politically, as the orthodox and revisionist cases suggest. In particular, both the army and local magistrates seemed to be quite adept in many instances at cooling down potential disorder, and special constables were enrolled at times of extra pressure (Leon 1990, 1991). In the longer term, philanthropy and poor relief were often mobil-ized to reduce the tensions generating disorder. Altogether it might be more appropri-ate to ask why in the acute economic distress and upheaval of the early nineteenth century, and with the revolutionary ideological example of France, there was not *more* political turbulence than there was. If the fear of riot and the 'dangerous classes' was as acute as both orthodox and revisionist historians suggest, the long delay in police reform remains a baffling mystery. 'A large-scale police force was not created in England before 1829 because the authorities were confident that they could maintain public order using the old system, with *ad hoc* modifications. In this they were more justified than has often been allowed' (Stevenson 1977: 47–8).

Hay's analysis of the eighteenth-century criminal justice system has been challenged by subsequent research. Styles (1977) pointed out that the proliferation of new capital statutes (especially the Black Act) which Hay, Thompson and the other revisionists saw as the spearhead of an 'extending tyranny of exclusive property' were the least used of all capital statutes. Furthermore, Hay and his associates emphasized primarily those criminal activities 'which involved a clear conflict of interpretation between authority and local communities', such as blacking, poaching and smuggling. They played down the routine thefts and assaults that were the bulk of prosecuted criminal offences, and over which there might have been more general consensus. The nub of Styles's critique was that Hay and his associates had not adequately explored the diversity and complexity of eighteenth-century criminal activity and public reactions to it. They were too ready to impart to the eighteenth century somewhat premature notions of 'class conflict' and 'resistance' (Styles 1977: 979–81).

Brewer and Styles's 1980 collection confirmed Hay's account of the highly discretionary character of eighteenth-century criminal law, and the ideological significance of 'the rule of law'. But they qualified the picture of it as a unilateral weapon of the ruling class. The judicial process *could* be used as a class tool, and to legitimate existing social arrangements or changes desired by the patrician class. As in any legal order, its benefits were disproportionately available to those with the greatest means. 'But this does not mean that we should regard the seventeenth- and eighteenth-century legal process as simply an instrument of an elite, or as serving only a class function' (J. Brewer and Styles 1980: 19). Men from all classes, with the notable exception of the labouring poor, were involved in the workings of a citizen judiciary (J. Brewer and Styles 1980: 20). Even the grievances of the poor tended to be expressed in terms of authority's dereliction of legal duty, rather than a challenge to authority *per se*.

P. King's analysis of prosecutions at Essex quarter sessions in the late eighteenth century extended these points. He found that 'the key decision-maker in the eighteenth-century criminal law was the victim himself'. Moreover, those bringing prosecutions for property crime were overwhelmingly from 'the middling sort' and artisans, but the unpropertied labouring poor also resorted extensively to the law as victims of theft and assault. He suggested that the pardoning prerogative was exercised according to consistent criteria of merit and justice, rather than used as an arbitrary or biased tool of the powerful. King was not suggesting that a consensus view of eighteenth-century society should be reverted to, or that the gentry lacked social power. Rather he presented a more pluralistic picture of the criminal law 'as a multiple-use right within which the various groups in eighteenth-century society conflicted with, and co-operated with and gained concessions from each other' (P. King 1984: 57–8).

Langbein (1983) launched the most vitriolic onslaught on Hay's 'fatal flaws'. He partly relied on his own data from mid-century Old Bailey cases, which suggested that 'we often cross a class line when we move from the offender to his victim, but not a class gulf'. He also pointed out that part of the reason for the apparently massive increase in separate capital property offences was the low level of principled and systematic codification of English law. Many apparently new laws were really only marginal extensions of existing statutes to closely analogous cases. The over-representation of the poor as defendants was an indication not of the intrinsic class character of the law or criminal justice system, but of the way that universal law impartially applied in an unequal society mirrored that inequality. 'To seize upon that as the *raison d'être* of the criminal justice system is, however, to mistake the barnacles for the boat' (Langbein 1983: 120).

In sum, then, later historical work suggested a much more complex view of the 'old' policing arrangements than either the orthodox or the revisionist police historians did. The eighteenth-century criminal justice system was enormously diverse and dis-cretionary, but not as ineffective as earlier writers had suggested. Nor was it the unilateral weapon of the ruling class portrayed by revisionism. Whatever motivated the establishment of the new police it was not the patent break-down or inadequacy of the old.

(iii) What were the motives for police reform?

The motive stressed by the police reformers, notably Peel in his introduction of the 1829 Metropolitan Police Bill in parliament, was fear of rising crime. But whether or not crime *was* increasing was unclear to contemporary opinion. The official statistics for committals to trial certainly registered an apparently inexorable upward trend. But there were those even in the 1829 debates who challenged the validity of these figures in the light of the greater ease of prosecution since the 1750s (D. Philips 1980: 179–80). By the time we come to the debates on the 1839 and 1856 Bills opponents were ready to jump in with the obvious argument that the police reformers were using rising crime statistics to justify the extension of a preventive police, the efficacy of which was called into question by those very figures. Edwin Chadwick (the social reformer primarily responsible for the 1834 Poor Law Amendment Act and for the modernization of public health in the nineteenth century) and the other proponents of police reform were forced to abandon the numbers game (Watts-Miller 1987: 43–7).

Nor does the contemporary argument (also taken up by such orthodox histories as Tobias (1967) that whatever the quantity of crime, it was of a more serious nature—the work of a growing professional criminal class—derive much sustenance from recent evidence. Outside London there is little indication that offending was the work of people rationally exploiting crime for a livelihood, or making rich pickings out of their offences. On the other hand, the revisionist notion of 'social' crime as proto-political protest is also hard to sustain. Most offences were 'prosaic and undramatic, involving small amounts being stolen, squalid robberies, burglaries and assaults . . . nor are there visible indications of social purpose, still less of the individualistic waging of the class war, behind most "normal" criminal acts.' (Philips 1977: 286–7. See also Emsley 1997: 58–65; D. Taylor 1998: chaps. 1–3).

The 1856 County and Borough Act was motivated partly by dread of vagrant criminality associated with the end of the Crimean War and the prospect of a footloose army of unemployed returning soldiers. There was also apprehension that the end of transportation meant that 'an organised race of criminals' released on tickets-of-leave would roam the countryside (Steedman 1984: 25). But these fears were only able to overcome concern about threats to liberty and rate-payers' purses after two abortive Police Bills had been defeated in 1854 and 1855, and after much parliamentary shenanigans and wheeler-dealing. Evidently the threat to social order posed by crime cannot have been so clearly overwhelming as either the police reformers (or the orthodox and revisionist histories) implied.

The same qualifications must be levelled at the fear of political and social disorder, which the revisionists see as the primary motive for police reform. True, reference to riot was not (as the orthodox view has it) entirely absent from Peel's 1829 parliamentary presentation. (He raised it in debate, although not in his introductory speech.) The disorders associated with Chartism were certainly very much at the forefront of the 1838 debates. But even here there was a strong current of influential contemporary opinion agreeing with Disraeli that expanding the police throughout the provinces amounted to a declaration of civil war against the people and would be counter-productive. Social harmony could be restored only by the privileged part of the nation once more recognizing their duties to the second nation (Watts-Miller 1987: 47–8).

Whatever fears for the survival of the social order there might have been, even at the height of Chartist agitation, these were not sufficient to overcome the traditional suspicion and miserliness of over half the counties of England and Wales, who refused to utilize the possibility of establishing a rural constabulary allowed by the 1839 Act. Nor was there any clear relationship discernible between counties which had experienced riots and those which had not in their readiness to institute a new police (Emsley 1983: 70–1).

Monkkonen has made similar points about the parallel thesis that the American city police were a straightforward response to rising crime or political and class conflict: 'If each city had adopted a uniformed police only after a riot, changing crime rate, or the need for a new kind of class-control agency, many places would not today have a uniformed police' (Monkkonen 1981: 57). Rather, he argued, 'growth of uniformed urban police forces should be seen simply as a part of the growth of urban service bureaucrats' (Monkkonen 1981: p. 55). The establishment of the English and Welsh provincial police was to some extent a product of a similar process of gradual and uneven diffusion of models of rationalized urban administration (Emsley 1983: 78–81, 1996: Chap. 3; Jones 1983: 157–9, 1996; Wells 1991; Taylor 1997, 1998). A detailed study of the development of the Portsmouth police suggests, for example, that it was not the product of any pressure for reform arising out of crime or disorder, and the local elite were well satisfied with the old policing arrangements. The Portsmouth police were a part of the national process of spreading Whig conceptions of rationalized local government (embodied in the 1835 Municipal Corporations Act) which made all boroughs like Portsmouth establish a Watch Committee and 'new' police force (J. Field 1981: 42–8).

In short, the police reformers certainly perceived those threats of crime and dis-order that orthodox and revisionist historians pick out as the motives for police reform. But influential sections of the elite did not share this panic. The entrepreneur-ial activities of the reformers themselves, who became dominant in central govern-ment, and the diffusion of their model of rational local government administration, played a large part in the setting-up of the new police throughout Britain. It was not an automatic reflex of urbanization and industrial capitalism.

(iv) Who opposed the new police?

The revisionist critique of orthodoxy's dismissal of opposition to the police as simply misguided or malicious is confirmed by subsequent research (D. Taylor 1997: chap. 2, 1998: chap. 4; D. Philips and Storch 1999). 'In the 1830s and 1840s opposition to the new police was part of a "rejectionist" front ranging from Tory to gentry to working-class radicals against an increasing number of government measures seeking to regu-late and control more and more aspects of productive and social life' (Weinberger 1981: 66). The reasons for upper- and middle-class opposition encompassed fears for traditional civil liberties, apprehension about central government encroachment in local affairs, and resentment at the expense to ratepayers. Working-class hostility was roused by police intervention in recreational activities, and the use of the police to control industrial and political reform organization.

Detailed analyses of the various parliamentary debates about the new police do suggest, however, that the complex and diverse currents of opinion among the proper-tied classes represented there do not fall neatly into any clear-cut politics of class interests. Whereas the manufacturers had perhaps more need for a new police than the gentry (as the revisionists argue) they were more influential in local borough government than at Westminster, so had an interest in resisting centralizing measures like the 1856 Act (and *a fortiori* its two abortive predecessors). Above all, however, a close reading of the debates suggests the importance of varying political philosophies and principles which were not reducible neatly to sectional interests (Hart 1978). Moreover, many contemporaries, lacking the benefits of hindsight (or perhaps even if they had them!), were genuinely unsure about the validity of conflicting arguments about the efficacy or counter-productiveness of new policing arrangements for crime control, social harmony and political order. Fears about threats to liberty, concern about fiscal prudence, anxieties about local democratic accountability of the police, were neither irrational nor readily correlated with identifiable sectional interests. But these partly independent conflicting ideological currents—misguided, laudable, or whatever—shaped not only the pace but the pattern of police reform.

(v) How long did opposition persist?

The evidence of sustained anti-police hostility and violence that the revisionists accumulated was certainly sufficient to dispel the orthodox notion of easy and early acceptance of the new police by the mass of the population. But the revisionists erred in the opposite way, neglecting the clear evidence of growing acquiescence and indeed support for the police among a broad section of the working class, as well as the middle class. In many places the police came to be accepted and used by sections of the working class quite soon after their inception. Nor can this be put down to their 'service' activities stitching a velvet glove of superficial acquiescence over the reality of the iron fist of repression (although the 'service' role of the police *was* significant (see Emsley 1983: 146–7, 158–9).

This was brought out clearly in D. Philips's (1977) study of the early years of the new police in the Black Country. Philips demonstrated that in many ways the police were resented by the working class. The incursion of the new police into working-class leisure activities through the enforcement of public order offences, or the use of the police by industrialists to control strikes and redefine traditional popular conceptions of the legitimacy of workers' 'perks' as pilfering, caused considerable disgruntlement. But it would be quite wrong to suggest that this amounted to a rejection of the legitimacy of the police. Analysis of the data on the social position of those victims who prosecuted offenders at quarter sessions in the 1830s and 1850s shows that although retail traders and industrial entrepreneurs were the most common prosecutors, a significant proportion of prosecutions (varying between 28 and 50 per cent) was brought by unskilled working-class people. Most assaults and property offences (then as now) were committed by working-class offenders against working-class victims. And although (for a variety of reasons) many victims did not prosecute, others did.

Many working-class people accepted the basic legitimacy of the laws protecting property, and the agents who enforced them, however much they may have resented certain specific aspects of property law (notably the Game Laws) which were clearly class-biased in intent and practice (D. Philips 1977: 123–9; Emsley 1983: 158–60, 1997; D. Jones 1983: 166–7). Working-class attitudes to the law and its enforcement were clearly complex and ambivalent, and varied between different times and places (D. Taylor 1997, 1998). But there seems to have been in many areas as early as the 1850s a large measure of working-class assent to the basic legitimacy of the legal order, based not on ideological manipulation but on the use of its coercive aspects by working-class victims against offenders. Nor was the 'domestic missionary' role of the police uniformly resented by the working class. Some radical leaders, and the emerging 'respectable' working-class strata, welcomed control of 'the most dissolute and abandoned' habits of the rougher elements, seen as not only an immediate menace in everyday life, but a threat to the political and social advance of the whole class (Emsley 1983: 157–8; Ignatieff 1983: 90–2; D. Jones 1983: 166). By the 1870s it seems that the police had attained a large measure of legitimacy in the eyes of the working class, even though this could be readily disrupted by specific actions, such as stricter enforcement of the vagrancy or licensing laws (Weinberger 1981: 88–9). But the rhetoric of resentment against individual practices came to be couched in the terms of the system itself rather than a rejection of its legitimacy. 'From opposing the very idea of a policed society, radical critics had come to judge the police by those abstract standards laid down by the system's pioneers; judicious discretion mixed with firm impartiality in enforcing laws that were often blatantly biased against working people' (J. Field 1981: 59).

(vi) What was new about the new police?

Local research on provincial forces suggests that often the 'new' police were not very new. There were many transitional policing innovations which paved the way (Emsley 1996: chaps. 2–4; D. Taylor 1997, 1999; D. Philips and Storch 1999).

In the provinces some towns and counties had small constabularies established by particular statutes in the 1820s, for example under the Oldham Police Act 1826 and Cheshire Police Act 1829. More generally the Lighting and Watching Act 1833 enabled ratepayers to set up their own police forces independently of local justices and their old constables, and several small town parishes utilized this Act. Davey's vivid account of the Horncastle force shows that it was able to satisfy most of the townspeople (who governed the force through an elected Inspectorate) by successfully controlling the routine crime and public disorder which worried respectable citizens (Davey 1983). By the time of the debates preceding the 1856 Act which did away with these small independent forces, the argument was about the distribution of costs and control of the professional police, not the principle itself. The effectiveness of these local forces has been minimized by orthodox historians, who see them through the perspective which Chadwick foisted on the parliamentary commissioners in 1839 and 1853 with his creation of the migrant criminal myth, implying the need for more centralized policing.

In many provincial forces, despite the establishment of nominally 'new' police as a result of the 1835 Municipal Corporations Act, 'policing hardly changed . . . the paid watch simply became the paid police' (Emsley 1983: 68. See also J. Field 1981: 43–7). Similar conclusions have been drawn about the Rural Constabulary Act 1839. This left it to county magistrates to determine whether or not to establish a force, and, if they decided to, who the chief constable would be, and the size of the force (up to a ratio of not more than one policeman per 1000 population). Less than half the counties of England and Wales took advantage of this permissive legislation, and even where they did, this did not usually signal a drastic change in either the style, personnel or intrusiveness of policing (D. Philips 1977: 64; Weinberger 1981: 78–9). Fiscal tightfistedness often vitiated the possibility that the police could be numerous enough to achieve close surveillance of any area (Emsley 1983: 73–4).

Nor does the evidence imply that the 'new' police represented a sharp break towards the establishment of a professional police with a significantly higher calibre of personal efficiency and virtue than the old constables. In many places they were, at least for a short time, largely the same men. The policy of not recruiting people with 'the rank, habits or station of gentlemen' (whether motivated by parsimony or political prudence)meant that the social status of the intake was similar to the old constabulary. Furthermore, all the studies document the very high turnover rates in the first decades of the new police, both as a result of dismissals for drunkenness or other peccadilloes, and through rapid resignation due to the discipline and demanding nature of the job (D. Philips 1977: 64–75; J. Field 1981: 52; Weinberger 1981: 79–84; Emsley 1983: 71–3, 1991; Steedman 1984: chaps 3–5; D. Taylor 1997: chap. 3). There was not as distinct a movement towards a powerful professional system of surveillance as suggested by both orthodoxy and revisionism, whether for protection *or* oppression of the population.

(vii) What was the social impact of the new police?

The previous section implies that, for good or ill, the impact of the new police was not as considerable as either its defenders or detractors claim. The immediate effect was primarily the processing of more minor public order offences (Emsley 1996: chap. 4; D. Taylor 1997: chap. 4). In the longer term, however, the police force were undoubtedly connected with a general increase in the orderliness and pacification of Victorian society. Gatrell shows that from the 1850s until the First World War 'the war against criminal disorder was palpably being won by the State, and contemporaries knew it' (Gatrell 1980: 240–1, see also Radzinowicz and Hood 1985, for contemporary views on the conquest of crime in this period). The 'Watchman State' was not constructed at a stroke, but it did emerge eventually (Gatrell 1990). However, recent research has questioned the statistical evidence for falling crime in the late nineteenth century, and suggests that the figures were manipulated to suit the joint interests of police and government in creating an appearance of order and pacification (H. Taylor 1998*a*, *b*, 1999).

Other authors, while broadly concurring with Gatrell's picture of declining crime, are sceptical about the precise contribution of the police to this (Emsley 1983: chap. 7; D. Jones 1983). However, it is arguable that the prime way in which the police affect law enforcement is not through their technical efficacy in apprehending criminals, which depends on many factors beyond their control, but by symbolizing the existence of a functioning legal order. In this light the effectiveness of the police depends not so much on the *proportion* of offences they clear up, as on their showing the flag by clearing up a sufficiently high absolute number (Gatrell 1980: 242–3). As Emsley crisply puts it, 'while policemen were not the ultimate answer to theft and disorder which they and many reformers claimed (and continue to claim), they became the placebo of property' (Emsley 1983: 162).

The police were also a factor in the declining extent of disorder, whether in the sense of riot or everyday standards of street conduct (P. Thurmond Smith 1985; D. Taylor 1997: chap. 4). Obviously riot did not disappear, and in some periods political and industrial conflict intensified, as in the 1880s or immediately before the First World War. On occasion the police not only were unsuccessful in controlling a crowd, but contributed to disorder by provocation or poor tactics (Bailey 1981*b*: 94–125; Emsley 1996: chap. 5). But overall, the degree of collective violence tended to decline secularly, although as much because of changes in crowd behaviour as police effectiveness. The everyday orderliness of the streets increased, which evoked the approval of respectable citizens whatever the impact on those reliant on the street economy.

In sum, while their initial impact on anything but the casual street economy and its marginal illegalities was small, eventually the police were implicated in a broader process of pacification or integration of Victorian society. Although the weight of their distinctive contribution to this is impossible to state precisely it was undoubtedly significant.

(viii) Who gained from the new police?

The orthodox view has it that the police brought universal benefits, but especially to the weaker sections of society. The revisionists argue the reverse. The police were an agent of oppression of the majority on behalf of the ruling class, with the middle class also deriving some gains from harassment of the street economy. The police institution also benefited police officers themselves, by providing a channel of social mobility to greater security, status and power (although chief officers came from privileged backgrounds: Wall 1998).

The implications of recent research support both views partially. The working class did benefit from the police in so far as they resorted to the formal criminal justice machinery when victimized by assault or theft. It is by no means clear, though, that they had as much confidence in the new police as in the old parish constables (D. Philips 1977: 78–9, 124–5; Weinberger 1981: 71–2). Ultimately, however, they probably gained from the process whereby the police came to take over responsibility for most prosecutions.

But while gaining in their capacity as victims of routine offences of theft and assault and from some police services, in other respects the working class were at the sharp end of many police activities (Weinberger 1981: 73–6; D. Taylor 1997, chap. 4). This is especially true, of course, of the lower strata within the working class, those dependent on the street economy or irregular employment. They were the targets of the routine public-order policing which the middle class supported enthusiastically. The regularly employed workers also suffered from police actions during periods of heightened industrial conflict. It is probable also that the quality of police respect would be inversely related to the social status of a person they were dealing with (Emsley 1983: 152; Steedman 1984: 6).

The middle and upper classes certainly gained a sense of security, which many contemporaries gratefully expressed. Others quickly began to take the police for granted as they became a socially invisible public servant (Steedman 1984: 6, 142–5). Some took this to the cynical conclusion that the police officer was a mere 'fool in blue' who did nothing but walk about, and some ratepayers wondered if he was worth his weight in higher rates (Steedman 1984: 7).

It is clear that at first police officers did not gain from the job in terms of social mobility and a career. They merely took advantage of it for short spells while unable to obtain other work. However, in the third quarter of the nineteenth century, the development of a notion of police work as a distinctive career, with a specific ideology of service, professional identity and craft skills, slowly emerged (Steedman 1984: chap. 8; Emsley 1996: chap. 5; D. Taylor 1997: chap. 3). Police work began to hold out an opportunity for social mobility to some working-class men.

(ix) Who controlled the police?

The middle class and working class had a greater capacity to influence their parish constables, or local forces under such legislation as the 1833 Lighting and Watching Act than they had after the creation of the new police. This was the basis of the working-class struggles over police control which have been documented for some northern towns (Foster 1974). It was also the source of the objections of many towns to incorporation under the Municipal Corporations Act 1835, or the amalgamation with surrounding counties as proposed in 1856. On the other hand, it was one reason why Chadwick and other reformers wanted to have more centralized control. To them local control smacked of corruption and inefficiency. Their objections to local democratic control of parish forces echo precisely the arguments of contemporary chief constables about the supposed threat to their professional independence (Davey 1983: 192).

The working class clearly had no possibility of influencing borough Watch Committees until the slow extension of the franchise to them. It was perhaps no coincidence that by that time Watch Committees had lost much of their power over the increasingly autonomous chief constables. The middle class had some degree of influence over Watch Committees, depending on the local political balance. They had less involvement in the gentry-dominated magistracy, which completely controlled the county police until 1888.

Nominally chief constables had the authority to control police policy and administration in the counties (Reiner 1991: chap. 2). However, as the magistracy chose men with a social background and standing which ensured a harmony of outlook, the gentry viewpoint dominated in county policing (Wall 1998). In the boroughs the powers in theory and practice of watch committee over chief constable remained paramount. Even the 1856 admixture of a measure of central control through the Home Office Inspectorate and Exchequer Grant did not change this pattern at first (Steedman 1984: 38–47). However, during the 1870s chief constables in both counties and boroughs began to assert and exercise a greater measure of professional independence. This was facilitated by a series of legislative changes conferring on the police more duties directly from national government, as well as more powers (Steedman 1984: 53–5, 62–3, chap. 10; Wall 1998).

In sum, the orthodox view has no foundation for the claim that the 'people' controlled the police, if by this is meant a concrete channel for the expression of this control. The new police signified a move away from a degree of popular control that had existed in some places over parish constables. They also emerged after the 1870s as increasingly autonomous of local government and magistracy. The police were on the route to becoming that autonomous body of professionals, the accountability of which has become a major source of controversy.

CONCLUSION: A NEO-REITHIAN/REVISIONIST SYNTHESIS

All historians of the emergence of professional policing in Britain have shown that it was surrounded by acute political conflict. The orthodox historians were clearly wrong in their lack of appreciation of the rational basis of opposition to the police, rooted in different social interests and political philosophies. On the other hand, the revisionists over-emphasized the extent of continued working-class opposition, and the overt role of the police in class and political control. While not securing the quick and relatively painless passage into acceptance suggested by the Reithians, the police did gain increasing acquiescence from substantial sections of the working class, not only as a result of 'soft' service activities, but in their 'hard' law enforcement and order maintenance functions. This anchored consent in substantial benefits and cooperation, not mere ideological manipulation. The police succeeded in acquiring this degree of legitimacy, in which they were no longer widely seen as a politically oppressive force, by a combination of specific strategies which did give the British police a unique character, implanting them firmly in national mythology. I would claim that a neo-Reithian/revisionist synthesis is the most appropriate for understanding this.[7] This is a perspective which gives due weight to the success of the police reformers and the tradition they created, but also recognizes that policing is embedded in a social order riven by structured bases of conflict, not fundamental integration. The manner of policing such a divided social order may be more or less harmonious and consensual, or overtly oppressive, with important consequences. The precise processes by which the comparatively benign British policing tradition was constructed in the century after their controversial introduction, the manner of their legitimation and depoliticization, will be the focus of the next chapter.

NOTES

1. Readers of Griffith's (1997) critique of the political partiality of the judiciary may not think this claim amounts to much. It should also be noted that in the formative years of the new police, far from parliament being the *vox populi*, the overwhelming majority of the population were not enfranchised.

2. The grant was increased in 1874 to half these costs (which it remained until 1985, when the local Government Act increased it to a symbolic majority of 51%). The 1856 Act distinguished two kinds of local police authority: (i) watch committees in boroughs, which were committees of the town council; (ii) county forces were the responsibility of magistrates in quarter sessions. The Local Government Bill 1888 established standing joint committees consisting of one-third magistrates, and two-thirds elected councillors, the structure which survived until 1964 (and was extended to all police authorities by the Police Act 1964). The nominal powers of watch committees over appointment, promotion, discipline and the administration of the force

in general far outstripped those of the county authorities. The 1856 Act also began the process of encouraging amalgamation of smaller forces. The 226 forces of 1856 had been reduced to 183 by the Second World War as a result of this and later legislative inducement.

3. Hart (1978), Bailey (1981), D. Philips (1983), Ignatieff (1983), D. Jones (1983), Styles (1987), Gatrell (1988), Hay and Snyder (1989), Knafla (1990), Emsley (1983, 1996, 1997), D. Taylor (1997, 1998), and W. Miller (1999) all address this revisionist position and offer a critique—or autocritique—from somewhat different perspectives. Whereas (with the exceptions of Hart and Radzinowicz) the 'orthodox' historians worked outside academia, the revisionists were mainly professional historians or academics in related fields. Their work was thus hedged in by more caution and qualification in style of presentation. None the less, certain commonalities, sharply contrasted with the orthodox view, can be discerned in Silver's seminal (1967) essay (which spearheaded the new approach with its subtle and stimulating account of police origins), Foster (1974), Storch (1975, 1976), J. Palmer (1976), Bunyan (1977), Spitzer and Scull (1977a, b), P. Cohen (1979), D. Philips (1980), and M. Brogden (1982, 1987). It is out of these that I construct the model of a revisionist perspective. Harring (1983) is an American counterpart. The perspective was found in its purest form in Scraton (1985).

4. Watts-Miller (1987: 51) raises this intriguing possibility:

The Metropolitan Police, Radzinowicz and others tell us, soon became an 'accepted institution'. This ignores continuing criticism and government attempts to stifle it . . . . Although central control kept the capital in more 'reliable' hands, it is open to question if a Bill such as Peel's could have passed after 1832, or 1835, the 'Magna Carta' of local self-government. All that is certain is Parliament's refusal to accept the 'accepted institution' outside London.

5. Silver (1971: 185) indicates the powerful support for this argument during the Reform Bill conflicts, including the King and the Duke of Wellington.

Wellington argued after the Reform Bill was passed: 'From henceforth we shall never be able to carry on a government without the assistance and support of a military body. If we cannot have a regular army in such a state of discipline and efficiency as that the King can rely on them, we must and we shall have a National Guard in some shape or other.'

6. As Watts-Miller (1987: 58) put it trenchantly: 'The executive of a modern state is also a committee to mismanage the affairs in common of the bourgeoisie.'

7. I call this neo-Reithian in order to emphasize the virtues of that ideal of pacific policing by popular consent which Reith attributes to the British police. However, as an account of history Reith requires drastic critical revision to recognize the structured conflicts which surrounded policing in a class-divided society (and continue to do so).

2

THE RISE AND FALL OF
POLICE LEGITIMACY
1856–1991

As shown in the last chapter the modern British police came into being as a deeply contested institution in the early nineteenth century. Yet by the middle of the twentieth century they had become a key component of national identity. The first part of this chapter analyses the achievement of legitimacy by the modern British police. In the latter half of the twentieth century this totemic status was increasingly contested and undermined. The nadir of police legitimacy was reached at the start of the final decade of the twentieth century, as indicated by many indices of public and police opinion. During the 1990s the position of the police in Britain seemed to move on to a new stage of development, reflecting a profound restructuring of state, society and culture. This may be characterized as 'post-legitimacy'. The police are in some senses a Teflon service: they have survived all manner of scandal and controversy and remain a powerful political and cultural force, more so than any other state institution in an increasingly neo-liberal, privatized world in which the state has 'hollowed out' (Bottoms and Wiles 1996, 1997; N. Walker 1996; Loader 1997b; McLaughlin and Murji 1995, 1996, 1997). However they are now only one element in an array of competing policing services, and are subject to increasingly rigorous audit to ensure efficiency, effectiveness and economy in their functioning. At a practical level policing policy has never been more fiercely controversial. But the deeper issues of legitimacy which were struggled over for more than two centuries—the contribution of the police to the shaping of the fundamental structure of power and advantage in society—have largely been bracketed out of debate.

FROM CRUSHERS TO BOBBIES: THE
DEPOLITICIZATION OF THE POLICE 1856–1959

The British police were established in the face of massive opposition from a wide range of political interests and philosophies. While middle- and upperclass suspicions were rapidly allayed, working-class resentment lived on, expressed in sporadic physical violence and symbolized by a stream of derogatory epithets for the new police: 'Crushers', 'Peel's Bloody Gang', 'Blue Locusts', 'Jenny Darbies','Raw Lobsters', 'Blue Drones'. Yet by the 1950s the police had become not merely accepted but lionized by the broad spectrum of opinion. In no other country has the police force been so much a symbol of national pride (Loader 1997b).[1]

Many contemporary statements testify to the almost universal acceptance the police had attained. A 1955 *Police Journal* (28/4: 245) editorial claimed: 'The law-abiding sections of the community (and in this we include the larger majority of all classes, working, professional and leisured, alike) have come to accept the police more as guardians and less as oppressors. Time and experience have dispelled old fears.'

In the same year, Geoffrey Gorer claimed 'that the bulk of the population has . . . incorporated the police man or woman as an ideal and become progressively more "self-policing"' (Gorer 1955: 311).[2] Michael Banton began his pioneering socio-logical study of the police with the 'idea that it can be instructive to analyse institutions that are working well in order to see if anything can be learned from their success' (Banton 1964: vii). Above all, the fictional character PC George Dixon, who first appeared in the 1950 film *The Blue Lamp*, and was subsequently resurrected for a long-running TV series, embodied the quintessential beloved British bobby, and still stands as a regularly evoked ideal (A. Clarke 1992; Reiner 1994; R. C. Mawby 1998c).

By the end of the 1950s there were indications of increasing tension. Recorded crime was rising at a rate described by the chief inspector of constabulary as an 'upsurge', 1958 saw race riots in Notting Hill and Nottingham, and there was growing police anxiety about their relations with the 'law-abiding', but increasingly car-owning, public. In the late 1950s some relatively minor incidents led to the November 1959 announcement by the home secretary of a Royal Commission 'to review the constitutional position of the police' (Bottoms and Stevenson 1990). But it is signi-ficant that the Royal Commission's national opinion survey found 'an overwhelming vote of confidence in the police'. As far as police acceptance by the public is con-cerned, the 1950s seem a 'Golden Age' of tranquillity and accord, with only hesitant harbingers of coming crisis (Weinberger 1995: 1–2).

POLICING BY CONSENT

The orthodox police historians saw the police as having already overcome any serious opposition to their presence by the early years of the twentieth century. Critchley (1978: 326), for instance, characterized the 1900s as 'the zenith' of police public relations in Britain. He cited a 1908 *Times* editorial which claimed: 'The policeman in London is not merely guardian of the peace; he is the best friend of a mass of people who have no other counsellor or protector.' This rosy portrait aroused the ire of the revisionists. Against its cosy complacency they posed a contrary picture. 'The "public" (meaning the middle and upper classes) . . . held their "bobby" in patronizing "affection and esteem" . . . but these sentiments were never shared by the undermass, nor in fact by the working class generally' (R. Roberts 1973: 100).

The Royal Commission on the Police's Final Report (1962) was criticized rightly for neglecting aspects of their own survey data which called into question the optimistic overall summary (Whitaker 1964: 151–7). However, an examination of the survey results suggests that there was no evidence of variation *by social class* in attitudes to the police. While 85.2 per cent of the professional and managerial classes had 'great respect' for the police, so too did 81.8 per cent of the skilled and 81.9 per cent of the semi or unskilled working class. 24.3 per cent of the semi and unskilled working class and 29.8 per cent of the skilled working class respondents reported 'unsatisfactory experience' of police conduct, but even more (33.3 per cent) of the professional and managerial strata did. Whilst 12.1 per cent of the police sample thought the 'upper classes' were more resentful of the police than they had been ten years previously, only 10.5 per cent of them felt this about the 'working classes'. This confirms those contemporary opinions that stressed the widespread acceptance of the police throughout the class structure. The Shaw and Williamson (1972) survey of public attitudes to the police, one of the few to include a class dimension, has often been cited as evidence of working-class reservations about policing (for example, M. Brogden 1982: 204). But their data showed only tiny inter-class differences, and some results went in the opposite direction to the one predicted. For example, they found that 86 per cent of respondents in class III had 'respect' for the police, compared to only 81.7 per cent in class I.

Apart from the empirical evidence, there are conceptual ambiguities in the much-debated notion of policing by consent. Both the orthodox and the revisionist approaches operate with absurdly absolutist conceptions of what consensual policing could mean. Policing is an inherently conflict-ridden enterprise. The essential function and distinctive resource of the police is the potential use of legitimate force (Bittner 1974). Of course, the art and craft of successful police work is to minimise actual recourse to force. But a 'benign bobby . . . still brings to the situation a uniform, a truncheon, and a battery of resource charges . . . which can be employed when appeasement fails and fists start flying' (Punch 1979: 116).

If there was universal consensus about norms, values and appropriate modes of social behaviour there would be no need for a police force. In most situations there is somebody being policed against, whose assent to policing, at any rate there and then, is bound to be brittle. At best they may utter a grudging 'It's a fair cop, guv' in the time-honoured tradition of British gangster movies. But those who are frequently at the receiving end of police authority are unlikely to give it much consent other than a sullen acceptance of *de facto* power. Realistically, the most that 'policing by consent' can mean is not universal love of the police, but that those at the sharp end of police practices do not extend their resentment at specific actions into a generalized withdrawal of legitimacy from the institution of policing *per se*.

By the 1950s 'policing by consent' had been achieved in Britain to the maximal degree it is ever attainable. The police enjoyed the wholehearted approval of the majority of the population who did not experience the coercive exercise of police powers to any significant extent, and *de facto* acceptance of the legitimacy of the institution by those who did. Police *power*, that is, the capacity to inflict legal sanctions including force, had been transmuted into authority, power which is accepted as at least minimally legitimate.[3] How did the police come to be accepted as legitimate authority figures rather than politically controversial bearers of power? How did their image change from 'crushers' to 'bobbies'?

THE CONSTRUCTION OF CONSENT

The achievement of consensus policing in Britain was partly the product of specific aspects of police organizational policy. It also was helped by (and helped) the process whereby the working class, the main source of initial hostility to the new police, came to be incorporated into the political and economic institutions of British society. Police acceptance was mutually interdependent with a wider process of pacification of social relations.

Police policy was crucial to this. The policies were by no means absolutely determined by the political or social character of Britain. They were more or less conscious choices between options, and could have been different. At the same time they were not free-floating decisions, independent of the political balance and cultural traditions of British society. Many sociologists have argued that the distinctive character of British policing, its relative legality and eschewal of force, is a product of social homogeneity and tranquillity, especially as contrasted with the USA (Banton 1964: chap. 8). But the opposite is the case. The architects of the benign and dignified English police image, Robert Peel, Colonel Rowan, and Richard Mayne, adopted the policies they did because of the strength of opposition to the very existence of the police. They encouraged a low-profile, legalistic stance precisely in the teeth of the bitter political conflict and acute social divisions of English society in the first half of the nineteenth century, not as an expression of underlying harmony.[4] In the USA by contrast, the more free-wheeling and aggressive style of policing evolved not as a consequence of social divisions, but because of the political integration of American society as something approaching a property-owning democracy (W. Miller 1999). Popular participation in government meant confidence that control of the police could be entrusted to the political process, rather than to a tight framework of legal rules and regulations.

The policy choices made by the creators of the British police were central to the way the force was accepted. But these policy-makers acted in conditions of class resistance and political conflict not of their own making, and were informed and limited by particular ideological traditions. There were eight specific policies laid down by Peel, Rowan, and Mayne which were crucial for the engineering of consent in the face of initial opposition, and which need to be explored before the process of legitimation down to 1959, and the subsequent repoliticization, can be understood.

POLICE POLICY AND LEGITIMATION

Bureaucratic organization

The basis of the 'new' police idea was the establishment of a full-time force of professional police officers, organized into a bureaucratic hierarchy. This contrasted with the previous reliance on a motley assortment of part-timers, entrepreneurial thief-takers and amateur volunteers. Entry and promotion were meritocratic not partisan or nepotistic. Rowan and Mayne set initial entrance requirements that were quite demanding and stringently applied to applicants by the two Metropolitan commissioners (W. Miller 1999: 267). We saw in chapter 1 that in many provincial forces established after the 1835 and 1839 Acts there was much more continuity than in the Met between the 'old' and 'new' police. But in the provinces, too, after 1856 and the introduction of a minimal element of standardization through the Inspectorate of Constabulary, this began to change (Emsley 1996: chap. 3. However, both private and amateur police are very much part of the scene today, in the shape of the security industry and the Special Constabulary; see South 1988, 1997; Johnston 1991, 1992, 2000; Leon 1991; M Gill and Mawby 1991; T. Jones and Newburn 1998).

Training was not taken very seriously in many forces until after the 1919–20 reports of the Desborough Committee, which introduced a much stronger element of standardization and central direction into all aspects of administration and conditions of service (Weinberger 1995: chaps. 1–2). The Committee had been appointed following the 1918 and 1919 police strikes in London and Liverpool, and resulted in a major shift towards centralization (G. Reynolds and Judge 1968; Critchley 1978: 190–4; Reiner 1978: 24–5). In the Metropolitan Police there had been some minimal training from the early days (W. Miller 1999: 41).

Rowan and Mayne elaborated a strict set of rules and regulations governing not only the internal standards of dress, deportment and discipline, but the prescribed demeanour for dealing with the public. (Critchley 1978: 52–5; W. Miller 1999: 37–42). These were inculcated during drill and training, and enforced by sanctions for disobedience. In the early years there was a high turnover due to dismissals, mainly for drunkenness.

A chain of command was constructed on quasi-military lines, and at first the policy was to appoint former non-commissioned military officers to the higher ranks, because of their experience as disciplinarians. This later changed in favour of internal promotion from the ranks (Wall 1998). But the promotion system itself became an instrument of bureaucratic control. Only those who obeyed orders 'readily and punctually' could aspire to be promoted, for 'he who has been accustomed to submit to discipline will be considered best qualified to command' (W. Miller 1999: 40).

The policy of bureaucratization was partly contradicted by low pay. This, plus the irksome discipline itself, meant that all early police forces had a massive problem of rapid resignations. But during the 1870s the notion of policing as a career offering status and security, if not high short-term pay, began to emerge, and a more stable body of professional officers developed.

Although never realized completely, the image of policemen as disciplined members of a bureaucratic organization of professionals was constructed by the 1850s in London. An 1856 article in the *London Quarterly Review* summed up the ever-uncertain process of conversion of human raw material into 'well-regulated machines', impersonal embodiments of bureaucratic authority: 'Amid the bustle of Piccadilly or the roar of Oxford Street, P.C.X. 59 stalks along, an institution rather than a man' (cited in W. Miller 1991: 15).

The rule of law

The way in which the police maintained order and enforced the law was itself supposed to be governed by legalistic procedures and constraints. Adherence to the rule of law was a prime requirement of the Metropolitan Police. At first the London 'police courts' were generally unsympathetic to the force, and they remained fiercely concerned to maintain their role and image as independent regulators of the legality of police conduct (J. Davis 1984: 332). On several occasions the magistrates laid down rulings which effectively halted particular law enforcement policies (J. Davis 1984: 328).

Although this was an impediment to the exercise of police power, which the commissioners resented, at a deeper level they were aware that subjection to legal regulation was a major factor in the legitimation of police authority. In any case, the magistrates seemed to have become less wont to question police behaviour after the mid-century, as indicated by a growing tendency to dismiss charges of assault brought against the police, and a greater readiness to convict on police evidence (J. Davis 1984: 329).

The commissioners were well aware of the importance of the police maintaining an image of subjection to the rule of law as a way of alleviating opposition. They laid down strict regulations and sanctions governing the use of the wide discretionary powers conferred on constables by statutes such as the Vagrancy Act 1824 (source of the notorious 'sus' law), and the Metropolitan Police Act 1839, which conferred on the London police broad stop-and-search powers. While the Commissioners believed such powers were needed by constables, they exerted strict disciplinary sanctions over abuse, and encouraged 'all respectable persons' to bring complaints to them (W. Miller 1999: 4–12, 56–66). The commissioners also laid down narrow rules on interrogation and treatment of suspects:

It is clear that the Commissioners sought, on the whole successfully, to commit their men to the cautious exercise of their powers within the framework of legal protections of civil liberties. This principle was a . . . key element in securing public acceptance of the force (Miller 1999: 94).

The strategy of minimal force

All police forces would claim to use as little force as necessary. The British tradition stands out, however, for its eschewal of arms. With characteristic forthrightness, in a television interview Sir Robert Mark, commissioner of the Met, once articulated the crowd control strategy of the Metropolitan Police thus: 'The real art of policing a free society or a democracy is to win by appearing to lose.' Their secret weapon was not water cannon, tear gas or rubber bullets, but public sympathy. To this end, he claimed, the Metropolitan Police had trained an especially comely horse the—'Brigitte Bardot'—of police horses to collapse, feigning death, at a word of command. This was guaranteed to win the support of the animal-loving British public. The British 'police advantage' of public support rather than lethal hardware as a means of crowd control was a carefully chosen strategy (Bowden 1978: 35, chap. 9). It was a calculated response to the fears of an oppressive *gendarmerie* which had motivated so much resistance to the force.

Rowan and Mayne limited constables' weapons to the truncheon, carried concealed until 1863. Its use was intended to be a last resort. Complaints of police violence diminished after the early 1830s, implying that the commissioner's regulations had some effect on behaviour (W. Miller 1999: 49). On specific dangerous assignments or beats, selected officers might carry a pistol or a cutlass, but each occasion of use or even drawing of such a weapon was closely scrutinized, and if not justified as self-defence would probably result in dismissal.

Some post-1839 county police forces, notably Essex, did adopt a military model of policing (Steedman 1984: 21–5). But the strategy of policing that the Home Office encouraged after 1856 was prevention by 'a police force essentially civil, unarmed and acting without any assistance from a military force' (Steedman 1984: 32–8; Emsley 1996: 54–9). The army was available as the ultimate backup should preventive policing fail, and it was used on many occasions in the latter part of the nineteenth and early twentieth centuries. But gradually the non-lethally-armed civilian police force became the sole means of riot control. Paradoxically, one of the last occasions troops acted in a public order role was in 1919 during the Liverpool police strike.

Although they have certainly never acted with kid gloves, there is no doubt that the British police developed a tradition of containing industrial disputes and political demonstrations with minimum force when contrasted with the experience of other countries. There have been periods of special anxiety and controversy about intensified political and industrial conflict, with attendant complaints of police brutality and right-wing bias. The most notable have been the series of clashes between police and the organized unemployed of 'Outcast London' in the late 1880s, the bitter industrial disputes immediately before and after the First World War, and the conflicts between the police and the unemployed movement and anti-Fascist demonstrators in the 1930s (J. Morgan 1987; Weinberger 1991). But the Home Office tried to ensure that police tactics were kept within legal limits (Bailey 1981*b*: 9–125; P. Thurmond Smith 1985).

In the unprecedented economic and political crisis of the 1930s public order became an issue in a way it had not been since the middle of the nineteenth century. The violence surrounding Fascist meetings was the stimulus for the Public Order Act 1936. Concern about the brutality used to suppress marches of the National Unemployed Workers' Movement, led to the growth of the National Council for Civil

Liberties after 1934. A detailed consideration of 1930s conflicts concludes, however, that, despite considerable evidence of bias and brutality by police officers against the NUWM and anti-Fascists, 'the police do seem to have reacted less in political terms than in response to the challenge to public order and to their own position as the custodians of law and order' (Stevenson and Cook 1977: 243). Certainly, the level of violence or police repression was not comparable to that in most other industrial countries suffering from the depression. Geary (1985) documents the declining levels of violence between police and pickets in industrial conflicts between the 1890s and the 1970s, arguing that industrial conflict changed from something resembling a war to something more like a sporting contest. This pattern of non-violent and non-confrontational policing of the 'normal' industrial dispute was confirmed by Kahn et al (1983 chap. 5). The policing of industrial disputes reverted to a higher level of violence in the mid-1980s, however, as we will see below.

As far as individual violence involving police is concerned, there is similar evidence of a sustained decline in the first century of policing. The revisionists have all taken assaults on the police as a sensitive index of working-class rejection (Storch 1975; P. Cohen 1979; Weinberger 1981: 67–71). Gatrell has shown that from the 1860s until the First World War there was a dramatic decline both in assaults in general, and specifically in assaults against the police. From a national annual average of 67.5 per 100,000 in 1857–60, the recorded rate of assaults on the police had fallen to 24.1 per 100,000 in 1911–14, with a consistent decline in between (Gatrell 1980: 286–93. The accuracy of the recorded figures is debatable in view of the long-standing police tendency to under-record such offences; see Weinberger 1995: 31–2). Whatever the totality of reasons underlying this long-run decline in violence, it is clear that the police reflected and contributed to it.

Non-partisanship

When the 'new' police force was established working-class leaders and Radicals saw it as a thoroughly political military and spy agency, 'the minion and paid servant of the Government' (Poor Man's Guardian, 11 October 1830, p. 3).

Peel, Rowan and Mayne recognized quite clearly that the key to legitimating the police was the presentation of an image of non-partisanship. Public acceptance depended upon the police not being seen as political. Rowan and Mayne declared that in the middle of acute social conflict they 'endeavoured to prevent the slightest practical feeling or bias, being shown or felt by the police . . . the force should not only be, in fact, but be believed to be impartial in action, and should act on principle' (cited in W. Miller 1999: 12).

The police were insulated from direct political control, and police authorities (the home secretary, local watch and standing joint committees) tended to abstain from interventions in operational policy. It was not until the 1920s, though, that this discreet stance began to be transmuted explicitly into a notion of constabulary independence from policy guidance, which would have been considered 'so unconstitutional as to be absurd' in the nineteenth century (G. Marshall 1965: 31).

Peel and the Metropolitan commissioners did insist on strict exclusion of patronage in appointments and promotions at a time when this was normal civil service practice. Police officers were also denied the vote until 1887. This tradition dies hard. In an article celebrating the 150th anniversary of the Metropolitan Police, the then commissioner, Sir David McNee, wrote: 'I no longer exercise my right to vote, nor have I since I was appointed a chief officer of police. Police officers must be men and women of the middle, bound only by the rule of law' (McNee 1979: 25). Although enfranchised in 1887, police officers remain forbidden to join, or affiliate to (and until 1972 even to associate with), outside trade unions on the ground that this would impugn their political impartiality (Reiner 1978: 111–2).

The insistence on suppressing indications of overt political control or partisanship softened the initial conception of the police as a tool of government oppression (Emsley 1996: chap. 5). As an 1864 article in *Chambers's Magazine* said of the police, 'they know nothing of politics; the man in blue preserves his neutral tint . . . the good old cause of order is the only side the policeman supports' (cited in Miller 1999: 13).

Accountability

Although the police were not formally controlled by any elected body, they were seen as accountable in two ways. First, the legality of police action was reviewable by the courts; the police were held accountable to the rule of law (as seen in (ii) above). Second, they were purported to be accountable through an almost mystical process of identification with the British people, not the state. Although lacking any tangible control by elected institutions, they were supposed to be in tune with the popular will because of their social representativeness and lack of special powers. The ideology developed of the constable as 'citizen in uniform', doing on a paid basis what all citizens had the power and social duty to do. This conception is most explicitly articulated by the 1962 *Report of the Royal Commission on the Police* (Para. 30, pp. 10–11). As Reith summed it up, 'the police are the public and the public are the police' (Reith 1956: 287). The recruitment policies of the police have always been attuned to this principle, drawing upon manual working class backgrounds representative of the mass of the people (Weinberger 1995: chaps. 1, 3). Since the First World War this principle has been supposed to govern even chief officer selection in all forces, and since the Second World War it has done, with all chief constables working their way up through the ranks and almost all sharing working–class origins (Wall 1998).

The service role

The notion of the friendly bobby is summed up for modern ears by the cliché, 'If you want to know the time, ask a policeman.' The meaning was rather different in the nineteenth century. 'The popular catchphrase . . . reflected not so much the confidence of the Victorians in the reliability of the police, as their assumption that any policeman who did not quickly . . . win . . . a watch from the pockets of a drunken reveller was unnaturally honest or dull' (Rolph 1962: 52).

The nineteenth-century police reformers cultivated the service role in order to secure legitimacy for more coercive policing functions. Edwin Chadwick was the most explicit about this. He urged that it would 'exercise a beneficial influence on the labouring classes . . . by showing them that they are cared for by the authorities, and are not, as they must but too commonly suppose, merely and exclusively the subjects of coercion' (Donajgrodski 1977*b*: 67).

Certainly in the nineteenth century the police carried out a number of tasks wider than law enforcement and order maintenance. Some were formal duties, such as inspecting weights and measures or inspecting bridges, others were informal, such as knocking people up early in the morning for work (Emsley 1983: 158–9). Then as now these were often regarded by the police themselves as unwelcome 'extraneous' duties (Steedman 1984: 53–4). Many of the service tasks benefited the middle class at the expense of the working class, such as the enforcement of nuisance laws. But others did benefit the working class too. How crucial the service role was in securing consent may be questioned, and to some it is mere ideological window-dressing (Brogden 1982: 208–19). Arguably the crime-control role of the police, in particular their taking over of most prosecutions, was a more valued and useful service to the mass of the population than the 'friendly' non-coercive 'services' to which the term is usually confined. But the 'service' role has played a part in securing police legitimation.

Preventive policing

The primacy of prevention over detection is emphasized in the famous opening lines of Peel's celebrated instructions to the Metropolitan Police (cited in Critchley 1978: 52–3), which are still taught to recruits:

It should be understood at the outset, that the object to be attained is the prevention of crime. To this great end every effort of the police is to be directed. The security of person and property . . . will thus be better effected than by the detection and punishment of the offender after he has succeeded in committing crime.

The practical implementation of this principle meant the concentration of the force's manpower on uniform patrol of regular beats in full and open public view (Weinberger 1995: chap. 2). This was motivated not only by a belief in the efficacy of the police constable's 'scarecrow function'. It was also a response to that element in the anti-police opposition which invoked fears of the abominable French experience of undercover police spies.

This hostility to the idea of plain clothes police delayed the formation of detective branches for many years. Mayne, in particular, was concerned to minimize use of detectives because of public fears about police spying (W. Miller 1999: 33–4). In 1842 Rowan was able partly to overcome Mayne's anxieties and they secured the home secretary's approval for a detective branch of six men. When it was proposed to expand the number of detectives in 1845, *The Times* declared: 'If it be dangerous, and perhaps unconstitutional, to maintain a few government spies, what will be the effect of impressing that character on the whole police force of this vast metropolis?' (cited in Baldwin and Kinsey 1982: 11). By 1868 when Mayne died there were still only fifteen detectives in a force of 8000. Mayne's successor, Lieutenant-Colonel Edmund Henderson, prompted partly by a moral panic about rising crime in the late 1860s, placed more emphasis on the detective branch, created permanent divisional detectives, and ended Mayne's policy of regularly rotating plainclothes officers back to uniform in order to reduce the risk of corruption (Petrow 1993). Mayne's fears were vindicated when, in 1877, the three top Scotland Yard detectives were involved in a major bribery scandal. Paradoxically, the response to this was the establishment of a separate Criminal Investigation Department (Emsley 1996: 72–3). By the late 1870s the trend towards increasing specialization and emphasis on detection was well entrenched, playing down the role of the general practice uniformed constable.

By the 1880s the police had become sufficiently well entrenched in public confidence for the formation of a specifically political unit, the Special Irish Branch, initially to deal with Fenian terrorism (B. Porter, 1987). It subsequently acquired a wider remit than Irish terrorism, and became the Special Branch. But in the early years the primacy of the idea of prevention by uniformed patrol was a factor in the achievement of legitimation, quelling fears about armies of undercover spies.

Police effectiveness

The previous factors in the legitimation of the police all point to ways in which strategy was more or less successfully directed to allaying fears about the harmful consequences of the police. But that the worst did not happen does not mean that anyone felt the police had any positive value.

The final aspect of police policy contributing to their legitimation was the cultivation of at least the appearance of effectiveness, in terms of not just service tasks but the core mandate of crime control and order maintenance. How effective the police actually were in crime control remains debatable (Gatrell 1980, 1990; Weinberger 1995; H. Taylor 1998a, b, 1999), but certainly the appearance of success in crime-fighting was cultivated. In the 1860s there was a moral panic in the respectable classes about a new 'crime wave', and the police, especially the aged Mayne, were blamed. Fear of crime was fuelled by anxiety about a supposed epidemic of garrottings (the Victorian equivalent of mugging) and by rising official statistics of recorded indictable offences. Conservative critics bemoaned the pernicious consequences of soft-hearted penal policies and demanded stricter control of ticket-of-leave men. They also campaigned for the police to be 'armed with preventive powers similar to those exercised by the Continental police'. This was precisely what working-class spokesmen feared. *Reynolds's Weekly Newspaper* claimed that 'The Government proposes converting the English Peeler into a species of continental policeman . . . the mouchard, or spy, will become an established institution among us.'

Gradually, however, the bulk of the working class became reconciled to the criminal justice system and availed themselves of its services. A sizeable proportion of the work of the police courts comprised prosecutions and summonses for theft and assault brought by working-class men and women. While most theft cases were brought by the 'respectable' working class, 'more surprisingly it was members of the casual poor, sometimes convicted criminals themselves, who predominated in making assault charges' (J. Davis 1984: 321). These prosecutions were usually a phase in the conduct of longer-running disputes between working-class people: 'a great many prosecutions brought by the working class did not so much replace informal sanctions as operate in addition to them' (J. Davis 1984: 330–1). Slowly, it seems, the new police and criminal justice system were inserting themselves into working-class life not only as an intrusive controlling apparatus but also as a potential means of redress. Historical understanding of this process is only now developing, but the growth of a sense of police effectiveness was probably at least as significant as the image-building aspects of legitimation. Police success 'in securing the cooperation of the public depended less on keeping a rosy image of impartiality than on securing a near-monopoly over the market in violence and redress. Street by street, the police negotiated a complex, shifting, largely unspoken "contract"' (Ignatieff 1979: 444–5). This was threatened by heavy-handed control of industrial or political conflict, or by over-zealous policing of working-class leisure pursuits. Recognizing this, the early Metropolitan Police Commissioners were discreet in their enforcement of laws which were unpopular with the working class, such as the Sabbath laws (W. Miller 1999: 129–38).

By the 1870s, then, the police had come to be seen as offering an effective law enforcement service to the middle and upper classes, who complained when its quality seemed to decline. The working class also made use of it, but the less respectable sections of this class were predominantly at the receiving end of law-and-order campaigns. As long as the working class was and felt largely excluded from even minimal political and economic participation, so too would their acquiescence to policing be fragile and grudging.

THE SOCIAL CONTEXT OF POLICE LEGITIMATION

The all-important final factor which facilitated the legitimation of the police was not an aspect of police policy, but the changing social, economic and political context. The working class, the main structurally rooted source of opposition to the police, gradually, unevenly and incompletely came to be incorporated as citizens into the political institutions of British society (T. Marshall 1950; Bulmer and Rees 1996; P. Waddington 1999).

The process of incorporation had very clear limits. It enabled the bulk of the working class to share in the growth of the economy. However, class inequality remained in proportionate terms virtually unaltered, and has widened substantially since the return of free market economics in the late 1970s (Goldthorpe, Llewellyn, and Payne 1980; Commission on Social Justice 1994; Hutton 1995; Levitas 1998; Davies 1998).

None the less, the wide gulf between the 'two nations', which was sharply manifest to all in the mid-nineteenth century as the new police came into being, had become hedged round and blurred by the 1950s, the high point of police legitimation. In the 'affluent society' there was supposed to be an 'end of ideology' and this included controversy about the police. In the late 1950s complacency was ending in many spheres of public life, and there was sufficient disquiet about policing to necessitate the announcement of the Royal Commission on the Police.

This should not detract from the accomplishment of the first century of policing. From a widely hated and feared institution, the police had come to be regarded as the embodiment of impersonal, rule-bound authority, enforcing democratically enacted legislation on behalf of the broad mass of society rather than any partisan interest, and constrained by tight legal requirements of due process. This was achieved by a variety of police organizational strategies, but they succeeded only because of the wider social context of working-class incorporation.

FROM PLODS TO PIGS: THE POLITICIZATION OF THE POLICE SINCE 1959

From a position of almost complete invisibility as a political issue, after 1959 policing became a babble of scandalous revelation, controversy and competing agendas for reform. The tacit contract between police and public, so delicately drawn between the 1850s and 1950s, began to fray glaringly. Evidence mounted of an increasing haemorrhage of public confidence in the police (T. Jones, McLean, and Young 1986; Crawford et al. 1990; Skogan 1990a).

The 1960 Royal Commission on the Police was the outcome of a series of causes célèbres which seem in retrospect pretty small beer. In 1956 and 1957 disciplinary or legal proceedings involving alleged corruption were brought against the chief constables of Cardiganshire, Brighton and Worcester. Again in 1957, allegations were made in parliament that a policeman had beaten a boy in Thurso (a small Scottish town), and that this complaint had not been properly investigated. In 1959 a row in Nottingham raised the fundamental constitutional issue of the respective responsibilities for law enforcement of chief constable and watch committee. Captain Popkess, the chief constable, was suspended by the Watch Committee because he refused to give them a report of an investigation into criminal allegations involving councillors. The home secretary told the committee to reinstate Popkess, but the case illustrated the lack of clarity about the roles of chief constable, watch committee and home secretary (G. Marshall 1965: 13–14).

Other anxieties about policing mounted in the background. After 1954 the crime statistics began to rise inexorably each year, heralding 'a crime wave unparalleled in modern times' (Critchley 1978: 254). The teddyboys and beatniks of the mid-1950s created new 'folk devils' and presaged perennial moral panic about the threats to law and order posed by new and ever more bizarre styles of youth culture (S. Cohen 1972; Pearson 1983; Loader 1996; Newburn 1997; M. Lee 1998). Future concerns about public order policing were signalled by the 1958 Notting Hill and Nottingham race riots, the 1956 anti-Suez demonstrations in Trafalgar Square, and the launching of CND and the Aldermaston marches in 1957.

The immediate trigger for the Royal Commission was none of these grave matters, but a Whitehall farce. In December 1958 Brian Rix the comedy star was stopped for speeding by a PC Eastmond. An obscure argument developed between Eastmond and a civil servant who intervened in the incident, resulting in mutual assault allegations, which were settled out of court. This provoked a parliamentary debate which raised all the fundamental issues of police accountability. During the debate the home secretary indicated his intention to institute the Royal Commission. It considered the case for a national police force, the roles of chief constable, local police authorities and the home secretary, the relationship between police and public, the complaints system and police pay.

Despite rejecting the argument that a nationalized police force would be a step towards a police state, the commission did not propose nationalisation, although the case for it was effectively argued in a highly respected memorandum of dissent by Dr A. L. Goodhart. The majority report claimed that the advantages of rationalization, coordination and efficiency could be achieved by a more limited programme of amalgamations and greater central control.

The commission's proposals on accountability and complaints, and their implementation in the Police Act 1964, were widely seen as vague, confused and contradictory (Whitaker 1964: chap. 7; G. Marshall 1965). The net effect of the Act was to strengthen the hands of the Home Office and of the chief constables at the expense of local police authorities (Jefferson and Grimshaw 1984b; Lustgarten 1986; Reiner 1991).

The continuing relevance of the problems that had led to the Royal Commission were highlighted by some scandals which occurred before the passage of the Police Act 1964, and which demonstrated the need for an effective system for complaints and accountability. One involved Challenor, a detective sergeant in the Meteropolitan Police, who planted false evidence on at least two dozen suspects, apparently unnoticed by colleagues and supervisors (Grigg 1965). The Sheffield Inquiry into allegations of brutality involving a 'rhino whip' underlined the reluctance of officers to 'hear, or speak, or see any evil' about their colleagues (Whitaker 1964: 136–7). There was also concern about rough police handling of the 1961 anti-nuclear protests.

Despite its inadequacies, the Police Act 1964 constituted a settlement which was generally accepted for a time. This was aided by the transformation of police organization in the mid-1960s, centring on the new, motorized Unit Beat System of patrol (a full account of it is given in Weatheritt 1986). The emphasis was on technology, specialization and managerial professionalism as the keys to winning 'the fight against crime'. 'The "British Bobby" was recast as the tough, dashing, formidable (but still brave and honest) "Crime-Buster"' (Chibnall 1977: 71).

Given the now universal bad press accorded the 'fire brigade' policing style that the Unit Beat System brought into being, it is salutary to recall that its birth was greeted with general acclaim (Weatheritt 1986). It was intended simultaneously to bolster efficiency, improve relations with the public, and advance the policeman's lot. As originally conceived, the area constables would have the function of preserving close relations with local communities, the Panda cars would provide a faster emergency service, the collator would analyse information provided by the patrol officers for use in detecting offences, and all policemen would gain enhanced status and job-interest. All birds were to be killed by the same stone. In practice, the system soon frustrated these hopes, partly because of shortage of manpower to implement it properly, but primarily because of the unintended consequences of the ability of rank-and-file culture to frustrate managerial purposes. The constables' action-centred perspective on policing was accentuated by the technology of fast cars, sirens and flashing blue lights. What was intended as professionalization ended up as the politicization of relations with the public (Holdaway 1977, 1983; Reiner 1978: 189–92). At first, however, the police image may have changed from the cosy 1950s Dixon of Dock Green to the more abrasive Inspector Barlow of the 1960s TV series *Z Cars*, (see A. Clarke 1992; Reiner 1994; Leishman 1995; R. C. Mawby 1998*c*), but neither was a politically controversial figure. The police were no longer Plods, but not yet pigs.

By the end of the 1960s the growth of the counter-culture, and police clashes with anti-Vietnam War and anti-Apartheid demonstrators in 1968–9, heralded a renewed politicization of policing. In 1970, the Police Federation chairman announced to the annual conference: 'We have been eyeball to eyeball with the fanatics, the lunatics and the hooligans.' Later that year, the Federation magazine drew attention to the institution of a 'Pig of the Month' contest in *Frendz*, an underground newspaper.

'Should we be upset? Not at all. The pig has made a notable contribution to our national well-being over the centuries. As such, it has a great advantage over hippy squatters . . . whose concepts of sanitation are far more primitive than its own . . . In America, they say P-I-G stands for Pride, Integrity and Guts' (*Police*, September 1970, p. 6).

What processes were transforming the police image from Plod to pig? All the factors that produced the earlier depoliticization of policing had question-marks placed against them.

BUREAUCRATIC ORGANIZATION?[5]

Recruitment, training, and discipline

The first element in the undermining of police legitimacy was the erosion of the image of an efficient, disciplined bureaucracy. Partly this was a question of standards of entry and training, which (though much higher than in the nineteenth century) had not kept up with general improvements (Weinberger 1995: 14–15). The generous pay award recommended by the 1960 Royal Commission had been intended to remedy this problem, but police earnings were rapidly outstripped by inflation. The poor educational standards of recruits—and in particular the shortage of graduates— which the Royal Commission had lamented, remained a concern (J. Martin and Wilson 1969). Despite increasing attention to training, which was straining the manpower capacities of forces (J. Martin and Wilson: 103), there were still many complaints that it was inadequate for the complex needs of modern society (P. Evans 1974: 187; Whitaker 1979: 215). The old emphasis on drill and discipline was also being eroded as a response to a growing ideology of 'man-management', and the need to match changing social fashions in order to attract recruits (Reiner 1978: 186–94).

There have been many attempts since the 1960s to raise educational and training standards. In the 1960s various schemes were introduced to attract graduates to the service, and encourage higher education for serving police officers (Adlam 1987). These included the Graduate Entry Scheme, the Bramshill Scholarships, and the Special Course at Bramshill for potential high-flyers. (These have played an increasing part in the careers of senior officers; see Reiner 1991; Wall 1998). However, significant results were not achieved until the 1980s, when as a result of the 1978 Edmund-Davies pay award (and unemployment outside the service) the intake of graduates accelerated sharply to about 12 per cent of recruits per annum. There was also increasing interest from serving officers in specialist criminal justice degrees (M. Brogden and Graham 1988; Tierney 1989; J. Brown 1996). Significant changes occurred in recruit training, as well, largely following from the 1982 Scarman Report (Fielding 1988; Southgate 1988; Bull and Horncastle 1989). Despite the merit of these developments, they have not prevented an erosion of public confidence in police professional standards.

CORRUPTION SCANDALS

The main way in which the image of the police force as a disciplined, impersonal bureaucracy came to be dented was the series of Scotland Yard corruption scandals that rocked it after 1969 (Cox, Shirley, and Short 1977; Punch 1985). Since then the police have experienced a repeated cycle of scandal and reform (Sherman 1978; Newburn 1999). In retrospect the establishment of the CID as a separate department in 1878, in the wake of a corruption scandal, had only aggravated the problem. The Met's own historian concluded that 'it is beyond argument that by the summer of 1922 the CID had become a thoroughly venal private army' (Ascoli 1979: 210). Allegations of malpractice by London detectives remained rife (Laurie 1970: chap. 10).

None the less, the revelations published by *The Times* in November 1969 were a bombshell that still reverberates. It was not simply that *The Times* had been able to tape-record discussions between detectives and a villain, thus proving their allegations beyond the shadow of a doubt. Nor was it just that the corruption uncovered was very grave (involving deals to cover up serious crimes, setting up criminals as *agents provocateurs*, perjury and planting of evidence). What was most shocking was the revelation of the systematic, institutionalized and widespread network of corruption, the so-called 'firm within a firm.' The Yard's initial attempt at investigation only confirmed this, with a pattern of obstruction, leaks, and disappearing documents. Eventually Frank Williamson, formerly a Manchester detective chief superintendent but in 1970 Her Majesty's Inspector of Constabulary (Crime), was brought in. Williamson's investigation was also frustrated, and he resigned prematurely, in disgust at his experiences.

During the mid-1970s there were two more major corruption scandals at the Met, one involving the Drug Squad, the other the Obscene Publications Squad. Both revealed systematic malpractice, and led to the imprisonment of several senior detectives. The Drug Squad under Detective Chief Inspector Kelaher was implicated in unorthodox methods, including fabrication and manipulation of evidence in order to achieve major 'busts'. The 'Porn' Squad was riddled with graft on a grand scale. Relations between crooks and criminals were warm and intimate. On one occasion a pornography dealer went into Holborn Police Station wearing a CID tie to examine seized material for 'recycling'. Confiscated blue films were shown on the squad's projector at regular Friday evening 'stag' parties (Cox, Shirley, and Short 1977: 168).

Home Secretary Reginald Maudling's answer was to appoint as commissioner an 'outsider', Robert Mark, who had been assistant commissioner since 1967 but had previously served entirely in provincial forces. Mark's appointment was seen as clearly signalling a battle against corruption: 'He had the reputation of a "Mr. Clean", the "Manchester Martinet", the "Lone Ranger from Leicester"' (Cox, Shirley, and Short 1977: 132).

Mark introduced a dramatic strategy of associated reforms, clearly seeing the excision of the 'cancer' at the Yard as the price of its continued independence (Mark 1978, chaps. 7–10). He established a new specialist elite department, A10, to investigate all complaints against police officers, put a uniformed officer in charge of the Yard CID and uniformed supervisors over all divisional detectives, abolished the 'Porn' squad, moved many detectives back into uniform, rotated detectives frequently, and cultivated more open relations with the press. As a result of this new climate some five hundred policemen left the force during Mark's period as commissioner, many voluntarily in anticipation of being investigated.

The resilience of corruption at the Yard was shown by new revelations in 1978. They alleged involvement of detectives, including some in the Robbery Squad, in major armed robberies (Ball, Chester, and Perrott 1979). The allegations were an unwelcome by-product of the 1970s strategy of developing 'supergrasses'—informants who are induced to reveal large numbers of names in return for immunity from prosecution. (This tactic was subsequently transported to Northern Ireland, with equally dubious results; see Greer, 1995a and b). The commissioner, Sir David McNee, responded by setting up Operation Countryman under the direction of the Dorset chief constable, Arthur Hambleton. Hambleton and his team claimed on several occasions that their work was being sabotaged by corrupt Yard pressure, and by the time the operation was wound up only two convictions had been achieved. Yard officers in turn spread smears about the incompetence of the 'Swedey', as the provincial detectives came to be contemptuously called.

The Countryman investigations cast doubt on any idea that the endemic corruption in the Yard detective squads had been eliminated. Research on professional criminals suggests a perennial web of corrupt deals and police malpractice (L. Taylor 1984: chap. 8; Hobbs 1988, 1995).

The Countryman inquiry was especially disturbing because it did not involve specialist detectives in the vice area, which criminologists had long argued was a special breeding-ground for police corruption. The 250 years' experience of thief-taking suggests that the standard methods of plain clothes criminal investigation, the cultivation of close relations with criminals as informants, operate perennially on the borderline of legality. During the 'Golden Age' of high public confidence in the police, the evidence of police and underworld memoirs and oral histories suggests extensive and routinized corruption occurred behind the façade of legitimacy (Mark 1978; White 1986; Weinberger 1995: chap.10; Emsley 1996: 241–7). No way has yet proven successful of promoting effective detection of serious crime without the dangers of corruption and other systematic illegalities and malpractices. As Tom Tullett, a former CID detective, and *Daily Mirror* chief crime reporter, put it in his eulogistic account of the 1960s Murder Squad investigation of gangland killings: 'In this kind of "war" the police had to think like villains themselves, using every ruse, trick and disguise' (Tullett 1981: 243). The trouble is that rule-bending which may be justified initially by a sincere determination to 'crack down' on serious crime may serve as the 'invitational edge' of the kind of wholesale and predatory wrongdoing revealed in the 1970s (Manning and Redlinger 1977). The explosion of corruption scandals was the product of the dangers inherent in traditional detective methods, coupled with the novel pressures of the 1960s and 1970s. These included the rise of large-scale organized crime, and growing toleration of some still illegal activities (like drug-taking or pornography) which increased their profitability and lessened the sense detectives had that conniving at them was harmful. The decline in public deference also made it much more likely that police wrongdoing would come to light and that allegations against them would be believed.

What is undoubtedly true is that the 1970s scandals fatally damaged the image of the police as impersonal and disciplined law enforcers, which the tradition built up by Rowan and Mayne had stressed. While in the 1960 Royal Commission survey 46.9 per cent of the public did not believe bribe-taking occurred, the 1981 Policy Studies Institute study of Londoners found that only 14 per cent believed the police 'hardly ever' took bribes (Policy Studies Institute 1983, i: 249).

During the 1980s there were fewer scandals involving personal corruption (although they revived during the 1990s, see Newburn 1999). Attention switched to abuses of police powers undermining the rule of law, what Sir Paul Condon, Metropolitan Police ommissioner for most of the 1990s, dubbed 'noble cause' corruption.

The rule of law?

The issue of police violations of legal procedures in the course of dealing with offences became acutely politicized in the 1970s. On the one hand groups like the National Council for Civil Liberties publicized evidence of widespread police malpractice, while on the other the police began to lobby for greater powers to aid the 'war against crime'.

Civil libertarians had been arguing for years that the rights of suspects (encapsulated in the 'Judges' Rules', the non-statutory administrative directions laying down procedures for questioning and taking statements) were routinely violated (Whitaker 1964: chap. 7; Laurie 1970: chap. 10). Such claims were crystallized by the 1972 conviction, on charges arising out of the murder of Maxwell Confait, of three teenage boys, one of whom was mentally retarded (Baxter and Koffman 1983). One boy's parents managed to get Christopher Price (then MP for Lewisham West) to take up the case, and after a three-year struggle the verdict was quashed by the Court of Appeal. (Evidence which emerged in 1979 completely exonerated the boys.) Concern about the case led to an official inquiry under Sir Henry Fisher, a high court judge, which reported in 1977.

The Fisher Report found that the boys' rights had been violated in several ways, leading to their false confessions. They were interviewed without an independent adult being present; they were not informed of their rights to phone a solicitor or friend under the Judges' Rules; there were several improprieties in questioning and charging, amounting to unfairness and oppressiveness. Altogether, Fisher found 'some of the Rules and Directions do not seem to be known to police officers'. He suggested that reform of the Rules should be conducted in the light of a broader inquiry—'something like a Royal Commission'. The hint was taken up shortly afterwards when the prime minister, James Callaghan, announced the Royal Commission on Criminal Procedure (RCCP), which reported in 1981.

Senior officers repeatedly claimed that police work could not be done effectively if legal procedures were properly adhered to (Mark 1978: 58). The same opinion was common among the rank and file (Reiner 1978: 77–81, 221–3). This view translated into practice, according to observational studies. Holdaway described a variety of tactics for controlling suspects which 'distance . . . officers from the constraints of legal rules and force directives' (Holdaway 1983: 101), such as 'verballing' or 'working the oracle' (fabricating statements) or physical force. A PSI study also found that while 'outright fabrication of evidence is probably rare . . . departure from rules and procedure affecting evidence are far more common. . . . There will be no fundamental change as long as many police officers believe that the job cannot be done effectively within the rules' (Policy Studies Institute 1983, iv: 228–30).

Apart from violations of rules concerning collection of evidence, there was also a mounting campaign in the late 1970s against police abuse of physical force, stimulated by a number of notorious cases (Box 1983: 82; Ward 1986). The refusal of the director of public prosecutions to prosecute any police officers in connection with these only fuelled critics' suspicions. The Home Affairs Select Committee reported in 1980 on the procedures for investigating deaths in police custody. It revealed a growing number of such deaths, from eight in 1970 to forty-eight in 1978, with a total of 274 in 1971–9. The proportion of these officially categorized as due to 'misadventure' or 'accident' doubled. These figures underestimate the number of deaths connected with police custody, for they exclude those which closely followed release. There is no warrant for saying that all such cases involved police misconduct, let alone abuse or brutality. Nevertheless, it was clearly an issue that provoked concern about police departure from the rule of law, and was an element in the politicization process.

The RCCP report was eventually transmuted into the Police and Criminal Evidence Act 1984 (PACE). This purported to provide a balanced codification of police powers and safeguards over their exercise, synthesizing the concerns of the 'law and order' and the civil liberties lobbies. (I shall consider how far it succeeded in this in Chapter 6.) What is certain is that the issue of police abuse of powers increased rather than abated, especially in the late 1980s and early 1990s. Between 1989 and 1991 police confidence in the police was shaken by a series of scandals revealing serious mal-practice. In October 1989 the Court of Appeal released the 'Guildford Four', the three men and a woman sentenced to life imprisonment in 1974 for the Guildford and Woolwich pub bombings. In the words of the Lord Chief Justice, Lord Lane, new evidence gathered by the Avon and Somerset Constabulary showed that some of the Surrey officers investigating the bombings 'must have lied' at the trial of the Four. In 1990 the Court of Appeal exonerated the 'Maguire Seven', who had also been jailed in connection with the bombings. A further blow to confidence in the police was the release in March 1991 of the 'Birmingham Six', who had been convicted in 1975 of the savage Birmingham pub bombings. Other causes célèbres considered by the Court of Appeal in the early 1990s included the cases of Judith Ward (whose conviction for a 1974 IRA coach bombing was quashed), and the four men convicted for the 1978 murder of a newsboy, Carl Bridgewater. There was also continuing concern about a number of even older miscarriages of justice, such as the cases of Craig and Bentley, and Timothy Evans,[6] stemming from the early 1950s (Woffinden 1990). Allegations of corrupt conspiracies to pervert the course of justice reached as high as the cabinet in the Stalker case, arising out of the removal of John Stalker from his inquiry into fatal shootings in Northern Ireland by the RUC (Stalker 1988). A particularly tragic case that of was Stefan Kiszko, who served sixteen years imprisonment for a murder which evidence suppressed by the police showed he could not have committed.

Although these cases profoundly shook public opinion, police representatives often argued they had occurred before recent reforms, and could not happen under the procedures now in force. This argument was itself weakened by a number of *causes célèbres* involving more recent abuses (C. Walker and Starmer 1999; Nobles and Schiff 2000). Some featured on-the-street violence not related to the bringing of a prosecu-tion, and thus untouched by PACE, of which the most notorious was a 1986 attack on a group of black youths in Holloway (Holdaway 1986). Directly calling into question police adherence to the rule of law was the scandal involving the West Midlands Serious Crimes Squad, which was disbanded in June 1989 by the then chief constable, Geoffrey Dear, after allegations of serious malpractice. (These led to a flurry of suc-cessful appeals by people convicted on the basis of evidence provided by the squad.) Perhaps the most damaging blow of all was the Court of Appeal decision in Novem-ber 1992 to uphold the appeals of the 'Tottenham Three', who had been convicted of the brutal murder of PC Blakelock during the 1986 Broadwater Farm riot (Rose 1992), on the basis of forensic evidence that the accused's statements had not been recorded contemporaneously (as PACE requires). These investigations had supposedly taken place under PACE procedures.

The anxiety produced by these revelations of abuse was enough to make the home secretary announce in March 1991 (after the release of the Birmingham Six), the establishment of a Royal Commission on Criminal Justice, chaired by Lord Runciman, the first Royal Commission in twelve years. The change in public views of the police was encapsulated by a *Guardian* cartoon following the successful appeal by the Tottenham Three. A man, late for a date, offers his girlfriend the excuse 'I asked a policeman the time, and he lied!'

The strategy of minimal force?

Had the traditional policy of 'winning by appearing to lose' been abandoned, perhaps to be replaced by one of losing while appearing to win? That was the question raised by a clear trend to harder-line policing of political and industrial conflict. The preparedness of the police to cope with public order problems began to be expanded and refined during the 1970s (Bowden 1978). The militarization of policing has proceeded apace in the 1980s in the wake of yet more serious disorder (Northam 1988; McCabe *et al.* 1988; D. Waddington, Jones, and Critcher 1989; Jefferson 1990; P. Waddington 1991, 1994, 1999*a*: chap. 3; Vogler 1991; D. Waddington 1992; Critcher and Waddington 1996; M. King and Brearley 1996; della Porta and den Boer 1998).

Without much public debate *de facto* 'third forces' developed, specifically trained and readily mobilisable to cope with riots. The Metropolitan Police Special Patrol Group, formed in 1965 as a mobile reserve, clearly developed a paramilitary role in dealing with public order and terrorism. All forces now have similar units (under various names), trained in riot control, use of firearms and sometimes CS gas. Since 1974 all forces have also formed Police Support Units(PSUs) to help in controlling crowds, strikes and demonstrations. All are specially trained for public order duties, including the use of shields, but are normally engaged in ordinary policing at local level. However, they are readily mobilizable to deal with problems arising outside their own force under mutual aid arrangements.

The PSUs are coordinated in a crisis by the National Reporting Centre, established in 1972 and located at Scotland Yard. When in operation it is controlled by the current president of the Association of Chief Police Officers (ACPO). Its most controversial and prominent use was during the 1984–5 miners' strike.

All these mutual aid arrangements are the fruits of the establishment panic in 1972, after the Saltley coke depot had to be closed during picketing by miners after a six-day struggle. While Saltley was seen as an abject defeat by many Conservatives and police officers, it was regarded by others as an example of the traditional 'winning by appearing to lose' strategy. Reginald Maudling, the then home secretary, believed it would have been possible for sufficient force to be used to clear the gates, but the long-run consequences for social stability would have been disastrous (Jeffery and Hennessy

1983: 236). After Saltley there was much debate about the need for a 'third force' specializing in riot control, along the line of the French CRS(Compagnies Républicans de Sécurité). The police succeeded in scotching the idea, but in effect created 'third forces' within their own organizations, as the 1984–5 miners' strike indicated. In this strike a massive, centrally coordinated police operation was directed by the National Reporting Centre, with much criticism of 'police-state' tactics (Reiner 1984, 1991: chap. 8; Fine and Millar 1985; McCabe *et al.* 1988; Green 1991). During the trials of miners on riot charges, it was revealed that in the early 1980s ACPO had produced a secret document, the Tactical Options Manual. This was the blueprint for a finely graded response to public disorder, culminating in the militaristic tactics used at Orgreave and elsewhere during the strike (Northam 1988). Altogether the trauma of the miners' strike for policing has been rightly compared to the impact of Vietnam on the US military (Graef 1989).

It is hard to remember the shock that greeted the bringing-out of police riot shields at Lewisham and Notting Hill in 1977, replacing the traditional protection of dustbin lids. But shields, strengthened helmets and other protective equipment are now regular sights. After the police failure to contain the 1980 Bristol riots and their lack of success in preventing widespread damage and police injuries in the 1981 Brixton, Toxteth and other disorders, police preparation for riot control redoubled, with Home Office support (Joshua, Wallace, and Booth 1983). During the riots themselves, of course, there was an evident intensification of police tactics, notably the first use of CS gas in riot control in mainland Britain, and high-speed driving of police vehicles to disperse crowds. Altogether in the 1981 riots levels of injury unknown for nearly fifty years in English disorders were inflicted on both police and civilians by boot, brick, fist, truncheon and petrol bomb.

The immediate response of Conservative politicians and police was to call for tougher tactics, equipment and legal powers for the police.[7] Mrs Thatcher told parliament that the government agreed to the use of water cannon, CS gas and plastic bullets if chief constables wanted them. A deputation of senior English police officers visited Northern Ireland to discuss riot control with the RUC and see what lessons could be learned from their 'success', and the advice of the Hong Kong police was also sought (Northam 1988).

John Alderson, then chief constable of Devon and Cornwall, who represented the liberal pole of police opinion, expressed grave doubts about this trend: 'There has to be a better way than blind repression. . . . We must not advance the police response too far ahead of the situation. It is even worth a few million pounds of destruction rather than get pushed too far down that road' (*Sunday Telegraph*, 12 July 1981).

In the end this more balanced approach prevailed over Lord Scarman's inquiry, set up by the government in the wake of the Brixton riots (Scarman 1981). Neither the tougher methods available after 1981 nor the wider Scarman-inspired reforms were able to avert even more serious urban riots in 1985, in the West Midlands, Liverpool and Brixton. The most serious conflict occurred on the Broadwater Farm estate in Tottenham North London (Gifford, 1986). Firearms were used against the police, and plastic bullets deployed (but not used) by them. Most tragically there was the savage hacking to death of PC Keith Blakelock, the first Met police officer to be murdered in a riot since PC Culley in the 1833 Coldbath Fields case. After the riots, the Met commissioner, Sir Kenneth Newman, warned that he would use plastic bullets should such violence occur again. His successor, Sir Peter Imbert, argued in a Howard League lecture in 1987 that the 'winning by appearing to lose' strategy had to be abandoned in the face of regular disorder of such magnitude, or it would amount simply to losing all the time.

Serious public disorder occurred again in an industrial context at Wapping in 1986–7, during picketing, by printworkers protesting at their displacement by new technology and non-union staff, outside the News International plant. Many complaints of undue violence were made against the police, and the Police Complaints Authority upheld some of them after an investigation. However, although charges were brought against several officers in 1989–91, they were all dismissed because the passage of time was held to make further proceedings unjust. Other apparently unjustified uses of tough public-order tactics occurred during the policing of hippie convoys converging on Stonehenge.

During 1990 anti-poll-tax demonstrations were the source of severe public order clashes, especially following a march and rally in Trafalgar Square on 31 March (P. Waddington 1994). In the worst rioting since 1985, over 300 officers were injured, and 300 arrests made. Damage, looting and violence fanned out from Trafalgar Square to neighbouring areas in central London, with tourists, theatre-goers, and shoppers caught up in the melee. Despite the levels of violence and disorder, criticisms of police abuse and overreaction surfaced quickly, and a Trafalgar Square Defendants' Committee was formed. In October 1990 a breakaway group from a south London anti-poll-tax rally marched on Brixton prison to support those sentenced for the Trafalgar Square troubles. This led to serious disorder, with forty-five police officers injured and 105 arrests.

In the early 1990s, the greatest public order concerns were not industrial or political conflicts. A 'moral panic' developed about disorder occurring in a variety of leisure contexts. In 1988 ACPO had raised fears about growing disorder in rural areas caused by 'lager louts' with 'too much beer in their bellies and money in their pockets'. Subsequent Home Office research questioned the idea of disorder growing in rural areas (as distinct from towns in county force areas), and the alleged connection with affluence (Tuck 1989). In 1989–90 there was great police concern about the spread of 'acid-house' parties, and the violence they stimulated, as several officers were seriously injured in raids. The most serious violence and disorder in a leisure context occurred in September 1991, in riots on the Blackbird Leys estate, Oxford, and Meadow Well estate, Tyneside, after police attempts to curb joy-riding (B. Campbell 1993; Power and Tunstall 1997). The police were subject to criticism both for underreacting to the joy-riding, and from other quarters for harassing teenagers suspected of joy-riding.

In the mid-1990s there arose a variety of new forms of political protest, and there was a spread of protest against specific issues such as live animal exports and the building of new roads in rural areas. These united groups with long experience of the hard end of public order policing with middle-aged, middle-class people, including many women, who would traditionally have been stalwart police supporters. The combination created especially acute policing problems. In the late 1990s there was also a resurgence of left-wing protest about financial globalization and its consequences of deepening inequality, including major clashes in the City of London in 1999 and 2000 (with counterparts in the USA in Seattle and Washington).

Although the British police response to riots remains lower in profile than that of most foreign forces, there has undoubtedly been a stiffening of strategy, and more resort to technology, equipment and weaponry. Dixon is out and Darth Vader is in, as far as riot control goes.

Apart from the growing use of riot control hardware, there has been a rapid proliferation of firearms use by the police in Britain (McKenzie 1996, 1998; Squires 2000a, b). Although still unarmed (apart from the traditional truncheon) on routine patrol, the frequency with which firearms are issued to the police has escalated inexorably. Many forces now deploy some cars carrying guns in their lockers, which can be used on orders from headquarters. The number of occasions when guns are fired by the police remains small, and the rules are tight (and were toughened following the most notorious 'cock-up' yet, the shooting of Stephen Waldorf in 1983. Waldorf, an innocent man, was mistaken for an escaped prisoner and shot many times at close range; fortunately, he survived). Most police officers are adamant in wishing to remain unarmed for routine work, but there is a growth of support for being armed. Whatever the justification in terms of the growing violence faced by police in public order and routine patrol work, the traditional unarmed image of the British bobby has been undermined. Debate has raged about whether this has aggravated the violence which it is supposed to deal with (Jefferson 1987, 1990, 1993; P. Waddington 1987, 1991, 1993b, 1994, 1999a; McKenzie 1996; Squires 2000a, b).

Accountability

Until relatively recently the independence of the British police from control by elected governmental institutions was often seen as a virtue, although there has also been a long-standing radical critique arguing that this was anomalous in a democracy. However, in the USA several generations of police reformers regarded the British model of insulation from political control as a solution to problems of corruption and partisanship.

As policing has become more controversial in Britain in the last two decades, so the perception of the mechanisms of accountability has changed. The old mystical substitute of police identification with the public has come under strain as the police came to be seen increasingly as unrepresentative in terms of race, gender and culture, and alienated from the groups they typically dealt with as offenders and victims (S. Jones 1987; Hanmer, Radford, and Stanko 1989; Holdaway 1991, 1996; Fielding and Fielding 1992; Walklate 1992; Heidensohn 1992, 1994, 1998; C. Martin 1996; J. Brown 1997; Holdaway and Barron 1997; Bowling 1999a; Macpherson 1999). Throughout the 1980s radical critics pinpointed the police as being not adequately controlled by any outside bodies, the dark side of their vaunted independence, and hence unresponsive to the popular will. They sought to reform the structure of police governance so as to make police policy-making fully accountable to the electoral process (McLaughlin 1994). Sophisticated critiques of the existing system were produced by constitutional lawyers (Lustgarten 1986; Lambert 1986; Uglow 1988). While the police themselves strongly resisted the full radical package, they have conceded increasingly the legitimacy of some aspects of the critique, especially about the complaints system (Goldsmith 1991; Maguire and Corbett 1991; Reiner 1991: chap. 11; G. Smith 2000). All governments have wanted to maintain the constitutional status quo. They have, however, become increasingly concerned to render the police more accountable for their use of powers and, even more crucially, the effective use of resources (Reiner and Spencer 1993; T. Jones, Newburn, and Smith, 1994; McLaughlin and Murji 1995, 1996, 1997; Leishman, Loveday, and Savage 1996; Morgan and Newburn 1997).

At the same time it was becoming increasingly evident that local accountability to police authorities has atrophied. It was being replaced by a degree of central control amounting to a *de facto* national force (Reiner 1991). (These issues will be fully explored in Chapter 6.) What is clear is that the perceived lack of adequate accountability has been a major factor undermining their legitimacy in recent years.

Non-partisanship?

The spectacle of James Anderton, Manchester's chief constable, or representatives of the Police Federation, preaching at the drop of a helmet about the sinking state of our national moral fibre became familiar in the 1970s. It is hard to appreciate quite how novel a departure from tradition this was (Reiner 1978, 1980a; Hall 1979; McLaughlin and Murji 1998; Loader and Mulcahey 2000).

When, in 1965, the Police Federation, then a humble professional association rather than the media opinion leader it has become, launched at a press conference a pamphlet, *The Problem*, which argued for police pay rises to help the fight against crime, the authorities were aghast. The official side of the Police Council hammered the Federation for its 'unprecedented breach of faith', while one member was quoted by the Federation's *Newsletter* (April 1996: 40) as saying, 'I never thought I would see the day when the representatives of law and order would be advocating anarchy.'

By 1980 the police, at all levels from chief constable down to the rank and file, seemed to set the terms of debate on law and order and social policy (Thompson 1980). This change was heralded by the Marksist revolution at Scotland Yard, when Sir Robert Mark delivered his controversial Dimbleby lecture on BBC television in 1972.

In 1975, the Police Federation launched an unprecedented campaign for 'law and order'. It aimed 'to harness the public's growing concern about the state of crime and public order in Britain into a programme for positive action'. The Federation modelled itself on the liberal pressure groups of the 1960s that had successfully campaigned for reform of the law on capital punishment, homosexuality, and abortion.

The intention was to mobilize 'the silent majority', to influence politicians to support the 'rule of law,' and to reverse the liberalizing trend in penal and social policy. The campaign was condemned by many as a dangerous departure from the tradition of police non-involvement in politics. The Federation justified itself by asking, 'What is "political" about crime?' It claimed the right to comment on legislation and policies which 'affected the working lives of police officers, who might have strong views on it'. In the event, the law and order campaign was shelved in 1976 as a bitter pay dispute developed which was to absorb Federation energies for nearly two years.

In 1978, the Federation relaunched the campaign specifically to influence the 1979 general election. A stream of strikingly similar and much-publicized pronouncements appeared from police spokesmen and Tory politicians as part of what the media dubbed the 'great debate' on law and order. Two high points, which marked the increasingly explicit political involvement of the police, occurred near the election. A fortnight before polling day, Robert Mark hit the headlines with a broadside comparing the relationship between the Labour Party and the trade unions to 'the way the National Socialist German Workers' Party achieved unrestricted control of the German state'. The way that the media structured the debate in the terms set by what the *Daily Mail* called 'The gospel according to Sir Robert Mark' was neatly illustrated by the headline chosen by the *Evening News* to report Prime MinisterJames Callaghan's response, 'JIM PUTS IN THE JACKBOOT', which precisely echoed Mark's imagery. The day after Mark's intervention, the Police Federation placed a long advertisement in most national newspapers under the heading, 'LAW AND ORDER. In essence, it blamed government policies for rising crime and urged support for a set of proposals, ranging from higher police pay to stiffer penalties. The police–Tory symbiosis was underlined when, four days later, the shadow home secretary, William Whitelaw, gave a six-point pledge on law and order, which matched all the Federation's points. Despite this, Jim Jardine, the Federation's chairman, disingenuously claimed that the £21,000 series of advertisements had not been intended to sway voters. If not, it was a cavalier waste of his members' money.

In the event the advertisements proved to be an investment which reaped handsome dividends. On the first working day after the Conservative election victory, Federation leaders were summoned with urgency to Downing Street to be told that the new government would immediately implement in full the pay increase recommended by the Edmund–Davies committee, (which in 1978 had recommended a large pay award and generous inflation-proof formula, which Labour was introducing in two stages). Symbolizing the more open accord between the police and the new Conservative government, the Federation broke with tradition (which had been that their parliamentary adviser was drawn from the opposition party) and reappointed Eldon Griffiths, a Conservative MP noted for abrasive speeches on law and order. Some members were distressed that the Federation had 'nailed its flag for all to see to the Conservative Party mast', but the Federation justified the move by 'his commitment to the policies which the Police Federation had been putting forward on law and order'.

The 1979 election seemed to presage a situation comparable to the open politicization of the American police. There so many candidates carry endorsements from rival police associations that even the voter concerned to support law and order may be confused about how to vote. American police not only wield considerable political clout in determining who is elected, but have many times successfully lobbied to destroy liberal policies (Reiner 1980: 379–90).

The climax of overt police involvement in political lobbying came in March 1982. This was a last-ditch backlash against a groundswell of establishment support for reforms in police policy and organization: the 1980 triennial report of the Police Complaints Board (which suggested the need for an overhaul of the system for investigating serious complaints), the 1981 Royal Commission on Criminal Procedure, and above all the reverberating impact of the Scarman Report. In addition the Labour Party had become politicized over the issue of law and order. (The dying tradition of cross-party accord was well symbolized by a conference on community policing held at Exeter University in March 1982. Unable to address the audience in person, Merlyn Rees, the former Labour home secretary, sent along instead a speech by William Whitelaw, his Conservative opposite number, to be read out, as it exactly expressed his views!)

In March 1982 when the Met released its annual crime statistics, it analysed them by the race of robbers as identified by victims, highlighting the stereotype of the black mugger. This was an unprecedented use of official statistics in a manner that had clear political implications. It was widely interpreted at the time as an attempt to 'mug' Scarman (Sim 1982).

Within the same week there was a blistering diatribe by James Anderton, in a hysterical speech condemning 'an enemy more dangerous, insidious and ruthless than any faced since World War Two', and exposing an alleged 'long-term political strategy to destroy the proven structures of the police' (cited in Prince 1988: 93). The Police Federation fuelled the growing panic by an advertisement in most national newspapers arguing for the restoration of capital punishment. Police pressure on law and order was echoed by growing criticism from the Tory right of Whitelaw's supposedly 'soft' approach to crime. In the event the Conservatives did hold a vote on the restoration of capital punishment soon after their election victory in the summer of 1983, but it was defeated.

The March 1982 events were the high-water mark of overt police lobbying for law and order. McNee's successor as Metropolitan commissioner, Sir Kenneth Newman, avoided the high-profile politicking of his predecessors, as have subsequent commissioners.

During the late 1980s the police at chief officer and Federation level were clearly trying to step back from the overtly politicized stance in favour of the Tories that reached its high point in the miners' strike of 1984–5. The love affair between the Tories and the police cooled as public expenditure cuts began to bite on the police, and they feared a hidden agenda of incipient privatization (Rawlings 1991). For its part Labour tried hard and ultimately successfully to repair broken bridges. The party's leader, Neil Kinnock in an interview in *Police Review* in 1986, said he had had a childhood ambition of becoming a policeman. Labour spokespersons assiduously attended Police Federation conferences, and criticized the Tories for cutting police expenditure. In March 1990, during the critical Mid-Staffordshire by-election, Federation leaders appeared on a Labour platform. It would be exaggerating to claim that the police switched partisan loyalties. Rather there was a gradual return to cross-party consensus on law and order. However this occurred largely because New Labour accepted many of the policy changes of the Thatcherite years in law and order as in other areas. Its electorally successful soundbite 'Tough on crime, tough on the causes of crime' increasingly emphasized the former. This was especially marked during the contest in toughness on law and order between the home secretary, Michael Howard and the shadow home secretary Jack Straw before the 1997 general election (Downes and Morgan 1997; Reiner 2000*b*).

The prototype of the outspoken chief constable, Sir James Anderton, retired in 1991. He had become even more controversial in the late 1980s for his supposedly divinely inspired utterances on aids and other topics, as well as his suspension, on the basis of rather dubious corruption allegations, of his deputy, John Stalker, who was investigating some shootings by the RUC in Northern Ireland (Stalker 1988). Despite this he retained the loyalty of his force throughout. A *Police Review* cartoon on his resignation well expresses their ambivalence: as Anderton is seen departing the station, one PC says to another: 'I'm sorry to see him go in a way. He was the only Chief Constable I've ever known who thought someone else was God!' By then most chief constables had come to believe overt police interventions in political and social debates were unwise (Reiner 1991: 210–19). None the less, the years of partisanship had tarnished, possibly irretrievably, the sacred aura hitherto enjoyed by the British police of being, like the Queen, above party politics.

The service role?

The service role continues to be paid lip-service by chief constables. Indeed, an influential current of police thinking stresses that, contrary to the growing image of the police as primarily crime-fighters, much if not most uniformed police work (measured by time or number of incidents dealt with) consists of service calls for help. This primacy of the service role was emphasized in the 1970s by John Alderson, then chief constable of Devon and Cornwall, and his philosophy of community policing (Alderson 1979, 1984*a*, 1998). He urged that the large proportion of service tasks in the actual activity of the police ought to be more explicitly recognized and rewarded, and encouraged in training and force organization. Community policing subsequently became an influential movement amongst progressive police chiefs in the USA and elsewhere (Skolnick and Bayley 1986, 1988; Greene and Mastrofski 1991; Friedmann, 1992; Rosenbaum 1994; Stephens and Becker 1994; Fielding 1995, 1996; Brodeur 1995, 1998; P. Waddington 1999*a*: 206–226; Herbert, 2000).

The very energy put into this campaign is an index of the degree to which the service aspects of policing were devalued and downgraded by the operative force status system. There is copious evidence that most rank-and-file policemen believe the service aspects of the work should have low or no priority. As one uniformed constable summed it up, 'This idea of performing a public service is a load of cobswobble as far as I'm concerned' (Reiner 1978: 213–7). In truth, the service work of the police is largely a by-product of their availability on a 24-hour basis, and their possession of coercive powers in order to perform their core mandate of order maintenance and law enforcement. When people call the police to a scene of trouble (even if there is no immediately obvious crime aspect) they do so not primarily because they require the services of an amateur priest, psychiatrist, nurse, or marriage guidance counsellor. They call the police because the problem needs authoritative resolution, by force if necessary (Bittner 1974).

Encouragement of the service role was an effective device in police legitimation. (This was also true in other countries; see Weinberger and Reinke 1991). The devaluing of it by rank-and-file culture, as crime-fighting was elevated to its glorified pedestal—a process encouraged unintentionally by Unit Beat reorganization was—problematic for police legitimacy. The response of many chief constables was to set up specialist community relations units to provide an artificial surrogate for what tradition had held to be part of basic constabulary duty (M. Brogden 1982: chap. 8). Such specialist liaison units began to proliferate in the late 1960s as forces grew larger with the post-1964 wave of amalgamations, more distant from their communities, and specialization of all kinds multiplied. After the Scarman Report endorsed a kind of community policing philosophy this became the orthodox analysis of the police role for all chief constables (Reiner 1991: chap. 6). The decline in public support in the late 1980s led to a redoubling of the effort to define policing in service terms, in the Met's Plus Programme and the ACPO Statement of Common Purpose and Values (Woodcock 1991; M. Hirst 1991; Waters 1996; Squires 1998).[8] However, these efforts were largely over-turned by the Conservative government's reform package launched in 1993, which explicitly sought to prioritize 'catching criminals' (in the words of the 1993 White Paper on Police Reform) as the primary if not sole job of policing. New Labour's Crime Reduction Programme continued this emphasis, albeit in a somewhat modulated form (Reiner 2000a, b).

Preventive policing?

Peel's original conception of policing emphasized patrol by uniformed constables as fundamental. This notion of the bobby on the beat as the essential bedrock of the force, to which all other specialisms are ancillary, remains a philosophy to which most chief constables pay constant homage. However, it is potent as symbol rather than practice (N. Walker 1996). Despite the rhetoric, specialist departments have proliferated, and foot patrol has been relatively downgraded (Bennett 1994a, b, 1995). It has been treated as a reserve from which high-flying potential specialists can be drawn, and a Siberia to which failed specialists can be banished (M. Jones 1980). Whereas specialisms are always kept up to strength by temporary 'manning-up', or by replacing personnel who leave, the uniformed branch is often below its nominal complement of officers. Beat work is an apprenticeship through which all police officers must pass, but seldom wish to stay in or return to, and most patrolling constables are young and inexperienced. Uniformed patrol is also devalued in the rank-and-file subculture, looked down upon by the CID in particular (Reiner 1978: 134–5; Graef 1989).

The Unit Beat reorganization represented a move towards specialization within the patrol function itself. It encouraged the development of the hedonistic action perspective on police work, and glorification of the thrills of car chases, combat and capture (Holdaway 1977, 1983). Relationships between Panda car drivers and the public were much more likely to be restricted to conflict situations than with old-style foot patrol. As a uniformed inspector put it to me: 'Before UBP you heard there was a fight round the corner, and by the time you got there, they were probably tucked up in bed together. Today the policeman is there in seconds, while it's still going on, and he has to sort it out.' The abrasive quality that was unintentionally imparted to beat policing by reorganization was augmented by the proliferation of mobile crime and disorder units, starting with the Met's Special Patrol Group in 1965.

Since the 1960s the meaning of crime prevention has shifted (Gilling 1997; Crawford 1997, 1998; Pease 1997; G. Hughes 1998). Originally it referred to the 'scarecrow' function of regular uniform patrol, augmented by the deterrent value of detection after the event. In the 1960s this was transmuted into a notion of prevention as pre-emption (as patrol became a 'fire brigade' emergency service). Pre-emption meant two things. First it meant the strategy, built into the Unit Beat system as its bedrock, of collecting and coordinating the lowlevel information provided by patrolling and area constables, who were to be evaluated by the quality and quantity of information they accumulated (Baldwin and Kinsey 1982). A central role in the system was given to the collator, the station-based officer whose task was to assemble and monitor the information provided from the streets. This largely consisted of hunches based on the political and personal proclivities of individuals who aroused the idiosyncratic suspicions of local police. With the proliferation of computers in police forces (and the growth in capacity of the Police National Computer) this information has become more centralized and widely and readily available, as well as acquiring an insidious status as 'hard data'. As Duncan Campbell anticipated, this has fundamental implications for the character of policing: 'In this "pre-emptive" view, any citizen, certainly any socially uncharacteristic citizen, is a target for suspicion and observation. This quite explicit development in police planning has virtually put the whole of society under surveillance' (D. Campbell 1980: 65). The development of 'intelligence-led', risk-oriented, inter-agency, and 'partnership' policing methods has accentuated the breadth and depth of pre-emptive surveillance and analysis in all police forces (Marx 1988, 1992; Fijnaut and Marx 1996; Maguire and John 1996a, b; Ericson and Haggerty 1997; den Boer 1997; P. Gill 1997a, b; Dunnighan and Norris 1999; Maguire 2000).

The second meaning of pre-emption is the development of specialist crime prevention departments, providing advice to citizens on methods of minimizing the risk of victimization, and alerting them to the dangers of some kinds of offences. At first crime prevention departments were Cinderellas of the service, low-status, low-budget, and low-key. However, as crime prevention became increasingly central to the government's law and order policy in the 1980s so they blossomed into belles of the ball (L. Harvey, Grimshaw, and pease 1989; Bottoms 1990; Reiner and Cross 1991: chap. 1). The impact of such vaunted crime prevention efforts as Neighbourhood Watch is mixed however (Bennett 1989, 1990; Forrester, Chatterton, and Pease 1989; Skogan 1990; McConville and Shepherd 1992; Laycock and Tilley 1995; Jordan 1998).

In the view of some critics the community policing philosophy, emphasizing both service and crime prevention work, is itself only a more covert (and therefore insidious) means of penetrating communities to acquire information (Gordon 1984). Its equally proactive cousin 'Problem-Oriented Policing' (H. Goldstein 1979, 1990; Leigh, Read, and Tilley 1996; Maguire 1998b) has been subject to the same accusation, although it purports to be more finely targeted, aimed at specific problems. What seems clear is that the pursuit of greater crime prevention effectiveness has meant a proliferation of proactive tactics, and specialist and plainclothes units, reversing the original strategy of Peel, Rowan and Mayne. These policies are themselves a response to the undermining of the eighth ingredient of legitimation.

Police effectiveness?

Police effectiveness is a notoriously slippery concept to define or measure. But the official statistics routinely produced by police forces and published by the Home Office seem to record an inexorable rise in serious offences and decline in the clear-up rate since the mid-1950s. Whereas in the mid-1950s there were less than half a million indictable offences recorded as known to the police in most years, this rose above half a million for the first time in 1957. By 1977 it was over 2 million, by 1982 more than 2.5 million, and by 1992 5.4 million. Recorded crime fell in the 1990s for five consecutive years after 1993, although it began to rise again thereafter (Home Office 1999: chap. 1, 2000). Before the Second World War the percentage of crimes recorded as cleared up was always over 50 per cent. By the late 1950s it had dropped to about 45 per cent, and by the end of the twentieth century was around 25 per cent.

The inadequacy of all these figures is well known (Walker 1995; Coleman and Moynihan 1996; Reiner 1996c; Maguire 1997). Many crimes are not reported to the police, so increases in the rate may mean a greater propensity to report rather than suffer victimization. The clear-up rate is affected by many determinants apart from detective effectiveness, including massaging the figures (M. Young 1991; H. Taylor 1998a, b, 1999; Davies 1999b). None the less it is hard to argue that the recent recorded trends (in particular the spectacular rise since the 1950s) do not correspond to basic changes in the same direction. They are certainly associated with a growing public fear of crime and a popular sense that police effectiveness is declining (Skogan 1994; Bucke 1996; Hale 1996; Walklate 1997, 1998; Hollway and Jefferson 1997; Hope and Sparks 2000; Stenson and Sullivan 2000).

The police's legitimacy has been undermined by their apparent inability to deal with crime in the suites as well as in the streets. As the salience of fraud problems has grown in the 1980s, so there has been increasing concern about police incompetence or partiality in this area (Levi 1987; Croall 1992; Nelken 1997; Slapper and Tombs 1999).

In the 1980s the Home Office Research Unit produced a growing volume of evidence (paralleling earlier American findings) indicating that current methods of patrol and detection were of dubious effectiveness (R. Clarke and Hough 1984). Taking a lead from this (as well as the Scarman Report) several chief constables attempted to redirect methods of policing towards a restoration of public confidence and cooperation—a new social contract, as Sir Kenneth Newman called it (Reiner 1991: chap. 7). During the 1990s there was, however, a rebirth of police and political belief in the possibilities of crime control by the police, with some support from criminological researchers (Sherman 1992, 1993; Weisburd, Uchida, and Green 1993; Kelling and Coles 1998; Dennis 1998; Bayley 1998; Jordan 1998; Weatheritt 1998). None the less, the consensus of researchers remains that policing alone can have only relatively marginal impact on crime (Bayley 1994; Loveday 1996b, 1997; R. Morgan and Newburn 1997; Reiner 2000b). Whatever the outcome of these debates is, there can be no doubt that public concerns about apparently declining police effectiveness, and the new tactics and law and order campaigns they stimulated, were a major factor in declining police legitimacy during the 1960s and 1970s.

THE SOCIAL CONTEXT OF DECLINING POLICE LEGITIMACY

Police activity has always borne most heavily on the economically marginal elements in society, the unemployed (especially if vagrant), and young men, whose lives are lived largely in the street and other public places (Stinchcombe 1963; Cohen 1979). Such powerless groups have aptly been named 'police property' (Cray 1972; Lee 1981). They are excluded from full 'citizenship' and bear the brunt of policing (Waddington 1999). Whereas the incorporation of the working class modified their systematic resentment at policing, police conflict with the residuum at the base of the social hierarchy remained. The police themselves recognize this and their argot contains a variety of derogatory epithets for their regular clientele drawn from this stratum. In California they are 'assholes' (Van Maanen 1978), in Canada 'pukes' (Ericson 1982), in London 'slag' or 'scum' (Policy Studies Institute 1983, iv: 164–5), and on Tyneside 'prigs' (M. Young 1991). Drawn mostly from the respectable working class, the police are responsive to their moral values and scorn those whose lifestyles deviate from or challenge them. But, however conflict-ridden, relations between the police and 'slag' are not usually politicized. Membership of the marginal strata is temporary (youths mature, the unemployed find jobs) and their internal social relations are atomized, so a sense of group identity is hard to develop. Moreover, police action against them has majority support, even (perhaps especially) from the respectable and stable adult working class (B. Johnson 1976).

One crucial factor which politicized policing after the 1960s was the development of social strata with a consciousness of antagonism towards (and from) the police. This was primarily the product of the development of more self-conscious youth cultures, the return of long-term unemployment, and the increasing militancy of industrial conflict in the 1970s and early 1980s.

A more crucial change, however, has been the catastrophic deterioration of relations with the black community. There is a long history of police prejudice against blacks and complaints of racial harassment. By the mid-1970s clear evidence had mounted of blacks (especially black youths) being disproportionately involved in arrests for certain offences, partly (though not only) because of police discrimination. A vicious cycle of interaction developed between police stereotyping and black vulnerability to the situations that attract police attention (Stevens and Willis 1979; Lea 1986; Jefferson 1988, 1993; Reiner 1989a, 1993; D. J. Smith 1997). Unlike the traditional marginal strata, however, blacks have a clear identity and consciousness of being discriminated against. Furthermore, the common experience of discrimination in other areas of social life means many 'respectable' black adults share an identification and common cause with black youths in their struggles with the police (Cashmore and McLaughlin 1991). The consequential disastrous ebbing away of black confidence in the police was crystallized by the Stephen Lawrence case, which dramatically illustrated the failure of the police to protect black people, who are in fact disproportionately victimized by crime (Fitzgerald and Hale 1996; Macpherson 1999; Bowling 1999a; Cathcart 1999).

Research on police–public relations suggests clearly that while these remain harmonious with the majority of the population (including most of the working class) they are tense and conflict-ridden with the young, the unemployed, the economically marginal and black people (Policy Studies Institute 1983, i: 314–5, iv: 162–8; Skogan 1994; Bucke 1996; Loader 1996; M. Lee 1998). What has happened to politicize policing since the 1970s is a growth in the size of these vulnerable groups, primarily because of the increasing social exclusion resulting from free market policies (E. Currie 1998a, b; I. Taylor 1999; J. Young 1999), and a heightening of their self-consciousness as targets of policing.

This reflects profound structural changes in the political economy of Western capitalism. Long-term structural unemployment (increasingly never-employment) has re-emerged, leading to the *de-incorporation* of increasing sections of the young working class, especially among discriminated-against minorities, 'who are being defined out of the edifice of citizenship' (Dahrendorf 1985: 98). A new underclass is forming not simply as a result of unemployment, but because of unemployment's apparent structural inevitability. There is much debate about the popular concept of an underclass, and its conservative, culturalist version has unacceptable connotations of 'blaming the victim' (Levitas 1998). But the structurally generated formation of a completely marginalized segment of society is a major source of the huge growth recently of crime, disorder, and tensions around policing (N. Davies 1998). Unemployment is certainly not linked to crime or disorder in any straightforward, automatic way, as the Conservatives are ever ready to tell us. But there is much evidence, since the 1970s, at any rate, that unemployment is a key part of the explanation of crime and disorder (Dahrendorf 1985; Farrington *et al.* 1886; Box 1987;

S. Field 1990, 1999; Downes 1998; Coleman and Moynihan 1996: chap. 6; Hale 1998; Witt, Clarke, and Fielding 1999; Reiner 2000*b*).

Conflicts between the socially marginal and the police are perennial, although the socially excluded are now more numerous than during the postwar boom. However, the key to how this is translated into political debate is a long-term cultural change in the opinion-forming middle class. The police have lost the confidence of certain small but crucial sections of the influential 'talking classes', what may be described roughly as the *Guardian*- or *Independent*- reading circles. This process of a developing gulf between the police and some educated middle-class opinion had a variety of roots, stretching back to the invention of the car (Weinberger 1995: chap. 4). But the most crucial developments were the growth of middle-class political protest from the early 1960s (CND, the anti-Vietnam War demonstrations, the 1960s student movement and counterculture, the 1990s live animal export and environmental protests), and the politicization of forms of marginal deviance which involve some middle-class people, notably drug-taking and homosexuality. This conflict with highly articulate and educated sections of the population has been of enormous significance in converting policing into an overt political issue.

CONCLUSION

This chapter has charted the process of police legitimation in the century after 1856, and its reversal since the 1960s. In Part II I shall consider the knowledge gained by studies of police culture and work. This historical and sociological understanding will be brought to bear on current developments and debates in Part III. In particular the Conclusion will argue that the politics of policing at the start of the twenty-first century is 'beyond legitimation'. Without recovering the status they had acquired by the middle of the twentieth century, the police have become less racked by political conflict and popular suspicion than in the late 1970s and 1980s. Controversy and complaint are focused more on the failure of police to achieve their widely agreed mission of crime control than any critique of their overall purpose or place.

The Stephen Lawrence case, the main cause célèbre of the 1990s, illustrates this. Although it raised once again the vexed issues of police racism and discrimination, they were manifest above all in the police failure to clear up the murder of a young black man, not in abuse of powers against him. The concern was a failure to deliver public protection from crime in an equitable and efficient way, rather than the allegations of heavy-handed policing that had dominated earlier controversies.

NOTES

1. Some other police forces have equal claims to a commanding place in their country's popular culture, for example the FBI (R. Powers 1983; Potter 1998). Canadians often point out that their most characteristic national emblem is the Mountie (Walden 1982). But in each case it is an elite force that is accorded prestige. The 'Yard' plays the same role in British popular mythology, but the mundane bobby is also a cornerstone of national pride, unmatched by the treatment of any other country's routine patrol force.

2. Too much weight should not be placed on Gorer's survey based on a self-selected sample of readers of the *People*. But it is worth noting (as Gorer does) that the *People* had a wide readership, and a disproportionately working-class one.

3. This is the standard Weberian distinction. Weber (1964: 327) emphasizes that the nature of legitimacy 'subjectively . . . may vary, especially as between "submission" and "sympathetic agreement"'. In other words, seeing an authority (like the police) as legitimate does not necessarily imply agreement with the concrete content of rules or their specific enforcement. It only means acceptance on some minimal basis of the authority's right to make or enforce rules. (For a critical exposition of the Weberian analysis of legitimacy, see Beetham 1991.)

4. The stance of compromise and co-option between classes, rather than outright conflict, was a wider historical pattern in English political development. 'Governing in the context of rapidly growing industrial capitalism, the landed upper classes . . . avoided serious defeat by well-timed concessions. This policy was necessary in the absence of any strong apparatus of repression' (B. Moore 1967: 39). It can be added that the absence of a strong apparatus of repression was itself a tactical choice deeming it (against strong countervailing

arguments) to be the course of political wisdom (Silver 1971).

5. I am using the Weberian concept of bureaucracy as the pursuit of administrative rationalization in an organization. This is to be contrasted with the pejorative image of red tape, bungling, and faceless oppressors, although these may well be dysfunctional consequences of the Weberian model (Albrow 1970).

6. Timothy Evans was (almost certainly wrongly) convicted and executed in 1950 for the murder of his wife and child while living at 10 Rillington Place. Their landlord there, John Christie, was subsequently revealed as a serial killer.

Derek Bentley was hanged in 1953 for the murder of a policeman: during a burglary he had called out the ambiguous words 'Let him have it' to his sixteen-year-old accomplice, Chris Craig. Craig, who actually shot the policeman, was too young to be executed. Bentley's conviction was finally overturned by the Court of Appeal in 1998.

7. The West Yorkshire police issued 'personal protective equipment', i. e., cricket boxes and jockstraps. Class discrimination within the police was complained of when it was discovered that those for sergeants and inspectors were bigger than those for constables!

8. The Plus Programme was launched in the late 1980s by the Met's commissioner, Sir Peter Imbert, as an attempt to convert the whole force to a community-policing and service ethic. The ACPO Statement was an attempt to define the police mission in service terms. It began: 'The purpose of the police is to uphold the law fairly and firmly; to prevent crime; to pursue and bring to justice those who break the law; to keep the Queen's Peace; to protect, help and reassure the community; and to do all this with integrity, common sense and sound judgement' (Johnson 1991: 206–7).

PART II

SOCIOLOGY

3

COP CULTURE

An understanding of how police officers see the social world and their role in it—'cop culture'—is crucial to an analysis of what they do, and their broad political function. This is not to suggest a one-to-one correspondence between attitudes and behaviour, as implied in two challenging critiques of the concept of police culture (P. Waddington 1999*a*: chap. 4, 1999*b*). Waddington stresses the gap between attitudes and behaviour that has long been established in social psychology. He also rightly notes that many observational studies of police work have shown that officers regularly fail to enact in practice the attitudes they have articulated in the canteen or in interviews, for example with regard to race (see, for example, Black 1971; Policy Studies Institute 1983, iv: chap. 4). An important distinction can indeed be made between 'cop culture'—the orientations implied and expressed by officers in the course of their work—and 'canteen culture'—the values and beliefs exhibited in off-duty socializing (Hoyle 1998). As Waddington points out, the latter clearly has an important function of tension release, which is why it so often characterized by mordant gallows humour (M. Young 1995). Waddington rightly criticizes many usages of the idea of police culture for identifying this completely with verbalizations gathered either through surveys or by observing canteen culture. Either has a problematic relationship with police work in practice. However, police culture does not simply mean police attitudes.

The *Oxford English Dictionary* defines the 'anthropological' meaning of culture as 'the whole way of life of a society: its beliefs and ideas, its institutions and its systems, its laws and its customs'. Cultures are complex ensembles of values, attitudes, symbols, rules, and practices, emerging as people react to the exigencies and situations they confront, interpreted through the cognitive frames and orientations they carry with them from prior experiences. Cultures are shaped, but not determined, by the structural pressures of actors' environments (what Chan (1997) calls their 'situs', following Bourdieu's usage). They are developed as people respond in various meaningful ways, which in turn create the situations that others act within. In short, to paraphrase Marx: people create their own cultures, but not under conditions of their own choosing.

Police culture—like any other culture—is not monolithic, although some analyses have tended to portray it as such (for example, Crank 1998). There are particular variants—'subcultures'—that can be discerned within the broader police culture, generated by distinct experiences associated with specific structural positions, or by special orientations officers bring with them from their past biographies and histories. In addition, cultures vary between forces, shaped by the differing patterns and problems of their environments, and the legacies of their histories. None the less, it will be argued that police forces in modern liberal democracies do face similar basic pressures that shape a distinctive and characteristic culture, discernible in many parts of the contemporary world, albeit with differing emphases across time and space, and with internal subcultural variations.

It is a commonplace of the now voluminous sociological literature on police operations and discretion that the rank-and-file officer is the primary determinant of policing where it really counts: on the street. As James Q. Wilson put it, 'the police department has the special property . . . that within it discretion increases as one moves down the hierarchy' (J. Wilson 1968: 7). It has often been argued that legal rules and departmental regulations are marginal to an account of how police work operates. Many observers have pointed out that a central tenet of the highly practical culture of policing is 'You can't play it by the book.' The core laws enforced by the police often seem to be the 'Ways and Means Act' and 'contempt of cop'. The original impulse for much of the early research on police discretion in the 1960s and 1970s was a civil libertarian concern about the extent and sources of police deviation from due process of law through their espousal of a 'crime control' model (Packer 1968. For a sample of these classic studies see Reiner 1996a).

In the late 1970s this approach came under fire from a structuralist critique, pioneered most notably and effectively by Doreen McBarnet (1976, 1978a, b, 1979, 1981).[1] She argued that the civil libertarians failed to distinguish between abstract rhetoric about the general values underpinning the rule of law, and concrete legal rules: there is 'a distinct gap between the substance and the ideology of law' (McBarnet 1981: 5). The rights of suspects presumed by ideological rhetoric are not clearly encapsulated in statutory or common law rules giving them practical effect. The laws governing police practice are sufficiently permissive to give officers a wide range of discretion. The courts have often seemed ready to accommodate extensions of the rules to legitimate police practice. The assumption of writers like Skolnick that the police routinely violate the law makes the low-level operatives 'the "fall-guys" of the legal system taking the blame for any injustices' (McBarnet 1981: 156). But responsibility ought to be placed on 'the judicial and political elites' who make rules of sufficient elasticity to assimilate departures from idealized values of due process legality, which the law effectively condones or even demands. McBarnet's detailed examination of the content and operation of the rules of criminal procedure is of immense value. But it does not displace the need for analysis of the police subculture and the situational pressures on officers' discretion. To say that the laws governing police behaviour are 'permissive' is only to suggest that they do not even purport to determine practical policing (contrary to legal ideology). That leaves considerable leeway for police culture to shape police practice in accordance with situational exigencies.

Legal rules are neither irrelevant to nor completely determining of police practice. The Policy Studies Institute study (1983) distinguished between three types of rules.

'Working rules' are those that police officers actually internalize so that they become the effective principles guiding their actions. 'Inhibiting rules' have a deterrent effect—officers must take them into account in their conduct, because they are specific, thought likely to be enforced, and refer to visible behaviour. 'Presentation rules' are used to impart an acceptable gloss to actions undertaken for other reasons. The relationship between any of these sets of rules and the law is problematic. Legal rules may well be used presentationally, rather than being operational working rules or inhibitors. They then act as an ideological façade whereby the public at large can turn a blind eye to the messy realities of policing.

This all means that the standard legalistic response to revelations of police malpractice—slap on a new rule—may be irrelevant or even counter-productive. On the other hand, formal 'black-letter' law is far from irrelevant to police practice. Legal rules may be 'inhibiting' or become the 'blue-letter' law of police 'working' rules, depending on a variety of factors. These have been illuminated above all by research on the impact of the 1984 Police and Criminal Evidence Act, examined in Chapter 6 (Reiner and Leigh 1992; D. Dixon 1997; D. Brown 1997; B. Dixon and Smith 1998).

The culture of the police—the values, norms, perspectives, and craft rules that inform their conduct—is neither monolithic, universal nor unchanging. There are differences of outlook within police forces, according to such individual variables as personality, generation, or career trajectory, and structured variations according to rank, assignment, and specialization. The organizational styles and cultures of police forces vary between different places and periods. Informal rules are not clear-cut and articulated, but are embedded in specific practices and nuances according to particular concrete situations and the interactional processes of each encounter.

None the less, certain commonalities of the police outlook can be discerned in the reports of many studies in different social contexts. This is because they are rooted in constant problems which officers face in carrying out the role they are mandated to perform, at any rate in industrial capitalist societies with a liberal-democratic political ethos. Cop culture has developed as a patterned set of understandings that help officers cope with and adjust to the pressures and tensions confronting the police. Successive generations are socialized into it, but not as passive or manipulated learners of didactic rules. The process of transmission is mediated by stories, myths, jokes, exploring models of good and bad conduct, which through metaphor enable conceptions of competent practice to be explored prefiguratively (Shearing and Ericson 1991). The culture survives because of its 'elective affinity', its psychological fit, with the demands of the rank-and-file cop condition.

COP CULTURE: THE CORE CHARACTERISTICS

The *locus classicus* for discussing the core police culture remains Skolnick's (1966) account of the policeman's 'working personality'.[2] What needs to be added to his discussion is the variations around his basic model, within and between police forces. Skolnick's portrait also failed to draw out the politically relevant dimensions of police culture. This culture both reflects and perpetuates the power differences within the social structure it polices. The police officer is a microcosmic mediator of the relations of power in a society—a 'street corner politician' (Muir 1977). The values of the police culture act as 'subterranean processes in the maintenance of power' (Shearing 1981a).

Skolnick synthesized earlier sociological research with his own findings to construct a pioneering sketch of the police 'working personality' (Skolnick 1966: chap. 3). This referred not to an individual psychological phenomenon (as the term 'personality' misleadingly implies) but to a socially generated culture. It was a response to a unique combination of facets of the police role: 'two principal variables, danger and authority, which should be interpreted in the light of a "constant" pressure to appear efficient' (Skolnick 1966: 44).

The 'danger' in the police milieu is not adequately represented by quantitative estimates of the risk of physical injury, although these are not small. People in other occupations—say, steeplejacks, miners, deep-sea divers, anyone working with asbestos—may be exposed to higher risks of job related disease or death. But the police role is unique in that its core tasks require officers to face situations where the risk lies in the unpredictable outcome of encounters with other people (Crank 1997: chap. 8). The police confront the threat of sudden attack from another person, not the more calculable risks of physical or environmental hazards. The extent of seriousness obviously varies. But the police officer faces, round every corner she turns or behind every door whose bell she rings, some danger, if not of firearms at least of fists.

Danger is linked to authority, which is integrally part of the police milieu. It is because they represent authority, backed by the potential use of legitimate force, that police officers face danger from those who are recalcitrant to the exercise of that authority. Traditional British police organization and tactics have been directed towards minimizing the use of force by converting power into authority, by making the individual constable a symbol of an impersonal and universally accepted law. But in each individual encounter this presentation is liable to be challenged when authority has to be exercised over someone. Danger and authority are thus interdependent elements in the police world, to cope with whose pressures cop culture develops as a set of adaptive rules, recipes, rhetoric, and rites.

Skolnick postulates a third environmental element producing cop culture: 'the pressure put upon individual policemen to "produce"—to be efficient rather than legal when the two norms are in conflict' (Skolnick 1966: 42, 231). Undoubtedly police officers experience external political pressure for 'results', more or less so at different times according to particular moral panics or trends in crime statistics. Under the pressure to get 'results' in the form of clear-ups, police may well feel impelled to stretch their powers and violate suspects' rights.

Skolnick overemphasized the degree of external compulsion in this. Public expectations of the police are themselves inflated by police propaganda about their capacities as professional crime-fighters, which they have elevated as their core mandate (Manning 1997). Police officers are for the most part intrinsically dedicated to the goals of 'maintaining order' and 'fighting crime'.

MISSION—ACTION—CYNICISM—PESSIMISM

A central feature of cop culture is a sense of mission. This is the feeling that policing is not just a job but a way of life with a worthwhile purpose, at least in principle. 'It's a sect – it's like a religion, the police force' (constable, cited in Reiner 1978: 247). The purpose is conceived of not as a political enterprise but as the preservation of a valued way of life and the protection of the weak against the predatory. The core justification of policing is a victim-centred perspective. As a constable put it to me: 'Speaking from a policeman's point of view it doesn't give a damn if we oppress law-breakers, because they're oppressors in their own right' (Reiner 1978: 79).

The mission of policing is not regarded as irksome. It is fun, challenging, exciting, a game of wits and skill. Many commentators have stressed the hedonistic, action-centred aspects of cop culture (notably Holdaway 1977, 1983; Policy Studies Institute, 1983, iv: 51–6; Skolnick and Fyfe 1993; Geller and Toch 1996; Crank 1998). They are undoubtedly very strong and of central importance. The main substance to which the police are addicted is adrenalin (Graef 1989). But the thrills of the chase, the fight, the capture, the 'machismo syndrome' (Reiner 1978: 161), although rare highlights of the work, are not merely a sport. They can be so uninhibitedly and delightedly engaged in because they are also seen as worthwhile. In a policeman's own eyes he is one of the 'good guys' and it is this which gives him the licence for action. He is not just a racing-driver or boxer in a blue uniform.

This moralizing of the police mandate is in many respects misleading. It overlooks the mundane reality of everyday policing, which is often boring, messy, petty, trivial and venal. It permits the elision of the universally approved elements of the police task (apprehending a murderer, say) and the political role of policing in upholding a specific state and social order. Certainly the 'sacred canopy' (Manning 1997: 21) often drawn over police work can be a tool of the organization, protecting and advancing its interest in gaining more resources, power, and autonomy from independent scrutiny. Nevertheless, it is important in understanding police work that it is seen as a mission, as a moral imperative, not just another job. This makes its established practices much more resistant to reform than if they were merely self-serving.

The elements of mission in the police perspective are reflected in their sense of themselves as 'the thin blue line', performing an essential role in safeguarding social order. The myth of police indispensability, of their essential social function 'to protect and serve', is central to the police worldview. Even much police wrongdoing has been attributed to arguably misguided pursuit of a 'noble cause', the 'Dirty Harry' dilemma of achieving essential ends by tarnished means (Klockars 1980; P. Waddington 1999: 112–4; R. Morgan 2000).

Nevertheless, police officers tend to acquire a set of views which have been rightly described as 'cynical', or 'police pessimism' (Niederhoffer 1967; Vick 1981). Officers often develop a hard skin of bitterness, seeing all social trends in apocalyptic terms, with the police as a beleaguered minority about to be overrun by the forces of barbarism (Reiner 1978: chap. 11). This pessimistic outlook is only cynical in a sense – in the despair felt that the morality which the police officer still adheres to is being eroded on all sides. It is not a Wildean cynicism which knows the price of everything and the value of nothing. Rather it resembles a Marxian account of commodity fetishism: price has sadly masked value. The very strength of the hardboiled outlook of policemen derives from the resilience of their sense of mission. Cynicism is the Janus face of commitment.

The salience of a sense of mission obviously varies between police officers. It was much more evident in the type I labelled the 'new centurions' (after the title of Joseph Wambaugh's seminal 1971 police novel) than those the argot calls 'uniform-carriers', who shirk the work as much as possible (Reiner 1978: chap. 12). But many (if not most) 'uniform-carriers', with their quintessentially cynical views ('It's the survival of the fittest . . . You've got to look after No. 1 . . . The policeman should exploit his job to the full advantage'), became that way precisely because of the effects of career disappointment destroying a prior sense of mission.

Undoubtedly many policemen see their combat with 'villains' as a ritualized game, a fun challenge, with 'winning' by an arrest giving personal satisfaction rather than any sense of public service. But this cynical view may well function as a self-protecting shield to reduce the anxiety that the thief-taker's many failures would otherwise induce.[3] One constable advised me:

All police work's a game. You get the people who do wrong and the people that try and catch them. Sometimes the wrong-doers get caught, sometimes they don't. If they get caught and copped, if they get nicked and weighed-off, fair enough. If they don't there's no point getting emotionally involved.

Cynicism about thief-taking as a game is thus functionally analogous to the role of humour as tension-release, expressed in the motto 'If you can't take a joke you shouldn't have joined this job' (Reiner 1978: 216–7; Holdaway 1983: 138–54; M. Young 1995; P. Waddington 1999: 114–6).

The core of the police outlook is this subtle and complex intermingling of the themes of mission, hedonistic love of action and pessimistic cynicism. Each feeds off and reinforces the others, even though they may appear superficially contradictory. They lead to a pressure for 'results' which may strain against legalistic principles of due process. *Pace* Skolnick's account, this pressure for 'efficiency' is not primarily derived externally but is a basic motivating force within police culture. It does, however, relate to the other facets of cop culture—suspicion, isolation/solidarity, conservatism—in the way Skolnick suggests.

SUSPICION

Most police officers are aware that their job has bred in them an attitude of constant suspicion that cannot be readily switched off. Suspicion is a product of the need to keep a lookout for signs of trouble, potential danger and clues to offences. It is a response to the danger, authority, and efficiency elements in the environment, as well as an outcome of the sense of mission. Police need to develop fine-grained cognitive maps of the social world, so that they can readily predict and handle the behaviour of a wide range of others, in frequently fraught encounters, without losing authority (Rubinstein 1973: chaps. 4–6; Holdaway 1983: chaps. 6–7; Kemp, Norris, and Fielding 1992; P. Waddington 1999: 101–2). Police stereotyping has been the subject of many critiques. They suggest that stereotypes of likely offenders become self-fulfilling prophecies as people with those characteristics are disproportionately questioned or arrested, leading to a vicious cycle of deviance amplification (J. Young 1971). However, stereotyping is an inevitable tool of the suspiciousness endemic to police work. The crucial issue is not its existence but the degree to which it is reality-based and helpful, as opposed to categorically discriminatory in a prejudiced way—and thus not merely unjust but counter-productive for the police force's own purposes (Banton 1983).

Suspicion does not only develop out of the intrinsic conditions of police work; it is deliberately encouraged by training. Skolnick cited an American manual giving detailed guidance for field interrogations which begins, 'Be suspicious. This is a healthy police attitude.' Among the Catch-22 tips for signs of the 'unusual' subject who should be stopped are: '7. Exaggerated unconcern over contact with the officer. 8. Visibly "rattled" when near the policemen' (Skolnick 1966: 45–6). A similar guide to the 'abnormal', embracing most of the population, was found in an English field manual by David Powis, a former Metropolitan assistant commissioner. Powis included in his list of suspicious types political radicals or intellectuals who 'spout extremist babble', or people in possession of a 'your rights' card (Powis 1977: 92).

While police suspiciousness and stereotyping are inescapable, the particular categories informing them tend to be ones that reflect the structure of power in society. This serves to reproduce that structure through a pattern of implicit discrimination.

ISOLATION/SOLIDARITY

Many commentators have emphasized the marked internal solidarity, coupled with social isolation, of police officers (Clark 1965; Westley 1970: chap. 3; Cain 1973; Reiner 1978: 208–13; Graef 1989; Skolnick and Fyfe 1993; Crank 1998: chap. 15; P. Waddington 1999: 99–101, 117). They have been referred to as 'a race apart' (Banton 1964), 'a man apart' (Judge 1972), 'a beleaguered minority' (Alex 1976).

Certainly, many police officers report difficulties in mixing with civilians in ordinary social life. These stem from shift-work, erratic hours, difficulties in switching off from the tension engendered by the job, aspects of the discipline code, and the hostility or fear that citizens may exhibit to the police. Social isolation is the price to be paid for Peel, Rowan, and Mayne's policy of elevating the British police as symbols of impersonal authority, and was to an extent a direct product of recruitment policies aimed at severing officers from their local communities (W. Miller 1999: 26–8). Internal solidarity is a product not only of isolation, but also of the need to be able to rely on colleagues in a tight spot, and a protective armour shielding the force as a whole from public knowledge of infractions. Many studies have stressed the powerful code that enjoins officers to back each other up in the face of external investigation (Stoddard 1968; Westley 1970: chap. 4; Shearing 1981b; Punch 1985; Skolnick and Fyfe 1993; Kleinig 1996; Newburn 1999). The offences that colleagues shield are not necessarily major infractions to be protected from external eyes. Rank-and-file solidarity is often aimed at concealing minor violations (what Cain (1973: 37) called 'easing behaviour') from the attention of supervisory officers.

This points to a misleading aspect of the emphasis on solidarity and isolation. First, it neglects the importance of conflicts inside the police organization. Some of these are structured within the rank hierarchy and the force division of labour, say between uniform and detective branches. It is true that internal conflicts may often be over-ridden by the need to present a united front in the face of external attacks. But this is not always so. The fundamental division between 'street cops' and 'management cops' can be reinforced in the face of external investigation (Ianni and Ianni 1983). 'Management cops' are derided by the 'street-wise' operational officers. The depth of the gulf is due to the different, often contradictory, functions of the two levels. The 'management' have to project an acceptable, legalistic, rational face of policing to the public. This may mean complicity with misconduct in some circumstances, deliberately hearing, seeing and saying nothing. But when reform pressures become intense, the 'management' may be forced into confrontation with the street level. To an extent, however, the apparent gulf and conflict between 'street' and 'management' orientations is functional for the organization itself (Grimshaw and Jefferson 1987). It allows presentational strategies to be adopted by management levels in real ignorance of what these might cover up, while at the same time the sacrifice of some individuals as 'bent' ratifies the effectiveness of the disciplinary process as a whole.

The 'them' and 'us' outlook which is a characteristic of police culture makes clear distinctions between types of 'them' (as well as of 'us'). The police perspective on social divisions in the population clearly reflects the structure of power as filtered through the specific problems of police work (Reiner 1978: chap. 11; Shearing 1981a, c; J. Lee 1981; Holdaway 1983: chap. 6; M. Young 1991).

The social structure as perceived by the police is one in which the hard class distinctions of the past have been eroded. Many policemen subscribe to an ideal of egalitarianism (epitomized by remarks such as 'nothing would give me greater pleasure than being able to nick the Lord Mayor'). At the same time they are acutely aware of the status distinctions which do exist (and their need to be finely tuned to them in giving and expecting the appropriate level of deference): 'You deal with everybody here. From the basic form of human life in the jungle conditions of the bad areas, to

the elite of the town. The posh dinner parties that go on. You have to handle them all'
(uniformed constable). Society does not bestow fair and equal chances. As one constable remarked to me: 'It's hard for a kid if his mother's tomming it, and his dad's
always in the boozer.'

The crucial divisions for the police do not readily fit a sociologist's categories of
class or status. They are police-relevant categories, generated by their power to cause
problems, and their congruency to the police value-system (Norris 1989; M. Young
1991; Kemp, Norris, and Fielding 1992). The fundamental division is between rough
and respectable elements, those who challenge and those who accept the middle-class
values of decency that most police revere. But finer distinctions within these categories can be made as generated by the police problematic. Seven key groups can
be distinguished: 'Good-class villains', 'police property', 'rubbish', 'challengers',
'disarmers', 'do-gooders', and 'politicians'.

'Good-class villains'

'Good-class villains' are professional (or at least experienced) criminals (Policy Studies Institute 1983, iv: 61–4). Pursuing them is seen as worthwhile, challenging, and
rewarding, indeed the *raison d'être* of the policeman's life, however infrequently the
ordinary officer may encounter such a case. Moreover, the villains are likely to play the
game with the same understandings as the police (Hobbs 1988, 1995). While obviously wishing to evade arrest, they do not normally challenge the basic legitimacy of
the police. Relations with them may well be amicable—indeed, this may be cultivated
by both sides for favours—the thin end of the corruption wedge.

'Police property'

'A category becomes police property when the dominant powers of society (in the
economy, polity, etc.) leave the problems of social control of that category to the
police' (J. Lee 1981: 53–4). They are low-status, powerless groups whom the dominant
majority see as problematic or distasteful. The majority are prepared to let the police
deal with their 'property' and turn a blind eye to the manner in which this is done.
Examples would be vagrants, skid-row alcoholics, the unemployed or casually
employed residuum, youth adopting a deviant cultural style, ethnic minorities, gays,
prostitutes and radical political organizations. The prime function of the police has
always been to control and segregate such groups, and they are armed with a battery
of permissive and discretionary laws for this purpose (added to recently by the Crime
and Disorder Act 1998; see Ashworth *et al.* 1998). The concern with 'police property'
is not so much to enforce the law as to maintain order using the law as one resource
among others. Stop and search has been a traditional and controversial tactic in this
(A. Sanders 1997: 1058–60; Fitzgerald 1999).

A major pitfall for the police is to mistake a member of a higher-status group for
police property. The danger is reinforced in policing ethnic minority groups where the
police officer is not as attuned to the signals of respectability. It is also a problem that
has become accentuated for the police with the growth of respectable middle-class

involvement in 'deviant' activities. The demonstrator or pot-smoker may turn out to be a university professor or lawyer.

'Rubbish'

'Rubbish' are people who make calls on the police which are seen as messy, intractable, unworthy of attention, or the complainant's own fault (Policy Studies Institute 1983, iv: 64–6). Domestic disputes are a common sort of call regarded as 'rubbish' by many police officers: 'With domestic disputes, the husband and wife going hammer and tongs, you've got to separate them, calm them down before you go. And you're not doing a policeman's job, you're doing a socialist's [sic]' (Reiner 1978: 214–5, 244–5). 'Rubbish' are essentially people from the 'police property' groups presenting themselves as victims or clients for service, as they often do. Indeed, a major finding of crime surveys is the social isomorphism of victims and offenders (Maguire 1997: 161–79; Zedner 1997: 580–86; Home Office 1999: chaps. 2, 3).

'Challengers'

'Challengers' are defined by Holdaway (1983: 71–7) as those whose job routinely allows them to penetrate the secrecy of police culture, and gives them power and information with which they might challenge police control of their 'property'. Doctors, lawyers, journalists, and social workers are in this position (as are police researchers!). Efforts will be made to minimize their intrusion, and presentational skills used to colour what they see. The Scarman-inspired development of schemes for lay visitors to police stations is an attempt to ensure regular penetration of the backstage areas of the police milieu by organized 'challengers' (Kemp and Morgan 1989). PACE attempted to facilitate access by relevant 'challengers' such as duty solicitors or 'appropriate adults'. The extent to which this has succeeded in piercing the low visibility which shrouds police decisions on the street and in the station remains debatable (see Chapter 6 in this volume; Thomas 1988; A. Sanders and Bridges 1990; McConville, Sanders, and Leng 1991; D. Brown 1997; D. Dixon 1997; Choongh 1998).

'Disarmers'

'"Disarmers" are members of groups who can weaken or neutralise police work' (Holdaway 1983: 77–81). They are groups who are hard to deal with as suspects, victims, witnesses, or in service work, because they are perceived as socially vulnerable and so allegations by them against the police may receive special sympathy. Holdaway specifies women, children, and the elderly as the main disarmers.

Anyone may turn out to be an unexpected 'disarmer' because of the limitless naivety of the public, so the police officer has to be wary of every encounter. One constable told me of an incident where he let off with a warning a man doing 65 m.p.h. in the city, after he explained that his wife was in labour. 'A fortnight bloody later he writes to the chief constable. He explains all the circumstances and wants to thank me. I got dragged in there and given the thickest bollocking ever for condoning him going at 65 m.p.h. He dropped me right in it' (Reiner 1978: 246).

'Do-gooders'

'Do-gooders' are principled anti-police activists who criticize the police and organize to limit their autonomy (Reiner 1978: 221–3). The prime example is the 'National Council for the Prevention of Policemen Doing Their Duty' (the National Council for Civil Liberties, now renamed Liberty). 'We're going through a spate of do-gooders who do no good! . . . They shout and shout to create problems or they'd be out of a job' (uniformed constables, *ibid.*). From the police perspective, the development in the 1980s of police monitoring groups represented a proliferation of such 'do-gooders' (Jefferson, McLaughlin, and Robertson 1988; McLaughlin 1994).

Politicians

Politicians are regarded suspiciously (Reiner 1978: 76–81). They are remote and unrealistic ivory-tower idealists, corrupt self-seekers, secret subversives, or simply too weak to resist villainy. Unfortunately, however, they have the power to make law. The lawyers and judges involved in its administration tend to be made from the same cloth and are regarded as no better.

'The trouble is the Government think they're legislating for educated men. . . . But the people here are animals, they're thick . . . MPs are out of context altogether . . . They live in a different world. I mean, every meal these politicians have is a six-course one!' (uniformed constable, *ibid.*).

Beset by all these threatening elements, the police become a solidary group: 'We're a tight-knit community. We've got to stand by each other because we're getting it from all angles. We get it from outside, the general public, we get it from solicitors, from QCs, we get it from our own bosses' (*ibid*: 246).

Running through the police perception of the social structure is a distinction between the powerless groups at the bottom of the social hierarchy who provide the 'rubbish' and the 'police property', and the respectable strata, each with distinct segments which in different ways threaten police interests. Police culture both reflects the wider power structure and reproduces it through its operations.

POLICE CONSERVATISM

The evidence we have of the political orientations of police officers suggests that they tend to be conservative, both politically and morally. Partly this is due to the nature of the job. The routine 'clients' of the police are drawn from the bottom layers of the social order. But control of the lumpen elements is not necessarily something which even politically conscious members of the working class would be averse to. However, in their public order role, and even more so in the work of their specifically political 'high policing' sections, the police have been routinely pitted against organized labour and the Left (Lipset 1969; Skolnick 1969; Bunyan 1977; Brodeur 1983; J. Morgan 1987; Weinberger 1991, 1995: chap. 9; Vogler 1991; P. Gill 1994, 1997*a, b*; Brewer *et al.* 1996; Mazower 1997; Huggins 1998; Della Porte and Reiter 1998). Furthermore, the force has from the start been constructed as a hierarchical, tightly disciplined organization. Thus the police officer with a conservative outlook is more likely to fit in. Processes of selection and self-selection lead police officers to be conservative.

However, there are contradictory pressures at work. Fiscal and political prudence from the start dictated pay and recruitment policies which meant that the bulk of officers were drawn from the working class, and these processes still operate today. Even chief officers come predominantly from working-class origins (Reiner 1991: chap. 4; Wall 1998). The police are an employee group whose grievances over pay and conditions of work have generated militancy and trade union organization analogous to that of other workers (Reiner 1978; Judge 1994). The 'deradicalization' of the policeman was not automatic, but had to be constructed (and continuously reconstructed), as Robinson (1978) cogently argued.

In the USA there has been copious evidence of police political support for the Right and the far Right. Skolnick (1966: 61) summed up his interviews and observations thus: 'A Goldwater-type of conservatism was the dominant political and emotional persuasion of police' (see also Bayley and Mendelsohn 1968: 14–30; Lipset 1969; Bent 1974: chap. 5). These attitudes have been openly translated into political campaigning. Police associations have on numerous occasions actively lobbied for reactionary political candidates, and in support of specific right-wing policies (Skolnick 1969: chap. 7; Ruchelman 1974; Alex 1976; Reiner 1980; Bernstein et al. 1982).

There is some comparable evidence of British police officers' political views. When I attempted to interview police in the 1970s about their political attitudes this was prohibited by the Home Office, as it was claimed that it would impugn the traditional notion of the police as outside any form of politics (Reiner 1978: 11, 283; 1979b). I have seen an unpublished 1977 dissertation by a police officer who interviewed a sample of colleagues in a northern city force, using the questions I had been prohibited from asking. He found that 80 per cent described themselves as Conservative—18 per cent of whom were to the right of the party. The remainder were evenly divided between Labour, Liberal, and 'don't know'. Of his sample, 80 per cent had voted in all recent elections. A slight rightward shift was indicated by the fact that 9 per cent had moved from Labour or Liberal to Conservative between 1974 and 1977, with no movement in the opposite direction. Despite this, 64 per cent affirmed that the police should remain politically neutral at all times, 21 per cent wished for the right to join a political party without taking an active role, while 12 per cent wished to be able to take an active part in politics.

More recently, a survey was conducted of 286 serving Metropolitan Police officers which included questions on voting patterns and intentions (Scripture 1997). This found that of those who had voted in the 1979, 1983, 1987, and 1992 general elections the overwhelming majority had supported the Conservatives (respectively 79 per cent, 86 per cent, 74 per cent, and 74 per cent: Scripture 1997: 172). However, only 44 per cent intended to vote Conservative at the next general election (the survey was conducted before the 1997 election). This was probably a result of police disenchantment with the Conservative government's reform package aimed at subjecting the service to market disciplines, embodied in the 1993 Sheehy Report and the Police and Magistrates Courts Act 1994 (Loveday 1995*a*, *b*; McLaughlin and Murji 1996, 1997; D. Rose 1996: chap. 6; Reiner 1997: 1030–9).

The trend in the 1970s towards more open involvement in political debate of chief constables and the Police Federation has already been described (Judge 1994; McLaughlin and Murji, 1998; Loader and Mulcahey 2000). It clearly expressed views which were symbiotically related to Conservative Party policies, and echoed (at a less explicit level) the American 'blue power' political campaigning of the 1960s and 1970s.

Apart from specific party politics, the police tend to hold views on moral and social issues which are conservative. 'Cops are conventional people. . . . All a cop can swing in a milieu of marijuana smokers, inter-racial dates, and homosexuals is the night stick' (cited in Skolnick 1966: 61). A 1960s survey of New York police attitudes found that the two most disliked categories of people after 'cop-fighter' were the homosexual and the drug addict (Niederhoffer 1967). I found similar support for a narrowly conventional morality in my interviews with British police (Reiner: 1978: chap. 11. See also J. Lee 1981 for Canadian evidence). Undoubtedly the very fact that some gay and lesbian police officers can now 'come out', and indeed form their own representative association, indicates a measure of progress in the last quarter of a century. However, they still experience considerable discrimination, and there remains considerable homophobia in police culture even if it is expressed more covertly (M. Burke 1993; P. Waddington 1994*a*, 1999: 109). The social philosophy of chief constables also tends to the conservative, albeit less stridently expressed for the most part (Reiner 1991: chap. 9).

Although there is an obvious elective affinity for police officers between their role as upholders of authority and conservative politics and morality, this is by no means a constant. During the early and mid-1990s, as the Conservative government increasingly applied to the police its market-oriented approach to public services, so police sympathy at all levels appeared to swing towards more radical views (D. Rose 1996: chap. 6; Scripture 1997). This not only involved sharing concern about incipient privatization and more rigorous controls on public expenditure with other services, but extended to an increasing sympathy for analyses of crime and other social problems in terms of social justice rather than individual responsibility (D. Rose 1996).

MACHISMO

Despite this moral conservatism, in many respects police culture departs from puritanism. The police world is one of old-fashioned machismo (Fielding 1994*a*; Crank 1997: chap. 14). Sexism in police culture is reinforced by discrimination in recruitment and promotion (Hanmer, Radford, and Stanko 1989; Graef 1989: chap. 6; M. Young 1991: chap. 4; Heidensohn 1992, 1994, 1998; Halford 1993; Walklate 1996; C. Martin 1996; J. Brown 1997). The contempt exhibited for such sexual deviance as homosexuality and paedophilia is accompanied by routinized 'sexual boasting and horseplay', often at the expense of women colleagues (Policy Studies Institute 1983, iv: 91–7). Policemen are not notorious for their aversion to illicit heterosexual activities. As one constable told me, 'Policemen have one of the highest divorce rates in the country. There's always a bit of spare round the corner, because of the glamour of the job' (Reiner 1978: 212).[4] Nor are policemen notably abstemious from alcohol, for all their contempt for users of other drugs. One hazard of police research is the taking of mental notes while sinking under a bar as the consumption of pints mounts. Police alcoholism has been a perennial problem since the early days of the force. The alcoholic and sexual indulgences of police are a product both of the masculine ethos of the force and of the tension built up by the work. Their significance in this regard is brought out best by the novels of Joseph Wambaugh, in particular *The Choir-Boys* (1976), with their central theme of policing as a morally (even more than physically) dangerous occupation. The decidedly non-puritanical ethos about heterosexual behaviour, drinking and gambling can expose the police officer to strains, tensions and charges of hypocrisy when enforcing laws in these areas. This factor helps explain the greater propensity for police corruption in the specialist enforcement of vice laws.

It has always been tough for women police officers to gain acceptance. The establishment of employment for policewomen in the first place came only after a protracted campaign (Carrier 1988). Despite formal integration, they continue to experience discrimination (Bryant, Dunkerley, and Kelland 1985; S. Jones 1986, 1987; Heidensohn 1989, 1992, 1994, 1998; Dunhill 1989; Walklate 1992, 1996; J. Brown, Maidment, and Bull 1993; J. Brown, 1997). The difficulties they face in achieving higher rank were illustrated by the highly publicized action claiming sex discrimination brought by Alison Halford, former assistant chief constable in Merseyside (Halford 1993). However, since then a number of women chief officers have been appointed.

RACIAL PREJUDICE

An important aspect of police conservatism is racial prejudice. A large number of American studies demonstrate police suspiciousness, hostility, and prejudice towards blacks, and vice versa (Crank 1997: chap. 16). It is usually argued that this is a reflection of the racism of American culture generally, and especially the social groups from which most police are drawn (lower middle or working class with no more than high school education). Bayley and Mendelsohn (1968) sum up their own and many other studies: 'Are policemen prejudiced? The answer is yes, but only slightly more so than the community as a whole. Policemen reflect the dominant attitudes of the majority people towards minorities' (p. 144). (See also Westley 1970: 99–104; Skolnick 1966: 81–3; Skolnick and Fyfe 1993) American police have also been prominent in political opposition to the civil rights movement and in support for far-Right political organizations with a racist character (Reiner 1980: 383–8).

There is similar evidence from many studies of British police racial prejudice. It is noteworthy that the earliest documentation of this prejudice pre-dates by many years official police allegations or statistical data claiming a problem of black over-involvement in crime. Up to the early 1970s police arrest statistics indicate an under-involvement of black people in crime compared to their proportion in the population (Lambert 1970). None the less, Cain's and Lambert's studies of city forces in the early and late 1960s show a clear pattern of rank-and-file police prejudice, perceiving blacks as especially prone to violence or crime, and generally incomprehensible, suspicious, and hard to handle (Lambert 1970; Cain 1973: 117–9). My own interviews in Bristol in 1973–4 found that hostile and suspicious views of blacks were frequently offered quite spontaneously in the context of interviews concerning police work in general (Reiner 1978: 225–6). Of the sample, 25 per cent volunteered adverse comments, while 35 per cent in the central division (which included St Paul's, an inner-city area with high tension between black people and the police; it was the scene of the of the first ghetto riot in 1980) did so. One uniformed constable summed up the pattern: 'The police are trying to appear unbiased in regard to race relations. But if you asked them you'd find 90 per cent of the force are against coloured immigrants. They'd never want you to do that research and come up with that sort of finding.' Later work, conducted in a period during which black crime and especially mugging became heated political issues, confirms the evidence of prejudice (Holdaway 1983: 66–71, 1995, 1996; Policy Studies Institute 1983, iv: chap. 4; Reiner 1989, 1991, 1993; Lea 1986; Jefferson 1988, 1993; D. Rose 1996, chap. 2; Holdaway and Barron 1997; Bowling 1999a, b; Macpherson 1999). However, the extent to which prejudice is expressed openly and virulently has generally lessened. This is primarily a result of changes in the demographic character of forces, such as more ethnic minority officers (albeit still a disproportionately small number), more officers with higher education, and a greater emphasis on multi-culturalism in training and the official force ethos since the Scarman Report (Bull and Horncastle 1989; Pearson et al. 1989; D. Rose 1996: chap. 6).

It cannot be assumed that police prejudice translates into behaviour expressing it. As a seminally important PSI study put it:

Our first impression after being attached to groups of police officers was that racialist language and racial prejudice were prominent and pervasive . . . on accompanying these officers as they went about their work we found that their relations with black and brown people were often relaxed or friendly (Policy Studies Institute 1983, iv: 109).

American research suggests a similar pattern of disjunction between prejudice and discriminatory behaviour (Black 1970, 1972; Friedrich 1979; Sherman 1980, 1983; P. Waddington 1999a, b).

The other qualification that must be made to the recital of evidence of police racial prejudice is that it is in part a reflection of general societal prejudice. The consensus of social research (in Britain and in the USA) suggests that, contrary to popular belief, police recruits do not have especially authoritarian or prejudiced personalities (Skolnick 1969: 252; Reiner 1978: 157; Scripture 1997; P. Waddington 1999a: 102–4). Rather, they share the values of the social groups from which they are drawn—the lower middle and respectable working classes, which constitute the bulk of society.

This is, of course, a double-edged finding, for while police recruits may not be more authoritarian than the general population, the 'normal' degree of authoritarianism is disturbing in an occupation which wields considerable power over minorities. As Stuart Hall has commented trenchantly, chief constables would not state so cavalierly the equally true proposition that the police force must contain its fair share of criminals (S. Hall 1979: 13). It must be noted, too, that prejudiced views are also common among chief constables themselves (Reiner 1991, esp. 204–10).

One influential article has challenged this orthodoxy (Colman and Gorman 1982). The authors administered several psychological tests intended to assess dogmatism, conservatism, and authoritarianism, as well as specific views on race relations, to three samples: forty-eight police recruits at the beginning and end of basic training; thirty-six probationer constables with an average of twenty months' experience; and a control group of thirty civilians supposedly matched to the police groups in socio-economic status. They found that 'the police force attracts conservative and authoritarian personalities, that basic training has a temporarily liberalizing effect, and that continued police service results in increasingly illiberal/intolerant attitudes towards coloured immigration'. Their results have been subject to severe criticism on methodological and substantive grounds (P. Waddington 1982b; Butler 1982a). The control groups had a higher average level of education, which could be at least part of the explanation for the more 'authoritarian' police recruit attitudes. Other studies of other samples of recruits do not suggest the police attract individuals with radically distinct value systems compared with matched civilian control groups (Cochrane and Butler 1980; Brown and Willis 1985.) What the research does reveal is that (although not necessarily sharply distinctive from the population norm) the police recruits did manifest hostile attitudes to ethnic minorities. Such attitudes seem to be accentuated with work experience, after a temporary liberalizing effect during training (Fielding 1988). The changes in selection and training since Scarman may have had some impact, but effects do not seem to survive practical policing experience to a significant extent (Bull and Horncastle 1989). Unless the pressures generating traditional cultural attitudes change as a result of more profound changes in the social structural context of police work, changes in the selection and training of individual officers' cannot achieve much (American and Australian experience confirms this; see Sherman 1983; Chan 1997).

Overall, it is both necessary and sufficient to explain the police outlook on ethnic minorities (and other issues) by the police function, and the circumstances of police work, rather than by peculiarities of individual personality. Even if at some times and places distinctive personality types are attracted to policing, it would still be necessary to analyse the nature of police work as the determinant of the attraction. The crucial source of police prejudice is societal racism, which places ethnic minorities disproportionately in those strata and situations from which the police derive their 'property'. This structural feature of police–ethnic-minority relations bolsters any prior prejudice police officers have (Jefferson 1988; Reiner 1989a, 1993).

PRAGMATISM

The final element of police culture it is important to stress is the very pragmatic, concrete, down-to-earth, anti-theoretical perspective which is typical of the rank and file, and indeed chief constables (with a growing number of exceptions). This is a kind of conceptual conservatism (Crank 1997: chap. 13).

Police officers are concerned to get from here to tomorrow (or the next hour) safely and with the least fuss and paperwork, which has made them reluctant to contemplate innovation, experimentation, or research. This has changed in recent years with the impressive growth of a significant body of practice-oriented research, through such bodies as the Home Office's Police Research Group and Research and Statistics Directorate, the Police Foundation, and police forces themselves (Reiner 1992a, 2000b; J. Brown and Waters 1993; J. Brown 1996). The limits of much in-house police research were, however, underlined by a study of it, which questioned the tendency to find favourable 'foregone conclusions' (Weatheritt 1986). This is less true of current work, due in part to a significant influx of graduates and indeed some experienced civilian researchers into police research departments (J. Brown 1996). In-house and other forms of official police research will be stimulated further by the increasing emphasis on intelligence-led policing. A research-based approach has become mandatory with the requirements encapsulated in the 1998 Crime and Disorder Act and the Crime Reduction Programme to analyse and evaluate crime patterns and the effectiveness of crime reduction strategies at local level (Home Office 1998; Jordan 1998; Reiner 2000b).

One review of the psychological literature on 'police personality' indicated that, while the evidence on such overtly political issues as distinctive authoritarianism or racial prejudice among policemen was mixed, it did seem that police officers have a markedly 'empirical' cognitive structure (Adlam 1981: 156). Training innovations have moved towards less didactic techniques to try and counter this (Adlam 1987).

VARIATIONS IN COP CULTURE

Police culture is not monolithic. The organizational division of labour is related to a variation in distinct types of perspective around the core elements of the culture. This has been noted by a variety of studies that have developed typologies of different police orientations and styles.

Muir's (1977) study, for example, used sensitive observations of twenty-eight police officers in an American city. It was unique in sociological studies of the police in centring on the question 'What makes a police officer good?' rather than on the more common analysis of deviation. Muir approached this by considering the way police officers deal with the problem of handling coercive power. The good cop has to develop two virtues. 'Intellectually, he has to grasp the nature of human suffering.

Morally, he has to resolve the contradiction of achieving just ends with coercive means' (Muir 1977: 3–4). Intellectual vision can be 'cynical', that is, based on a dualistic division of people into 'us' and 'them', fault-finding, and individualistic; or 'tragic', seeing mankind as of one unitary substance and moral value, seeing action as complexly produced by chance, will and circumstance, and recognizing the important but fragile nature of social interdependence. Moral understanding may be 'integrated', that is, accommodating the exercise of coercion within an overall moral code; or 'conflictual' where it creates guilt because it is not related to basic moral principles. The two dimensions yield a fourfold typology of police officer. The 'avoider' (with cynical perspective and conflicted morality) shirks duties; the 'reciprocator' (tragic perspective and conflicted morality) hesitates to use coercive power even when appropriate; the 'enforcer' (cynical perspective and integrated morality) acts in the heat of conflicts and without understanding the need for restraint; the 'professional' (tragic perspective and integrated morality) is the 'good' cop. He or she is able to use violence where necessary in a principled way, but is adept at verbal and other skills that enable solutions to be resolved without coercive force wherever the opportunity exists.

Muir's four types were similar to those found in my own research: the 'bobby', the ordinary copper applying the law with discretionary common sense, in a peace-keeping role; the 'uniform-carrier', the completely cynical and disillusioned time-server who'll 'never answer the phone if he can help it—it might be a job at the other end!'; the 'new centurion' (see Wambaugh 1971), dedicated to a crusade against crime and disorder, seeing detective work as the central function, and emphasizing the street cop as the repository of all truth, wisdom, and virtue; the 'professional' policeman, ambitious and career-conscious, with an appropriately balanced appreciation of the value of all aspects of policing from crime-fighting to sweeping the station floors, equipping him for the largely public relations functions of senior rank (Reiner 1978: chap. 12).

Other studies have identified very similar perspectives, albeit with different labels (Broderick 1973; Walsh 1977; Shearing 1981a; M. Brown 1981). The types seem to be as follows (translating the other authors' labels into my terminology):

(i)   The 'bobby' (= Broderick's 'optimist' = Walsh's 'street-cop = Muir's 'professional' = Shearing's 'wise officer' = Brown's 'professional').

(ii) The 'new centurion' (= Broderick's 'enforcer' = Walsh's 'action-seeker' = Muir's 'enforcer' = Shearing's 'real officer' = Brown's 'crime-fighters').

(iii) The 'uniform-carrier' (= Broderick's 'realist = Walsh's cynical 'street-cop' = Muir's 'avoider' = Shearing's 'cautious officer = Brown's 'service type 1').

(iv) The 'professional' (= Broderick's 'idealist' = Walsh's 'middle-class mobile' = Muir's 'reciprocator' = Shearing's 'good officer').

The differences in nomenclature reflect differing purposes of particular studies, as well as conflicting conceptions of the 'good' police officer—is it possible to play it by the rules (Broderick), must we resign ourselves to the tragic inevitability of coercive power (Muir), or is the apparent conflict of roles ideologically functional for class control (Shearing)? This leads to explicitly opposed notions of the 'professional': the ideal embodiment of legalistic policing (Broderick), the wise, empathetic but untutored intuitions of Dixon-style beat work (Muir), a legitimating ideology for individual and collective social mobility (Reiner).

But the same underlying types are postulated: an alienated cynic, a managerial professional, a peace-keeper and a law-enforcer. These correspond with the basic organizational division of labour between management and rank and file, and between CID and uniform patrol. But the differing orientations are already discernible in samples of uniformed patrol officers, prefiguring future career developments.

The culture of chief constables itself varies, with different perspectives typically related to the pattern of previous careers, the character of the force, and the experience of particular generations (Reiner 1991: chap. 12). Overall, British chief officers do not have fundamentally different cultural styles from the rank and file, having come from similar backgrounds and worked their way up the force hierarchy (M. Young 1993). However, they are more likely to espouse different policing philosophies, shaped by the need to accommodate to pressures from governmental and social elites. In the 1980s the conventional wisdom of chief officers was moulded by the Scarman Report (Reiner 1991). During the 1990s, however, it increasingly adopted a managerialist, 'businesslike' flavour (Wall 1998).

The differing orientations do not seem related to demographic characteristics such as ethnic group and gender. No research on these issues exists in Britain as yet. But American work suggests there is no tendency for black officers to be different in work style from whites (Alex 1969), or to be less punitive towards other blacks (Black 1971; Geller 1983; P. Waddington 1999: 111–2). It may be, though, that increasing the proportion of black officers changes the whole ethos of a department in ways which cannot be discerned in individual comparisons (Sherman 1983). Nor is there evidence of significant differences in policing style between male and female officers (Bloch and Anderson 1974; Sichel 1978; Heidensohn 1992). Again, though, it is plausible that raising the proportion of women in the department might alter the masculine ethos (Walklate 1996). On the other hand, the whole burden of the argument of this chapter so far is that the culture of the police depends not on individual attributes but on elements in the police function itself. Research on differing department styles implies that there is some scope for change, although this is constrained by the social and political context in which the department is embedded.

VARIATIONS IN ORGANIZATIONAL CULTURE

The *locus classicus* for considering differences in the styles of whole police organizations is J. Q. Wilson's (1968) study, *Varieties of Police Behaviour*. Wilson suggested that three departmental styles could be distinguished. The 'watchman' style emphasized order maintenance and the patrolman perspective. Bureaucratization, standardization, and professionalization were barely developed, and political influence was rife. Patrol officers had much discretion in handling their beats. The 'legalistic' style operated with a law enforcement approach, attempting to impose universalistic standards impartially on all communities in the city. The organization was bureaucratic and professionalized. The 'service' style prioritizes the consensual, helpful service functions of the police. If it has to deal with deviations from the law, it attempts to do so wherever possible by cautioning, not prosecution (but they are dealt with formally, not ignored). There is much stress on public relations and community involvement. Although partly a product of departmental policy choices, the styles reflected social and political balances. 'Legalistic' departments replaced 'watchman' ones either after a corruption scandal bringing in a reform administration, or as a result of a slower process of change in the balance of power between class elements, elevating groups with an interest in rational and universalistic authority as a framework for long-run planning. It could run into paradoxical difficulties if introduced in an adverse social context. For example, while less racially discriminatory, the 'legalistic' style enjoined higher levels of law enforcement, and might thus adopt aggressive methods of patrol which blacks saw as harassment. The 'service' style was only developed in middle-class suburban communities with a value consensus.

There is not much British evidence about differences in culture between police forces. Cain's (1973) study of a rural and a city force in the early 1960s indicated that the country police officers were more closely integrated into the communities they policed. The city officers were by contrast much more closely interdependent with their police colleagues, and alienated from the populations they policed, with more abrasive encounters. This was probably a consequence of the different conditions of policing in rural and urban areas rather than a function of organizational styles readily open to policy change. Urban/rural differences in style are a frequently recurring motif (Shapland and Vagg 1988; Shapland and Hobbs 1989).

S. Jones and M. Levi (1983) collected data on police and public attitudes in two forces whose chief constables stood at opposite poles in the spectrum of police debate. Devon and Cornwall's chief constable, John Alderson, was the foremost exponent of the 'community policing' philosophy, emphasizing the importance of a close and positive relationship between police and public as the essential precondition of effective policing, and seeing the police role as a broad one with a strong social service component. Manchester's James Anderton had the highest public profile of all chief constables, standing for a tough law-and-order approach.

Jones and Levi found that on a variety of indicators the public in Devon and Cornwall had more favourable opinions of their police than people in Manchester. Moreover, the police in Devon and Cornwall had a more accurate perception of their public standing than the Manchester police, suggesting a closer relationship. One common criticism levelled against the community policing policies of John Alderson was that, while they might be appropriate for tranquil rural counties, they would be impracticable in a city. Jones and Levi found, however, that the contrast held true when Plymouth (the second largest city in the south-west) was compared to Wigan (a relatively small northern country town), although Plymouth did have the lowest levels of expressed public satisfaction in the Devon and Cornwall force area. This suggests that, while it is indeed harder to cultivate positive police–public relations in cities, organizational culture and style are also important variables.

The clearest evidence of the possibility of introducing changes in police culture comes from an important ethnographic study (Foster 1989) comparing two inner-city London police stations. In one, substantial changes in policing style and practices were introduced successfully, altering the culture in the direction intended by the Scarman Report with its espousal of a community policing philosophy. The key ingredient of this achievement was the overall commitment and solid backing of the whole management hierarchy. In the other station, where this was lacking, traditional police culture remained resilient. A similar message of the possibilities of reform even in tough city areas is provided in a study of six innovative police chiefs in the USA, who set out to reorient their departments in a community policing direction (Skolnick and Bayley 1986). However, it is left somewhat unclear how far this translated successfully into sustained change in practices on the ground. Chan's (1977) account of the failure of attempts to change police culture in Australian reform attempts underlined the limited possibilities in the absence of fundamental transformation of the police role.

Altogether it seems that there are significant differences in the culture of policing between different areas. What is less clear is the extent to which the differences are the products of policy choices which can effectively be made in areas with different social and political structures and cultural traditions. Do societies get the policing they deserve, or can they do significantly better or worse? It is impossible to foreordain the degree of freedom facing reform strategies, although it is undoubtedly never very great. But the variations found in departmental style do imply that the emphasis on the autonomy of rank-and-file culture in the interactionist research tradition may need some qualification. (Although the resilience of cop culture even in extreme situations is shown by Brewer and Magee's (1990) study of routine policing in Northern Ireland). Further development of systematic comparative work would allow us to analyze just how much is constant in police work across a variety of contexts, and how much is variable and why (Punch 1979a, 1985; Bayley 1985, 1991, 1992, 1994; R. I. Mawby 1991, 1999; Miyazawa 1992; M. Brogden and Shearing 1993; Brodeur 1995; Marenin 1996; Manning 1997; Backman 2000).

CONCLUSION

There seem to be certain commonalities in cop culture as discovered by many studies in several different places and periods (P. Waddington 1999: 111–2). These arise from similar elements in the police role in any advanced industrial liberal democracy, notably authority and danger.

Police culture and its variations are reflections of the power structures of the societies policed. The social map of the police is differentiated according to the power of particular groups to cause problems for the police, with the least powerful elements in society becoming police 'property'. The power structure of a community and the views of its elites are important sources of variation in policing styles (with 'divided' societies constituting an extreme case; see Brewer 1991). The different orientations within the police reflect the two ways police organizations have to face in a class-divided hierarchical social order: downwards by the rank and file, to the groups controlled with varying degrees of gusto or finesse; and upwards by the professional police chiefs, to the majority public and elite who want an acceptable gloss to be placed on what is done in their name.

Police culture is neither monolithic nor unchanging. But the predicament of the police in maintaining order and enforcing the law in liberal democracies generates a typical cultural pattern. Officers vary in their responses, however, according to structural factors like their role in the organizational division of labour, their own demographic background, and their individual personalities and interpretations. None the less the nature of police work does seem to generate a recognizably related culture in all forces which have been studied. Fundamental change in this requires not just changes aimed at individual officers (for example in selection and training), nor grand policy declarations, but a reshaping of the basic character of the police role as a result of wider social transformation.

NOTES

1. Her critique was in many respects similar to Gouldner's (1968) debate with Becker (1963, 1967) and the 'labelling' perspective in general, which Skolnick and the other interactionist studies of rank-and-file policing were part of. Her arguments pointing to the need for a structuralist analysis of the operation of police discretion, rather than a culturalist one, were developed by Shearing (1981a, b), Ericson (1982), and M. Brogden and Brogden (1983). The most comprehensive and sophisticated presentation of this structuralist account was the rigorous attempt to develop a Marxist analysis of police culture and operations in Grimshaw and Jefferson (1987). For attempts at synthesis between interactionism and structuralism see McConville, Sanders, and Leng 1991; Reiner and Leigh 1992; D. Dixon 1997.

2. The police world remains aggressively a man's world, notwithstanding equal opportunities legislation in the USA and Britain (Fielding 1994a). In America despite the Equal Employment Opportunity Act 1972 women remain grossly under-represented in most forces (Heidensohn 1989). Although some forces have sent women on routine patrol for many years now, they still face formidable barriers of an informal kind in 'breaking and entering' into this male preserve (Ehrlich 1980). British research has also found unequivocal evidence of both informal and formal discrimination against women, in flagrant breach of the law (Policy Studies Institute 1983, ii: 163–8, iv: 91–7; Bryant et al. 1985; S. Jones 1986, 1987; Hanmer, Radford, and Stanko 1989; M. Young 1991; Heidensohn

1992; Fielding and Fielding 1992; Walklate 1992, 1996; J. Brown, Maidment, and Bull 1993; C. Martin 1996). To talk of policemen is thus not shorthand but for the most part a literal description.

3. It also serves to resolve the 'Dirty Harry' problem, whereby 'policing constantly places its practitioners in situations in which good ends can be achieved by dirty means.' This is 'a genuine moral dilemma ... from which one cannot emerge innocent no matter what one does' (Klockars 1980: 33). Cynicism is a clearly possible psychological result.

4. I well remember the experience in 1971 (soon after I began research on the police) of attending a conference where, after the learned seminars a local officer took me, two other sociologists, and two out-of-town policemen to a local drinking club. There were about fifty men there, and just three women —two strippers and the barmaid. To the amazement of the observing but not participating sociologists, at the end of the evening the three policemen managed to walk off with the three women, whom they had been assiduously chatting up while fending off earnest discussion of police sub-cultural normative patterns.

4

DEMYSTIFYING THE POLICE: SOCIAL RESEARCH AND POLICE PRACTICE

There are various conflicting political mythologies about policing which have bedevilled debate. The 'law and order' myth portrays the police as an effective force for the prevention and detection of crime, and advocates police power as the panacea for law enforcement and public order problems. It is the primary representation of policing in the mass media, and in both police and popular culture. It was the position espoused by the Conservatives and the police in the late 1970s (Downes and Morgan 1997), and surfaced again in the 1990s in much of the enthusiasm for 'zero tolerance' policing (Bowling 1996, 1999c; Dennis, 1998; R. Burke 1998; Weatheritt 1998; Innes 1999a, b; Walklate and Evans 1999). Its antithesis, the 'repressive state apparatus' myth, flourished in the radical criminology of the 1970s and 1980s. It depicted the police as an essentially oppressive political force creating crime and criminals through its labelling activities. In this view, community safety and harmony require the curbing of police power (see, for instance, Scraton 1985, 1987; Farrell 1992).

We can also discern a variety of 'third way' mythologies about policing, which have burgeoned in the 1990s, reflecting the broader quest for social policies that have moved 'beyond left and right'. 'Community policing' was and remains a fashionable label internationally in police policy discussions, largely because of its apparently benign and uncontentious 'cherry pie' connotations (M. Brogden 1999). The fundamental premise is that effective police work is possible only on the basis of public consent and co-operation (Alderson 1979; Skolnick and Bayley 1986, 1988; M. Moore 1992; Friedmann 1992; Stephens and Becker 1994; Bennett 1994a, 1995b; Fielding 1995). In much political and police rhetoric this innocuous proposition often becomes a broader mythology of policing as ideally a species of social service delivering good works to a harmonious community of satisfied customers. In so far as this idyll is not realized in today's harsh and conflict-ridden world, policy must be aimed at restoring it.

A tougher version of 'third way' policing can be called the 'magic bullet' myth. Through research and analysis of policing problems it is possible to develop tactics that deliver precisely the right degree of force necessary for effective yet legitimate crime control and order maintenance. This forensic crime reduction myth is a sophisticated version of the 'law and order' myth. It believes that intelligently targeted policing can, using laser-like precision, excise crime and disorder with minimal negative side-effects for civil liberties or social justice. At one level it is impossible to question the project. Who but Al Capone and his disciples would prefer stupidity-led to intelligence-led policing? As with community policing, the question marks are over not the desirability of the approach but its feasibility.

What all the mythologies over-simplify or ignore is the extent to which policing reflects the conflicts and contradictions of the wider social structure, culture, and political economy. Policing alone cannot achieve an orderly society, whether this is seen as desirable or repressive (P. Hall 1998). On the other hand it can never operate in the fully harmonious way implied by some prophets of community policing (Manning 1997; P. Waddington 1999*a*: 206–26).

Research evidence, as opposed to presumption about what the police do (and especially the determinants of their actions), has proliferated in America, Britain, and elsewhere in the last four decades (Reiner 1992*a*, 1996*a*, 1997*b*, 2000*a*). However, it remains inconclusive when it comes to the question of assessing possible reforms and alternatives to current practice. The evidence that exists does suggest the one-sidedness of all the above mythologies. Police work is more complex, contradictory, indeed confused, than any of them allows.

The research evidence about police practice will be considered in this chapter in relation to three specific questions. What is the police role? How effectively is it performed? How fairly is it performed? There has been a clear dialectic in the development of police research about all these issues. Early research tended to emphasize a debunking of the pre-research conventional wisdom about policing, offering an antithesis to the tacit thesis of popular assumptions. More recently the critical deconstruction offered by early research has itself been called into question, although not to the extent of rehabilitating the original conventional wisdom. Rather, a degree of synthesis between the rational kernel of pre-research common sense and the debunking offered by early research has developed.

WHAT IS THE POLICE ROLE?

A perennial chestnut of debate about the police role has been whether the police are best considered as a force, with the primary function of enforcing the criminal law, or as a service, calming a sea of social troubles. The starting-point for debate was the empirical 'discovery' that the police (contrary to popular mythology) operate not mainly as crime-fighters or law-enforcers, but rather as providers of a range of services to members of the public, the variety of which beggars description.

Banton (1964), on the basis of an analysis of field diaries kept by a sample of Scottish policemen, observation, and interviews (both in Britain and in the USA) concluded (p. 127):

The policeman on patrol is primarily a 'peace officer' rather than a 'law officer'. Relatively little of his time is spent enforcing the law in the sense of arresting offenders; far more is spent 'keeping the peace' by supervising the beat and responding to requests for assistance.

Cumming, Cumming, and Edell 1965 found in an analysis of phone calls by the public to an American force that over half involved demands for help or support in relation to personal and interpersonal problems, in which the police performed as 'philosopher, guide, and friend'. This was replicated by Punch and Naylor (1973) in an analysis of the calls by the public to the police in three Essex towns in a two-week period. In the 'new town', 49 per cent were service calls, in the 'old town' 61 per cent, and in the 'country town' 73 per cent. Of the service calls, the largest categories were 'domestic occurrences' (such as family disputes or noisy parties) and 'highway accidents'. J. Martin and G. Wilson (1969) found that only 28 per cent of duty time in provincial forces (and 31 per cent in the Met) was spent on crime-related work. Very similar results have been found in many subsequent studies (McCabe and Sutcliffe 1978; Hough 1980; Antunes and Scott 1981; P. Morris and Heal, 1981: chap. 3; Ekblom and Heal 1982; D. A. Smith and Klein 1984; Bennett and Lupton 1992a; P. Waddington 1993a, 1999a: chap. 1; Bayley 1994, 1996; Hough 1996; Fielding 1996; Police Foundation/Policy Studies Institute 1996; R. Morgan and Newburn 1997; Johnston 2000: chap. 3).

The empirical findings about the nature of police activity stimulated two contradictory reactions. For the most part they were used to bolster a liberal argument which became the orthodoxy among progressive police administrators, chiefs, and commentators between 1965 and 1975. This was that 'is' meant 'ought'. The police were *de facto* social workers, although not recognized as such. They were a 'secret social service' (Punch 1979b). But because this was covert and seldom articulated, there was a need for the police to be better trained and organized to cope with the work that anyway accounted for most of their activity. If the law and order panacea for police problems was bigger guns, the liberal's was a sociology degree.

Some argued that the mandate of crime prevention should mean more than that the police engage in the traditional techniques of patrol and detection. They should collaborate with other social service agencies and government to tackle the underlying social causes of crime, as well as the symptoms (Stephens and Becker 1994). In British police circles this view was championed above all by John Alderson, chief constable of Devon and Cornwall, in his community policing philosophy (Alderson 1979, 1984a). There are also close affinities with the idea of 'problem-oriented' policing, that instead of reacting to crime and other problems on a reactive, piecemeal basis, police should analyse and tackle proactively the source of recurrent problems (Goldstein 1979, 1990; M. Moore 1992; A. Leigh, Read and Tilley, 1996).

By the late 1980s this had become the new post-Scarmanist orthodoxy of nearly all chief officers (Reiner 1991: chap. 6). The *Operational Policing Review* mounted in 1989 by all three staff associations seemed to indicate public preference for a more community-oriented style of policing. This inspired the 1991 'Statement of Common

Purposes and Values' in which the police staff associations committed themselves to a mission based on the idea of service. Following the Plus Programme in the Met, HM Inspectorate and ACPO aimed to reconstruct police culture and practice around an ethic of 'quality of service' service to the consumer (*Policing* Special Issue on 'The Way Ahead', autumn 1991; I. Waters 1996).

While this consensus was emerging at the top, there was a developing underswell of protest in the police rank and file. Research had shown that street-level police culture rested on an action and crime-fighting orientation. This was pithily summed up by one American patrolman: 'Every time you begin to do some real police work you get stuck with this stuff. I guess 90 per cent of all police work is bullshit' (Reiss 1971: 42). The 1990 *Operational Policing Review* survey of national samples of senior and rank-and-file police confirmed that this gulf still existed. While senior ranks favoured community policing initiatives, the operational ranks remained wedded to a 'strong' crime-fighting approach. However, the 1993–4 reform package—the White Paper, the Sheehy Report, the Police and Magistrates' Courts Act 1994, and the *Review of Police Core and Ancillary Tasks* (Posen 1995)—explicitly sought to restructure the police on a 'businesslike' model aimed at the sole priority of 'catching criminals' (Reiner 1997b: 1030–9). Although the Labour government re-emphasized the importance of police partnership with local government and other agencies, it continued to prioritize crime reduction as the primary purpose of policing and criminal justice policy (Home Office 1998; Downes 1998; Walklate 2000).

The force–service debate that has long bedevilled discussions of the police role rests on a false dichotomy. In so far as the two roles are distinguishable, they are inter-dependent, and derive from a more fundamental mandate of first-aid order mainten-ance. To clarify this, let me define the basic concepts. There are two dimensions underlying police work: (a) is there consensus or conflict between the civilians and the police in an interaction? And (b) does the police action invoke the legal powers of arrest, prosecution, and so on? Putting the two dimensions together yields a typology of four possible types of police intervention (Table 4.1).

The first cell (law enforcement in a consensus situation) is a controversial area. If there is genuinely no conflict about desired outcomes between civilian and police participants in an interaction, there is no need for the invocation of legal powers, which are inherently coercive. However, the police regularly stop and question and/or search people, or detain them at police stations 'assisting with enquiries', without formally exercising their legal powers, claiming that the compliance of citizens has

Table 4.1 Dimensions of police work

	Police use legal powers ('law officer')	Police do not use legal powers ('peace officer')
Consensus	'voluntary compliance'	'service'
Conflict	'law enforcement'	'order maintenance'

been voluntary. There must be doubt about how often such 'voluntary' compliance is whole-hearted and genuine, and how often it is based on ignorance about rights, and bluff by the police (D. Dixon, Coleman, and Bottomley 1990; McKenzie, Morgan, and Reiner 1990; D. Dixon, 1997).

The categories are all 'ideal types' and concrete incidents can be classified into them only after a contingent process of interaction in which different outcomes are possible. Take an incident I observed where police were called out because of incessant barking of a neighbour's dog. The police officer discovered that the owners were not in and climbed over the back garden fence to investigate because the dog sounded in distress. In the course of this the owners returned. The neighbours and the constable explained what had happened, and everyone was satisfied. The outcome was a good example of 'service' work. But it is possible that the neighbours might have got into an argument about the propriety of involving the police, and an 'order maintenance' situation developed. Depending on many factors, but primarily the officer's orientation to his job, his assessment of the moral characters of the disputants, and his skills at defusing conflict, it is quite possible that the eventual outcome would have been an arrest for assault. Then the outcome would have been classifiable as 'law enforcement' work. The nature of a police intervention is not totally foreordained by the initial 'call for service' made by a member of the public.

In terms of these more precisely defined types, most police work is neither social service nor law enforcement, but order maintenance—the settlement of conflicts by means other than formal law enforcement. Moreover, this is accomplished in the main by the distinctive police capacity, which is not possession of legal powers of arrest (though police powers do considerably exceed those of the ordinary citizen) nor social work skills, but 'the capacity for decisive action', as Bittner has put it. 'The policeman, and the policeman alone, is equipped, entitled and required to deal with every exigency in which force may have to be used' (Bittner 1974: 35). The police mandate is the very diffuse notion of order maintenance, what Bittner (ibid) has graphically called 'a solution to an unknown problem arrived at by unknown means'. But beneath the diversity of problems and means is the core capacity to use force if necessary. This does not mean that the police typically (or even often) use coercion or force to accomplish the resolution of the troubles they deal with. The craft of effective policing is to use the background possibility of legitimate coercion so skilfully that it never needs to be foregrounded. Several observational studies have given impressive accounts of how 'good' patrol officers can maintain peace in threatening situations, with their legal powers (including force) as a latent resource (Bittner 1967; Muir 1977; Kemp, Norris, and Fielding 1992). The successful police officer draws on the authority of her office, as well as her personal and craft skills in handling people, rather than the core of coercive power—although sometimes this will not be possible. These skills are not adequately recognized, rewarded or understood, largely because popular and police preconceptions about the nature of the police task have precluded analysis of the craftsmanship involved in effective peace-keeping (Bittner 1983; Bayley and Bittner 1984; Norris and Norris 1993; Reiner 1998).

However, order maintenance is just as problematic in terms of social and political justice as the higher-profile issue of crime control (P. Hall 1998). The observational studies that vividly depict many examples of good peace-keeping work fail to grapple with these problems adequately. For example, Chatterton (1983: 211–5) gives a detailed account of the calming-down of a domestic dispute without the arrest of the husband, who had assaulted his wife. In Chatterton's analysis this was ultimately due to the officer exercising his sense of the justice of the man's position. As he described the case, an arrest accomplishing 'legal' justice would have been both unjust and troublesome to all concerned.

This clearly raises the problem of whether we can rely on the personal sense of justice of patrol officers, and how its exercise can be made accountable. The typical handling of domestic 'disputes' as non-criminal, order-maintenance matters, rather than assaults, has been criticized effectively for many years by feminists, and has produced change in forces around the world. One common reaction has been the encouragement of mandatory arrest policies, shifting this large category of calls unequivocally into 'law enforcement'. There has been much debate about the effectiveness and desirability of such innovations (Sherman and Berk, 1984; S. Edwards 1989, 1994; Hanmer, Radford, and Stanko 1989; Sheptycki 1991, 1993; Sherman 1992b; Dobash and Dobash 1992; Hoyle 1998). The issues of achieving and reconciling fairness, effectiveness, and accountability are just as acute for order-maintenance work as for the areas of law enforcement where they have been most widely discussed. This is brought out clearly in American quantitative research on police handling of interpersonal disputes, which shows evidence of class, sex, and race discrimination in the police reaction to such incidents, analogous to similar evidence in crime work (D. A. Smith and Klein, 1984). Even those commentators (among them some eminent neo-conservatives) who have most passionately extolled the virtues of beat policing and a renewed emphasis on order-maintenance work have recognized the acute problems of equity and accountability that are raised (J. Wilson and Kelling 1982: 35–6; Skogan 1990b; Kelling and Coles 1998).

That order maintenance is the core of the police mandate is attested to in a variety of ways. It is reflected in the pattern of specific demands placed upon the police by calls for service. Most involve some element of conflict, not harmonious service requests like fetching cats out of trees, but do not relate unequivocally to a criminal offence. Second, it was a core mandate historically. The main *raison d'être* for the 'new police' was crime prevention by regular patrol (that is, intervention in situations before crimes occurred) as well as order maintenance in the sense of crowd control. The unique character of British policing lies partly in merging the tasks of law enforcement and order maintenance (including crowd and riot control) into the same organization.

However, to say that the primary police role is order maintenance is not to give the police responsibility for all elements of social order. Their task is the emergency maintenance of order, not the creation of its preconditions, as the broadest philosophies of community policing seek (Alderson 1979, 1984a). As P. Waddington has

put it: 'The police are the social equivalent of the AA or RAC patrolmen, who intervene when things go unpredictably wrong and secure a provisional solution' (P. Waddington 1983a: 34). In this analogy, they are neither service-station mechanics nor
car-makers. But, like the AA, they have a role in advising on policy relevant to their
duties and co-operating with other agencies.

The influential 'new left-realist' school of criminologists in Britain argued for a
'minimalist' policing approach (Kinsey, Lea, and Young 1986). They argued that
police intervention should be confined to cases where there was clear evidence of law-
breaking, and then should take the form of the invocation of legal powers and criminal process (Johnston 2000: 48–50). Only in this way, it was claimed, could police
work be fully accountable to the law. This ignores, however, the large bulk of calls for
service which are not unequivocally reports of crime. On a 'minimalist' strategy this
would mean either not responding to such requests, or forcing the police response
into a Procrustean bed of legalism untempered by discretion. While the problem of
ensuring equity and efficiency in order-maintenance or service work is daunting, the
'minimalist' approach would achieve the confinement of the police to a 'constitutional corral' (Uglow 1988) only by excluding as illegitimate many problems which
people call the police for.

Recent empirical work suggests that a growing proportion of calls for police service,
at least in urban areas, are indeed reports of crime or 'potential crime' (T. Jones,
Maclean, and Young 1986; Shapland and Vagg 1988: 36–9; Shapland and Hobbs 1989.
This is also true in a number of other countries; see Bayley 1985: 120–7). This may
partly be a result of reconceptualization of some types of incident (such as domestic
disputes) into the criminal category, by citizens, police, and researchers. It is also
plausible, however, that more criminal victimization is occurring as well as more
being reported by victims (Home Office 1999: chaps. 1, 2). Certainly recorded crime
rates have risen dramatically and constitute a greater pressure on the police. Forces
have responded by increasing the number of specialists with law-enforcement functions (Dorn, Murji, and South 1991a, b; Audit Commission 1993; Loveday 1996b,
1997; Murji 1998; Sheptycki 2000; Maguire 2000), even though uniformed patrol still
constitutes the bulk of personnel deployment (Tarling 1988: 5; Bayley 1994; Morgan
and Newburn 1997). As discussed earlier, under both the Conservatives and Labour,
during the 1990s government sought to define the police mandate in crime-control
terms. However, uniformed patrol remains the bedrock of policing, and this will
continue to be pre-occupied with order-maintenance, rather than criminal
investigation.

Order maintenance is clearly a political enterprise, raising questions of definition,
equity and accountability. The recognition that the distinctive police resource is the
authority derived from the potential for the legitimate use of force places policing at
the heart of the functioning of the state. The 'hollowing-out' of the state in the last
three decades has of course vastly complicated this (Bottoms and Wiles 1996, 1997).
Policing is increasingly diffused between a complex variety of agencies and processes
apart from the traditional police provided by the state (Shearing and Stenning 1983,

1987; South 1988, 1997a; M. Davis 1990, 1998; Shearing 1992, 1996; Johnston 1992, 2000; Stenson 1993, 2000; O'Malley and Palmer 1996; Reiner 1996b, 1997b; Braithwaite 2000; P. Hirst 2000; N. Rose 2000).

None the less order maintenance remains the core function of the police, and one which they are still primarily deployed towards. It has recently been argued in an influential study that in contemporary 'risk society' the police task has shifted away from being primarily order maintenance or crime control (Ericson and Haggerty 1997). The police have become knowledge workers. Their main function is to broker information about risks to public and private organizations concerned with the regulation and governance of people and territories. Ericson and Haggerty provide a rich account of police work involving the accumulation, analysis, and transmission of knowledge about risk to other institutions. Their analysis is based on extensive observation and interviews, and certainly establishes the significance of risk-related information-processing in contemporary policing. However, the extent to which this has supplanted order maintenance or crime control remains debatable. Their data was derived from theoretical sampling of police with 'knowledge-work roles' (Ericson and Haggerty 1997: 128). This concentration on what they regard as the prototypical aspects of policing is theoretically justifiable to allow analysis of police knowledge-work. It does mean, however, that the material cannot itself establish empirically the extent to which this now characterizes police work in general. In any event, the police function of knowledge-brokering derives from their traditional patrolling and surveillance activities, and their power as the specialist carriers of the state's monopoly of legitimate force. It is this that gives them uniquely privileged access to risk knowledge.

Both the Bittner conception of policing as emergency order maintenance deploying the capacity for legitimate force, and Ericson and Haggerty's analysis of policing as risk information-brokering, agree that popular and political notions of the police as crime-fighters cannot be sustained. To regard the primary task of the police as crime control is dangerous not least for the police themselves, for there is now a substantial body of evidence suggesting not only that this is not being accomplished effectively, but that it cannot be.

HOW EFFECTIVE ARE THE POLICE?

The police were part of a process that made cities less violent, crime-ridden and disorderly during the nineteenth century. The police's precise contribution to this, compared with more general processes of social pacification, is hard to pinpoint, but it is probable that they were a significant factor. Even if they were no more successful in detecting crime than nowadays, the impact-effect of creating a regularly patrolling force which recorded, and where possible prosecuted, violations probably increased the risks facing offenders. The nineteenth-century police's accomplishments established a baseline of order and crime control that the present-day police continue to maintain more or less successfully.

Since the Second World War in most industrial countries there has been a dramatic rise in recorded crime rates, public fear of crime, and anxiety about law and order as a public issue (Hale 1996; I. Taylor 1996, 1997a; Walklate 1997, 1998; Hollway and Jefferson 1997; Reiner 2000; Hope and Sparks 2000; Stenson and Sullivan 2000; Garland 2000, 2001). Discussions about criminal justice policy, and the police specifically, have usually reflected the law-and-order myth that given adequate resources and powers the police could tackle the problem of rising crime. The only opposition to the law-and-order lobby was on the civil libertarian grounds that police effectiveness must not be bought at too high a price: the undermining of civil rights. However, in the 1970s and 1980s research in the USA and Britain began to question the assumption that increased police power and resources can control crime (R. Clarke and Hough 1980, 1984; P. Morris and Heal 1981; Heal, Tarling, and Burrows 1985; Bayley 1994; Morgan and Newburn 1997). This cautionary attitude to the effectiveness of increased police spending struck a harmonious note with the fiscal parsimony of the conservative regimes dominant in Britain and North America, if not with their traditional soft spot for the guardians of law and order (Reiner and Cross 1991: chap. 1). It also chimed in with the more general mood of 'nothing works' in criminal justice (Martinson, Lipton, and Wilks 1974; J. Wilson 1975; S. Cohen, 1997a).

STUDIES OF PATROL WORK

Since 1954 many studies have been carried out in the USA and Britain aimed at evaluating the effectiveness of foot and car patrol in crime-control work.[1] The initial American research suggested that crime rates did decline if patrol strength was significantly increased. However, this early work was flawed methodologically and through data-rigging by the police (P. Morris and Heal 1981: 21–2). Some small-scale research conducted by the Home Office in the 1960s suggested that when an officer was introduced to patrol a hitherto uncovered beat recorded crime decreased, but that there was no significant further reduction from increasing the number of officers on the beat (P. Morris and Heal 1981). This was in line with the general finding of patrol studies that increasing police coverage does not affect crime control beyond the baseline achieved by having police at all (Hough 1996).

The most sophisticated study of motorized patrol was the celebrated Kansas City preventive patrol experiment (Kelling et al. 1974). This evaluated the effects of systematically varying patrol strengths between five sets of three beats, matched demographically, in crime rates, and in patterns of demand for police services. In each set one beat was chosen at random for 'normal' levels of patrol and acted as 'control' beat. Another set was designated for 'proactive' patrol, and patrolled two or three times as frequently as the 'controls'. In the third set 'reactive' patrol was carried out, with cars entering only in response to specific calls for service. The study found no significant differences between the areas in reported crime, rates of victimization, levels of citizen fear, or satisfaction with the police. It was as if the level of preventive patrol made no difference to any policy goals at all. The experiment was subject to methodological criticism by Larson (1976), who claimed that the design of the study was not adhered to in practice, and visible police presence in the experimental and control areas was much the same. But the study (after some very hostile early responses from American police chiefs) has come to be generally accepted as establishing that increasing car patrol (at least within feasible limits) is not significantly related to crime levels.

Nor is this surprising:

Crimes are rare events and are committed stealthily—as often as not in places out of reach of patrols. The chances of patrols catching offenders red-handed are therefore small ... a patrolling policeman in London could expect to pass within 100 yards of a burglary in progress roughly once every eight years—but not necessarily to catch the burglar or even realize that the crime was taking place (Clarke and Hough 1984: 6–7).

If the preventive patrol car does not have much of a 'scarecrow' function and is unlikely to come across crimes in progress, might not cars' faster response to emergency calls increase the chances of apprehending criminals? After all, many of the technological developments in policing in the last twenty years—cars, radios, command and control computers—have been geared to this end. But again, research suggests that few if any offenders are caught as a result of faster response by police. The main reason is that most offences (70–85 per cent) are discovered some time after the event, and most victims do not call the police immediately (Silberman 1978: 330–4; R. Clarke and Hough 1984: 8–9). There is some evidence, however, that if fast response can be directed accurately to the minority of cases reported while they are in progress it can make an impact (Coupe and Griffiths 1996; Jordan 1998: 69).

In recent years it has commonly been argued that car patrol may even be counterproductive with regard to crime control. It cuts the police off from non-adversarial contacts with the public, thus reducing cooperation and information flow. Cars may also accentuate the hedonistic action elements in police culture, producing a fruitless overreaction to incidents (Holdaway 1977, 1983).

The limited utility (and evident expense) of car patrol stimulated a renewed enthusiasm for foot patrol in Britain and the USA. Early studies of foot patrol suggested it was no more effective than motorized patrol (Clarke and Hough 1984: 6). But the 1981 Police Foundation study of foot patrol (based on surveys in twenty-eight cities and an experiment in Newark, New Jersey) had encouraging results (Clarke and Hough 1984). The Newark experiment was based on sets of matched beats of which some were randomly to discontinue foot patrol, some to continue it, and some to introduce it for the first time. Crime levels (measured by victimization surveys and recorded crime rates) were not affected by the varied patrol methods. But in other respects the foot patrols had beneficial effects. Fear of crime declined, confidence in neighbourhood safety increased, and citizens evaluated police services more positively. Foot-patrol officers were more satisfied with their work, had a more benign view of citizens, a more community-oriented conception of policing, and lower absenteeism rates. However, the study was not able to indicate whether these attitudes led to or resulted from the officers' assignment to foot patrol. Altogether, while confirming that policing had little impact on crime rates *per se*, the foot-patrol experiment did imply that it had a beneficial impact on the communal sense of security and order. The research inspired the highly influential 'broken windows' hypothesis, that policing could impact on crime by preventing spirals of neighbourhood decline through timely intervention to prevent minor nuisances tipping over into broader, more embedded, and serious problems (J. Wilson and Kelling 1982; Skogan 1990*b*; Kelling and Coles 1998). This idea was the theoretical inspiration for what came to be known in the 1990s as 'zero tolerance' policing (Bowling 1996, 1999*c*; Dennis 1998; R. Burke 1998; Weatheritt 1998; Innes 1999*a, b*; Stenson 2000).

However, the possibilities of limiting crime by routine policing strategies remain limited, for reasons spelled out by the Audit Commission (Audit Commission 1996; Morgan and Newburn 1997: 126). They calculate that on current police strengths, a patrolling officer typically covers an area containing: 18,000 inhabitants, 7500 houses, 23 pubs, 9 schools, 140 miles of pavement, 85 acres of parks or open space, and 77 miles of road. The number of potential targets of crime, especially in urban areas, is simply too large to be effectively covered by police patrols of any feasible visibility and frequency—unless limited police resources can be proactively focused on the most probable targets for criminal victimization through intelligence or crime-pattern analysis (Maguire 1998*b*, 2000). Although variations in the quantity of patrol do not seem to affect crime levels, it has long been argued that qualitatively different, innovative styles or strategies of policing might do (Wilson 1975: chap. 5; Sherman, 1992, 1993). I shall examine the evidence about this after considering research on the effectiveness of detective work.

STUDIES OF DETECTION

The lack of success of criminal investigation work is in one sense apparent from the low (and declining) proportion of crimes reported to the police that are cleared up. Before the Second World War the clear-up rate for recorded offences was usually over 50 per cent, but it is now down to 29 per cent (Home Office 1999: 30). The clear-up rate varies widely for different crimes. It remains high for violent offences such as homicide (90 per cent), violence against the person (79 per cent), and sexual offences (77 per cent). It is however far lower for property offences, which constitute the vast majority of all recorded crimes. Clear-up rates in the late 1990s were around 27 per cent for robbery, 24 per cent for theft and handling, and 19 per cent for criminal damage (Home Office 1999: 30).

However, the clear-up rate is a notoriously inadequate measure of detective effectiveness (Audit Commission 1990*b*; M. Walker 1992, 1995; Coleman and Moynihan 1996; Maguire 1997). For one thing the denominator—crimes known to the police—can vary independently of offending behaviour if a higher or lower proportion of victimizations is reported by the public and/or recorded by the police. The British Crime Surveys show that fluctuations in victim reporting and police recording practices have indeed been major factors underlying the rise of recorded crime rates in recent decades, as well as the fall in the mid-1990s (Hough and Mayhew 1983; Mayhew, P., and Mirrlees-Black, C. 1993; Reiner 1996c). The falling clear-up rate is in large part a reflection of rising recorded crime levels rather than declining detective efficiency.

Since the 1970s police manpower has increased, but the absolute number of crimes cleared up increased even more, so that the proportion of crimes per officer which are cleared up has grown. This may indicate an increase in detective efficiency, despite the fall in the proportion of recorded crimes cleared up. One British study has attempted to quantify the relationship between possible increases in manpower and likely improvements in clear-up rates. From a comparison of the clear-up rates of different forces in England and Wales, this concluded that a 10 per cent increase in overall manpower, directed entirely to the CID, would raise the clear-up rate by less than 1 per cent (Burrows and Tarling 1982; Tarling and Burrows 1985).

The measure of crimes cleared up is fundamentally problematic in itself as an index of police efficiency or effectiveness. Studies of the detective function show that many of the crimes recorded as cleared up are not solved as a result of investigative effort. Only a relatively small number of major incident enquiries fit the model of 'classical' detection, starting from the crime itself and systematically investigating those with motive and opportunity to commit it (Maguire and Norris, 1992; Ericson 1993; Innes, 1999c, d, 2000)

Critical analysis of police investigative activity has indicated that it traditionally follows one of two patterns, both of which have the discriminatory and invidious social consequences of stigmatization and criminalization of vulnerable groups through a process of 'deviance amplification' (Matza 1969; J. Young, 1971). The first method is what Matza called the 'bureaucratic' mode, which echoes the famous lines uttered at the end of *Casablanca* by police chief Claude Rains: 'Round up the usual suspects.' In this mode successful detection depends upon knowledge of the 'underworld'. Crimes are solved by culling the group of people 'known' to commit offences of a certain type, or by cultivation of informants. The second method is that of stereotyping and suspicion. People are apprehended because they fit the investigator's preconceived notion of particular kinds of offender. Vice work is especially likely to rely on both the bureaucratic and suspicion methods, because the discovery and clear-up of vice offences relies entirely upon proactive policing as there are no co-operating 'victims'. Similarly, the more minor and vague 'public order' offences, which form a high proportion of patrol arrests, are heavily dependent on 'suspicion'. But the majority of offences are not cleared up by either of these modes of detection.

The major finding of studies of the process by which crimes are cleared up is that the prime determinant of success is information immediately provided by members of the public (usually the victim) to patrol officers or detectives when they arrive at the scene of a crime. If adequate information is provided to pinpoint the culprit fairly accurately, the crime will be resolved; if not, it is almost certain not to be (Bayley 1994). This is the conclusion of all the relevant studies, whether conducted by observation (Reiss 1971; Chatterton 1976; W. Sanders 1977; Ericson 1993), analysis of records (R. I. Mawby 1979; Zander 1979; Bottomley and Coleman 1981; Burrows and Tarling 1982; D. Brown 1991), or a combination of both (Greenwood, Chaiken, and Petersilia 1977; Steer 1980; Maguire and Norris 1992; Innes 1999c, d). This pinpointing of the crucial importance of initial information emphasizes not only the central role of the public in clearing up offences, but also the important part played by the uniformed branch. The proportions of crimes cleared up almost immediately (as a result of the offender still being at the scene when the police arrived, or being named or fully and accurately described by victim or witnesses) was as high as 57 per cent in Steer's study and 62 per cent in Mawby's.[2]

Research has also emphasized the significant proportion of crimes deemed to be cleared up by 'secondary' means, that is the questioning of suspects and offenders in order to elicit admissions that they have committed other crimes for which they will not be charged separately. Before the Police and Criminal Evidence Act 1984 (PACE) some studies suggested that as many as 40 per cent of property offences were cleared up by being 'taken into consideration' ('TIC') when offenders were sentenced for other offences (Lambert 1970; R. I. Mawby 1979). Steer (1980) and Bottomley and Coleman (1981) found a lower proportion of TICS (20 and 25 per cent, respectively), and nationally, around 26 per cent of clear-ups were by TIC (Burrows and Tarling 1982). PACE made it harder to use legally dubious 'tactics' of interviewing suspects which had led them to admit large numbers of offences to be taken into consideration (Irving and McKenzie 1989a, b; Williamson 1996; D. Brown 1997). Only 2 per cent of clear-ups are now by TIC according to official statistics (Home Office 1999: 30).

A major scandal about manipulation of the clear-ups attributed to TICS and 'prison write-offs' (where detectives question convicted prisoners in order to get them to admit other offences) occurred in Kent in the late 1980s (Observer, 8 October 1989). Such dubious ways of clearing the books by massaging the statistics had been rife for many years in other forces (P. Gill 1987; M. Young 1991; H. Taylor 1998a, b, 1999), and official estimates indicate that prison interviews still account for 4 per cent of clear-ups (Home Office 1999: 30). Recent revelations in several forces suggest that the government's increasing emphasis on meeting performance targets may have led to the revival of statistical book-cooking (Davies 1999b). Indeed a police force that is assiduous in its crime recording may appear inefficient in comparison with less scrupulous neighbours (Farrington and Dowds 1985).

Thus only a small proportion of crimes are cleared up by investigative techniques bearing any resemblance to either the 'classical' or the 'bureaucratic' modes beloved by fiction. Most solved cases are essentially self-clearing. This does not mean that detectives are useless or inefficient. 'The detective has a variety of skills. These include gathering information from the public; locating suspects; interviewing and, on the basis of information derived from both the public and suspects, of preparing cases for the prosecution' (P. Morris and Heal 1981: 33). There is also of course the relatively small but significant category of cases where the perpetrator is not initially known ('whodunits' in detectives' jargon) but are none the less successfully cleared up by methods including the 'classical' and 'bureaucratic' modes (Innes 1999*c*, *d*). However, the pressure on detectives to achieve more 'primary' clear-ups (not based on post-arrest or sentence interviewing) has led to increasing use of innovative methods which may themselves be ethically, legally, and practically problematic. These include pro-active tactics such as undercover work, technological surveillance, and informers who are themselves offenders (Marx 1988, 1992; Audit Commission 1993; Greer 1995*a*, *b*; Maguire and John 1996*a*, *b*; Fijnaut and Marx 1996; den Boer 1997; Sheptycki 1997, 2000; P. Gill 1997*a*, *b*; Colvin and Noorlander 1998; Norris and Armstrong 1999; Dunnighan and Norris 1999; Norris and Dunnighan 2000; Heaton 2000; Maguire 2000; Innes 2000; Billingsley, Nemitz, and Bean 2000). There is scope for more effective management and coordination of the detective function, especially through 'case-screening' to distinguish crimes according to 'solvability' (and whether they should be allocated to CID or uniformed branches for investigation), and more effect-ive proactive 'targeting' of some serious offences and offenders. However, given the proliferation of recorded crimes and other demands for service relative to police resources (Audit Commission 1993; R. Morgan and Newburn 1997: 57), and the constraints on legitimate tactics in a liberal democracy (Weisburd, Uchida, and Green 1993), the prospects of successful investigation will always be limited.

INNOVATORY POLICING STRATEGIES

The realization as a result of evaluative research that more of the old police tactics cannot work in reducing crime stimulated advocacy of a variety of innovative policing strategies (Sherman 1992*a*, 1993). Two diametrically opposed suggestions emerged in the late 1970s in the wake of the research debunking traditional tactics: 'aggressive' patrol and crackdowns, and several variants of 'community policing'. More recently these have been synthesized in a variety of 'third way' approaches.

'Aggressive' patrol was championed initially by James Q. Wilson in the USA. A cross-sectional study of twenty-three police departments purported to show that patrol aggressiveness produced a greater likelihood of arrests for robbery, and lower robbery rates as a result of a deterrent effect (J. Wilson and Boland 1978). The findings were criticized by a later study which showed that robbery rates increased (rather than declined) with greater police expenditure over time (Jacob and Rich 1980). Wilson and Boland's (1981) reply argued that their thesis concerned the effects on crime of the structural characteristic of a departmental style of aggressive patrol, and was not refuted by longitudinal data about relatively small and short-term fluctu-ations in police expenditure. However as Jacob and Rich replied (1981), this limits the significance of the original claim. 'Aggressive' patrol is not a readily adoptable tactic, but a structural element of departmental style which can be altered (if at all) only in line with more fundamental reforms of municipal government and wider socio-political change. Subsequent reviews of a variety of experiments in targeting 'hot spots' for aggressive crackdowns suggest occasional success, but on the whole mixed results (Sherman 1992a; Jordan 1998).

A further caveat about aggressive tactics was already implied by the San Diego Field Interrogation study (Boydstun, 1975) cited by Wilson and Boland (1978) in support of their thesis. Boydstun showed that heavy use of 'field interrogation' (that is, stop-and-search) reduced crime. However, the price was a considerable increase in public hostility. British research shows the same result. A substantial absolute number of mainly petty offences can be uncovered by stop-and-search methods (P. Waddington 1999a: 50). However, as the 'hit' rate of successful searches is usually small (less than one in ten) the price in alienation of some sections of the public (primarily young males, especially blacks) is very high (Tuck and Southgate 1981; Willis 1983; Policy Studies Institute 1983; Norris *et al.* 1992; J. Young 1994; Skogan 1994; Bucke 1996, 1997; Mirrlees-Black and Budd 1997; McPherson 1999; Fitzgerald 1999; Yeo and Budd 2000). Since the disastrous 'Operation Swamp', a saturation police operation aimed at reducing robbery, which was launched shortly before the 1981 Brixton riots, and is widely regarded as a precipitating factor, the British police have broadly accepted Lord Scarman's message, which was reinforced by the 1999 Macpherson Report on the Stephen Lawrence case. Any marginal gains in law enforcement due to aggressive tactics are not worth the cost in endangering public tranquillity.

The other type of innovative strategy that developed after the late 1970s stressed the central importance of public support, and advocated measures to enhance community consent and cooperation with the police. These community-oriented strategies became the central post-Scarman orthodoxy in Britain, and increasingly throughout the world (Manning 1997; M. Brogden 1999). As one review put it trenchantly: 'police departments in the western world can only remain legitimate if they genuflect before the altar of "community policing"' (Herbert 2000: 114).

The team policing schemes that flourished in the USA in the early 1970s, were progenitors of this approach, but had ambiguous messages. According to the evaluation of seven such projects by Sherman, Milton, and Kelley (1973), the problem was that they were never really tried. Initial indications about crime rates, community cooperation and information flow were encouraging; but organizational problems, in particular middle-management and lower-rank hostility, frustrated full or sustained implementation. Unfortunately this verdict has been echoed by many subsequent evaluations of similar community-oriented approaches.

Community policing schemes have proliferated since the 1980s in several American cities under a number of progressive police chiefs (Skolnick and Bayley 1986, 1988). While there have been some notable success stories, the outcome of community policing in the USA remains uncertain and variable (Skolnick and Bayley 1986, 1988; Greene and Mastrofski, 1988; Trojanowicz and Bucqueroux 1990; Bayley 1994, 1998; Rosenbaum 1994; Skogan and Hartnett 1997; Manning 1997; Herbert 1997, 2000).

The record of British initiatives in the community policing direction is similarly patchy. Many schemes have received positive in-house evaluations, but these are usually by partisans, and suffer from the 'foregone conclusions' syndrome of predictably happy endings (Weatheritt 1986: 18–19). Independent evaluations of community policing innovations seem to have the opposite tendency (Pawson and Tilley 1994; Bennett 1996; Jordan 1998). 'Nothing works' has been the bottom line of studies of a variety of such tactics. These include community constables (D. Brown and Iles 1985; Bennett and Lupton 1992*b*), crime prevention officers (L. Harvey, Grimshaw, and Pease 1989), focused patrol (Chatterton and Rogers 1989), neighbourhood policing (Irving *et al.* 1989), community policing (Fielding Kemp, and norris 1989; Bennett 1994*a*, *b*; Fielding 1995), sector policing (B. Dixon and Stanko 1995), and neighbourhood watch (Bennett 1989, 1990; McConville and Shepherd 1992; Laycock and Tilley 1995).

In many if not most of these cases the problem lies in 'programme failure', difficulties in implementing the schemes as intended, and it is far from established that community-style strategies in general, or specific tactics like neighbourhood watch in particular, cannot work (Jordan 1998; Bayley 1998). It is hard to measure the effect of innovations on broad outcomes like recorded crime or victimization rates, which are affected by numerous factors besides the policing initiative, and truly experimental research designs which could overcome this problem in principle are almost impossible to arrange. This difficulty blights even the one celebrated case of a rigorously evaluated scheme with a positive result: the Kirkholt Burglary Prevention project which used 'cocoon neighbourhood watch', intensive mutual watching of houses immediately adjacent to houses already victimized at least once (Forrester, Chatterton, and Pease 1988; Bottoms 1990; Tilley 1993).

The Kirkholt experiment is, however, a pointer to the key concept on which 'third way' policing initiatives pin their hopes. Traditional tactics fail in large part because they spread scarce police resources much too thinly across all victims, targets, and perpetrators of crime, whether in the form of preventive or detective activities. Improvements in crime reduction and detection can occur through pro-active, problem-oriented and intelligence-led approaches (A. Leigh, Read, and Tilley, 1996; Maguire 1998*b*, 2000). By analysing crime and disorder patterns it is possible to target prevention and detection efforts at the most likely victims and offenders. This would allow adequate levels of protection to be offered to the most likely victims, and the apprehension of offenders together with sufficient evidence to achieve convictions. While such approaches are likely to be more effective than traditional ones, there remains much doubt about their efficacy in achieving substantial degrees of crime reduction (Jordan 1998). There is also considerable potential for unethical practices and encroachments on civil liberties, for example through intrusive forms of surveillance, and the abuse of informers and other undercover tactics (Marx 1988, 1992; Greer 1995*a*, *b*; Fijnaut and Marx 1996; den Boer 1997; Jordan 1998; Norris and Armstrong 1999; Maguire, 2000; Innes 2000; Norris and Dunnighan 2000; Sheptycki 2000*b*; Billingsley, Nemitz, and Bean 2000). None the less, government's search for 'magic bullets' has encouraged the proliferaton of such approaches.

A crucial difficulty in evaluating policing innovations is the absence of reliable and valid measures of police performance (Reiner 1998). One of the most methodologically self-conscious projects to evaluate policing initiatives concluded that measures of good practice could be developed meaningfully only in relation to specific areas of police work, not globally, and were inescapably political (Horton 1989). None the less, since the 1980s successive governments' hunt for value for money in public services has led to the search for more adequate performance indicators in policing (Audit Commission 1990*a*, *b*). HM Inspectorate of Constabulary in particular have developed an ever more elaborate matrix of indicators for their annual assessments of forces (Bradley, Walker, and Wilkie 1986; Hough 1987; Chatterton 1987*a*; Reiner 1988, 1998; Weatheritt 1993; Butler 1992; McLaughlin and Murji 1995, 1996; Leishman Cope, and Starie 1996; R. Morgan and Newburn 1997). It is unlikely that these have yet overcome the possibly intractable problems of measuring police effectiveness.

Altogether the research on crime control implies that the police more or less successfully maintain a bedrock of effectiveness. Neither more of the same nor any innovative tactics are likely to improve their capacity for detection or prevention to any substantial degree. The final aspect of research on police practices which is of crucial importance to analysis of their political significance is the question of how fair the police are in their pursuit of effective law enforcement and order maintenance.

HOW FAIR ARE THE POLICE?

Since the 'discovery' by early research on the police that they routinely exercise a considerable amount of discretion in the way they enforce the law, there has been a plethora of work on the pattern and determinants of this (some key examples are collected in Reiner 1996*a*). A central concern has been the question whether discretion really meant discrimination, in particular against black people. Do police discriminate against ethnic and other minorities, women, and the socially less powerful, when dealing with them as suspects, victims, or fellow employees?

RACE AND POLICING

This issue is more complex and harder to resolve than most polemics imply. Contrary to the implications of much radical criticism of the police, the evidence of a pattern of social differentiation in the use of police powers from which the young, the lower working class, and blacks suffer most—although undeniable—does not in itself establish discrimination. The radical critique implies that the differential exercise of police powers against the socially disadvantaged and relatively powerless is the product of bias, stereotyping, and the amplification of the apparent deviance of these groups (D. Chapman 1968; Cashmore and McLaughlin 1991). On the other hand, more conservative writers would argue that this unjustly vilifies the police. The differential exercise of powers reflects not police discrimination but the varying deviance of different social groups (Wilbanks 1987; D. J. Smith, 1997; P. Waddington 1999a: 49–50). If studies of police culture reveal hostile attitudes to minority groups, this is the product, not the determinant of police work (P. Waddington 1983b, 1984a, 1999a: 118–9). Both positions embody an element of truth, but it has been clouded by abrasive either/or polemics. There is a complex interaction between police discrimination and the differential criminogenic pressures experienced by different social groups (Jefferson 1988, 1993; Reiner 1989a, 1993).

Some terminological issues must be resolved before the evidence can be reviewed. I shall adopt the following definitions:

(a) 'Prejudice': the belief that all or most members of a particular group have certain negative attributes, a preconception which is carried into encounters with individuals in the category who may or may not actually have these traits. Examples are 'The people here are animals' (constable, quoted in Reiner 1978: 80), and 'All coppers are bastards.'

(b) 'Bias': the view that some types of people should have preferential treatment regardless of their specific conduct on any particular occasion.

(c) 'Differentiation': a pattern of exercise of police powers against particular social categories, which varies from their representation in the population (such as a disproportionate arrest-rate of young black males).

(d) 'Discrimination': a pattern of exercise of police powers which results in some social categories being over-represented as targets of police action even when legally relevant variables (especially the pattern of offending) are held constant.

The attitudinal characteristics of prejudice and bias may, but need not, result in differentiation or discrimination. They may not be translated into action if legal, ethical, organizational, or situational constraints preclude this. Nor does differentiation necessarily indicate discrimination. It may result from legally relevant differences between groups, for example, varying patterns of offending.

Even when the police do discriminate, in the sense of treating people differently without any legal justification, this may not be the product of prejudice, bias, or unilateral police decision-making. It is necessary to distinguish five forms discrimination might take. Banton (1983) proposes a distinction between 'categorical' and 'statistical' discrimination. The former refers to invidious treatment of members of a group purely on account of their belonging to a certain social category, regardless of the relevance of this to any particular performance criteria. The latter refers to differentiated treatment of members of a group on the grounds of a belief that they are disproportionately likely to have certain characteristics, but without reference to specific behaviour of individuals. An obvious example is police stopping, say, long-haired youths or young black men disproportionately because of the belief that they are more likely to get a 'result' (Norris et al. 1992; Fitzgerald 1999). This does not constitute a legally valid basis for 'reasonable suspicion', and is explicitly ruled out by the Code of Practice on stop-and-search powers under PACE (D. Brown 1997: 20). None the less, it is undoubtedly a factor in stop-and-search practices (D. Brown 1997: 22). It is an example of statistical rather than categorical discrimination against black people *per se*.

To Banton's two types of discrimination I would add three further types.

The first is 'transmitted' discrimination, whereby the police act as a passive conveyor-belt for community prejudices. For example, white citizens' racial prejudice may make victims label attackers disproportionately as black, leading the police to search for black suspects. This is supported by the fact that victim identification of the ethnic group of their assailant (for those offences where there is some contact between them) roughly matches the pattern of arrests (D. J. Smith 1997: 737–8).

The second is 'interactional' discrimination, whereby the process of interaction (say, the rude demeanour of a suspect) produces a differential outcome which is dubiously justifiable legally. Observational studies have often noted that a key factor triggering the use of police powers is 'contempt of cop' (P. Waddington 1999*a*: 153–5). There is substantial evidence that young black men have more negative attitudes than other groups towards the police (P. Waddington and Braddock 1991; Skogan 1994; Bucke 1996, 1997), mirroring the long-standing police prejudice directed towards them. It is likely that many police encounters with young black men generate a vicious spiral of hostility culminating in an arrest (D. Brown and Ellis 1994; D. Brown 1997: 56).

The third is 'institutionalized' discrimination, whereby the consequences of universalistically framed organizational policies or procedures work out in practice as discriminatory because of the structural bias of an unequal society. An example is the way that the institutions of privacy make certain actions (say, drinking) actionable by the police only in public contexts, such as the streets or public bars, to which the poorer classes are disproportionately restricted (Stinchcombe 1963).

The concept of institutional discrimination has long been a controversial one. Lord Scarman considered two possible interpretations in his 1981 Report on the Brixton Disorders. One was official discrimination that occurs 'knowingly, as a matter of policy'; the second was indirect and unintended: 'practices may be adopted by public bodies as well as private individuals which are unwittingly discriminatory' (Scarman 1981, para. 2.22). Scarman adopted the former definition and came to the conclusion that it did not occur in the Metropolitan Police. However, he did clearly show that the police were discriminatory in the second, institutionally mediated, sense.

The latter interpretation is the standard one used by most sociological analyses, and I have used it above. The Macpherson report on the Stephen Lawrence case adopted it, and concluded that the Met *were* institutionally racist in that sense. Macpherson's definition of 'institutional racism' is now treated as authoritative. It is: 'The collective failure of an organisation to provide an appropriate and professional service to people because of their colour, culture, or ethnic origin. It can be seen or detected in processes, attitudes and behaviour which amount to discrimination through unwitting prejudice, ignorance, thoughtlessness and racist stereotyping which disadvantages minority ethnic people' (Macpherson 1999: para. 34). The emphasis is clearly on the *unconscious* processes that bring about the objectively identifiable outcome of discrimination by an organization.

All these forms of discrimination may operate at either the policy level of senior echelons or rank-and-file discretionary decisions on the street. The two are interdependent. Rank-and-file discrimination, for example, may produce a higher recorded crime rate in areas with a high black population, which might trigger differential deployment policies, leading in turn to even higher recorded crime rates.

The weight of the research evidence supports the following propositions:

(1) There is a clear pattern of differentiation in police practice. Young males, especially if they are black and/or unemployed or economically marginal, are disproportionately subject to the exercise of police powers. (They are also disproportionately victimized by violent offences; see Fitzgerald and Hale 1996; Bowling 1999*a*).

(2) Part of the disproportionate police exercise of powers against young, black, economically excluded men can be explained by their disproportionate involvement in some offences (mainly minor and marginal ones), as a result of their life circumstances (D. J. Smith 1997; Waddington 1999*a*). Even given this, however, there is evidence of police discrimination not explicable by differential offending.

(3) Part of this police discrimination is 'transmitted', 'interactional' or 'institutionalized'; that is, although not based on criteria sanctioned by law, it does not result from individual bias. For example, if a person approached by the police for a minor offence, over which the officer would normally not proceed, formally fails 'the attitude test' (is not sufficiently deferential) he might be sanctioned nominally for the offence, but really for 'contempt of cop'.

(4) However, there is also evidence of 'statistical' and 'categorical' discrimination. Statistical discrimination violates legal specifications of adequate grounds for 'reasonable suspicion', but it arises out of a concern to police effectively. In Shearing's terminology it is 'organisational police deviance', in that it is 'designed to further organisational objectives rather than promote personal gains' (Shearing 1981*b*, *c*: 2). Statistical discrimination is a good example of what Sir Paul Condon referred to as 'noble cause corruption'. 'Categorical' discrimination, the translation into practice of bias, is illicit from any point of view. While it is probably a significant factor, it is hard to isolate by either statistical or observational analysis (Reiner 1993).

(5) The evidence reviewed in Chapter 3 clearly documents police bias and prejudice. However, as argued there, the bulk of the research evidence suggests these attitudes are not the product of prior peculiarities of the individual personalities of police officers, but are a reflection of wider societal prejudice, accentuated by the characteristics of police work.

I shall now examine some of the research that establishes the above propositions.

Differentiation

The police stop and search, arrest, charge, and use physical force against young, black, lower-status males disproportionately to their representation in the population. At the same time, they have disproportionate contact with them as victims or complainants for violent offences (Policy Studies Institute 1983, i: 62–4, 124–6; Hough and Mayhew 1983; T. Jones, McLean, and Young 1986; Crawford et al. 1990; Skogan 1990a, 1994; Bucke 1997; Percy 1998; Bowling 1999a).

The North American evidence supports of all these points, as does research in many other countries (J. Lee 1981; Chan 1997). The San Diego Field Interrogation study found that 100 per cent of people stopped were male, 66 per cent were black or Mexican-American, and two-thirds were juveniles (Boydstun 1975: 61). A 1973 study of stops in Dallas found that young and/or black males were stopped more than proportionately to their representation in the population or in arrest statistics (Bogolmony 1976). Young, black, and/or lower-class suspects are more likely to be arrested (Black 1970, 1972; Sykes and Clark 1975; Lundman, Sykes, and Clark, 1978; Lundman 1974, 1979, 1980; Sherman 1980; D. A. Smith and Visher 1981; D. A. Smith and Klein 1984). According to the Black–Reiss study, young or lower-class suspects are more likely to be treated harshly (Sherman 1980: 82–3). All those subject to excessive force were lower-class. But this study found that a smaller proportion of black suspects were physically abused, although, given their greater chance of being suspects, the prospects of blacks or whites being at the receiving end of police force were the same (Reiss 1968). However, blacks are far more likely than whites to be killed by police. The black death rate from police shootings is about nine times the white, while over half the victims of police shootings are black, although blacks are only 10 per cent of the US population (Takagi 1974; Meyer 1980; J. Fyfe 1981; Binder and Scharf 1982; Geller 1983; Sherman 1983; Dunne 1991; Skolnick and Fyfe 1993; Geller and Toch 1996). The evidence about the treatment of suspects after arrest is more equivocal. Several studies of juveniles do not find that higher proportions of black or lower-class suspects are referred to court, although others do (Sherman 1980: 80–3; Wilbanks 1987).

The British evidence points in the same direction (Choongh 1997: 52–9). Being young, male, black, unemployed, and economically disadvantaged is associated with a higher probability of being stopped, searched, arrested, detained in custody, charged, making complaints against the police (especially of assault), and failing to have these complaints substantiated.[3]

Differential arrest rates of the young, male, black, and economically marginal are found by all research after the mid-1970s (until then the evidence is clear that black people were disproportionately less likely to be arrested than white people; see Lambert 1970; Lea and Young 1984). The first study, and one of the most systematic, was the Home Office analysis of the 1975 Metropolitan Police statistics (Stevens and Willis 1979). This showed higher black than white arrest rates in all offence categories, but especially for assault, robbery, 'other violent theft', and 'other indictable offences'. Asians were under-represented in all offence categories except assault.[4]

Unemployed or unskilled working class young men, especially if they are also black, are also much more likely to be detained in police custody after arrest and before being charged (R. Morgan, Reiner, and McKenzie 1990; Reiner and Leigh, 1992; Choongh 1997: 52–9; Phillips and Brown 1998, Chap. 1). Juveniles who are working-class (Bennett 1979; C. Fisher and Mawby 1982) or black (S. Landau 1981; S. Landau and Nathan 1983; Fitzgerald 1993; D. Brown 1997: 66; Phillips and Brown 1998: chap. 6) are less likely to be cautioned than to be charged and prosecuted.

Blacks are more likely than whites to say they have wanted to make a complaint against the police (Tuck and Southgate 1981: 38–9). Blacks, especially young ones, and older Asians are more likely than whites to bring complaints, and the proportion is increasing. Blacks are more likely to make serious complaints, especially of assault (Stevens and Willis 1981; Maguire and Corbett 1989, 1991). Nearly a quarter of all complaints alleging brutality are made by blacks or Asians (who constitute about 6 per cent of the population). On the other hand, ethnic minorities and the unemployed or economically marginal are less likely to have their complaints substantiated (Box and Russell 1975; Stevens and Willis 1981; Box 1983: 82–91). Black people are more likely to claim knowledge of police use of excessive force on the basis of personal experience (Policy Studies Institute 1983, i: 26–57). Unsurprisingly, ethnic minorities view the complaints system even less favourably than whites do (D. Brown 1997: 230).

Altogether the evidence shows that the groups upon whom the differential exercise of police powers falls disproportionately are those characterized as 'police property' in the exploration of 'cop culture' in Chapter 3. It remains to be seen, however, to what extent the clear pattern of police differentiation involves discrimination—that is, use of police powers unjustified by legally relevant factors—and further what kind of discrimination is involved.

Discrimination

To a large extent the pattern of differentiation described so far can be accounted for by differential rates of offending. The degree of police discrimination is less than what would be implied by a superficial reading of the social distribution of stops, arrests and other exercises of police power.

This is least true, however, of the lower-level occasions of police intervention, especially street stops. In some American research black youths constitute a much higher proportion of stops of 'innocent' than of 'guilty' suspects (Piliavin and Briar 1964: 212). In that research, the likelihood of police stopping black males is disproportionate not only to their representation in the population, but also in arrest statistics (Bogolmony 1976: 571).

The British data do not replicate this pattern. An equal proportion of stops of whites and blacks produces a 'result' in the sense of the recording or prosecution of an offence (Willis 1983: 1; Policy Studies Institute, i: 116), although it must be stressed that the 'hit' rate for all stops is very small (around 10 per cent): most people stopped are innocent of an offence (Fitzgerald 1999). When age and class are controlled for, much of the ethnic variation disappears (D. Brown 1997: 19–27). However, there is considerable variation in the patterns found in different local surveys, and it is likely that some of the ethnic differences are the result of discrimination. Certainly Afro-Caribbeans are much more likely to be stopped repeatedly, and if stopped also to be searched (D. Brown 1997; Bucke 1997).

The American studies of arrest patterns generally show that much, but not all, of the disproportionate arrest rate of blacks, youths, and the lower class can be accounted for by differences in the seriousness of offences which are alleged (that is, a legally relevant criterion. See Black and Reiss 1970; Black 1971; Lundman, Sykes, and Clark 1978; D. A. Smith and Visher 1981; P. Waddington 1999*a*: 49–50). With regard to physical abuse of suspects, and especially the most controversial issue of police shootings, the American evidence is mixed. While some studies find that most of the disproportionate shooting rate of blacks is accounted for by varying arrest patterns, the weight of the evidence suggests that black and lower-class suspects are victims of police force more often than would be expected on the basis of arrest or other legally relevant differences (Meyer 1980; Sherman 1980: 81–3; Geller 1983; Skolnick and Fyfe 1993).

In Britain too, the evidence suggests that the disproportionate arrest rate of young black males is partly the product of police discrimination. However, it is also due in part to differential rates of offending (largely attributable to the age-profile and socio-economic deprivation, as measured by such indices as unemployment or home-ownership rates, of the black population. See Stevens and Willis 1979; Policy Studies Institute 1983, i: 121, 71–5, iii: 96–7; Fitzgerald 1993; D. Brown 1997: 55–6; D. J. Smith, 1997: 737–9). The precise balance of these two factors is hard to ascertain. But the role of police discrimination can be adduced from the fact that blacks were most heavily arrested for offences which allow particular scope for selective perception by police officers: 'other violent theft' and 'sus'—for which the black arrest rate was 14 or 15 times the white (Stevens and Willis 1979). Cain and Sadigh's (1982) study also showed disproportionate black prosecutions for 'victimless' crimes dependent upon police initiative. However, several studies (for instance, Stevens and Willis 1979; D. J. Smith 1997: 737–9) point to victim identifications of the race of offenders as support-ing the claim that the disproportionate black arrest rate reflects varying involvement in offences, as well as police stereotyping (although victim identifications may them-selves be, at least in part, a consequence of public stereotypes). However, the extent of the black–white arrest differential is so great that it would be implausible to attribute it all to police discrimination. Stevens and Willis (1979: 28–34) calculated that, on the hypothesis that black and white crime rates were identical, and the arrest imbalance was entirely due to 'mistaken' arrests of blacks, 76 per cent of all black arrests would have to be 'mistaken'.

Lea and Young (1984), in the book that pioneered the 'left-realist' analysis of crime, accepted the validity of the Home Office and PSI analyses. They explained the disproportionate black arrest rate as the consequence of two mutually reinforcing processes: 'increased … black crime and police predisposition to associate blacks with crime become part of a vicious circle' (Lea and Young 1984: 167; see also Lea 1986).

Lea and Young were subjected to a torrent of criticism for this, accusing them of capitulating to 'the weight of racist logic' and of lending 'sociological credibility to police racism' (Gilroy 1982, 1983; Bridges 1983a, b; Scraton 1985, 1987). In this plethora of vituperation there was no serious attempt at a rebuttal of Lea and Young's argument. Any such engagement with the issue of explaining the black arrest rate as the outcome of anything but a protean and all-pervasive racism was dismissed as 'empiricist haggling over official crime statistics' (Gilroy 1983: 146). But this sort of characterization of all police and all aspects of policing as equally and undistinguishably racist precluded any serious analysis of how and why policing changes, and of separating out potentially positive developments within police strategy and thinking. The state and its coercive apparatus, the police, were blanketed together as a monolithic reflex of the racist logic of capital.

Against this position Lea and Young mounted several powerful arguments. First, for many years during which there was clear evidence of widespread prejudice in the police force, official arrest statistics (which probably exaggerate black involvement in crime) did not depict blacks as arrested disproportionately. That was the clear conclusion of Lambert's (1970) study of Birmingham crime statistics in the late 1960s, and of the police evidence to the House of Commons Select Committee on Race Relations in 1971–72. But by the time of the 1976–77 Commons Select Committee on Race Relations and Immigration, in their evidence to the hearings the police were claiming that the position had changed, and that there was a disproportionately high rate of young black crime.

Apart from the implausibility of the changing black arrest pattern in the 1970s being the result of a sudden shift in police thinking, Lea and Young stressed that it would be strange if the life circumstances of young blacks did not produce some increase in offences. 'The notion that increasing youth unemployment . . . a high young population in the black community . . . racial discrimination and the denial of legitimate opportunity, did not result in a rising rate of real offences is hardly credible' (Lea and Young 1984: 167–8).

All this is not to deny that 'moral panics' are often created by the practices of the police, the judicial apparatus, and the media. This was shown, for example, by *Policing the Crisis*, with its detailed account of the 'mugging' scare of 1972–73, and how it was constructed by police, judiciary, and media (S. Hall *et al.* 1978). However, there can be little doubt that during the 1970s 'mugging' (robberies involving street attacks on strangers) had became more prevalent, and was a not insignificant risk for vulnerable categories of people in some areas (although not for the population overall). Black over-representation in arrests for this were unlikely to be the product exclusively of police policy or prejudice (P. Waddington 1986a). Indeed *Policing the Crisis*, for all its emphasis on the moral panic associated with mugging as symbol of increasing state and societal authoritarianism, did not deny its underlying reality (S. Hall *et al.* 1978: 390).

It seems clear that the disproportionate black arrest rate is the product both of black deprivation and of police stereotyping—and of the interaction between these factors amplifying both. To recognize that the police statistics have some basis in a reality of black crime, which is itself related to structures of institutionalized and direct discrimination in economic and social life, is important. It underlines the point that more needs to change than just setting straight mistaken police stereotypes or prejudices.

The most systematic evidence of pure police discrimination came from S. Landau's two studies (1981; S. Landau and Nathan 1983) of the processing of juvenile offenders by the Metropolitan Police. The first concentrated on decisions by station officers about whether to charge offenders immediately or refer them to the juvenile bureau. Holding constant the legally relevant variables of offence type and previous criminal record, blacks were more likely to be charged immediately than to be referred to the juvenile bureau (S. Landau 1981).

Landau's later study examined the decisions of the juvenile bureau itself about whether to charge or caution those referred to it. He noted that, given the assumption that the earlier police decision would have screened out the 'worst' cases, it might be expected *a priori* that more people would be cautioned in those categories which are treated more harshly at the earlier stage. But in fact for 'crimes of violence' and 'public order' offences blacks were more likely to be treated harshly at both stages: they were less likely to be referred to the bureau, and less likely to be cautioned by it, holding constant the nature of the offence and past record. This might partly be accounted for by a lesser likelihood that cases involving blacks satisfied the legal preconditions for the cautioning process: an admission of guilt, and the consent of the victim. But part of the difference is 'pure' discrimination not explicable by 'legal' factors (S. Landau and Nathan, 1983).

A similar conclusion emerges from data about complaints. Some, but not all, of the class and ethnic differences can be accounted for by legally relevant factors (Stevens and Willis 1981). Black complainants were disproportionately involved in trouble with the police at the time of the complaint. A higher proportion of them were under arrest or had previous records. Police were more likely to allege suspect's provocation (that is, assault or violent struggling) as a justification in the cases of black complaints of assault by the police. In other words blacks (and other vulnerable groups like young unemployed men) were more likely to have the characteristics of 'discreditability' which made it improbable that their complaints will be substantiated (Box and Russell 1975).

The evidence clearly suggests that part but not all of the social differentiation apparent in the exercise of police discretion is accounted for by legally relevant factors like offence patterns. But there is a further element of class, age, and race discrimination, encompassing 'transmitted', 'interactional', 'institutionalized', and 'statistical' as well as pure 'categorical' discrimination.

Transmitted discrimination. The role of 'transmitted' discrimination (that is, where the police act as transmitters of public discrimination) is indicated in several ways in the research. It is implied in the key role of victim and witness information and identification in the clear-up of crime. It is also indicated in the significance attached by police to victim specifications of the race of their assailants in the case of crimes like robbery (D. J. Smith 1997: 737–9). American research has also underlined the central importance of complainants' wishes as a determinant of arrest decisions, after controlling for legal variables like offence seriousness (Black and Reiss 1970: 70–1; Lundman, Sykes, and Clark 1978: 84; Smith and Visher 1981: 173).

Interactional discrimination. Many researchers have stressed the context and process of interaction itself (especially the respect accorded by a suspect, which may itself depend upon the officer's approach) as a crucial determinant of police decision-making (P. Waddington 1999a: 153–5). Such penalizing of 'contempt of cop' is not, of course, a valid legal basis for arrest. But many apparently legally proper arrests may result from the suspect's failing the 'attitude test', thus incurring sanctions for an offence which might otherwise be overlooked. This is largely a result of the cop cultural imperative that the police officer should appear to maintain control, especially in public situations—which is why the presence of bystanders increases the probability of arrest or the use of force (Smith and Visher 1981: 172–3; Waddington 1999a: 154).

Institutionalized discrimination. A key example of institutionalized discrimination is the directing of extra police resources or more aggressive tactics to 'high-crime' areas suffering from social deprivation. The result will be a greater probability of stop and search, arrest, and so on, for those people living there who are vulnerable to police attention, such as young black and/or unemployed men (Blom-Cooper and Drabble 1982).

Another example is the use of indices of the risk of re-offending (which themselves are an example of 'statistical' discrimination) in a routine way to determine decisions such as cautioning or charging. These indices of 'problem family' backgrounds and the like, even if used universalistically by the police bureaucracy, will result in discriminatory decisions (S. Landau and Nathan 1983: 143–5).

Finally the long-standing complaints about police inattention to racial attacks are partly due to unthinking application of standard preconceptions and procedures which assume individual motivations for offences. The 'normal' procedures of the police institution may indirectly disadvantage ethnic minority victims (Home Office 1981; Klug 1982; Gordon 1983: 48–59; Saulsbury and Bowling 1991; Bowling 1999a; Bowling and Phillips 2000a, b). As the Stephen Lawrence case made clear so dramatically, however, the failure to deal adequately with racist crimes may often be due to more direct forms of discrimination. The Macpherson Inquiry revealed many instances of incompetence and malpractice, which it attributed in large part to institutionalized racism in the Metropolitan Police (Macpherson 1999; Cathcart 1999).

Statistical discrimination. This is pinpointed in several studies as the main cause of discrimination in stop-and-search, due to stereotypical police presuppositions that particular groups (including young black men) are more likely to be offenders (Stevens and Willis 1979: 31–3; Willis 1983: 25; Policy Studies Institute 1983, iv: 230–9; Norris *et al.* 1992; J. Young, 1994; Fitzgerald 1999). This is certainly not a legally acceptable basis for 'reasonable suspicion'. Stops based on statistical discrimination are a form of 'noble cause' corruption. They derive from a concern with effective policing, however misguided (as well as illegal) this might be in that frequent stops and searches of innocent people magnify hostility to the police in vulnerable groups, and in the end undermine law enforcement.

Categorical discrimination. Undoubtedly much discriminatory use of police powers is a reflection of categorical bias of the kind found in police culture. However it is hard to pinpoint it as a separate factor from the overall context of encounters. That is why observational studies of policing tend to emphasize the absence of pure discrimination which cannot be justified or at least explained in some sense by the process and context of encounters (Reiner 1993). At the same time observational studies do portray a prevalence of prejudiced opinions, which are not necessarily directly translated into police practice (Black 1971; Holdaway 1983; Policy Studies Institute 1983, iv: chap. 4; P. Waddington 1999a: chap. 4). But it is likely that prejudices do also overdetermine the conflict-ridden character of many police encounters with black people, generating the perceived 'contempt of cop' that is the trigger for some discriminatory arrests. Bias and prejudice also underlie the failure to recruit and retain ethnic minority officers in proportion to their numbers in the population, due to their experience of discrimination at the hands of white officers (Holdaway 1991, 1996; Holdaway and Barron 1997).

GENDER AND POLICING

The issue of gender discrimination has also been a vexed one. A clear difference between the debates about race and sex discrimination is that women are disproportionately infrequently at the receiving end of police powers, whereas one of the key questions in relation to race is the disproportionate policing of black people. The very small proportion of female suspects or offenders at every stage of the criminal justice process is one of its most striking and consistent patterns (Heidensohn 1996, 1997).

It does not follow, however, that the police do not deal with women in discriminatory ways. It has plausibly been suggested that police officers tend to view women with a conventional imagery, bifurcating them as either 'wives' or 'whores' (M. Brogden, Jefferson, and Walklate 1988: 119–20; Heidensohn 1996). A consequence may be that the low rate of formal processing of women as suspects masks a complex web of discrimination. Some women may escape suspicion because 'chivalry' places them outside the frame of likely offenders in the stereotypes of investigating officers (A. Morris 1987: 80–1; Heidensohn 1997: 770–2). Yet others, such as teenage girls behaving in sexually precocious or deviant ways, or prostitutes, may be dealt with by the police at a lower threshold of entry into the system because they violate the officers'codes of acceptable behaviour, or may be seen paternalistically as in need of 'protection' from themselves (M. Brogden, Jefferson, and Walklate 1988; Dunhill 1989). As one study concluded, 'evidence . . . on this topic is patchy, and conclusions necessarily tentative' (Heidensohn 1997: 770).

There is much clearer evidence of police discrimination in their treatment of women as victims of crime. Calls to domestic disturbances have always been a significant part of the police workload, but notoriously have tended to be treated by officers without recourse to criminal proceedings, even when evidence of assault is present (Stanko 1984; S. Edwards 1989, 1994; Hanmer, Radford, and Stanko 1989). 'Domestics' were seen as messy, unproductive and not 'real' police work in traditional cop culture (Reiner 1978: 177, 214–5, 244–5; M. Young 1991: 315–6). This issue has become highly charged since the 1970s, and around the world police forces have attempted to improve their response to domestic assaults, with debatable results (Sheptycki 1991, 1993; Dobash and Dobash 1992; Sherman 1992b; Hoyle 1998).

There has also been much concern about insensitive or even hostile treatment of rape victims, an issue dramatically highlighted in 1982 by a celebrated episode of Roger Graef's TV documentary on the Thames Valley Police which showed a very disturbing interrogation of a rape victim (BBC 1, 18 January 1982). Despite considerable improvements since then (Blair 1985; Temkin 1987: 158–62), the treatment of rape victims by police remains problematic (Hanmer, Radford, and Stanko 1989; Gregory and Lees 1999).

It is also clear from a growing volume of evidence that women are discriminated against as police officers, in terms of career prospects as well as harassment in the job. Until the 1980s discrimination within police forces was open and institutionalized in the existence of separate departments carrying out radically different functions. This itself followed from widespread resistance within (and outside) the force to the initial recruitment of policewomen in the early decades of the twentieth century (Carrier 1988). Since the Sex Discrimination Act 1975, women have been formally integrated into the same units as male officers. None the less, the continuation of discrimination has been documented by numerous studies.[5] The issue was vividly highlighted by the much-publicized action brought by the former assistant chief constable of Merseyside, Alison Halford, alleging discrimination against her in her attempts to be promoted (Halford 1993).

Many commentators have argued that the unequal employment and promotion of policewomen is important not only as an issue of justice, but to dilute the machismo element in police culture, which has been seen as an important source of abuse. Although this argument is not firmly founded on research evidence that women officers do in fact police differently from their male colleagues, it remains plausible (Heidensohn 1992, 1997; Walklate 1996). A related issue of discrimination relates to the treatment of gays and lesbians, as victims or suspects or as police officers.

Although again the position has certainly improved in the last two decades, there remains evidence of bias and discrimination (M. Burke 1993; Walklate 1996: 201–2).

CONCLUSION

The pattern of discrimination and the map of the population found in police culture are isomorphic. They are interdependent, and bound up within the wider structure of racial and class disadvantage (M. Brogden, Jefferson, and Walklate 1988: chap. 6; Jefferson 1988; Reiner 1993; Bowling and Phillips 2000a). Although it may sometimes be that discrimination is associated with prior individual police attitudes of a prejudiced kind, the fundamental processes are structural. Even if recruits were not especially prejudiced at the outset, the evidence on the impact of the experience of policing suggests they tend to become so.

The young 'street' population has always been the prime focus of police order-maintenance and law-enforcement work (Loader 1996; M. Lee 1998). The processes of racial disadvantage in housing, employment, and education lead young blacks to be disproportionately involved in street culture. They may also become engaged in specific kinds of street crime, for reasons that have already been indicated. At the same time, the relative powerlessness of ethnic minorities and lower-working-class youth means that the police may be less constrained and inhibited in dealing with them. In times of economic crisis and competition for jobs and other resources, the majority group (especially the white working class) may indeed benefit from the effects of over-policing of blacks, because black stigmatization as criminal, the acquisition of criminal records, reduces their competitiveness (Johnson 1976: 108). For all these reasons, the economically marginal ethnic minorities, and especially their youth, are prone to become 'police property' (J. Lee 1981). These structural aspects are the hard core of police conflict with the underclass who constitute their main clientele (Crowther 2000a, b). But they are exacerbated by cultural factors such as police prejudice, which, if reflected in verbal and other abuse, can make even normally uncontroversial service work fraught with tension. Finally, once conflicts become common a vicious cycle develops whereby police officers and their 'property' approach encounters with pre-existing hostility and suspiciousness, and interact in ways which only exacerbate the tension.

Overall, this chapter has argued that the primary mandate of the police is emergency order-maintenance, for which they are entrusted as specialists in (if not monopolists of) the use of legitimate force on behalf of the state. At certain times and places much if not most of their role will be service work, but since the 1970s the crime demands have been increasing. Their effectiveness in law enforcement is apparently declining, but this is largely because of pressures on crime rates arising from wider social and cultural processes. Attempts to measure police effectiveness are bedevilled by the absence of adequate performance indicators even in relation to crime work, and certainly for the broader aspects of policing (Brodeur 1998). The exercise of police powers has throughout history been operated primarily against the economically and social marginal, especially those from ethnic minorities, and it still is. The growth in the size of 'police property' groups that has resulted from government economic and social policy since the 1980s has been the major factor undermining police effectiveness and legitimacy, and the apparently discriminatory use (or, rather, misuse) of powers.

NOTES

1. In addition to the experimental studies reported in the text, there have been attempts to discover the relationship between aggregate levels of crime and policing (McDonald 1976: chap. 6; Carr-Hill and Stern 1979; P. Morris and Heal 1981: 16–18). These found a positive relation between police force size and crime rate, which they attributed to the recording phenomenon: the more police, the more crime recorded.

2. The crucial information was usually provided by victims, but another important source of clear-ups was professional security personnel such as store detectives (Bottomley and Coleman 1981: 45–6).

3. Evidence showing disproportionate stops and searches of young males, especially if unemployed and/or black, is presented by A. Brogden 1981: 44–52; Tuck and Southgate 1981: 26–7; Field and Southgate 1982: 50–53; Willis 1983: 14; Policy Studies Institute 1983, i: 95–102, iii: 96–7; Southgate and Ekblom 1984: 15–19; Norris et al. 1992; J. Young 1994; Skogan 1990a, 1994; Crawford et al. 1990; D. Brown 1997: 19–27; Bucke, 1997; Mirrlees-Black and Budd 1997; MacPherson 1999; Fitzgerald 1999; Yeo and Budd 2000. Lidstone

(1984: 454) gives evidence of discrimination in the use of powers of search of premises without warrant.

4. On low Asian involvement as suspects with the police, see R. I. Mawby and Batta 1980; Jefferson and Walker 1992, 1993; Jefferson, Walker, and Seneviratne 1992; Fitzgerald 1993; D. J. Smith 1997; Bucke 1997. Other evidence for disproportionate arrests of blacks, young males and the unemployed is found in Field and Southgate 1982: 50–53; Policy Studies Institute 1983, i: 118–26, iii: 88–91; Cain and Sadigh 1982; Painter et al. 1989; Jefferson and Walker 1992; Jefferson, Walker, and Seneviratne 1992; Fitzgerald 1993; D. Brown and Ellis 1994; D. Brown 1997: 55–6; Phillips and Brown 1998: chap. 1.

5. For evidence of discrimination against women police officers, see Bryant, Dunkerley, and Kelland 1985; S. Jones 1987; Graef 1989: chap. 6; Heidensohn 1989, 1992, 1994, 1998; M. Young 1991: chap. 4; Fielding and Fielding 1992; Walklate 1992, 1996; R. Anderson, Brown, and Campbell 1993; Brown, Maidment, and Bull 1993; Fielding 1994a; C. Martin 1996; J. Brown, Hazenberg, and Ormiston 1999.

5

MYSTIFYING THE POLICE: THE MEDIA PRESENTATION OF POLICING

Mass-media images of the police are of considerable importance in understanding the political significance and role of policing. We have seen that neither uniformed patrol nor plainclothes investigation work is very successful in crime control. However, it should not be concluded from this that the police are not an effective and important part of the processes of order maintenance. Their symbolic significance is profound (N. Walker 1996; Manning 1997; Loader 1997b; C. P. Wilson 2000). They are an integral aspect of the presentation of society as governed by the rule of law. They signify that there exists an agency charged with the mandate of apprehending offenders, so that there is always some prospect (however small statistically) of penal sanctions—a deterrent function. Moreover, the processes of detection, apprehension, and punishment are supposedly bound by fair, legalistic constraints of due process—they represent deterrence as justice not brute force. In Chapter 2 we saw that the architects of the British police tradition, particularly Peel, Rowan and Mayne, were concerned to construct an image of the bobby as both effective and the embodiment of impersonal rational legal authority.

In large, complex and class-divided societies, however, the practical experience of different segments of the population with the police is very uneven. Police activity bears most heavily upon a relatively restricted group of people at the base of the social hierarchy, who are disproportionately the complainants, victims,or offenders processed by the police (Yeo and Budd 2000). Politically, though, the most crucial sectors for determining police prestige, power, and resources are the majority higher up the social scale, whose contacts with the police (and certainly adversarial encounters) are confined mainly to the police's traffic-control functions. For these strata the mass media are the main source of perceptions and preferences about policing. Moreover, even in the lower-status groups where police contacts are more frequent, contacts are largely restricted to a distinct segment: young males. The attitude to the police of the women and older men in these groups is crucial, in particular for the flow of information, and the probability that routine encounters can be conducted relatively peaceably, without the ever-present potential of explosion into collective confrontations.

   The media-constructed image of policing is thus vital for the attainment of that minimum of 'consent' which is essential for the preservation of police authority. This image does not float free of the actualities of policing, but it is not a mirror reflection of them, either. It is a refraction of the reality, constructed from it in accordance with the organizational imperatives of the media industries, the ideological frames of creative personnel and audiences, and the changing balance of political and economic forces affecting both the reality and the image of policing.

   The crucial political significance of media presentations of policing has long been recognised by police officers themselves. There are many examples of use of the media by police to construct 'crime waves' as devices for accruing organizational prestige and resources (Fishman 1978; S. Hall *et al.* 1978; Christensen, Scmidt, and Henderson 1982; R. Powers 1983; Potter 1998; Surette 1998). More recently they have begun to use the media more systematically as a means of presenting a desirable image, and even as an investigative resource (Ericson Baranek, and Chan 1987, 1989, 1991; Schlesinger and Tumber 1992, 1993, 1994; R. C. Mawby, 1998*a*, *b*, and *c*, 1998*c*; Innes, 1998; Fishman and Cavender, 1998). The long tradition of respectable anxiety about subversive media effects is embodied in continuous demands for more censorship and control. Conceptions of the political and social implications of media presentations of crime and law enforcement can be broadly divided into two opposing perspectives (Reiner 1997).[1] The first view holds that the media ought responsibly to inculcate respect for legal and moral norms and their appointed guardians. Commercial exigencies, however, exert constant pressure to pander to base appetites and emotions, leading all too often to sensationalist and exploitative glorification of the criminal and denigration of the police. The opposing view regards the media as propagators of a dominant ideology sanctifying the existing institutions of the social order, the laws by which their operations are expressed, and the repressive apparatuses that maintain them. Struggles for or against dominant values and rules are transformed by the media into metaphysical confrontations of universal good and evil. They are thus depoliticized, as is the role of the police as an arm of the state.

   Both the 'subversive' and the 'hegemonic' view of the role of media images of law and order are too simple. In an unequal and hierarchical society, competition in presenting ideas is as structurally loaded as all conflicts. Very broadly, the weight of images portrayed by the mass media will be supportive of the existing social order in any relatively stable society. These images reflect and reinforce the views and self-perceived interests of the majority, not just an elite. On the other hand, demands of credibility and comprehension produce a reflection in media presentations of changing patterns of conflict. Images across the range of media may be contradictory, or even present a consensus for reform at particular times. The key to understanding the content of the media is knowledge of the organizational dynamics, ideology, and professional imperatives of the productive personnel and institutions (Ericson, Baranek, and chan 1987, 1989, 1991; Schlesinger, Tumber, and Murdock 1989; Ericson, 1991, 1995; Sparks, 1992; Reiner 1997*a*).

This chapter will examine the pattern and implications of media presentations of the police, both in purportedly 'factual' and in fictional products.[2]

'FACTUAL' IMAGES

Sir Robert Mark, Commissioner of the Metropolitan Police in the early 1970s, initiated a policy of unprecedented openness between the Met and the news media. He justified this by referring to the relationship between police and journalists as 'an enduring, if not ecstatically happy, marriage'. Overall the treatment of the police by the news media has been such as to legitimate their role and activities. But this outcome has been neither smooth nor unruffled. Conflict has frequently arisen between police and journalists over specific issues, and many police officers have a genuine sense of the media as biased against them. These perceptions are not unfounded. The media, even while reproducing perspectives fundamentally legitimating the police role, none the less criticize and question many particular police actions and individual officers. So long as that is not carried too far, the existence of the media as apparently independent, impartial and ever-vigilant watchdogs over state agencies on behalf of the public interest is conducive to the legitimation of these apparatuses (but not all individuals working within them). The process of legitimation could never be effective if the media were seen as mere propaganda factories.

Law and order is a staple of news reporting. As one major study expressed it, 'deviance is *the* defining characteristic of what journalists regard as newsworthy' (Ericson, Baranek, and Chan 1987:). Many studies have tried to calculate the proportion of news devoted to crime stories. Their estimates vary considerably (from 5 per cent; to over 60 per cent;), partly because they used different definitions and methods, but also because there is a variation in the prominence of crime news across time and space, and between different media and the market they are aimed at. (Useful reviews of this literature include Dominick 1978; Garofalo 1981; Marsh 1991; Sacco 1995; Reiner 1997a: 194–9; Surette 1998: 67–8.) The overall proportion masks the special prominence given many crime reports, in terms of placement, story length and headlining. The amount of attention given to crime news is generally greater in popular than in 'quality' media (Roshier 1973; Ditton and Duffy 1983; Marsh 1991; Williams and Dickinson 1993; Cumberbatch Woods, and Maguire 1995; Reiner, Livingstone, and Allen 2000a, b). However, Ericson, Baranek, and Chan (1991) found the reverse to be true when a broad definition of deviance was adopted, which encompassed 'straying from organisational procedures' and thus included reports of business and government malpractice. The proportion of news devoted to crime, and especially to criminal justice and policing, has tended to increase over time (Reiner 1997 a: 196–9). Broadcast media typically have a higher proportion of crime stories than print media, although not all studies concur in this (Reiner 1997 a: 195–8).

Both American and British research finds an emphasis on reports of specific crimes, rather than analyses of trends, causes, or remedies (Roshier 1973; Dominick 1978: 108; Marsh 1991; Sacco 1995; Reiner 1997 *a*: 199–203; Surette 1998). The amount of attention given crime bears no relationship to trends in official crime statistics (Roshier 1973; Graber 1980: 24; Garofalo 1981: 322–3).

There are structured differences between the characteristics of crime and criminals reported by the media, and the picture conveyed by official statistics, victimization or self-report studies (Reiner 1997 *a*; Surette 1998; Allen, Livingstone, and Reiner 1998). The following divergences have been found by all the British and American research:

(i) The media over-report serious crimes, especially murder, crimes against the person, or ones with a sexual element. This may not be surprising, although one Norwegian study (Hauge 1965) showed it is not a universal phenomenon. But it has ideological consequences for perceptions of the police role.

(ii) The media concentrate on crimes which are solved. Offences which are reported by the media at the time of their occurrence are disproportionately the serious offences of interpersonal violence which have the highest clear-up rates. Most other offences are reported only after an arrest. Indeed, reports are frequently based on trials, especially the opening prosecution stage and the judge's summing-up and sentencing.

(iii) Offenders reported in the media are disproportionately older adults, and from a higher social class than their counterparts in reality. (The same is true of victims.)

In short, the news media present a picture of crime which is misleading in its focus on the serious and violent, and the emphasis on older, higher-status offenders and victims. Reporting also exaggerates police success in detection.

The corollary of this is a presentation of the police that is without doubt generally favourable. The police are cast in the role they want to see themselves in—as the 'thin blue line' between order and chaos, the protectors of the victimized weak from the depredations of the criminally vicious. The media (with particular inflections ranging from the more liberal 'quality' organs like *the Guardian* or *The Times*, to the more overt vigilantism of the popular tabloids) generally support the police role and even extensions of police powers. As one study concluded, 'the news media are as much an agency of *policing* as the law enforcement agencies whose activities and classifications they reported on' (Ericson, Baranek, and Chan 1991: 74).

Chibnall's study (1979) of Fleet Street crime reporters found that they explicitly saw it as their responsibility to present the police in a favourable light. A typical quote was: 'If I've got to come down on one side or the other, either the goodies or the baddies, then obviously I'd come down on the side of the goodies, in the interests of law and order' (Chibnall 1977: 145).

Since the 1980s this picture has altered considerably. Specialist crime reporters used to be found only on tabloid newspapers, and they tended to see themselves as extensions of the working team of the detectives whose crime-busting exploits they glamorized and celebrated. More recently, reflecting the politicization of 'law and order' (Downes and Morgan 1997), broadsheet newspapers, as well as the BBC and ITV, have employed specialist correspondents in the criminal justice area, though often under labels such as 'home affairs' or 'legal' correspondents rather than crime specifically (Schlesinger and Tumber 1994). This has gone hand in hand with not only an increase in the proportion of crime-related stories in the broadsheets but a shift towards stories concerned with criminal justice issues rather than crime as such (Reiner 1997 *a*: 198).

In the last couple of years another profound change in crime-news production has become apparent: the virtual disappearance of newspaper court reporters (Davies 1999 *a*). This is due in part to the increasing news emphasis on celebrities, to a point where even the sensational murder story is squeezed out (unless there is also a celebrity element, as in the murder of Jill Dando). It is also a result of the more commercial orientation of the multimedia conglomerates that own an increasing number of news outlets, which has restricted editorial budgets severely. The result is that many crime and criminal-justice stories, cases, and issues fail to get aired at all, even in the sensational manner that used to be a core news staple.

None the less, belief in their watchdog role has always led reporters assiduously to pursue stories of police wrongdoing. The most notable example was *The Times's* (1969) revelation of widespread corruption in the Metropolitan Police, which sparked off the major scandals of the 1970s. But police corruption stories were traditionally located within a 'one bad apple' framework, implying that the discovery and punishment of the rare evil individual was proof that the police institution remained wonderful. As the number of corruption scandals proliferated, it became increasingly difficult to maintain the 'one bad apple' mode of legitimation. The metaphor increasingly became the 'rotten barrel', and in the late 1990s the 'poisoned tree', from which the 'bad apples' came.

However, media reporting has continued generally to place corruption stories in a framework that legitimates the police institution at the same time as reporting widespread deviance. The main legitimatory device now is the 'scandal and reform' narrative. Simultaneously with reports of malpractice, there are accounts of the reforms the police and government are undertaking to ensure that future wrongdoing will be prevented (Schlesinger and Tumber 1994). A good example is a front-page story which reported serious corruption in the National Crime Squad and other elite investigative units, and which also reported on the fundamental reforms of the complaints process which would be introduced to deal with the problem (*Observer*, 14 May 2000: 1–2).

The sources of this basically favourable framework of news about the police are threefold. First, a variety of concrete organizational pressures underlying news production have unintended pro-police ideological consequences. The tendency to report cases at the stage of the trial derives partly from the economy of concentrating reporters at institutional settings like courts, where newsworthy events can be expected to occur regularly, but it results in exaggerating police success. The police control much of the information on which crime reporters rely, and this gives them a degree of power as essential accredited sources. The institutionalization of crime reporters itself became a self-generating cause of regular crime news, and over time they can be expected to develop a symbiotic relationship with their reliable contacts, notably the police (Chibnall 1977: chaps. 3, 6; Schlesinger and Tumber 1994). The need to write reports to meet the deadlines of news production contributes to their event orientation, the concentration on specific crimes at the expense of analysis of causal processes or policies (Rock 1973: 76–9). Considerations of personal safety and convenience lead cameramen covering riots typically to film from behind police lines, which structures the image of the police as vulnerable 'us' confronting menacing 'them' (Murdock 1982: 10–89). These and other production pressures lead to a propolice stance quite independently of any conscious bias (Ericson, Baranek, and Chan 1987, 1989, 1991; Ericson 1991; Schlesinger and Tumber 1992, 1993, 1994).

Second, the professional ideology of reporters, their intuitive sense of newsworthiness, what makes a 'good story', can be analysed as a system of values which both emphasizes crime incidents, and underlies their particular representation (Hall *et al.* 1978; Ericson, Baranek, and Chan 1987, 1989, 1991: Schlesinger and Tumber 1994). Such elements of perceived newsworthiness as immediacy, drama, personalization, titillation, and novelty are conducive to an emphasis on violent and sensational offences (Chibnall 1977: 22–45).

These processes are most apparent in the handling of explicitly political issues with law-and-order dimensions, such as coverage of political demonstrations or Northern Ireland (A. Clarke and Taylor 1980; Hillyard 1982; Iyengar 1991; della Porta and den Boer 1998). This was shown in a detailed behind-the-scenes study of the production process of news reports about the 27 October 1968 anti-Vietnam War demonstration outside the US Embassy in Grosvenor Square, London, (Halloran, Elliott, and Murdock 1970). The media constructed their reporting around the issue of violence, crystallized in the famous 'kick photo', showing a policeman being held and kicked by two demonstrators, which appeared prominently on most front pages the day after the event (S. Hall, 1973). This achieved the subordination of the wider political questions involved in the demonstration to one dramatic incident of anti-police brutality. Similarly, news coverage of the May Day 2000 'anti-capitalist' rally in London concentrated above all on the daubing of the Cenotaph and Winston Churchill's statue, occluding discussion of the issues the protestors sought to highlight. The professional values of newsworthiness are a crucial determinant of the character of crime and police reporting, quite independently of any overtly political considerations.

Third, the nature of law-and-order coverage is also, of course, profoundly affected by the explicit political ideology of the press, which is predominantly conservative. The broadcasting media are dominated by a viewpoint representing the 'moderate middle', taking for granted certain broad beliefs and values—what Stuart Hall has succinctly called 'a world at one with itself'. The master concepts of news ideology include such notions as the 'national interest', the 'British way of life' and the 'democratic process'. These are seen as threatened by mindless militants manipulated by a minority of extremists representing anarchy and subversion, with only the 'thin blue line' to save the day for law and order (Chibnall 1977: 21). Both straightforward crime and political conflict are presented as the same pathology, with the police celebrated as guardians of the normal (Ericson, Baranek, and Chan 1991; Ericson 1991; 1995; Iyengar 1991; Schlesinger and Tumber 1992, 1993, 1994; della Porta and den Boer 1998).

The police, however, often see themselves as denigrated and under attack in the news media. Criticisms of the press are frequently made by police spokesmen, as epitomized in Robert Mark's complaint in a speech to the London Press Club in 1974 that 'Without doubt the most abused, the most unfairly criticized and the most silent minority in this country' were the police.

Part of the explanation of this discrepancy between police views and content analyses of media presentations lies in police officers' anxiety about the headline revelations of police malpractice, which is not assuaged by 'one bad apple' or 'scandal and reform' editorializing. Criticisms are perceived bitterly, while favourable comments seem less salient. Another factor is the police sense that they are inhibited from giving their side of many stories which may be *sub judice* or subject to official inquiries (Tumber 1982: 14–21). Because of anxieties about their coverage, and realization of its importance, the police have tried to handle their relations with the media carefully (Chibnall 1977, 1979; Schlesinger and Tumber 1994; Loader 1997*b*; Crandon and Dunne 1997; R. C. Mawby 1998*a, b, c*, 1999; Innes 1999*c*). Scotland Yard opened a press office in 1919, largely because of fears about unauthorized leaks produced by reporters bribing officers.

Since then relations between the press and the police have fluctuated. In the 1920s and 1930s Yard cooperation with the press remained relatively cool, and reporters gained their information largely by *sub rosa* tactics. The advent of Sir Harold Scott as commissioner in 1945 marked a high spot in police—press cordiality, the dawn of the 'Golden Age' of crime-reporting (coinciding with the 'Golden Age' of public confidence in the police), when a few detectives, notably Robert Fabian, achieved superstar status. Scott anticipated Sir Robert Mark in his appreciation of the value of good relations with the media. The late 1950s causes célèbres which heralded the Royal Commission on the Police marked a new strain on police—press cordiality, as the police became concerned about media highlighting of their peccadilloes. However the mid-1960s were glowing ones for press treatment of the police. The reorganization of the police was welcomed as a modernizing breakthrough, and their gang-busting successes against the Krays and Richardsons duly celebrated. The high point in press eulogizing of British police virtue was the laudatory way their handling of the counter-cultural manifestations of the spirit of 1968 (notably Grosvenor Square) were contrasted with repressive foreign heavy-handedness.

The police—press accord was threatened by the 1969 and later corruption scandals, but Mark dealt with these not by shutting out the media, but manipulating them skilfully through a policy of openness, enunciated in a memorandum of 24 May 1973. This was part of a coherent strategy of reform intended to fend off threats to police independence (Chibnall, 1979).

Following Mark's replacement by Sir David McNee as commissioner in 1977, relations with the media seemed to become more abrasive. A number of incidents led to harsh police criticism of the media, especially the BBC. The most prominent *cause célèbre* was the virulent police reaction to the *Law and Order* series of TV plays written by G. F. Newman, broadcast in April 1978. The Prison Officers' Association and the Metropolitan Police for a time withdrew facilities from the BBC in protest.

The abrasiveness in police—press relations in this period was not so much a consequence of personalities, of McNee being a less adroit media manipulator than Mark, as a symptom of the politicized state of policing. The 1979 general election was the culmination of the process of more partisan police interventions in politics (A. Clarke and Taylor 1980; I. Taylor 1980; Reiner 1980; Reiner and Cross 1991; Downes and Morgan 1997). The media were used by the law-and-order lobby to build up a climate conducive to their demands, but at the same time there was an undercurrent of questioning of police practices, perceived most clearly by the police themselves (McLaughlin and Murji 1998; Loader and Mulcahy 2000).

These contradictory currents became especially acute and apparent in media coverage of the 1981 urban riots in Brixton and Toxteth and their aftermath (Sumner 1982*b*; Tumber 1982). The most detailed analysis was Wren-Lewis's (1981–2), which distinguished three different discourses in media coverage. The 'law-and-order discourse' portrayed the clashes as an inexplicable eruption of sheer hooliganism requiring firm repression by an adequately equipped police force. The 'contra-discourse' was a radical one standing the first on its head. The riots were seen specifically as anti-police demonstrations provoked by heavy-handed police harassment. The 'social causality discourse' (favoured by the Labour Party's leaders) emphasized the importance of the failure of government economic policy as the root cause of discontent, but accepted the need for effective policing to suppress the unacceptable symptoms, the street disorders. Wren-Lewis emphasized the novelty of presentation of the contra-discourse during media analyses of Brixton. In 1981 the contra-discourse was given some prominence in the 'interpretive' stage after the riots died down. The initial 'revelation' stage of reporting Brixton was heavily loaded by the law-and-order discourse, carried above all by the vivid pictures of violent clashes in the early newscasts. However, after the establishment of the Scarman Inquiry into the April disorders, the media discussions moved into a stage of closure, attempting to play down the contra-discourse and re-emphasized the law-and-order discourse. When the July 1981 disorders erupted in Brixton, Toxteth, Moss Side, and elsewhere, far less attention was allowed to the contra-discourse, and reportage was heavily weighted to the law-and-order frame. Wren-Lewis thus pointed to the novel appearance in media discussions of Brixton in April 1981 of some critical views on policing. But he found a strong move to displacement of this by a pure law-and-order discourse following the appointment of Scarman, and the July riots.

In the event, the Scarman Report incorporated elements of the contra-discourse, seeing policing mistakes as a core factor sparking the disorders. The report united the contra- and social causation discourses, largely rejecting the law-and-order one. It was lapped up by the media, which gave much attention to Scarman's criticisms of police tactics. Media coverage of the long-term impact of the riots and the Scarman Inquiry allowed considerable scope to critical discourses, and on the whole rejected the law-and-order framework (Murdock 1982: 110–15). This was undoubtedly a major factor allowing the riots and the Scarman Report to presage a move to a climate of reform within the police during the late 1980s (Reiner 1991).

The general coverage of police matters since the mid-1980s has become increasingly critical. Much news footage revealed apparent abuses, for example during key public order clashes (notably the miners' strike, Wapping, and the 'Battle of the Bean Field' in 1986 when hippies travelling to Stonehenge were shown being violently handled by police officers). Even the 1990 Trafalgar Square anti-poll-tax demonstration, during which the media initially portrayed the police favourably, was subsequently subject to media analyses probing allegations of mishandling and malpractice. Above all the media have been prominent in the process by which the major causes célèbres of police abuses leading to miscarriages of justice have been revealed, notably the Guildford Four, the Birmingham Six and the Tottenham Three. In each case individual investigative journalists and documentaries were pivotal factors in discrediting the police evidence (Mullin 1989; Wolffinden 1989; D. Rose, 1992, 1996). Media coverage of the apparent police failure to cope adequately with rising crime has also become increasingly negative. The emerging critical consensus in the early 1990s was best encapsulated in a celebrated editorial in *the Independent* (26 January 1990) which spoke of 'institutional rot' in the police.

While the media played their part in the development of a crisis of confidence in policing in the early 1990s, they reflected rather than created this conjuncture. There were deeper sources of loss of faith in the police by government and opinion-formers, as well as the general public, not least the convenience of the police as a scapegoat for more fundamental failures of the criminal justice system and law-and-order policy. However, the police contributed to their own problems by the way their own 'law and order' campaigns of the late 1970s and early 1980s used the media to create unrealistic expectations of what more police powers and resources could achieve.

Since 1993 there have been contradictory trends in news coverage of policing. The police themselves have tended to withdraw from overt campaigning to influence public debate in the manner of such crusading chief constables as Sir James Anderton. Instead they have adopted a more corporate approach to cultivating a favourable public image, through the Association of Chief Police Officers (Reiner 1991; Savage, Charman, and Cope 1996; Wall 1998; Loader and Mulcahy 2000). The overall presentation remains highly favourable to the police mission, increasingly defined exclusively as crime control, and the capacity of innovations such as 'zero-tolerance' policing to deliver results. Fortuitously, the 1990s were a decade in which recorded crime rates fell in most years, and there was only spasmodic public disorder. However, the favourable media presentation of policing is uncertain, and constantly liable to be sabotaged by scandals or spectacular failures. The Stephen Lawrence case, which united the issues of police ineffectiveness, racism, and corruption, epitomized the brittle character of the representation and public standing of the police in the 1990s (Macpherson, 1999; Cathcart 1999). What is clear is that media presentation of police issues is now much more complex and contradictory than either the 'hegemonic' or the 'subversive' perspective implies.

FICTIONAL IMAGES

Crime and law enforcement have always been staple parts of the mass entertainment media. Historians of detective fiction are fond of tracing roots back to the Bible and Greek mythology, seeing Cain and Abel or the Oedipus myth as crypto-crime stories (Sayers 1928). In the eighteenth century there was a flourishing trade in broadsheets, ballads, 'memoirs', and novels about the exploits of highwaymen like Dick Turpin or Jack Sheppard, and thief-takers like Jonathan Wild. But the real take-off in crime and detective fiction occured with the formation of modern police forces in Europe in the early nineteenth century. There was a mushrooming output of fictionalized memoirs of ex-detectives from the Sûrete or the Bow Street Runners. The prototype was the publication in 1828–29 of the *Mémoires* of Vidocq, a thief turned thief-taker who ran the Paris police detective bureau after 1817. Modern detective fiction is usually traced back to Edgar Allan Poe's trilogy of short stories about C. Auguste Dupin, the arche-typal ratiocinative sleuth, starting with *The Murders in the Rue Morgue* (1841). The birth of detective fiction coincides with the development of modern police forces. Both can be traced to anxieties of similar kinds among the respectable literate strata, fears about the threat to social order represented by the 'dangerous classes' (Ousby 1976, 1997; J. Palmer 1978; Knight 1980; D. Porter 1981; Rubin 1999). They embody similar models of the solution to these concerns about conspiracy and subversion: the rational and unfailingly resourceful individual symbolizing a superior ideal of self-disciplined initiative, who is symbiotically related to a well-ordered social organization.

Since the mid-nineteenth century crime and detective fiction has been a prominent part of the output of all the dominant mass media. Popular heroes, including Sherlock Holmes, Charlie Chan, the Saint, Dick Tracy, Sam Spade, whatever medium they originated in, remain perennial favourites in all entertainment forms: novels, pulp magazines, comics, theatre, cinema, radio, television. About a quarter of all fictional works sold in Britain and America are crime stories. During the last fifty years in Britain about 25 per cent of the most popular television programmes, and around 20 per cent of all cinema films have been crime stories (Reiner 1997*a*: 206; Allen, Livingstone, and Reiner, 1998: 60–61).

Crimes and police officers are even more ubiquitous than that, appearing in almost all fiction, from Punch and Judy through Dostoyevsky to *Singin' in the Rain* (with Gene Kelly dancing round a bewildered cop). None of these is without some significance for images of the police, but I shall concentrate on the crime genre specifically as the richest source of such conceptions.[3] In this genre (fictions with crime and law enforcement as the central thematic elements) a broad division can be drawn between criminal tales (in which the central character is a person or persons—professional or amateur—engaged in criminal activity) and law-enforcement stories (in which the central character is a crime-fighter, whether amateur or professional).

Some interesting work has analysed quantitatively the content of prime-time crime shows in American TV (Dominick 1978; Pandiani, 1978; Garofalo 1981: 325–7; Lichter, Lichter, and Rothman 1994). The most striking finding was the remarkably similar pattern of representation of crime, criminals, and law-enforcers between news coverage and fiction (and consequently a similar pattern of divergence from official statistics). Four important structural characteristics were found in TV crime shows:

(i) Most crimes depicted were serious, involving considerable violence, large-scale theft, or extensive damage to property. Murder, assault, and armed robbery constituted about 60 per cent of all TV fiction offences.

(ii) Criminals were rational and purposive, not impulsive, confused, drifting, or driven. They were high-status, middle-aged, white men. Their main motive was greed, although they usually had to engage in violence to achieve their ends.

(iii) Law-enforcers were more likely to be amateur than professional. If professional police, they were usually detectives. They were predominantly unattached, economically comfortable, white males in middle adulthood.

(iv) The law-enforcers almost invariably solved or foiled the crime(s), usually through the exercise of remarkable personal skill and daring.

All these elements are the precise opposite of the pattern of real offending and policing. On the other hand, the characters, themes and milieux have similar features to most other prime-time TV entertainments, which portray predominantly comfortable-to-affluent middle-class, middle-aged lifestyles.

These are the basic features of the crime genre which seem to transcend the particular inflections of specific sub-types which vary between times and cultures. They constitute the core myth of law and order around which numerous variants can be constructed. Crime is portrayed as a serious threat, certainly to the property and person of individual victims, but often extending to the social order *per se*. Even if any single crime does not endanger civilization itself (although in fiction it often does), the volume of criminal activity shown in crime entertainments amounts to such a threat. However, the forces of law and order can and do regularly contain it. They are thus portrayed as essential and valuable, even pivotal, institutions in our society. Furthermore, although crime seldom prevails, criminals are formidable and worthy foes of the law-enforcers. They are not defeated because they are unintelligent, resourceless or puny, but because of the superlative prowess and dedication of the law-enforcers. Around this core myth, however, there can be quite varied permutations, with radically conflicting perspectives on the virtue, justice, likeability, and sympathy accorded to law-enforcers, the criminal justice system, and offenders. There are also changes over time in the basic pattern of representation of crime. Since the Second World War there has been a broad tendency towards media narratives which are more critical of the police, increasingly questioning their integrity, and their effectiveness in dealing with crime (Lichter, Lichter, and Rothman 1994; Powers, Rothman, and Rothman 1996; Sumser 1996; Allen, Livingstone, and Reiner 1998).

There have been numerous more or less scholarly analyses of crime films.[4] The fictional treatment of the police has been the subject of only a handful of studies (for example, C. P. Wilson 2000), and specialist studies examining police novels (Dove 1982; Dove and Bargainnier 1986), police films (Reiner, 1981b; Park, 1978; Inciardi and Dee 1987; Parish and Pitts 1990b; N. King 1999) and TV cop shows (Weiner 1973; Fiske and Hartley 1978: Chap. 12; Hurd 1979; Kerr 1981; Carter 1982; A. Clarke 1992; Sparks 1992, 1993; Reiner 1994; Leishman 1995; Eaton 1995). The paucity of studies of police fictions reflects the fairly recent elevation of the cop to hero status, coinciding with the advent of TV as the primary mass entertainment medium in the early 1950s. Novels and films with police heroes (the 'police procedurals') did not really emerge as a distinctive sub-genre until the late 1940s, so that television, since its early days in the 1950s, is the only medium where the professional police officer has always featured as an heroic figure.

To facilitate discussion of the varying kinds of law enforcement story (whether in literary, film or television form), their fluctuating dominance and social meanings, I have classified them into twelve ideal-type models, shown in Table 5.1. These are distinguished by their treatment of seven elements: the hero, crime, villain, victim, social setting, the police organization and narrative sequence.

Law enforcement narratives are connected to some other closely related genres, such as the espionage, investigative reporter or lawyer/district attorney/courtroom stories. They also have been subject to many comic or parodic treatments. The criminal protagonist side of the crime genre could similarly be analysed into different recurring patterns, although none of these leads will be pursued here.

I shall now give a brief account of the image of the police in each type.

THE 'CLASSIC SLEUTH'

The majority of detective stories between the heyday of Sherlock Holmes at the turn of the twentieth century and the l930s were classic sleuth mysteries. This sort of story remained popular in the last quarter of the twentieth century, in the form of the lavish screen versions of Agatha Christie novels which were big commercial successes for the British cinema in the 1970s and 1980s, and still flourishes on television in such series as *Inspector Morse* (Sparks 1993). The story revolves around a puzzling crime by an unknown offender—often one that was seemingly impossible to commit. There are a

Table 5.1 Law enforcement stories

Type	Hero	Crime	Villain	Victim	Setting	Police organization	Plot structure
Classic sleuth	Grey-celled wizard (usually amateur).	Murder by person(s)/ method unknown.	Personal motive – outwardly respectable.	Exceptionally murderable.	Respectable upper-class, often rural.	Honest, well-meaning, rule-bound plods.	Order – crime – red herrings – deduction – order restored.
Private eye	Self-employed. Motive: honour. Skill: dedication, moral intuition.	Greed and/or passion murder. Mystery not crucial.	Apparently respectable and/ or professionals. Several cross-plotting.	Not always clear. Client (i.e. apparent victim) often morally dubious.	Respectable upper-class façade masking corruption, and underworld.	Brutal, corrupt, but may be tough and efficient.	Moral disorder – private eye hired – blows, brawls, bullets, broads and booze – use of moral sense – 'solution' – moral disorder continues normally.
Police procedural	Routine cops, using footwear, fingerprints and forensic labs.	Murder, usually for gain. Whodunit less important than how apprehended.	Usually professional, and not sympathetic.	Ordinary, respectable folk. Weak, guileless innocents.	Cross-section of urban life, including cops' homes.	Team of dedicated professionals. Hierarchical but organic division of labour.	Order – crime(s) – one damn thing after another – use of police procedures – order restored.
Vigilante	Lone-wolf cop or amateur. Skill: ruthless fanaticism.	Bestial behaviour by habitual, not necessarily economic, criminal.	Psychopathic. Unsympathetic even if 'analysed'.	Tortured innocents, though gullible.	Urban jungle, ruled by naive, incompetent elite.	Rule-bound bureaucrats vs. wise street cops.	Rampage in urban jungle – ruthless chase – elites try to restrain vigilante – defiance – 'normal' jungle life restored.

Civil rights	Professional, dedicated, legalistic cop.	Mystery to allow hero to exhibit professionalism.	Usually personal motive, with modicum of sympathy to justify concern for rights.	Respectable/influential: strong pressure for 'results'.	Unequal society. Money and status 'talk'.	Servants of power.	Unfair order – crime – innocent accused – professionalism – solution – fairer order.
Undercover cop	Skill is courage + symbiosis with underworld: ability to 'pass'.	Organized racket.	Professional organized structure. Leader unknown (or proof required).	Ordinary citizens.	Underworld.	Team of professionals to give hero back-up.	Order – crime – infiltration – hero's rise in racket – solution – combat – order.
Police deviance	Honest 'loner' cop.	Police brutality or corruption.	Other law-breaking cops.	Suspects or ordinary citizens.	Police station + underworld.	Rotten basket, or bad apples.	Police deviance – investigation – control of deviance or of investigator.
Deviant police	Rogue cop or Freudian fuzz.	Police protagonist's brutality or corruption.	Professional crooks who 'invite' his brutality or corruption.	Suspects, processed by protagonist, or general public.	Police station + underworld.	Generally honest but bad apple(s).	Temptation – fall of protagonist – chance of redemption – redemption/death.
Let 'em have it	Elite gangbusters.	Organized racket.	Known gang (maybe unknown leader).	Ordinary folk.	Underworld vs. overworld.	Tough combat unit.	Order – rackets – battle – victory – order.

Table 5.1 continued

Type	Hero	Crime	Villain	Victim	Setting	Police organization	Plot structure
Fort Apache	Team of routine cops.	'Raids', skirmishes with ethnic minority enemy.	Ghetto toughs, and renegade or foolish whites.	Ordinary folk.	Police outpost in hostile enemy territory.	Beleaguered minority. Camaraderie broken by discipline and deviants.	Cold war – incident – threat of all-out war – troublemakers neutralized – cold war.
Police community	Routine patrol cops: very human.	Many petty misdemeanours. Tempt cops to cynicism.	No specific person. Real villain is despairing cynicism.	Ordinary citizens. Many are unsavoury 'assholes'.	Police station/car, contrasted with city jungle and domestic tensions.	Brotherhood, 'family' of disparate types.	Picaresque. Will cop save or lose his soul?
Community police	Routine patrol bobby: very human.	Petty, if any.	Prodigal son, if any.	Ordinary folk. Salt-of-the-earth types.	Organic, integrated community.	Microcosm of larger community. Non-divisive hierarchy and specialization.	Order – everyday human problem – police use moral wisdom + social bonds – order restored.

variety of possible culprits, but by the use of what Agatha Christie's Hercule Poirot called his 'little grey cells', the eccentric hero with supercharged neurons eliminates all the red herrings and points the finger at an unlikely culprit. The police are usually portrayed as bumbling buffoons or, at best, unimaginative bureaucrats, capable of handling routine offences but quite out of their depth with a case of any complexity. Their lack of perceptiveness (as well as that of the hero's companion and chronicler, the Dr Watson figure) operates as a device to show up the hero's genius. The sleuth is usually an amateur or a consulting detective. Sometimes, however, he may be a professional policeman, such as Freeman Wills Crofts's Inspector French, Ngaio Marsh's Roderick Alleyn, Michael Innes's Inspector Appleby, Earl Der Biggers's Charlie Chan and, more recently, P. D. James's Adam Dalgleish, Ruth Rendell's Wexford, and Colin Dexter's Inspector Morse (most of whom have featured in several types of media). But these are mostly unusual and exceptional police officers, of independent means and elite education, spouting poetry, esoteric allusions, and classical quotes with the snootiest amateur sleuth. These men clearly never joined police departments for anything so vulgar as a modest but secure pay cheque. Rather, the job provides them with a more predictable and plausible supply of mysterious corpses than their amateur counterparts' reliance on invitations to spend weekends at creepy country mansions. Unlike later models of fictional police, these supersleuths are in the great detective tradition, relying on brainpower not police power or firepower.

Contrary to the theory expressed by Rex Stout (creator of Nero Wolfe, and a master of the classic tradition) 'that people who don't like mystery stories are anarchists', the classical sleuth story is not really a law-and-order fable. The generally dim picture of the regular police militates against this. So does the image of a society with so ordered, predictable, and regular a daily round that the minutest deviation from routine constitutes a clue to the eagle-eyed sleuth. But above all it is a structural probability built into the plot requirements that the victim had it coming and merits no sympathy. He or she must be an 'exceptionally murderable' person, so odious a bundle of unpleasant qualities that all the other characters have ample motive for murder, supplying an abundance of red herrings (Grella 1970: 42). Furthermore, the sleuth does not want to be burdened with anything so mundane as legal requirements of proof. A good way out of this is for the murderer to be so sympathetically motivated that the sleuth, having demonstrated his prowess by discovering the culprit's identity, does not turn him or her over to the police. The detective in effect acts as a vigilante, invoking his private sense of justice, not due process of law (Ruehlman 1974).

PRIVATE EYE

The novels and stories of Dashiell Hammett in the late 1920s and early 1930s, heralded a new kind of detective mystery: the tough, hard-boiled private-eye story. In the hands of his successors, notably Raymond Chandler, Ross MacDonald and Mickey Spillane, the private eye became the dominant model of the law-enforcer during the 1940s, on screen as well as in literature. The model lives on in such characters as

Robert Parker's Spenser and James Lee Burke's Dave Robicheaux, (Geherin 1980), and more recently various feminist incarnations such as Sarah Paretsky's V. I. Warshawski. In Chandler's (1944) famous puff for the superiority of the private eye over the classic mystery, its virtue is said to lie in its greater realism. This doesn't really hold water. The milieux and characters of the private eye may be more sordid and seedy, but the hero was a far more romantic figure than the sleuth, and especially in Chandler's hands became a modern knight errant, the lone man of the mean streets. Further-more, there was a strong vein of social criticism and political commitment, usually of a radical or at least populist kind. (Spillane was an exception only in the sense that his politics were of the radical Right.) The private eye was plunged into a quixotic quest through the murky corruption of a modern metropolis, by a client who more often than not was as treacherous as the initial suspects. A particular mystery might eventu-ally be solved (although the puzzle element was never of real importance), but society itself could never be set to rights by such individual action as the hero was capable of. The police were often part of the network of corruption, on the take and/or brutal. But they were not stupid or weak. Some could even be effective law-enforcers in a bureaucratic way. The private eye's superiority was not special skill, but moral integ-rity and dedication compared with the corrupt run-of-the-mill cops, and an ability to violate bureaucratic procedure and cut corners.

THE POLICE PROCEDURAL

The police procedural story emerged in the late 1940s as an apparently more realistic successor to the private detective (Dove 1982: chap. 2). It appeared more or less simultaneously in all media: novels, in the hands of such pioneers as Hilary Waugh in the USA, and John Creasey in England (especially his *Gideon of the Yard* series, written under the pseudonym J. J. Marric); the cinema, spearheaded by *Naked City* in 1947 (later a long-running TV series); radio and TV, with Jack Webb's *Dragnet*—the quintessential police procedural. Webb's famous catchphrase, 'Just give us the facts, ma'am', sums up the procedural's distinctiveness. The heroes are ordinary, unglamorous, routine cops, with more or less happy domestic lives (which are often depicted, as in Nicolas Freeling's Van der Valk and Castaing novels), doing a job with professional skill and dedication, but no exceptional talent. They solve cases success-fully because they have the back-up of an efficient organization, technological aids, and legal powers. Often they are harassed and must work on several cases simultaneously, an early device to lend an aura of verisimilitude that rapidly became a cliché. The organization is an integrated one, with differences of rank or function not leading to conflict. Authority is accepted without undue deference or resentment. At the same time professional pride and camaraderie do not lead to alienation from the public. The cop has a private life which is meaningful and humanizing. At the level of physical detail and iconography the procedural is clearly more 'realistic' than the earlier kinds of mystery. But they really give scarcely more accurate an account of police work in general.

THE VIGILANTE

The vigilante is either a lone-wolf cop or an aggrieved private citizen. The prototype of the former is Clint Eastwood's Dirty Harry, and of the latter the character played by Charles Bronson in *Death Wish* (1974), based on a Brian Garfield novel.

The vigilante story is an implicit denial of the procedural's values. Police procedure is impotent in the face of crime. Only the street-wise cop, understanding the vicious nature of criminals, can deal effectively with them, defying any restraints posed by legal or departmental rules and regulations. The vigilante tale is a quite explicit law-and-order fable, proposing police power as the only solution to the major menace of crime. The obvious plot device for achieving this end is the representation of ordinary city life as an urban jungle, and the specific crime/criminals focused on as especially bestial. The department is not the integrated organization depicted in the procedural. Above all it is divided by the absolute gulf and conflict between street cops and the management cops who restrain them for 'political' reasons. The citizenry, although nominally the justification for the vigilante's battle, do not adequately appreciate or support his actions, preferring to know as little as possible about the men who remove their moral garbage.

The vigilante story was a clear reflection of the law-and-order politics which Richard Nixon used to secure his 1968 presidential victory. From early 1968 until the mid-1970s—the heyday of the vigilante story—law and order was regularly named as the main domestic problem by opinion polls in America. The cop became the rallying symbol for white 'backlash' and middle-aged 'kidlash', with 'Support your local police' as the effective code words. The vigilante films were peppered with specific references to the contemporary law and order debate, as in Dirty Harry's attack on the controversial Supreme Court decisions of the early 1960s (such as *Miranda* and *Escobedo*) which strengthened suspects' rights. The vigilante cop model was translated for British audiences by the exceptionally popular TV series *The Sweeney*, and its derivatives like *Target*.

So successfully did the vigilante story articulate widely shared sentiments, not only about law and order but also about the counter-cultural and radical (as well as conservative) disenchantment with bureaucracy, that it has come to seem *the* archetype of cop fiction (N. King 1999; Rubin 1999). Vigilante stories remained popular throughout the 1980s and 1990s, for example the *Lethal Weapon*, *Die Hard* and *Beverly Hills Cop* film series, which were huge box-office successes (Allen, Livingstone, and Reiner 1998: 62–3). Although these more recent incarnations display fashionably postmodern humour, knowing cool, and reflexivity, they remain stories about rule-bending cops, such as Ian Rankin's Inspector Rebus. The prevalence of the vigilante model is why police stories are widely regarded as law-and-order mythology, although there have been radically different fictional models of policing which have been popular at different times.

THE CIVIL RIGHTS STORY

The civil rights cop story was the vigilante narrative stood on its head. The police organization (and its political masters) were depicted as so concerned with 'results' that they trampled over due process and legal procedures. The hero was a cop in the procedural mould (who would have been happy in Jack Webb's team) but who confronted an unprofessional organization. The plot allowed the hero to prove that cops can have their cake and eat it. Only by following due process could they avoid fitting up the wrong suspect, and thereby allowing the guilty (and dangerous) villains to go free.

The quintessential example of this narrative was John Ball's 1965 novel *In the Heat of the Night*, which was made into an enormously successful, Oscar-winning 1967 film. Virgil Tibbs (Sidney Poitier) a black, big-city detective was arrested as a murder suspect merely because he was a black stranger passing through the small Georgia town of Sparta. Tibbs used his professional skills coolly and calmly to find the real culprit, teaching the sloppy and bigoted local police chief (played by Rod Steiger) that the college degree is a more effective tool of detection than the third degree.

The civil rights phase in cop stories only lasted a few years—from about 1965 to 1968. Although in general it would be misleading to see fiction as directly reflecting political events, in this case the connection was quite plain. Throughout the 1960s until 1968 the major domestic problems (as indicated by opinion polls) were seen as 'racial problems' or 'civil rights'. The emergence in 1968 of law and order as the prime domestic political issue coincided with the displacement of the civil rights by the vigilante cop story.

THE UNDERCOVER COP

Although the undercover cop tactic may be used by any style of policing, there is a special symbiosis between it and vigilantism. This is partly because it involves the hero in morally dubious practices of deception and conniving at crime (if not being an *agent provocateur*). It is also because, for it to be plausible that the hoods accept the hero as one of them, he has to have the image of a deviant. When clean-cut procedural cops like Mark Stevens in the 1948 film *Street with No Name*, or Edmond O'Brien in the 1949 *White Heat* infiltrated gangs, it was hard to credit the crooks' gullibility. It was much more plausible when James Cagney, with his established gangster persona, did undercover work in the 1935 *G-Men*. Indeed, what needed explaining was his employment as an FBI agent! The same was true of Edward G. Robinson's similar role in the 1936 *Bullets or Ballots*.

POLICE DEVIANCE (GOOD APPLE IN ROTTEN BARREL)

The police deviance story has affinities with the civil rights stories. It portrays the struggle of a single honest cop against a corrupt organization. The difference is that the civil rights narrative concerned the violation of rights to achieve convictions, rather than exploitation of the job for personal financial reward.

The police deviance story was very much a development of the 1970s, following the Knapp Committee investigations revealing pervasive corruption in the New York Police Department. The quintessential example was the book and film based on the experiences of Frank Serpico, the honest cop whose revelations stimulated the Knapp Commission. Many other individuals involved in those events have produced memoirs or fictionalized accounts (such as *Prince of the City*, 1982). Police deviance stories continue to be a vigorous sub-genre (*Year of the Dragon*, 1985; *The Untouchables*, 1987; *Q. and A.*, 1990; *Internal Affairs*, 1990; *Cop Land*, 1997; *LA Confidential*, 1997; *Night Falls on Manhattan*, 1997).

In Britain, too, the Scotland Yard scandals stimulated several novels and plays focusing on the issue of police corruption. Bernard Toms's *The Strange Affair*—(1968 also filmed, starring Michael York) focused, like *Serpico*, on the (unsuccessful) struggles of a lone honest policeman. G. F. Newman's *Bastard* series of novels, the even better-known *Law and Order* novels and play trilogy, and the play *Operation Bad-Apple* all explored the world of policing in a critical light reflecting the impact of the 1970s corruption scandals. More recent British television series have continued to focus on police deviance, as in *Between the Lines*, *Cops*, and *The Vice*.

DEVIANT POLICE (BAD APPLE IN CLEAN BARREL)

There are two subvariants of this category. In the 'Freudian fuzz' stories the central character is a cop who is driven into vigilante-style brutalities, which (unlike in the vigilante narrative) are not approved of. His rule-breaking is the product of the combined pressure of the general cynicism induced by police work and some special psychological weakness of the hero, which although 'analysed' by the narrative does not morally justify his actions. The quintessential example was Sidney Kingsley's play *Detective Story* and the 1951 movie version of it. (For other examples, see Reiner 1981*b*: 205–7.) The 'Freudian fuzz' was not a bad man, so he was allowed some chance to redeem himself, even though it usually cost him his life.

The other variant was the 'rogue cop' story, in which the protagonist was led into deviance at least partly for personal gain, although the 'invitational edge' of temptation was stressed so that his actions were seen as comprehensible if not condonable. Good examples were the 1950 Joseph Losey film *The Prowler*, and the 1954 *Rogue Cop*. Because the protagonist was not thoroughly evil, he was also usually allowed redemption through self-sacrificing death.

Where the police deviance/deviant police narratives are combined (bad apple in rotten barrel), as in G. F. Newman's work, the bleakest image of the police in popular fiction is achieved. Recent American police deviance stories have also tended to increasing pessimism, with corruption seen as endemic rather than episodic (for example, *Internal Affairs*, *LA Confidential*, *Cop Land*).

'LET 'EM HAVE IT'

Unlike the other categories there are no examples of this type with any pretensions to seriousness. It was the province of the 'B' movie, the pulp magazine or novel, the Saturday-morning cinema serial, and the comic-strip. None of the moral, political, or even practical problems or dilemmas of policing was touched upon, as they are in some way by all the other categories. Rather, this type formed the bedrock imagery of 'cops versus robbers' stories from which the others constructed more complicated permutations. The stories were simple sequences of planning and executing skirmishes, raids and battles in the 'war against crime' between police and hoodlum organizations. Examples are such G-men films of the 1930s as *Let'Em Have It*, *Muss'Em Up*, *Don't Turn'Em Loose*, and *Show'Em No Mercy* (vigilante stories without this being seen as a controversial stance), or the perennially popular Dick Tracy character (originating in a 1930s comic-strip, but graduating to 'B' feature and serial films and radio, and revived in Warren Beatty's 1990 blockbuster film). With the growing sophistication of post-1950s cinema, this type disappeared from the large screen. But it continued in such popular TV series as *The Untouchables* or *Starsky and Hutch*, although with inflections reflecting the fashions of the day (the procedural in the former, the vigilante in the latter). Since the early 1990s there has been something of a big screen comeback, in *Dick Tracy*, *Lethal Weapon* and lesser offspins, part of a Hollywood return to nostalgic escapist adventures which began with *Star Wars* and *Superman* in the late 1970s and continued with *Batman* in the law enforcement genre.

'FORT APACHE'

The 'Fort Apache' story was distinguishable more by its setting than its narrative structure. The quintessential example was Heywood Gould's novel *Fort Apache, the Bronx*, and the 1981 Paul Newman film it inspired. This was partly a picaresque account of the police community, partly (unsolved by the cops) murder mystery, partly a 'civil rights' story. The distinctive feature was embodied in the title. The police were portrayed as the old US cavalry, a beleaguered garrison in hostile territory. The military metaphor invited comparison with the 'Let'em have it' sagas, but the depiction of the 'enemy' was crucially different. In the G-Men or Dick Tracy stories the hoods were unequivocally evil. In the Fort Apache type the police were opposed by people of a different race. Not only did distinctions have to be made between the 'good' and 'bad' members of it (the hero of *Assault on Precinct 13* was a black cop), but even the hostiles who attacked the police were reacting to oppression (in the liberal variants like *Fort Apache, the Bronx*, or Tony Richardson's 1982 *The Border*), or at least represented a distinct if alien culture. (Even the savage gangs who callously murdered a little girl in *Assault on Precinct 13* were shown as having a code and rituals, and had taken to the warpath because of police harassment.) Implicitly the tense relations between the police and the ghetto residents whose borders they patrolled were the products of the racism and uneven economic development of white America, although the prime focus of sympathy was the cop who had to carry the can for the sins of the majority. In all these films the evil action of renegades on both sides threatened (or produced) all-out war, although the hero struggled to contain it. Ultimately, however, the police could at best lower the temperature of the cold war between ghetto and suburb, not remove the sources of conflict. The Fort Apache stories reflected the civil rights *vs.* law-and-order debates some years on, with a pessimistic, albeit usually liberal, slant. There was little faith in the efficacy of either civil rights or repressive policies to do more than contain a 'dreadful enclosure'.

POLICE COMMUNITY

Police community stories are everyday tales of ordinary cop folk. They are best illustrated by the novels of ex-Los Angeles police sergeant Joseph Wambaugh, and their film derivatives, especially *The New Centurions, The Blue Knight, The Choirboys*, and the TV series *The Blue Knight* and *Police Story*. The more recent and very successful *Hill Street Blues* continued some of the same themes, with much less reverence for the police force.

Although crimes featured in these stories, they were not central to the narrative, and were mainly petty misdemeanours rather than serious offences. The true theme of the stories was the moral development of the police officer, and the internal relations of the police community. The narratives were a picaresque portrayal of the bewildering array of incidents the patrolling cop encounters. The linking question giving these episodes coherence was whether the cop could safeguard his soul, or would surrender to the besetting sin of cynicism, and take refuge in alcohol, suicide, or brutalization. While the police formed an internal community of sorts, they were divided from ordinary citizens, who if not themselves corrupt were unappreciative 'assholes' who did not back up the police. Whereas the domestic life of the procedural policeman was happy (with the occasional trivial tiff over missed Christmas dinners and the like just adding a touch of verisimilitude), and the vigilante's home life non-existent apart from casual sexual encounters, the 'blue knight' reluctantly and sadly watched his marriage and family fall apart as a necessary consequence of his higher calling. The police community stories embodied the cop culture portrayed by American sociological studies, emphasizing the social isolation and internal solidarity of the police fraternity.

COMMUNITY POLICE

Community police stories are the British equivalent of the American police community narrative, the differences reflecting the divergent images and predicaments of the bobby and the cop. The quintessential exemplar was the *Dixon of Dock Green* television series (although *The Blue Lamp*, the 1950 film that introduced PC George Dixon—and killed him off within the first hour—was much more of a straightforward crime-fighting procedural than the television series that resurrected Dixon).

Although displaced by the harsher *Z Cars* and the later vigilante style of *The Sweeney*, the community police narrative staged a remarkable comeback in the 1980s in the successful *Juliet Bravo, Heartbeat*, and *The Bill* series (and other spin-offs like *Rockcliffe's Babies* or *Specials*), reflecting the new fashion for 'community policing' in the political debates about law and order (Reiner, 1994).[5]

The keynotes of the community police story are an emphasis on the harmonious relations within the police force, and between it and the wider society. This perspective is shared with the procedural, which originated in the same period. But unlike in the procedural, the emphasis is on the non-crime-related tasks of the police, and even, when crime-fighting, the human rather than organizational or technological resources of the police are stressed. Like the procedural policeman (but unlike the vigilantes or police deviants), the community police not only stick to the rules but are more effective as a result.

A recent variant in some British TV series is the bureaucratic police story, which focuses on senior management levels of the police (for example *Waterfront Beat* and *The Chief*). This is a variant of the police community/community policing stories in that it portrays the whole gamut of police work, not just crime, and is primarily concerned with the internal politics of the police bureaucracy rather than any mystery plot. Unlike earlier versions, however, the story is told from the management not street cop perspective. The emergence of this variant is clearly a response to the politicization of policing, and the comparatively greater salience in public debates of policing policy issues as opposed to individual cases. None of these examples has been particularly successful, however, and the more immediately crime-oriented work of street-level police, especially detectives, is likely to retain its fictional centrality.

THE CHANGING IMAGE OF THE POLICE

The crucial break in the police's fictional image came in the late 1940s when for the first time routine police officers (rather than G-men and the like) begin to appear as hero figures, in the American and British procedurals, and the British community police stories. Before then the ordinary copper was a background not a leading character; a servant figure, and like other servants, public or private, socially invisible. This was illustrated well by Thomas Burke's classic 1912 short story 'The Hands of Mr Ottermole', later filmed as an episode of Hitchcock's 1950 television series. In this the mysterious mass murderer whom nobody observes was in fact a patrolling bobby, seen by everyone but noticed by none.[6]

The precondition for the emergence of the police officer as a credible figure was the professionalization of the police, and their espousal of the important social mandate of crime control (Manning 1977). Jack Webb in the 1950s received unprecedented facilities for making *Dragnet* from William Parker, chief of the Los Angeles Police Department and a leader of the professionalization movement. (James Ellroy's novel

LA Confidential and the 1997 movie derived from it—in which the imaginary TV series *Badge of Honour* is modelled on *Dragnet*—offers a more jaundiced picture of Parker's LAPD). Webb (1959) responded by writing a eulogistic account of the LAPD 'from the inside'. *The Blue Lamp* also began with introductory shots and voice-over emphasizing the importance of both the uniformed bobby and technological professionalism in the battle against 'the crime wave'.

If the precondition for police heroes was professionalization, the demand for them (and for professionalization) came from the notion that other informal and amateur means of peacekeeping were no longer adequate. The procedural and the community police story implied a society where order maintenance required a professional organization, but this could operate democratically, with community consent and according to the rule of law.

The deviant police and civil rights stories, which emerged in the later phases of the procedural cycle but before the vigilante boom, implied that legalistic policing was breaking down, at least for some cops in some forces. But it was still maintained as an ideal. The 1970s vigilante stories rejected the model of liberal policing altogether as naive wishful thinking. They suggested a society so deeply threatened by extremes of evil that only the most drastic and unrestrained forceful measures could save it. Although the heyday of vigilantism suppressed any civil rights stories, the police deviance mini-cycle of the 1970s flourished simultaneously, emphasizing the unacceptable face of the law-and-order policies that vigilantism encouraged. The police community stories of that period also pointed to the dangers for the police themselves of the law-and-order mentality.

The overall trend throughout these developments was clearly towards an increasingly critical view of policing, and the culmination of this for the US cop fictions was the Fort Apache story. Although portrayed as a gallant band patrolling the borders between civilization and the chaos that the racism and ruthless economic advance of that 'civilization' had engendered in its ghetto areas, there was little faith in the prospect of any solution, either liberal reforms or total repression. In British police fiction a similar bleak conclusion was proposed by G. F. Newman's combination of the police deviance/deviant police models in a portrait of endemic corruption and rule-breaking. The only alternatives in his world were to let the villains carry on without any regulation, or to attempt control with the inevitable consequence of the corruption of the controllers, even as they did the job as well as possible while themselves on the take. Crime control conforming to a legalistic conception was unattainable. The deepening darkness of the mood of police fictions matched the politicization of law-and-order issues in the late 1960s and 1970s, as well as a growing undercurrent of apprehension by conservatives and liberals alike (fed by criminological and penological research) that 'nothing works'.

In Britain the 1981 Scarman Report stimulated a flurry of 'community policing' initiatives. This cautious attempt at relegitimating the police was reflected in the renewed fictional enthusiasm for community police stories like *The Bill* and *Heartbeat*, as well as such great sleuth-style police detectives as *Morse*. In the USA too, there was some softening of the police image on television in the early 1980s indicated by shows like *Hill Street Blues*, *Cagney and Lacey*, and *T. J. Hooker*. However, there was no return to *Dixon*-style harmony in the TV police image. The police community was shown with its own internal conflicts based on gender, race, age, rank, and specialism, and as dealing with a much more fragmented outside world (A. Clarke 1992; Eaton 1995; Leishman 1995; R. C. Mawby 1998*c*).

During the 1980s there was a bifurcation of images of the police. Critical and vigilante narratives coexisted with nostalgic throwbacks like *Heartbeat*. As a frequently appearing police soap opera with a large team of regular characters *The Bill* represented a dialectical synthesis of 1940s–1950s consensus and 1960s–1970s critical representations (Reiner 1994). In this milieu the police are not represented automatically as either 'goodies' or 'baddies'. Their moral status is contestable, and has to be established anew in each narrative (Allen, Livingstone, and Reiner 1998).

CONCLUSION

Both the 'factual' and the fictional presentations of the police broadly legitimate the police role in presenting them as necessary and for the most part effective. But critical analyses of the media treatment of law-and-order issues over-emphasize this legitimizing function. It coexists with media criticism not only of specific police actions and individuals, but even of the whole direction of police policy, at times building up to a consensus demand for reform. Moreover, the media image of the reality or ideal of policing is not monolithic, either in any one period or between different times. Nevertheless, a broad threefold pattern of change can be discerned corresponding to the trends in police politicization. The culmination of the long process of police legitimation led to the 'Golden Age' of crime-reporting as well as consensual police fictions of the 1940s and 1950s (procedurals and community police stories). The unintended outcome of professionalism became in the late 1960s a renewed politicization. Law and order became a major political issue, reflected in (and stimulated by) news and fictional media presentations. In the early 1980s, however, there was a struggle to restore legitimacy manifested both in police policy and debate, and in media accounts, both 'factual' and 'fictional'.[7] There is no new legitimating myth, however. A more sophisticated public awareness of conflict, inside and outside the police organization, precludes anything but a pragmatic, conditional legitimation in specific narratives, challenged by others. For every *Heartbeat*—style attempt at affirmative nostalgia there are critical revisionist excavations of the police, like *LA Confidential*. Having lost the automatic trust they once enjoyed, the police cannot retrieve it wholesale: public confidence is tentative and brittle and has to be renegotiated case by case.

NOTES

1. This overlooks a fundamentally different perspective, which is probably the predominant one among media professionals themselves. With regard to news production it is what has been called the 'cock-up' theory (Murdock 1982). In relation to crime fictions it is the view of them as mere innocent 'entertainments'. The common theme to these practitioners perspectives is the denial of coherent or consistent social or political implication, on the grounds either that the media 'tell it like it is', or that they are 'only' stories. I assume that media presentations are never innocent of social and political implications, though not conscious or intentional for the most part. Furthermore, although neither monolithic nor unchanging, the meanings of media accounts are structured by industrial and ideological pressures and processes.

2. This distinction is somewhat tenuous, and is based on the pretensions of producers. The edges are fuzzy. Crime fictions have often been at the frontiers of realism in style, while 'real-life' police are undoubtedly affected by media images. When I went on patrol in 1980 in the precinct of Los Angeles where Joseph Wambaugh's novel The Choirboys (and its film spin-off) was set, many officers wore belt-buckles sporting the legend 'I am a ChoirBoy' (I was not, sadly, invited to any 'choir practice'). The difference between 'factual' and 'fictional' presentations has been further eroded by the rise of 'fly-on-the-wall' documentaries like those pioneered by Roger Graef in his seminal 1981 Thames Valley Police series, called simply Police, and the new genre of 'reality' programmes (Kidd-Hewitt and Osborne 1995; Fishman and Cavender 1998). Fictional series such as Between the Lines and Cops blur the line further by using documentary styles of filming.

3. One important kind of fiction this leaves out is children's literature (Morrison 1984). One of the most interesting aspects of this is the frequent message that the police (however laughable, lovable, or large-footed) are essential for social order. In Enid Blyton's Mr Plod and Little Noddy, for instance, when Mr Plod is injured the Toytown populace bemoan their plight. 'Who is going to protect us against robbers?' asks Miss Fluffy Cat, and Mr Wobbly Man echoes her concern. The inconceivability to most modern people of social order without police presumably owes a lot to repetition of such stories.

4. These studies include, for analyses of crime films, McCarthur 1972; Shadoian 1977; Rosow 1978; Clarens 1997; Rubin 1999; of detective fiction, Haycraft 1941, 1946; Watson 1971; Symons 1972; Cawelti 1976; J. Palmer 1978; Knight 1980; D. Porter 1981; Benstock 1983; Most and Stowe 1983; Mandel 1984; Ousby 1997; of detective films, Everson 1972; Tuska 1978; Parish and Pitts 1990a; of detective TV shows, Meyers 1981, 1989; and of fictional images of specific, highly prestigious elite police forces, Walden 1982; R. Powers 1983; Potter 1998.

5. Juliet Bravo symbolized a new fashion for female cop heroes, also found in Police Woman, Charley's Angels, The Gentle Touch, Cagney and Lacey, and Prime Suspect, for example. Other programmes and films tried to transcend the previous domination of the genre by WASP males by having a variety of ethnic minority protagonists.

6. The device of the socially invisible uniformed lackey was exploited by G. K. Chesterton in a Father Brown story in which the murderer is a similarly unnoticed postman; it is also used in the clichéd denouement 'The butler done it.'

7. The crime genre (especially its law-enforcement side), more than any other popular entertainment form, has always presented itself as topical and bringing the public the facts 'hot from the headlines'. Although with differing devices for conveying verisimilitude (all of which have a very short shelf-life, rendering yesterday's forms palpably artificial), police movies have always striven for what counted as 'realism'. So it is no puzzle that the police genre should so quickly register changing styles and debates in the police. This also true of non-genre representations of the police in mainstream fiction (D. Miller 1981).

PART III

LAW AND POLITICS

6

POLICE POWERS AND ACCOUNTABILITY

The last two decades have seen profound changes in the legal and constitutional status of the police. Their powers and accountability have been transformed by a set of overt changes in statute and case-law, and by covert changes in policy and practice (D. Dixon, 1997; W. Dixon, 1999). The landmark Police and Criminal Evidence Act 1984 (PACE) attempted a codification of the powers of the police to investigate crime, and the safeguards over their exercise (D. Brown 1997; Phillips and Brown 1998: part I). The Prosecution of Offences Act 1985 created the Crown Prosecution Service, removing this major law-enforcement responsibility from the police, and purporting to intro-duce an extra element of accountability in the processing of cases (McConville, San-ders, and Leng 1991; A. Sanders 1997; Phillips and Brown 1998: part II). The Criminal Justice and Public Order Act 1994 made further changes in this significant area, including in s.34 putting pressure on suspects not to exercise their right of silence by permitting courts to draw adverse inferences from a suspect's refusal to answer ques-tions (D. Dixon 1997: chap. 6; D. Brown 1997, chap. 8; Bucke and Brown 1997; Bucke, Street, and Brown, 2000). These statutes derived from the only two Royal Commis-sions to have reported in the last twenty years (Royal Commission 1981, 1993). The Public Order Act 1986, the Criminal Justice and Public Order Act 1994, and the Crime and Disorder Act 1998 all extended police powers in the key area of public order (P. Waddington 1994; D. Brown and Ellis 1994; Ashworth *et al.* 1998; Bucke and James 1998).

Legal change and political practice have transformed fundamentally the doctrine of constabulary independence and the tripartite system for police governance instituted by the Police Act 1964 (Lustgarten 1986; Reiner 1991; Reiner and Spencer 1993; T. Jones, Newburn, and Smith 1994; Loveday 1996*a*, 1999; T. Jones and Newburn 1997; B. Dixon and Smith, 1998). The Police and Magistrates Courts Act 1994 (PMCA) was a key legislative step in this process. Chief constables have become less accountable to local government, while their accountability to central government has grown apace. Arguably we now have a *de facto* national police force.

The year 1981 was a major climacteric for the politicization of policing, most obviously because of the urban riots, unprecedented in the twentieth century, and the ensuing Scarman Report. The early 1990s were another major turning-point, as policing became more centralized and 'businesslike', above all through the Report of the Inquiry into Police Responsibilities and Rewards 1993 (Sheehy 1993), the White Paper *Police Reform* (Home Office 1993), and the PMCA 1994 (Reiner and Spencer 1993; Leishman, Loveday, and Savage 1996; Saulsbury, Mott, and Newburn 1996; R. Morgan and Newburn 1997). Police accountability, a perennially vexed issue in all criminal justice systems (Stenning 1995; Loveday 1999), was the subject of heated debate throughout these years.

The Royal Commission on Criminal Procedure (RCCP) had been announced to parliament by the prime minister, James Callaghan in 1977. It was a response to opposing political pressures concerning police powers and accountability which had been growing for years. On the one hand, there was mounting evidence and complaint about police abuse of powers (revealed by the 1977 Fisher report on the Confait case, which found that abuse of powers and violation of suspects' rights were common in the Met). On the other, the law-and-order lobby lamented that suspects' rights made the police operate with 'one hand tied behind their back' (as the Police Federation chairman Jim Jardine, put it). The RCCP mounted an extensive programme of research, and was also inundated by evidence from the opposing lobbies. Police organizations presented a 'shopping-list' of demands for new or enhanced powers, while civil liberties groups argued for tighter control over existing police powers.

When the RCCP Report was published in January 1981 it was greeted with almost universal condemnation by the Left and civil liberties groups (for examples, see the article by Harriet Harman, then of the National Council for Civil Liberties, in the *New Statesman*, 2 January 1981: 6–7; Hewitt 1982: chap. 1). The police had regarded the establishment of the RCCP with, in the words of the Superintendents' Association' 'almost universal pessimism', fearing that against 'law and order . . . will be ranged the big guns of every minority group and sociological agency'. But when the Report was published the police reception was very favourable (*Police*, February 1981: 3, 14–22).

In October 1982 the home secretary, William Whitelaw, published the first version of the Police and Criminal Evidence Bill (henceforth called 'Mark I'). It was claimed that this was based largely on the RCCP Report. However, it drew on the report in a one-sided way. The RCCP proposals for greater police powers were incorporated or extended, but many of the safeguards were omitted or weakened. The RCCP had placed great weight on the concept of 'a fundamental balance' between suspects' rights and the powers of the police, seeing the proposals it made as an integral whole. Mark I aroused a storm of controversy which united the Left and the civil liberties groups with a broad spectrum of middle-of-the-road and even conservative opinion. Altogether Mark I had a very rough parliamentary ride before it fell with the announcement of the 1983 General Election.

A revised Bill (Mark II) was introduced in the Commons in October 1983, with a number of new features. These were a response to some of the criticisms and amendments of Mark I. Mark II regained the support with reservations that had been accorded the RCCP by the mainstream professional law bodies, and had a much better press reception. The Left, civil liberties groups, and many academics continued to oppose it (Christian 1983; Freeman 1984). The police reception to Mark II was distinctly cooler than to its predecessor

The issues of police powers and accountability are of course interdependent and intimately related. The fundamental problem raised by both debates is how to control police actions, especially in the light of their considerable discretion (Reiner and Leigh 1992; Dixon 1997). The police inevitably have discretion in the enforcement of laws, for at least two reasons. One is that they do not, and never could, have adequate resources for full enforcement of every law. There is thus an inescapable necessity for choice about priorities. Second, even the most precisely worded rule of law requires interpretation in concrete situations. The logically open texture of rules in application makes inevitable an element of at least implicit discretion. These considerations make discretion unavoidable, but it is also desirable. Full enforcement would violate generally accepted criteria of justice, as recognized in cases where it is uncontentious that prosecutions should not occur, such as those involving exceptionally old or young offenders. In addition, with the more amorphously defined 'public order' offences, criteria of what constitutes a disturbance are situationally variable. What is accepted in Soho might scandalize in Suffolk (A. Smith 1987; Sherr 1989). The Anti-Social Behaviour Orders (ASBOS) instituted by the Crime and Disorder Act 1998, for example, constitute indirect criminalization of amorphous and ill-defined behaviour perceived by complainants and the police as nuisances (Ashworth *et al.* 1998).

The problem of how the inescapable and justifiable discretion enjoyed by the police can be controlled exists at two levels: the level of policy-making for the force as a whole—the assessment of priorities in resource allocation and broad overall strategy and style—and the street-level actions of rank-and-file officers. In addition, there is the task of providing channels for complaints about abuse and dissatisfaction. At present mechanisms exist only for complaints about individual officers and their specific actions. But it would be desirable to have means for citizens to raise complaints about policy and tactics. Before examining the recent changes in these areas, some fundamental principles for assessing police powers must be considered.

FIRST PRINCIPLES: THE SIGNIFICANCE OF FORMAL POLICE POWERS

There are two related and fallacious assumptions common in public policy debate about policing. They are shared by the otherwise opposed law-and-order and civil liberties lobbies. Both emphasize law enforcement as the central police function, and adopt the rational deterrence model of classical criminology, albeit at different stages of the argument. In this sense both fail to take on board the implications of social research on the police. Neither has adequately considered or explained the fundamental question 'What are police powers for?' but that issue must be addressed before it can be decided what powers are necessary and how they can be regulated.

If pushed on the issue both camps would say the police are primarily concerned with preventing and detecting crime. Civil libertarians might be more cautious in their statement: but it is implicit in many denunciations of police activities (for example, Christian 1983: 12–13; Kinsey, Lea, and Young 1986). The historical and sociological evidence should have made clear that crime-fighting has never been, is not, and cannot be the prime activity of the police, although it is part of the mythology of media images, cop culture, and, in recent years, government policy. The core mandate of policing, historically and in terms of concrete demands placed upon the police, is the more diffuse one of order maintenance. Only if this is recognized can the problems of police powers and accountability really be confronted in all their complexity. The vaguely defined 'public order' offences like breach of the peace or the 1998 Crime and Disorder Act's ASBOs (which appear to be a scandalous embarrassment from either a crime control or due process approach) speak to the very heart of the police function.

Given this, the implicit goal of many civil libertarian critiques—a precisely and unambiguously defined set of criminal offences and police powers to deal with them—becomes an unattainable chimera. Moreover, it is a dangerous rather than merely confusing chimera. For it makes conduct that should really be approached as a low-level nuisance come to be assimilated to an all-encompassing omnibus category of 'crime' (as the Crime and Disorder Act 1998 arguably does). Given that people frequently place demands upon the police for control of low-level disorderly conduct, such as rowdyism, there are only two possibilities. Either the police are restricted absolutely to consensual methods, or they are given graduated powers to deal with people coercively in the (not unlikely) event that they do not respond to firm but mere exhortation. Giving the police formal powers may reduce the incentive to develop tactics for a consensual resolution. But this problem has to be dealt with by adequate safeguards, not by denying powers to cope with the most common kind of request for police action. This is what the Public Order Act 1986, the Criminal Justice and Public Order Act 1994, and the Crime and Disorder Act 1998 intended to do, albeit with debatable success (A. Smith 1987; Sherr 1989; Newburn et al, 1991; P. Waddington 1994; D. Brown and Ellis 1994; Critcher and Waddington 1996; Lacey and Wells 1998: chap. 1; Ashworth et al, 1998; Bucke and James 1998).

It is not just civil libertarians, of course, who tend to discuss police powers as if the only function of policing should be crime detection. PACE was argued for by the Conservative government in 1984 as its 'main current policy initiative in the field of police powers to combat crime' (Home Office Working Paper Criminal Justice, 1984). The 1993 White Paper Police Reform, and New Labour's Crime Reduction Programme explicitly prioritize crime control as the police mission (Home Office 1993, 1998). In Chapter 5 it was shown that the clear-up of crimes is only marginally dependent on police initiative, and largely results from information provided by the public. Changes in police powers do not significantly increase police effectiveness in crime control.

There is no evidence that the rules of criminal procedure allow a significant proportion of suspects to avoid conviction, *pace* the 1979 claim of the Police Federation chairman that, if these rules had been suggested as a new board-game, 'Waddingtons would have turned it down because one player, the criminal, was bound to win every time'. The Royal Commission on Criminal Procedure's own research concluded that 'There are no obvious powers which police might be given that would greatly enhance their effectiveness in the detection of crime' (Steer 1980: 125).

Around 90 per cent of trials result in conviction, mainly because of guilty pleas, although the majority of contested trials also result in conviction (J. Baldwin and McConville 1977, 1979; McBarnet 1981; McConville, Sanders, and Leng 1991; A. Sanders, 1997; Phillips and Brown 1998: chap. 12; Home Office 1999: chap. 4). The police often claim that it is more serious professional criminals who are most likely to take advantage of their rights, whereas minor offenders ('small fry') are less likely to. Most research finds this is not the case, but the issue remains controversial, and some recent studies do suggest that serious criminals may exercise their rights more often. (Zander 1974; Mack 1976; J. Baldwin and McConville 1977, 1979; Williamson and Moston 1990; Greer and Morgan 1990; Zander and Henderson 1993; McConville and Hodgson 1993; Williamson 1996; D. Brown 1997: 175–7; Phillips and Brown 1998: 77–80).

If the law-and-order lobby errs in postulating the rational deterrent model with regard to policing crime (more police power + greater deterrence = less crime), the civil liberties lobby adopt the same model for policing the police. For years it has been the refrain of radical and liberal criminologists when arguing against the 'hang 'em, flog 'em' brigade that policing and penal policy have a limited and primarily symbolic role in restraining deviance. This analysis should extend to police deviance. The main way that the sanctions and enforcement machinery proposed by a rational deterrence model can be effective is by the impact they may have on the cultural controls in a community, including the police. It is these cultural understandings which are the immediate determinants of law-abidingness or deviation. What needs more precise analysis is the relationship between formal rules of law and procedure and the sub-cultural rules that are the guiding principles of police conduct. How do they result in 'blue-letter' law (Reiner and Leigh 1992), that is the police practice that results from interpretation of black-letter law 'in the books' as refracted through police culture and the situational exigencies and organizational sanctions of policing (McConville, Sanders, and Leng 1991; D. Dixon 1997)?

There are two competing views on this in the research literature. In the interactionist tradition it has largely been assumed that formal rules are primarily presentational (Manning 1979; Holdaway 1979, 1983, 1989, 1995; Chatterton 1979, 1995; Punch 1979a,; Fielding 1984, 1989). They are the terms in which conduct has to be justified, but do not really affect practice. It is the police subculture that is the key to understanding police actions. This sometimes amounts to an extreme rule scepticism. As McBarnet (1979: 25) has put it, 'Sociologists of the police have tended to treat the notion of legality as unproblematic, not because they assume the police operate according to these principles, but rather because they assume the opposite, that they are largely irrelevant in practice.'

But what is the relationship of subcultural norms to the formal rules? First, the interactionist studies themselves point to some impact of formal rules, for example in the emphasis on rank-and-file solidarity aimed at shielding deviant practices from the senior ranks, and the need always to have a good story to 'cover your ass'. Rank-and-file subcultural autonomy is thus limited to a degree by formal controls, but how much, when, and in what way has not been fully explored. Second, the police subculture is by no means radically distinct or deviant in its values from either legal or popular morality. The police are broadly representative of the population (P. Waddington 1999a, b).

While there is some tolerance for rule-bending in police subculture, that does not mean there is carte blanche for gross abuse. All studies of the informal understandings of police culture (even quite critical ones) imply that there are moral norms which, while tolerating malpractices like 'verballing' or even physical force in some circumstances, and certainly permitting non-legally-justified exercises of discretion, proportion these to moral judgements of desert and necessity (Klockars 1980; R. Baldwin and Kinsey 1982: 49–50; Chatterton 1983: 210–15; Holdaway 1983: chaps. 8, 9; Policy Studies Institute 1983, chap. 5; Kemp, Norris, and Fielding 1992; P. Waddington, 1994, 1999a, b; Geller and Toch 1996). The police sense of justice as revealed in these studies, while often deviant from the formal rules, is bound by constraints that probably reflect widely shared sentiments in the community, and are not absolutely autonomous.

The danger with relying on the police subculture's sense of justice becomes acute, however, when there is moral conflict, confusion, or change in a society, and police ethics are at odds with those of their 'clients' (Kleinig 1996). When the police deal with those regarded as 'alien', disreputable, and 'police property', the constraints of traditional communal morality are not an adequate protective guide or check. The problem in contemporary liberal democracies is not how to protect the majority, the 'public', from police oppression, but how to protect vulnerable minorities. This limits the potential of 'democratic accountability' as a panacea against abuse. While arguing the case for accountability of the police to the electoral process, Lea and Young (1984: 270) frankly admit that 'One of our constant nightmares is that if there was a completely democratic control of police in areas such as Hackney, the resulting police force would look exactly the same as the present'.

A crucial issue in the police accountability is the 'tyranny of the majority' problem. The rules of criminal procedure are dangerously stretched in relation to suspects drawn from relatively vulnerable and powerless social groups, but these constitute the vast majority of cases (Choongh 1997; Phillips and Brown 1998: chap. 1). 'Democratic controls' through the electoral process are not much help here. What has to be achieved is the incorporation within the operative police subculture of working procedures and norms which embody universal respect for the rights even of weak or unpopular minorities, which the rhetoric of legality purports to represent (Goldsmith

1990). The task of reform is neither just laying down the law, nor achieving majority control. It is knowing what policy changes can achieve their desired objectives, bearing in mind the refracting effects of the rank-and-file subculture, and the situational exigencies structuring police work (Chan 1997; D. Brown 1997; D. Dixon 1997).

The second, more recent, strand in research literature on the police is a structuralist one. It argues that the source of police deviance is not primarily rank-and-file subcultural autonomy. The problem is the tacit encouragement, by senior officers, judges, and the state elite, of deviations from the ideal of legality. This is accomplished through a permissive structure of vaguely stated legal rules, and the accommodation of case law to police practices (McBarnet, 1979, 1981; Jefferson, 1980; M. Brogden 1982; Jefferson and Grimshaw 1984a, b; Grimshaw and Jefferson 1987; McConville, Sanders and Leng 1991; Ericson 1993; B. Dixon and Smith 1998). But the interactionist emphasis on police subcultural fears about the need to 'cover your ass' implies that senior officers are not content to connive at every type of malpractice (P. Waddington, 1999, b). The structuralist case needs qualification in terms of specifying which rules, in which circumstances, may be bent, and in what ways. The fact that police work is dispersed and of low visibility, and that judges may accommodate police practices in many judgements, so that sanctions are often effectively weak, does not mean that the formal rules have no impact or that anything goes (Reiner and Leigh 1992; D. Brown 1997; D. Dixon 1997; B. Dixon and Smith 1998).

The prime problem in controlling police deviations from legality is not the permissiveness of law but conflicts of evidence about whether malpractice has occurred. In such arguments the suspect is usually at a structural disadvantage, which is why complaints are so seldom upheld (Box and Russell 1975; Maguire and Corbett 1991; Goldsmith 1991; T. Landau 1994; D. Brown 1997, chap. 11; G. Smith 2000). One consequence of tighter regulation of detention and interrogation in police stations since PACE is that more suspects seem to take the 'scenic route' to the police station (R. Morgan, Reiner, and McKenzie 1990; McConville, Sanders, and Leng 1991). This suggests that the law is less permissive than the structuralists claim, in that tactics have to be used by the police to circumvent the law's rigours, although it also confirms that such rule avoidance is often possible. A similar implication can be drawn from the high proportion of exercises of power which are by 'consent' (D. Dixon, Coleman, and Bottomley 1990; McKenzie, Morgan, and Reiner 1990; D. Brown 1997: 17–19, 68–71; D. Dixon 1997), although this raises the problem of knowing how full, voluntary and informed citizen agreement is. The rules do prohibit many forms of police conduct, which can none the less be engaged in frequently because of the problems of enforceability due to the low visibility of police work (Reiner and Leigh 1992).

Much of the criticism of PACE and other extensions of formal police powers rests upon what I have called 'a law of inevitable increment: whatever powers the police have they will exceed by a given margin' (Reiner 1981a: 38). As Ole Hansen of the Legal Action Group put it: 'If they exceed their present powers why should they not exceed wider powers?' (letter to New Society, 22 January 1981: 161). But police abuse is not the product of some overweening constabulary malevolence constantly bursting the seams of whatever rules for regulating conduct are laid down. It is based on pressure to achieve specific results, using traditional techniques that may often be inadequate. The pressure is derived partly from public expectations, as mediated by the police organization and subculture. If the police can achieve their proper objects within the law, one strain making for deviation disappears. This does not mean that unacceptable practices should be legitimated. But it does suggest that the police must have adequate powers to perform the core tasks that are expected of them. If they do not, the police culture may develop disdain for legality, which will multiply abuses. It is a criminological commonplace that it is counter-productive to pass unenforceable laws because this breeds general contempt for the law. The same is true of rules of criminal procedure drawn so narrowly that the police are regularly inclined to violate them in pursuit of objectives which would probably have wide popular approval.

Effective regulation of police powers and accountability requires that the rules of criminal procedure should be enforceable in the sense that they are broadly acceptable to and respected by the police. Internal disciplinary procedures must mesh with the external structure. If external controls are forced on a hostile police they are likely to prove empty or even counter-productive gestures.

The art of achieving accountability. . . . is to enlist the support of the police in disciplinary activities. . . . For processes of external regulation. . . . to be more than a highly publicised morality play, the police must become convinced that they will be trusted to bear. . . . the active responsibility for ensuring correct performance Bayley 1983: 158).

Accountability institutions will only be truly efficacious in affecting police practices if they win over and work in conjunction with internal disciplinary and self-controlling processes. None-the-less there is a need for competent and vigorous external account-ability, both to symbolise police subordination to law and democracy, and to ensure that internal disciplinary and management processes operate effectively.

One objection that could be levelled against the above argument is that the nature of police policy and organization has changed so fundamentally in recent years that there can be no prospect of internal reform. Since the 1980s it has been argued frequently that, as a response to increasing crime and disorder in late modernity, policing has moved away from a supposed 'consensus' style bound by the rule of law. Increasingly it has a more militaristic and coercive character, targeted by sophisti-cated surveillance and pre-emptive intelligence-gathering, above all on the socially excluded (S. Hall *et al.* 1978; Christian 1983; Lea and Young 1984; Kinsey, Lea, and Young 1986 Jefferson 1987, 1990; Northam 1988; Kraska and Paulsen, 1997; Choongh 1997; Maguire 2000; Sheptycki 2000*b*). This depiction has many valid elements, and recent trends such as so-called zero-tolerance policing seem to bear it out (Innes 1999*a*,; Stenson 2000; Johnston 2000: 63–7), as will be discussed further in the conclusions.

What is misleading is the implication that police abuse or disregard of legality is increasingly prevalent, although there have been, of course, many highly disturbing causes célèbres recently. But police lawlessness was rife in the past too. A fascinating illustration is Sir Robert Mark's autobiographical account of his youthful indiscretions as a pre-war Manchester constable, such as breaking a drunken navvy's leg with an illegal truncheon (Mark 1978: 28–9). He also documents the prevalence in the late 1940s of interrogation by physical force (such as holding suspects' heads down lavatories) and the meting out of brutal summary justice to those who assaulted the police. There is similar evidence in oral history of policing in the first half of the twentieth century (M. Brogden 1991; Weinberger 1995). I am not suggesting that the police are now more law-abiding, rather that we don't really know what the trend is. The extent of police deviance at any time is an unknown 'dark figure'. Increasing concern is as likely to be due to changing public sensitivity and values as to a growth of real police misconduct. Public perceptions of what constitutes intolerable police behaviour are likely to have changed as deference declined in the post-war period, making complaints against the police more widely credible. At the same time there have been profound changes in police organization and tactics since the 1960s: more centralization, specialization and utilization of technology, and an increased mobilization of coercive capacity to deal with public disorder, which, as seen in Chapter Two, threatened police legitimacy. But critics often over-emphasize the degree of conscious rationality, consistency, and intent in the changes they document. The development of 'militaristic' and 'fire brigade' tactics in the 1970s and 1980s was largely the unintended consequence of strategies aimed at enhancing professionalism and efficiency, while retaining or even improving a cooperative public relationship. The Unit Beat reorganization had been intended to improve community relations along with efficiency (Weatheritt 1983, 1986). That this was not how it worked out was due to the resilience of rank-and-file subculture, the growth of concern with crime and disorder, and lack of resources for adequate implementation (Holdaway 1977, 1983). The episode constitutes an important warning about the prospects of achieving rational and purposive change.[1]

Textbook expositions of legal powers usually suggest a mechanistic relation between rules, policy and practice. The findings of observational research imply that there are structural and cultural impediments in the way of reforming police practice by simply tightening rules or their enforcement. The low visibility of police work and the low status, and hence low political credibility, of the typical recipients of police power make this unlikely as a straightforward strategy of reform.

The function of formal rules and accountability mechanisms in the regulation of police work is more indirect and subtle. We can distinguish four such functions.

The constitutional function. Rules and accountability structures have a symbolic function in asserting the ideal of police subordination to democracy and the rule of law. They must express values and norms that are defensible with respect to the principles of due process legality.

The co-optive function. Formal rules will only become routinely effective to the extent they are co-opted into the informal values of police subculture. Because of this they should not be expressed in so purist or hostile a fashion that they result in a defensive closing of police ranks.

The communicative function. Some signalling mechanism registering the need for change is necessary to spark off internal reforms, a task often performed by 'scandals' in the absence of adequate channels for the routine communication of grievance and complaint (Sherman 1978).

The control function. Visible and demonstrated deviance must be sanctioned effectively. However, this cannot be relied upon by itself, because of the low clear-up rate of allegations of police deviance, few of which are officially sustained.

The relationship between legal rules and police practice is complex. Rules do not determine practice but they are not irrelevant to it (McConville, Sanders, and Leng 1991; Reiner and Leigh 1992; D. Dixon 1997). The relationship is highly variable between times, places, and different aspects of law and practice. This is demonstrated by the impact of recent legal change, above all PACE (D. Brown 1997).

POLICE POWERS: PACE AND AFTER

PACE is the single most significant landmark in the modern development of police powers. Much of its content had already been prefigured by piecemeal changes in statute and case-law (not to mention *sub rosa* police practice) in the years leading up to it (Reiner and Leigh 1992.) None-the-less, as a statutory codification and rationalization of police powers and the safeguards over their exercise, it had enormous symbolic and practical importance. The Act's many critics saw it as signifying a lurch towards 'policing by coercion' (Christian 1983) or 'a draconian increase in police powers' (Lea and Young 1984: 254). The official claim was that it balanced powers and safeguards, with the 'objective of encouraging effective policing with the consent and cooperation of society at large' (Home Office *Working Paper on Criminal Justice*, 1984: 15).

PACE purported to implement the RCCP's principle that 'a fundamental balance' had to be struck between 'the rights of the individual in relation to the security of the community'. This notion was built into its terms of reference, which were to have regard 'both to the interests of the community in bringing offenders to justice and to the rights and liberties of persons suspected or accused of crime'. As many critics pointed out, this sharp dichotomy between 'individual' and 'communal' interests is untenable. The 'communal' interest is ill served by abrogation of 'individual' suspects' rights which leads to wrongful convictions and the continued freedom of the truly guilty. An adequate framework of civil liberties is as much in the interest of any civilized community as is security from crime.

But if the contrast between 'communal' and 'individual' interest as presented by the RCCP is flawed, it none the less bears a kernel of truth. In relation to any specific investigation, the tighter the protections afforded individual suspects the greater the difficulties of securing a conviction. From the point of view of both the legislature and the police officer this gives rise to what has aptly been called 'the Dirty Harry dilemma' (Klockars 1980). Rules constructed too loosely undermine the pretensions of the system of criminal procedure to sift out offenders accurately and fairly from innocent people. If they are pitched too restrictively, not only do obviously guilty offenders escape justice but police respect for the rule of law is undermined, with the counterproductive consequence that violations of due process may increase. Wherever the balance is drawn, the individual officer in some cases will confront the Dirty Harry dilemma of either violating the rules or allowing offenders of whose guilt he is convinced to go free.[2] The problem is to place the balance so that there is neither an abandonment by the legal system of its role of enunciating and protecting just procedures, nor demoralization of the police through too frequent exposure to Dirty Harry situations.

THE CONTENT OF PACE

How adequately PACE achieved the aspiration of a 'fundamental balance' between police powers and safeguards is highly debatable. On one hand, the Act gave the police a plethora of powers that they had not possessed before, at any rate on a statutory basis. To a degree this extension of powers was nominal rather than real, for much was a rationalization and codification of hitherto haphazard statute and common law, or a legitimation of what was already police practice.

On the other hand, the exercise of statutory powers was governed by safeguards which were set out partly in the Act itself, partly in the accompanying five Codes of Practice. These Codes provided detailed procedures regulating stop and search; search and seizure; detention and questioning of suspects; identification parades; and tape-recording of interviews. Revised sets of Codes, incorporating lessons from the experience of PACE in practice, came into effect on 1 April 1991, and further revisions were introduced on 10 April 1995 (Brown, Ellis, and Larcombe, 1992; D. Brown 1997: 15, 36–9, 68, 76–90; Bucke and Brown 1997).

These Codes were under-pinned by s.67 of PACE, which made failure to comply with them a disciplinary offence, and made a breach admissible as evidence in criminal or civil proceedings, if thought relevant by the judge(s). The Act also implemented the RCCP's solution to the difficulties of reviewing police actions posed by the low visibility of routine police work. This was to establish a variety of recording requirements for each exercise of a police power, giving reasons for what is done. There was also a requirement that interviews be contemporaneously recorded. Backing up particular safeguards for specific powers, the Act also included sections purporting to enhance police accountability more generally. There was an obligation imposed on police authorities to make arrangements for consulting the views of the local community (s.106), and Part IX established the Police Complaints Authority, which enhanced the independent element in the complaints system.

This basic scheme, combining extension and rationalization of powers with procedural safeguards resting fundamentally on reporting requirements, ran through all the major provisions of PACE. A clear illustration was stop-and-search powers. These were boosted by s.1, which extended nationally the power to search for stolen goods, previously only granted by local legislation to some metropolitan areas. New powers were given to stop and search for articles made or adapted for use or intended to be used for burglary, theft, obtaining property by deception, or taking a motor vehicle without authority. Finally a power to stop and search for offensive weapons (defined as weapons made or adapted for use to cause injury, or intended by the person carrying it to be so used was provided).

Altogether, stop-and-search powers were clearly extended by PACE. There were two main safeguards over them, of debatable effectiveness. First, record-keeping: constables must make detailed records of each search, and of the reasons for it, and tell the suspect he has the right to request a copy within twelve months. Second, Code of Practice A specified that stops and searches must be justified by 'reasonable suspicion', for which there must be an objective basis, connected to the individual searched. It cannot arise only from an individual's membership of a category stereotyped as more likely to offend, such as black or young or long-haired people.

This same schema, combining extended powers with new safeguards based on record-keeping monitored by internal discipline, ran through all the main sections of PACE. It can be seen in the provisions on powers to arrest suspects, to enter and search their premises and seize evidence, and to detain them for questioning.

The detention and questioning sections contained a particularly complex set of safeguards, resting on the custody officer (CO), a new police specialism with a duty to supervise the detention of suspects (s.36). The CO (normally a sergeant) has the duty of informing a new detainee of his rights (to see a solicitor, to have someone informed of his arrest, and to consult the Codes of Practice). The CO must maintain a custody record on which are entered all significant events in the period of detention. A complex timetable of reviews of the necessity of detention, and of processes that can extend it up to an absolute maximum of ninety-six hours in exceptional cases, was elaborated in the Act and Code C.

THE INTERPRETATION OF PACE AT COMMON LAW

PACE clearly extended the key investigative powers of the police, subject to a regime of internal disciplinary safeguards for each power. In addition some general safeguards were introduced. Perhaps the most significant was the possible exclusion of evidence obtained in violation of PACE procedures. Confessions are admissible only if the prosecution can show they were not obtained by oppression, or by methods rendering them unreliable (s.76). Judges are obliged to warn juries of the dangers of convicting a mentally handicapped person on the basis of a confession (s.77). A more general

discretion was provided for judges to exclude evidence if it appears that 'the circumstances in which the evidence was obtained' mean it would have 'an adverse effect on
the fairness of the proceedings' (s.78). This rather loose discretion (a watered-down
version of an amendment introduced by Lord Scarman) fell far short of the tough
exclusionary rule hankered after by civil libertarians and experienced in the USA
(Sieghart 1985; A. Sanders 1988; N. Walker 1993).

However, one of the surprises of experience since PACE has been the much tougher
attitude adopted by the judiciary towards police breaches of the Codes than their
permissive toleration of violations of the old Judges' Rules. There is some unevenness
in the reaction of individual judges. None the less a review of the post-PACE common
law on the pivotal detention and questioning provisions concluded that 'the judges
now see themselves as having a disciplinary and regulatory role in maintaining the
balance between the powers of the police and the protection of suspects' (Feldman
1990: 469. See also Zuckerman 1987; Choo 1989; A. Sanders and Young, 1994; Zander,
1995; Lidstone and Palmer 1996; A. Sanders 1997; Ashworth 1998; B. Dixon and
Smith 1998).

There has been a plethora of empirical evaluations of the core aspects of PACE. This
represents an impressively 'reflexive' approach to policy in this area, embodying a
dialectic of research, scandal and reform.

PACE IN PRACTICE: THE RESEARCH VERDICT

Empirical studies of police work prior to PACE suggested that the powers of the police
were formulated in so loose a fashion, and interpreted so permissively by the judiciary,
that police practice frequently departed from principled statements of the 'rule of law'
(McBarnet 1981). Of particular concern was the evidence of discriminatory use of
police powers, as outlined in Chapter 4. This underlay much of the civil libertarian
opposition to PACE. It was feared that the police would exceed their new extended
powers just as they had prior to PACE. The safeguards were expected to be ignored,
relying as they did on police internal discipline and judicial discretion. These fears
were exacerbated by the evidently jaundiced views expressed towards the cumbersome
paperwork of the safeguards, not only by the police rank and file but even by many
senior officers (Reiner 1991: 144–60).

The controversial character of the Act ensured that a considerable body of evaluative empirical research, commissioned by a variety of bodies, has accumulated on the
effects of PACE. The Royal Commission on Criminal Justice (RCCJ), launched in 1991
under the chairmanship of Lord Runciman in the wake of the Guildford Four and
Birmingham Six miscarriage of justice revelations, also assembled a significant
research programme (summarized in the *Home Office Research Bulletin*, no. 35, 1994.
For critical views of its 1993 Report see McConville and Bridges 1994; S. Field and
Thomas 1994). Despite this growing volume of material, there is still much controversy about the overall impact of PACE, the RCCJ, and the subsequent changes (notably
the Criminal Justice and Public Order Act 1994).

The evidence so far suggests a much more complex picture than was implied by the polarized polemics that attended the birth-pangs of PACE. Research has thrown up more questions calling for further research and analysis, rather than definitive conclusions.

PACE certainly seems to have had a profound effect on the nature and outcomes of police handling of suspects. Routine practice has incorporated much of the rituals and procedures of the Codes of Practice, and many indices of suspects' access to rights indicate improvement. On the other hand, assimilation of the PACE rules into police culture and working practices has been uneven and incomplete. Much is ritualistic and presentational and affects little of substance in the experience of suspects (Adams 1995, 2000; Choongh 1997). Furthermore, there are signs that some early changes may have been an impact effect of new procedures, and that old working practices are creeping back in.

On the plus side, research evidence suggests that:

(i)   Suspects are almost invariably informed of their rights on reception at the police station (Sanders and Bridges 1990; McKenzie, Morgan, and Reiner 1990; Morgan, Reiner, and McKenzie 1990; D. Dixon 1997: 147–52; D. Brown 1997: chap. 6; Bucke and Brown 1997: chaps. 2, 3; Phillips and Brown 1998: chaps. 3, 4).

(ii) As a result, the proportion receiving legal advice has increased between two and four times, and is now about a third of all suspects (Maguire 1988; D. Brown 1989; Morgan, Reiner, and McKenzie 1990; D. Dixon, Coleman, and Bottomley 1990; D. Brown 1997, chap. 6; Bucke and Brown 1997: chap. 3; Phillips and Brown 1998: chap. 4). However, legal representation is frequently inadequate (McConville *et al.* 1994). Forty per cent of suspects interviewed now receive legal advice (Bucke, Street, and Brown 2000: 21).

(iii) The special extended powers available for 'serious arrestable offences' (on the authority of senior officers or in some cases a magistrates' court) are obtained relatively infrequently, in about 2 per cent of cases (D. Brown 1989).

(iv) The extent of the use of dubious 'tactics' to extract incriminating statements by interrogation has declined (Irving and McKenzie 1989*a, b*; D. Brown 1997, chap. 7).

(v)   Tape-recording of interviews seems to have reduced arguments in court about what occurred in them, and is now welcomed by police who were long opposed to it (Willis, Macleod, and Naish 1988; D. Brown 1997: 146–56).

(vi) The average period of detention in police stations for all cases remains roughly the same, about six hours and forty minutes (Morgan, Reiner, and McKenzie 1990; D. Brown, 1997: 63–5; Phillips and Brown 1998: chap. 7).

(vii) The Police Complaints Authority's supervision of the police investigation of complaints can be vigorous and active, especially in some serious cases (Maguire and Corbett 1991).

There is also much evidence from the same research, however, which paints a more negative picture:

(i)   Detention is authorized almost automatically and invariably. The idea of the custody officer as an independent check on this has proved chimerical (Morgan, Reiner, and McKenzie 1990; McConville, Sanders, and Leng 1991; A. Sanders, 1997: 1060–8; Choongh 1997; Phillips and Brown 1998: chap. 3).

(ii) The information to suspects about their rights is often given in a ritualistic and meaningless way. This may account for the overwhelming majority of suspects who do not take them up (Morgan, Reiner, and McKenzie 1990). It has been claimed also that 'ploys' are frequently used to dissuade suspects from taking up their rights (McConville, Sanders and Leng 1991 A. Sanders 1997), though the extent of this is debatable.

(iii) Some recent research has suggested that the right to silence may benefit serious offenders disproportionately (Williamson and Moston 1990; Williamson 1996), although other studies question this (Bucke, Street, and Brown, 2000: 6–7). Relatively few offenders have ever exercised their right of silence, in part or completely, and the proportion has declined since the Criminal Justice and Public Order Act 1994 permitted adverse inferences to be drawn (McKenzie and Irving 1988; Greer and Morgan, 1990; D. Brown 1997: chap. 8; Phillips and Brown 1998: chap. 5; Bucke, Street, and Brown 2000: chap. 3).

(iv) Later stages in the detention process (such as reviews, or regulating access to suspects by investigating officers) are less punctiliously followed than the reception rituals (D. Brown 1997: 62–3, 163–5). Custody officers are also less scrupulous about monitoring pre-detention events (such as delay between arrest and arrival at police stations: see Morgan, Reiner, and McKenzie 1990; D. Brown 1997: 159–63).

(v)   PACE procedures can frequently be side-stepped by securing 'voluntary' compliance by suspects with police requests. Such 'consent' is especially important for the stop and search powers, where it is often circumvented (D. Dixon 1990; D. Dixon, Coleman, and Bottomley 1990, McKenzie, Morgan, and Reiner 1990; D. Dixon 1997).

(vi) After PACE bedded in, the use of 'tactics' in interrogation increased, compared to its virtual elimination immediately after the Act took effect, but it did not return to its pre-PACE level (Irving and Mckenzie 1989; D. Brown 1997: chap. 7).

(vii) The provision of 'appropriate adults' and defence solicitors to assist vulnerable suspects like the mentally disordered is inadequate (Gudjonsson et al. 1993; R. Evans 1993; Bean and Nemitz 1994; Thomas 1994). In many cases no 'appropriate adult' is called or attends (Phillips and Brown 1998: 52–7). However, appropriate adults are obtained in most cases involving juveniles (97 per cent; according to Phillips and Brown 1998: 53–4).

(viii) However adequate PACE supervision of complaints investigations may be sometimes, public confidence and complainant satisfaction are disastrously low, while the rank-and-file police have simultaneously been alienated (Maguire and Corbett 1989, 1991; D. Brown 1997: chap. 11).

(ix) Consultative committees do more to impress police views on the public than *vice versa*, and act as a legitimating device more than a means of accountability (R. Morgan 1989, 1992; N. Fyfe 1992; G. Hughes 1994).

(x) The socially discriminatory pattern of use of police powers remains as marked as before. The burden of police powers still falls disproportionately on the young, economically marginal, ethnic minority males, who are the overwhelming majority of those who are arrested and detained (Morgan, Reiner, and McKenzie 1990; McConville, Sanders, and Leng 1991; A. Sanders 1997; Choongh 1997; Phillips and Brown 1998: chap. 1).

PACE: AN INTERIM CONCLUSION

The resilience of the social pattern of policing and its basic practices in the face of PACE is due to the unchanging role of the police, primarily as regulators of public space and those who live their lives there predominantly. PACE can do little to alter the impact of this on the culture and organization of policing.

None the less the Act *has* impacted on police practices, albeit unevenly and patchily. This is because of the symbolic consequences of the legislation, which puts safeguards on a statutory basis that carries more weight in police culture than the less formal Judges' Rules did. It is also because of a variety of changes making punishment of breaches more likely. These include the tougher line taken by the courts, and the deterrent value of internal disciplinary sanctions (however little it may be appreciated by outsiders). Of particular importance has been a variety of devices which have begun to open up the 'low visibility' backstage areas of routine policing, although not adequately as yet. Key examples are the recording requirements, lay station visitors (Kemp and Morgan 1989), enhanced access to solicitors (D. Brown 1997: chap. 6; Phillips and Brown 1998: chap. 4; Bucke, Street, and Brown 2000: 21–7), and 'appropriate adults' in cases involving juvenile or mentally disordered suspects (D. Brown 1997: chaps. 9, 10; Phillips and Brown 1998: chap. 3). The legislation has achieved far more than its civil libertarian critics initially expected, if far less than they would wish.

Deterrence, symbolism, organizational and training changes are all important in understanding how PACE has affected police culture and practice. If powers are precisely rather than permissively formulated, procedures to render visible occasions of use are constructed, and supervisors and courts determined to police the police, change can occur in line with the law. Thus the booking-in procedures, which are precise, relatively visible to supervisors, and clearly enjoined in training, are religiously followed. However, the danger of precisely formulated rules is also evident here. They can be satisfied by ritualistic observance with little meaning, defeating their intended objectives.

In short, PACE has in part accomplished the constitutional, co-opting, communicative, and control functions outlined earlier. However, given the low visibility and hence inevitable discretion of much routine police work, the key changes must be in the informal culture of the police, their practical working rules. These may be affected through symbolism, training, organization, and discipline, but they are not determined by the formal rules. Police culture is a function of the structurally determined social role of the police, which has not altered in any fundamental way. Policing in a hierarchical and divided society can never be even in its impact, and the socially discriminatory use of police powers continues. Thus legal regulation alone will always be inadequate to secure legitimacy and genuine consent. This is true also of the mechanisms for rendering the police organization accountable, to which I now turn.

CONTROLLING THE CONTROLLERS: DEVELOPMENTS IN POLICE ACCOUNTABILITY

The basic objectives and rules of criminal procedure are framed by parliament in its enactment of substantive and procedural law. The issue of accountability is the question of how to keep police practice, in particular the operation of discretion, within that broad framework and in line with communal values. This itself resolves into three analytically distinct functions: a 'judicial' function of determining whether specific police actions have breached legal or procedural rules; a quasi'legislative' function of setting priorities in the allocation of resources between different legitimate policing duties; and an 'executive' one of managing the performance of these duties in as efficient and effective a way as possible. Debates about accountability revolve around how satisfactorily existing mechanisms perform these functions. Underlying the debates are differing conceptions of who should have the ultimate power of decision when there is a conflict of viewpoints, over what range of issues accountability operates, and in terms of what political conceptions of justice should policing arrangements be evaluated (Reiner and Spencer 1993; Stenning 1995).

Conventional police rhetoric makes much of the democratic character of the British police (Pike 1985; Oliver 1997). As Robert Mark (1977: 56) put it: 'The fact that the British police are answerable to the law, that we act on behalf of the community and not under the mantle of government, makes us the least powerful, the most accountable and therefore the most acceptable police in the world.' This illustrates the central role played in official ideology by the notion of police accountability to the law (D. Dixon 1997; B. Dixon and Smith 1998; G. Smith 1997a).

There are four main ways in which the courts may operate to regulate police conduct: (i) police officers may be prosecuted for crimes, for example arising out of serious complaints alleging criminal misconduct, if the director of public prosecutions (DPP) recommends prosecution; (ii) civil actions may be brought against police officers for damages in cases of wrongful arrest, trespass, assault, and so on, or for negligent performance of their duties; (iii) judges have discretion to exclude evidence obtained in violation of due process of law, as embodied primarily in PACE and its accompanying Codes; (iv) judicial review of police policy decisions may be sought, if they are claimed to be *ultra vires*. In practice none of these has operated effectively so far. This may change after 2000, when the Human Rights Act 1998, which incorporated the European Convention on Human Rights into domestic UK law, becomes operational (Patten 1999: chap. 4).

Police officers are rarely prosecuted for crimes arising out of wrongful performance of their duties (G. Smith 1997*a*). The DPP and Crown Prosecution Services (CPS) have demanded stricter standards of evidence before recommending the prosecution of police officers than they require for ordinary suspects, because they believe it is harder to convince juries to convict police officers (Loveday 1983: 42–3; D. Rose 1996: chap. 7). During the 1990s there was an increase in the number of officers convicted of criminal offences (other than traffic offences) from 35 in 1992 to 65 in 1998 (G. Smith 2000: 5–6). However, the number remains small when compared with the approximately 35,000 complaints against the police recorded per annum, or the 1367 people awarded damages for police wrongdoing after a civil action was settled or won (G. Smith 2000: 5–6). The burden of proof in civil actions is the lesser standard of 'balance of probabilities', but the problems of cost, time, and access to lawyers mean that such actions are rarely resorted to (and rarely successful), even though they have significantly increased in recent years. Before PACE judicial decisions had whittled away the control functions of judicial discretion to exclude evidence. In the 1979 House of Lords *Sang* case which concerned police use of agents provocateurs, Lord Diplock stated: 'It is not part of the judge's function to exercise disciplinary powers over the police or prosecution as respects the way in which evidence to be used at the trial is obtained by them.' We have seen that judicial attitudes to breaches of PACE have become more robust, although this has been uneven, and many critics would still welcome a tougher rule for excluding evidence obtained improperly.

THE COMPLAINTS SYSTEM AND CIVIL ACTIONS

The Police Act 1964 laid down the basic pattern for the current system for making complaints against the police. From the start it was subject to severe criticism for relying on entirely internal police investigation and adjudication of complaints. After many years of pressure to introduce an independent element into the assessment of complaints against the police, resisted by most police opinion, the Police Act 1976 established the Police Complaints Board. (For an excellent critical account of the history of attempts to reform the complaints process see Maguire, 1991.) The board received a copy of the investigating officer's report on any complaint made under the procedures instituted by section 49 of the Police Act 1964, together with a memorandum stating whether the deputy chief constable had decided to bring disciplinary charges against the officer. After studying the papers, the board could recommend and, if necessary, direct that disciplinary charges be brought.

The board—a political compromise—was greeted with dismay both by the police and by civil libertarians. The latter deplored the impeccably establishment character of the board's members, the lack of independent investigative powers, and the greater facilities for police officers to sue complainants for libel, which was won by the Police Federation during the political wrangling preceding the Act.

In the early 1980s pressure mounted for a more vigorous and independent scrutiny of allegations of serious police misconduct. The Police Complaints Board's own 1980 Triennial Report set out several recommendations to improve its functioning. The board's new chairman, Sir Cyril Philips (who was also chairman of the RCCP), committed himself to a tougher policy, declaring that 'the existing Board had kept so low a profile that it has climbed into a ditch' (*Guardian*, 19 March 1981). The RCCP stated that public confidence required the implementation of the Police Complaints Board's proposals (para. 4.119). The Scarman Report and the Commons Select Committee on Home Affairs strongly argued for the independent investigation as well as adjudication of complaints. Finally, in a surprising volte face, the Police Federation retracted its long-standing opposition to independent investigation, as did a few chief constables.

Despite this pressure PACE did not establish a completely independent system. Rather, it replaced the Complaints Board with the Police Complaints Authority (PCA), which was required to supervise the investigation of complaints alleging death or serious injury, and empowered to do so in any other case where it considered this is in the public interest. When supervising an investigation, the PCA has power of veto over the appointment of the investigating officer, and can issue directions. It also receives the report of the investigation, and has to certify whether it is satisfied with the quality of it. The Act established procedures for resolving minor complaints informally, if complainants agree to this. It also strengthened police rights, for example by guaranteeing legal representation in cases where an officer might lose his job or rank.

While enhancing the degree of independent scrutiny of complaints (and police rights) the PACE reforms fell far short of a fully independent system. That a scheme involving completely independent investigators can work (in the sense of not impeding ordinary police work while sometimes reaching conclusions which are different from those of internal enquiries) is attested by overseas experience (Loveday 1988; Goldsmith 1991; T. Landau 1994). In 1998 the Police (Northern Ireland) Act established a fully independent ombudsman to investigate and adjudicate complaints against the police; the system was to become operational in the autumn of 2000 (Patten 1999: 36–8).

It is unlikely that pressure in the area of complaints will cease until such a scheme is established in the UK. Research on the new procedures since PACE suggests that the PCA and the system as a whole lack the confidence of both complainants and the police (D. Brown 1987, 1997: chap. 11; Maguire and Corbett 1989, 1991; Reiner 1991:

286–300). However, the much-maligned PCA, and the new procedures for informal resolution of minor complaints work reasonably well, given the severe resource constraints (Maguire and Corbett 1991; Corbett 1991).

By the late 1990s pressure for fundamental reform of the system had mounted to a crescendo once again, following several years of gradual reform in the wake of the miscarriage of justice scandals and the Royal Commission on Criminal Justice (RCCJ) Report of 1993 (G. Smith 2000). The Police and Magistrates Courts Act (PMCA) 1994 s.37 repealed the double jeopardy rule whereby officers acquitted of a criminal offence could not face a disciplinary charge which was substantively the same (G. Smith 1999).

The pressure for reform increased after the 1997 Labour general election victory. During 1997 the PCA and several police chiefs, including the Metropolitan commissioner, Sir Paul Condon, began to emphasize what they saw as a growing problem of police corruption. In 1997 there were also several divisional court judgments against the DPP for failures to prosecute police officers in serious cases (G. Smith 1997b). Shortly afterwards, the new Labour home secretary, Jack Straw, set up the Macpherson Inquiry into the murder of Stephen Lawrence murder, including in its brief an examination of the police complaints process. The new government also declared its intention to incorporate the European Convention on Human Rights into UK law, culminating in the 1998 Human Rights Act.

In late 1997 the Parliamentary Home Affairs Committee (HAC) began an inquiry into police discipline and complaints. Its report, *Police Disciplinary and Complaints Procedures*, was published in January 1998. It recommended radical overhaul of the system. It supported the principle of independent investigation, and recommended that the Home Office mount a feasibility study of how to implement this. It also concluded that the terms on which officers were investigated was as important as who did the investigating. Consequently, it recommended the removal of the 'right of silence' from police disciplinary proceedings, and held that the civil, balance of probabilities, standard of proof should apply, not the criminal one of 'beyond reasonable doubt'. It also recommended enhancing the PCA's role in investigation and adjudication of complaints, and that the PCA should be able to receive complaints directly. The report concluded that the complaints process should be more open and transparent, with disclosure of the reports of investigations, and public disciplinary hearings. It also suggested the establishment of a fast-track disciplinary procedure with a higher standard of proof than balance of probabilities, where this would not be prejudicial to subsequent criminal proceedings. The HAC Report supported the earlier agreement between the Home Office and the police staff associations for a procedure to handle unsatisfactory performance by police officers. It expressed concern about CPS decisions about the prosecution of police officers, urging the DPP to give written reasons when prosecution was not recommended.

The home secretary's response was largely favourable, broadly accepting the HAC Report's main recommendations. KPMG was commissioned to conduct a feasibility study of an independent system for investigating complaints against the police, to report in 2000.

On 1 April 1999 new regulations for dealing with police conduct and efficiency replaced the old discipline regulations, intended to bring the police in line with standard employment practice (G. Smith 2000). The Macpherson report on the Stephen Lawrence case, also published in 1999, gave further support to the establishment of an independent complaints procedure. Finally, in May 2000 the Home Office announced a consultation document on independent investigation of complaints against the police, based on the KPMG feasibility study and an unofficial report by Liberty ('Civilian Squad to Investigate Police Crimes', *Independent*, 15 May 2000: 1).

It seems as if radical overhaul of the complaints system will at last introduce the procedures long called for by civil libertarians, such as independent investigation and adjudication, and a civil standard of proof for non-criminal allegations, with officers having no more rights than ordinary employees. This will undoubtedly increase the confidence of complainants and the general public in the system. The changes will also probably raise the rate at which complaints are substantiated from its current very low level (only about 2 per cent of recorded complaints are substantiated, and of these only about 20 per cent result in either criminal or disciplinary proceedings; see G. Smith 2000: 6).

However the results may not be as dramatic as many hope. The low rates of clear-up of complaints against the police are probably not due mainly to cover-ups by police investigators, or even the high standard of proof required (though abandoning the criminal standard will definitely make a difference to the outcome of many complaints). A key factor is the 'low visibility' of the operational situations that give rise to most complaints. Frequently they turn on conflicts of testimony between complainants and police officers, with no independent evidence. Irrespective of who does the investigating and adjudicating, many are unlikely to be sustained even on a civil balance-of-probabilities standard of proof, still leaving many complainants with a sense of grievance.

In the light of the poor prospects of substantiation of complaints against the police, it is hardly surprising that civil actions have become a major growth industry as an alternative means of redress (Clayton and Tomlinson 1992; Harrison and Cragg 1995; G. Smith, 1997*a*; B. Dixon and Smith 1998). The door was opened in effect when s.48 of the 1964 Police Act made chief officers, and thus police forces, vicariously liable for wrongs committed by police officers, reversing the common law position established by *Fisher v. Oldham* in 1930 (B. Dixon and Smith 1998: 427). This made it financially worthwhile to sue officers for torts they might have committed. The means for suing frequently came from legal aid. The lower burden of proof in civil actions compared to the criminal standard required for complaints also made the prospects of success much greater. In the Met, in particular, settlements and damages for civil actions rose from £471,000 to 127 claimants in 1991 to £2,309,000 to 295 claimants in 1998–9 (G. Smith 2000: 6). In 1998–9, the first year that the HM Chief Inspector of Constabulary's Annual Report included these statistics, claims against all police forces had reached 5961 of which 1302 were settled and 65 successful in getting damages. The total paid out for damages and settlements came to nearly £4.5 million (G. Smith

2000: 6). Small wonder that the commissioner's policy appears to have changed in the mid-1990s from settling to contesting actions wherever possible. In the 1997 Appeal Court case *Thompson and Hsu v. Commissioner of Police of the Metropolis* the Met was successful in getting the court to suggest more restrictive guidelines for damages in such cases (B. Dixon and Smith 1998: 428). On the other hand, the grounds for civil actions were extended in 1996 by the Court of Appeal. In *Swinney v. Chief Constable of Northumbria* the police force was held liable for negligence, despite the stringent tests for such actions established by the House of Lords in 1989 in *Hill v. Chief Constable of West Yorkshire* (B. Dixon and Smith 1998: 424–6). It will have to be seen whether the tougher line taken by the police, and the more restrictive guidelines for damages, coupled with the reforms of the complaints system, will limit the growth of civil actions. At present, however, they appear to many an attractive means of redress for police wrongdoing compared to the complaints system.

POLICE GOVERNANCE

Some of the most contentious issues of police accountability arise in relation to the quasi-legislative and executive functions of determining the priorities and efficiency of force policy. The Police Act 1964 consolidated and rationalized the governance structure for provincial policing which had developed in the previous century. The two London forces (the Met and the City of London) retained their own accountability structures (in the former to the home secretary alone, in the latter to the Common Council of the City of London as well as the home secretary). The 1964 Act defined the general duty of the police authority as being 'to secure the maintenance of an adequate and efficient police force for the area' (section 4.l). The precise relationship constitutionally and in practice between police authority, chief constable and Home Office has long been a complex and much-debated matter (G. Marshall 1965, 1978; Loveday 1983, 1984, 1985, 1991, 1996*a*; P. Waddington 1984*b*; Lustgarten 1986; Reiner 1991; Reiner and Spencer 1993; Jones, Newburn, and Smith 1994; Jones and Newburn 1998; W. Dixon 1999). Although the 1964 Act purported to clarify and rationalize the situation, it failed to do so. Its statements were self-contradictory or vague at the crucial points. The police authority were explicitly empowered to appoint the chief constable, to secure his retirement (subject to the home secretary's agreement) 'in the interests of efficiency', and to receive an annual report from him. They could also ask him to submit further reports on 'matters connected with the policing of the area' (Section 12.2). However, the chief constable could refuse to give such a report if she deemed it inappropriate, and the dispute was to be referred to the home secretary as arbiter. Nor was the 1964 Act clear about the possibility of the police authority being able to instruct the chief constable on general policy concerning law enforcement in the area (as distinct from the immediate, day-to-day direction and control of the force, which is clearly precluded). Again, in cases of conflict it was for the home secretary to arbitrate. But the Act's thrust was to limit responsibility for 'operational' matters to the chief constables (Jefferson and Grimshaw 1984*a*, chap. 2). Lustgarten (1986) elegantly but devastatingly exploded this hackneyed, untenable distinction between 'operational' and 'policy' matters. These categories necessarily overlap and are arbitrary and tendentious classifications, without a basis in the Act itself.

Altogether the Act, together with the organizational changes in policing already discussed (amalgamation, technological advance, professionalization, growth of the police lobby), strengthened the power of the chief constable and the Home Office at the expense of the local authority. The police authorities paid the piper (or more precisely shared policing costs with central government) but did not call any tunes. They determined the force's establishment and rank structure, and appointed the chief constable (both subject to Home Office approval). But the chief constable had sole responsibility for deployment of the force, as well as for appointments, promotion and discipline. The authority could dismiss the chief constable for good cause, but only subject to Home Office veto. In practice most police authorities did not even use the limited powers envisaged by the Act, deferring normally to the chief constable's 'professional' expertise (M. Brogden 1977; Regan 1983; R. Morgan and Swift 1987; Reiner 1991: chap. 11). This was even more the case with the joint boards that replaced the Metropolitan authorities abolished by the 1985 Local Government Act (Loveday 1987, 1991).

In the late 1970s there developed several initiatives from the Left campaigning for police authorities to exercise their dormant powers, as well as seeking an expansion of them. Jack Straw, then Labour MP for Blackburn, introduced an unsuccessful Private Member's Bill on police authorities in November 1979. It aimed to increase the influence of police authorities (to be democratically elected by the local community, removing the JP element) over general policy issues, as distinct from day-to-day operational decisions, which would remain the chief constable's prerogative.

Controversy was particularly acute over the Metropolitan Police, for whom the authority was the home secretary, so that Londoners lacked even the limited form of financial accountability available in the provinces. In March 1980 Jack Straw, then a vigorous campaigner for radical police reform, introduced another unsuccessful Bill, aimed at creating a Greater London police authority to control the Met. However, it was not until 1999 that the Greater London Authority Act ended the anomalous lack of a local police authority in London, with the establishment of the Metropolitan Police Authority (MPA).

After the sweeping Labour victories in the May 1981 local government elections, the GLC established a Police Committee with a strong support unit to monitor police policy. In the early 1980s several London boroughs, aided by GLC funds, established local 'monitoring groups'. Many provincial councils also moved into radical Labour hands in 1981, and there followed a series of much-publicized battles between the police authorities and chief constables, especially in Greater Manchester and Merseyside (Loveday 1985; McLaughlin 1994; W. Dixon 1999).

The 1984–5 miners' strike stimulated even sharper conflicts, with several Labour-dominated police authorities protesting at their lack of control over the manner of policing the strike or the extent to which the national operation produced a potentially disastrous depletion of resources for local policing needs (Fine and Millar 1985; McCabe *et al.* 1988; Green 1991). South Yorkshire Police Authority attempted to curb its chief constable's spending on the miners' dispute, but was stopped by a high court ruling. In September 1984, the police authority instructed the South Yorkshire chief constable to disband the mounted police unit, and most of the dog section. They justified this on financial grounds, although the Chief Constable (and most of the press) saw it as retaliation for the controversial use of horses in controlling pickets. The next day the home secretary warned the authority that it might be acting in contravention of the Police Act 1964, and the authority backed down on legal advice. Overall the miners' strike indicated that police authorities could be ignored if chief constables and the Home Office were in agreement.

Developments after the miners' strike continued this trajectory of centralization, reducing the role of local police authorities to virtual insignificance. PACE introduced a statutory requirement (s.106) that consultative arrangements be established in each force area. Whilst apparently enhancing local accountability, pressure was exerted by the Home Office for these to take the uniform shape of consultative committees, illustrating how the growing number of nominally advisory Home Office circulars have come to be effectively regarded as binding by most forces (J. Morgan 1987). Consultative committees also function as a key means of legitimating the consti-tutional *status quo* (R. Morgan 1989; N. Fyfe 1992; G. Hughes 1994). The Local Government Act 1985 abolished the six metropolitan councils, replacing their police authorities by more quiescent joint boards. It also enhanced the home secretary's control over financial resources in these forces (Loveday 1987, 1991).

The court of appeal judgment in *R* v. *Secretary of State for the Home Department ex.p. Northumbria Police Authority* [1988] 2 *Weekly Law Reports* 590, established that local police authorities had no power to challenge policy decisions by a chief constable if he secured Home Office support, even if this involved spending matters. Home Office Circular 40/1986 had stated that, if chief constables were not permitted by their police authorities to purchase CS gas or plastic bullets for training in riot control, they could obtain them from a central store if the HM Inspector of Constabulary felt it necessary. The Northumbria Police Authority sought a judicial review of this circular as outside the home secretary's powers under the 1964 Police Act, which placed primary responsibility for 'maintaining an adequate and efficient' police force on the authority (s. 4[1]). The court of appeal rejected the argument. It held that the home secretary had power under the royal prerogative to do what he felt necessary for preserving the queen's peace, irrespective of the Act. It also interpreted the home secretary's powers to supply common services under s.41 of the Police Act, and to use his powers so as to promote general police efficiency (s.28), as enabling him to over-ride the police authority's views on necessary expenditure and equipment. This seemed to underline the impotence of local police authorities vis-a-vis the other two legs of the tripartite system of police governance, making them a fig leaf of local influence in a highly centralized, *de facto* national structure (Reiner 1991: 25–8).

In the late 1980s and early 1990s a number of other developments continued this clear centralizing trend. Talk of a 'hidden agenda' of regionalization or even a national force was common among the police elite. Central government increasingly achieved effective control of policing, but by proxy rather than by the overt creation of a national force. Its instruments for this were Her Majesty's Inspectorate of Constabulary (HMIC), the Association of Chief Police Officers (ACPO), the Met, and the creation of specialist national policing units.

The cutting edge of the thrust to greater centralization was the government's tightening control of the police purse-strings. Concern about 'value for money' from policing, as from all public services (although rather less stringently), was a major theme of the Thatcher government throughout the 1980s. Home Office Circular 114 of 1983 signalled the government's intention to make additional police resources conditional on evidence that existing resources were being used as efficiently, effectively, and economically (the dreaded three Es) as possible. The even tougher Circular 106 of 1988 cast over police managers and staff associations a chill which has continued ever since. The alarm that permeated policing circles at all levels was indicated by the unprecedented joint study of the threat to 'traditional policing' which was sponsored in 1989 by all three staff associations (*Operational Policing Review* 1990).

The new financial regime was not only tighter but more centralized. The Audit Commission, the independent body established by the government to monitor local authority spending, became a key player in the policing field with a series of hardhitting reports aimed at enhancing value for money (Weatheritt 1993: 32–6). It argued itself that 'The balance has now tilted so far towards the centre that the role of the local police authorities in the tripartite structure has been significantly diminished. Accountability is blurred and financial and management incentives are out of step' (Audit Commission 1990a).

The role of HM Inspectorate of Constabulary was considerably enhanced after the mid-1980s, as the linchpin of a more centralized coordination of standards and procedures (Weatheritt 1993; Leishman, Cope, and Starie 1996; Savage and Charman 1996; R. Morgan and Newburn 1997: 146–7; Savage 1998). This process began in the early 1980s with the financial management initiative, and developed apace (Weatheritt 1993: 29–32). In 1987, the inspectorate launched a complex computer-based management information system, the Matrix of Police Indicators. This is used by HMICs in preparation for inspections. Since 1990 inspection reports on individual forces have been published. Inspections are evidently no longer the perfunctory affairs of police legend, but involve the collation of considerable data on a standardized basis, shaping police activity into centrally determined channels. In late 1989, a Home Office Treasury report was launched, aimed explicitly at enhancing the role of the HMIN as the vehicle of a more standardized system of resource allocation (Jordan 1991).

Until recently the inspectorate was something like a House of Lords for the police. It was a place to which distinguished former chief constables could aspire after completing long and worthy operational careers, or occasionally to which less successful ones could be kicked upstairs. The change in the role of the HMIC from dignified to effective has been accompanied by a change in the character of appointments to it. Appointments are now relatively young chief constables, in the prime of their careers, and with the prospect of advancement in terms of operational command still ahead of them. There are also specialist civilian HMIS.

The Home Office has also encouraged (ACPO) to develop a much higher profile and expand its role, as a means of enhancing the standardization and centralization of policing (Reiner 1991; Leishman, Cope, and Starie 1996; Savage and Charman 1996; McLaughlin and Murji 1996, 1997; Wall 1998; Loader and Mulcahy 2000). ACPO first made a significant impact on public debate about policing when it established and operated the National Reporting Centre as a means of coordinating the massive national mutual aid policing operation during the 1984–5 miners' strike. It was widely argued that ACPO was acting as a medium of government control of policing, or at least as a proxy for it.

Successive home secretaries have encouraged ACPO to become the pivotal body for harmonising policies between forces. To deliver this enhanced function the Home Office increased funding for the ACPO secretariat, which has become more professional and streamlined. It had until the 1960s been run entirely by serving chief officers, and until 1989 remained a shoestring operation managed by retired police officers. In October 1989 ACPO appointed a firm of management 'headhunters' to find a suitable candidate for the Home Office-funded post of general secretary, at a salary comparable with that of servicing chief officers, and responsible for a policy analysis unit. Although ACPO rules required the post to be offered first to the membership, in the event a civilian was appointed: Marcia Barton, former secretary of the official side of the Police Negotiating Board. ACPO is the linchpin of what has become a central 'policing policy network'. This encompasses also the home secretary and Home Office civil servants, HMIC, the Audit Commission, with some input, too, from the staff associations representing lower ranks (the Police Federation and Superintendents' Association), individual chief officers, and police authorities (Leishman, Cope, and Starie 1996: 18).

In addition to the growth in importance in recent years of HMIC and ACPO as coordinating bodies between the Home Office and individual chief constables, there has been a proliferation of specialist national policing units. The most significant have been the National Criminal Intelligence Service and National Crime Squad, established by Parts I and II of the Police Act 1997, growing out of a variety of specialist national and regional organizations that had proliferated in the previous decade. They are the core agencies in the development of intelligence-led and proactive policing throughout the country, and have strong links with international policing bodies.

One of the key sources of the impetus towards centralized units and the tighter national control of policing generally is the belief that it was an essential requirement of European integration after 1992 (M. Anderson and den Boer 1992; M. Anderson et al. 1995; Hebenton and Thomas 1995; den Boer 1999). More generally there has been concern about the growth of international crime leading to a perceived need for higher-level national (and indeed international) police bodies to cope with it

(M. Anderson, 1989; Dorn, Murji, and South 1991a, b; N. Walker 1993; M. Anderson and den Boer 1994; Sheptycki 1995, 1997, 1998a, b, 2000a; R. I. Mawby, 1999).

Concern about the quality of police leadership has been a major source of the impetus towards centralization in recent years. A parliamentary Home Affairs Committee (HAC) Report in 1989 attributed most of the shortcomings of police leadership to lack of adequate central control leading to a deficient career structure and uncoordinated training. It recommended a number of measures to enhance the extent of rational central control over the careers and training of senior officers, such as making successful completion of the senior command course at Bramshill a condition of promotion above assistant chief constable rank. This was a formal ratification of the *status quo*, in which the Home Office already exercised a considerable measure of control over who becomes a chief constable (Reiner 1991: chap. 5). The career patterns of chief constables clearly show them to be 'cosmopolitans' not 'locals'. The Police Federation's caustic portrayal of them as 'butterfly men' is not that far off the mark.

The Home Office already had the power to approve the shortlist of candidates interviewed by police authorities, as well as to veto the police authority's selection, according to the 1964 Police Act. Even in the period before the Second World War, the Home Office could exercise considerable influence over chief officer appointments (for vivid examples, see St Johnston 1978: 61–3; Wall 1998; Stallion and Wall 1999).

Greater centralization is not a new development but the accentuation of a process that goes back to the initial creation of policing on a uniform basis throughout the country, the 1856 County and Borough Police Act. Since then every major piece of legislation concerning the police has imposed greater uniformity on policing. Nor is this just a question of the overt level of formal organization of the police. Historical work, notably Jane Morgan's (1987) important study of the policing of industrial conflict and the labour movement in the first four decades of this century, shows that the Home Office were often closely involved in the day-to-day operations of policing disputes. The 1984–5 miners' strike was far from being a new departure. National labour disputes and other serious public disorders were a major impetus towards nationalisation of policing disputes in the twentieth century.

Routine crime has also been a stimulus to greater centralization, and to the more efficient coordination of the 'war against crime' that it is expected to provide. This was the rationale used by the 1962 Royal Commission Report to justify its advance towards greater control by the Home Office, although it balked at the overt national force advocated in Dr A. L. Goodhart's influential dissenting memorandum. However, what Dr Goodhart and others forecast in 1962 has come about. Rejecting a *de jure* national police force, we have ended up with the substance of one, but without the structure of accountability for it that the explicit proposals embodied. You cannot have accountability for something that is not supposed to be there.

The centralizing trend became more apparent still as a result of the profound restructuring of police governance in the 1990s. Originally announced by home secretary Kenneth Clarke in March 1993, and published by his successor, Michael

Howard, in June 1993 in the White Paper *Police Reform*, the reforms culminated in the Police and Magistrates' Courts Act 1994 (which received its Royal Assent in July after a conflict-ridden passage). The Police Act 1996 consolidated the Police Act 1964, the Police and Criminal Evidence Act 1984 Part IX, and the Police and Magistrates' Courts Act 1994 into the currently definitive statutory statement of the structure of police governance.

The most controversial changes were to the structure of police authorities. S.4 of the 1996 Act limits the normal size of police authorities to seventeen (although the home secretary has discretion to increase this under ss.2). This identical size, regardless of the area or population covered, itself signified a departure from the conception of police authorities as primarily representative local bodies. The specified functions of police authorities are subtly altered from the 1964 Act s.4 formulation, which was the 'maintenance of an adequate and efficient' force. S.6 of the 1996 Act changed this to 'efficient and effective'. The precise scope of this responsibility remains as gnomic as in the 1964 version, but the symbolism is obvious. The prime motif of the new-fangled police authorities is that they are to be 'businesslike' bodies—the local watch-dogs of the managerialist, value-for-money, private-enterprise ethos underpinning the whole reform package (Leishman, Loveday, and Savage 1996: chaps. 1, 3; McLaughlin and Murji 1996, 1997).

The democratically elected councillor component of police authorities was reduced from two-thirds to just over a half (nine out of the normal total of seventeen members, Police Act 1996 Schedule 2 s.1(1)(a)). Three members are magistrates (that is, just under one-sixth instead of one-third: s.1(1)(b)).

The remaining five members are appointed under an astonishingly complex and arcane procedure detailed in Schedule 3 of the 1996 Act. The rationale running through the fourteen sections and umpteen sub-sections of the mind-numbingly labyrynthine selection game seems to be to allow the home secretary as many bites at the cherry as possible, without simply letting him or her choose the members directly. The original version of the Bill did indeed do precisely that, but so overtly centralizing a measure drew the wrath of a number of former Conservative home secretaries in the House of Lords, and the Lords staged a revolt against this aspect of the legislation. Hence the smokescreen of the tortuous process in the final version of the Act. Under it, the home secretary appoints one of the three members of the selection panel, the police authority itself appoints another, and the two members thus selected appoint the third. They then nominate to the home secretary four times as many people as the number of vacancies on the authority, applying criteria specified by the home secretary. The home secretary shortlists half the nominees. If the selection panel nominate fewer people than twice the number of vacancies to be filled, the home secretary makes up the shortfall. This brief summary of the arrangements cannot do justice to their cumbersome complexity—but it does show how the home secretary remains the pivot of the process.

The chair of the police authority is chosen by the members themselves. This was another concession resulting from the House of Lords revolt against the clear

centralizing thrust of the original Bill: it was originally intended that the home secretary would appoint the chair directly. Overall the final version of the Act leaves
police authorities with a slight preponderance of elected members, but this is a figleaf
to hide the centralization that was nakedly apparent in the Bill as originally presented
to Parliament.

The intention was to make police authorities more 'businesslike', but the business
they should be doing is that of central government rather than the local electorate.
This is despite the fact that the new police authorities have more explicit functions
and powers than their 1964 Police Act predecessors. They have new duties to issue an
annual policing plan for their area (Police Act 1996 s.8) and local policing objectives
(s.7). The chief constable has the same general function of 'direction and control' of
the force as in the 1964 Act, but must now exercise it with regard to the local policing
plan and objectives that the authority draws up in liaison with her (s.10). This is an
empowerment of the police authority compared to the 1964 Act, but it has to act
primarily as a conduit for the home secretary's priorities. The home secretary decides
the codes of practice for police authorities (s.39), sets national objectives and performance targets which local plans must incorporate (s.37, s.38), determines the
central government grant to police forces which covers most of their expenditure
according to formulae which are at his discretion (s.46), and can direct police authorities about the minimum amount of their budgetary contribution (s.41) and any
other matters (s.40).

Overall it seems clear that the Police and Magistrates' Courts Act 'substantially shifts the balance of power away from local government towards central
government' (Leishman Cope, and Starie 1996: 21). None-the-less it was officially
represented by the Conservative government as doing precisely the opposite. This
claim was based on the relaxation of the detailed controls that used to exist on
precisely how chief officers spent their budgets. Chief constables are now free to
allocate their budgets in whatever way they feel is best suited to carry out the policing
plan (Savage 1998). The White Paper on *Police Reform* (Home Office 1993) anticipated explicitly that chief officers would pay attention to the advice of the Audit
Commission and HM Inspectorate of Constabulary. These bodies have been
encouraging devolution of decision-making to basic command units in forces on the
model of schemes like sector policing in the Met (B. Dixon and Stanko 1995; W.
Dixon 1999). It was assumed that the pursuit of nationally determined performance
targets would (paradoxically) drive chief officers to devolve a considerable measure of
responsibility to local commanders (Hough 1996: 66–8).

This new independence may prove somewhat illusory, when the changes in police
governance are considered in the context of the other elements of the government's
police reform package. The Sheehy Inquiry into Police Responsibilities and Rewards,
which reported (Sheehy 1993) in the same week of June 1993 as the Police Reform
White Paper was published, recommended that all police officers should be appointed
on short-term contracts and subject to performance related pay (PRP). The criteria
for successful performance, and the assessment of whether these have been satisfied,

would be governed by the home secretary via the new police authorities (which on the White Paper's original plan would be controlled by central government appointees).

This would have constituted a formidably centralized system of control over policing. Without abandoning the constabulary independence doctrine in any formal way, the home secretary would colour the use of discretion by constables by setting and assessing the criteria for performance that determine pay and job security. The police would no longer be accountable in the gentlemanly 'explanatory and cooperative' style that characterized the impact of the 1964 Police Act (G. Marshall 1978). Nor would they be subject to the 'subordinate and obedient' style of accountability to democratically elected local authorities which was demanded by the Act's radical critics (G. Marshall 1978). Instead they would be subject to a new market-style discipline which can be called 'calculative and contractual' (Reiner and Spencer 1993). In the fashionable terminology of new public management, the government would be 'steering' but not 'rowing' (Osborne and Gaebler 1992). While not concerned directly with the details of policing (as under the other modes of accountability it purported to be), central government could in practice penetrate the parts of policing that they could not reach hitherto, the day-to-day operation of discretion. It would be accomplished by attaching offers that could not be refused to the attainment of the targets specified in policing plans.

The clear centralization apparent in the original version of the reforms was not fully incorporated into the ensuing legislation (Loveday 1995, 1999). The Police and Magistrates' Courts Act reached the statute book in considerably modified form because of Peer pressure exercised mainly by Conservative former home secretaries. The toughest aspects of Sheehy's recommendations were defeated by a storm of opposition from police representative associations. The watered-down versions of these measures that has resulted leaves a lot open to detailed argument and development. As Newburn and Jones (1996: 125) show, 'the nexus of control is a complicated one, and how it works in practice will, like the previous arrangements, be heavily dependent on how the relevant parties choose to use their powers'.

The potentially centralising thrust of the Police and Magistrates' Courts Act is not apparent as yet. National policing plans have tended to be along 'motherhood and apple pie' lines, with key objectives that were unlikely to cause controversy with local police authorities and chief constables (T. Jones and Newburn 1997). There are likely to be all sorts of unintended consequences of the changes. The new independent members of police authorities, for example, may well confound the expectations of both advocates and opponents of the legislation. Given their local concerns about the quality of service delivery, they might well align themselves with elected police authority members and chief police officers against the central government, on such matters as the effect of tight centrally set budgets.

A 1998 House of Lords judgment underlined the significance of the home secretary's national policing plan and objectives in setting the framework for operational policing throughout the country (*Regina v. Chief Constable of Sussex Ex Parte International Trader's Ferry Limited*, available on the House of Lords website). It upheld the legality of a chief constable's decision (restricting the level of police protection for live animal exporters against protestors). The decision was based in part on the chief constable's statutory obligation to pursue the objectives set by government. 'The Chief Constable has operational command of the force. . . . But he is now also required to have regard to the objectives and targets set out in an annual plan issued by the Police Authority pursuant to section 8 [of the 1996 Police Act]. . . . In preparing the plan, the Authority will have regard to what it perceives to be the policing priorities of its area and also to any national objectives and performance targets set by the Home Secretary under sections 37 and 38. The 1995–6 police plan said that the police would concentrate their efforts on the prevention and detection of crime and answering and attending calls from the public. The Home Secretary had also determined certain "key objectives" which had to be included in the plan, such as increasing the number of detections for violent crime and targeting crimes which were a local problem such as drug-related criminality' (per Lord Hoffmann). At one level these objectives are the kind of 'motherhood and apple pie' ones that nobody could dispute. However, in the case in question they were held to override both the general police duty to keep the peace (which had to be reasonably balanced against other concerns, including budgetary limitations) and also EC Treaty obligations to protect the free movement of goods.

The traditional common-law doctrine of constabulary independence was given lip-service in the House of Lords judgment, and indeed in this case it was supporting the chief constable's decisions. However, there was also recognition of the way that the Police and Magistrates Courts Act 1994 and subsequent legislation obliged the chief constable to pursue objectives specified by central government. This leaves the doctrine of police operational independence an empty shell. The police are free to 'row' in any way they decide, so long as it is in the direction 'steered' by the home secretary.

Whatever the eventual impact of the reforms in practice, there has certainly been a profound transformation in the formal organization of police governance since 1994. Almost as much criticism was levelled at the style in which these changes have been carried out as their their substance. Unlike previous major changes in police accountability there was no preceding Royal Commission or major public deliberations. The reforms emanated from internal Home Office inquiries with minimal outside consultation. Although the measures were predicated on a clear, contentious conceptualisation of the police role as primarily 'catching criminals' (as Para. 2.2 of the White Paper Police Reform specified) there was no public debate about this narrowing of the traditional police mandate. In theory and practice this had hitherto been seen as encompassing a much broader spectrum of concerns, including crime prevention and management, order maintenance and peace-keeping, emergency and other services (Bayley 1994; R. Morgan and Newburn 1997; Chapter 4 above). The narrow emphasis on crime detection, pushed to the forefront by the government's White Paper, had hitherto been seen by most official enquiries (notably the Scarman Report of 1981) as a deformation of rank-and-file police culture. It was to be rebutted by management as much as possible, not actively promoted by policy and performance targets.

Arguably, attempts to relocalize control now are like pushing a stream uphill. As 'law and order' has become increasingly politicized it is ever more unlikely that governments would wish to relinquish ultimate control over policing. On the other hand, the complexly mediated mechanisms that ensure central government dominance also shield it from responsibility for mishaps. Why should any government relinquish a position which gives it power without responsibility? This is after all an ancient if rather unroyal prerogative. The myth of a tripartite structure of governance for essentially local policing, with constabulary independence for operational decisions, is useful for legitimating a system of *de facto* national control.

None-the-less, concern to give local communities effective control over policing remains a live issue. Given the proliferation of policing agencies and processes apart from the state police, discussed above in the Introduction, and Chapter 7, and embodied in the Crime and Disorder Act 1998, the issue has become even more complex. It has been argued, most authoritatively by the Patten Independent Commission on Policing for Northern Ireland, that instead of talking about accountability for 'police' we should talk of 'policing', hence its recommendations for a Policing Board (Patten 1999: chap. 6). The proliferation of policing institutions and processes beyond the conventional Home Office police clearly poses even more acute accountability problems, given how chimerical the pursuit of adequate police accountability has been in the past (Shearing 1996; Johnston 2000: chap. 10; Loader 2000).

NOTES

1. Both the police and their critics often tend to exaggerate the efficacy of technology. One nice example (*Police*, September 1984: 6) of its subjection to human limitations was the introduction in the Metropolitan Police of a computer that gave patrol officers the precise map reference for responding to incidents. The utility of this was rather reduced by the fact that the computer references were to the AA *Greater London Atlas*, while police stations and cars used the *Geographer's AZ*, which had incompatible references!

2. The reference is to the 1971 film in which Clint Eastwood as Detective Harry Callahan is faced with the choice of violating procedures or failing to apprehend a palpably dangerous psychopathic murderer.

7

CONCLUSION: FIN DE SIÈCLE BLUES: A HISTORY OF THE FUTURE

Policing is undergoing momentous change throughout the world, as the previous chapters have already indicated. A fundamental break with the past appears to be occurring globally. 'Future generations will look back on our era as a time when one system of policing ended and another took its place' (Bayley and Shearing 1996: 585). The dominance of the Peelian model of state police, established slowly and painfully in the nineteenth century, is being challenged by a growing diversification of policing provision (Braithwaite 2000). The police are increasingly cooperating and competing with a variety of other policing agencies and processes, within and between states (Sheptycki, 2000). Their functions are also becoming more diverse and complex. The police are increasingly acting as 'knowledge workers', brokering information to public and private organizations concerned with regulating sundry kinds of risk (Ericson and Haggerty 1997). This partially displaces the traditional function of order maintenance and law enforcement. At the same time the police face increasing demands for adequate accountability for the effectiveness and the legitimacy of the delivery of their traditional functions (Leishman, Loveday, and Savage 1996; McLaughlin and Murji 1996, 1997; B. Dixon and Smith 1998; W. Dixon 1999; Loveday 1999; G. Smith 2000). In particular they face continuing challenges about race and gender discrimination (Heidensohn, 1992, 1997; Walklate, 1996; J. Brown, Hazenberg, and Ormiston 1999; Macpherson 1999; Bowling 1999a).

NEW MILLENNIUM, NEW ORDER?

The transformation of policing itself reflects and reinforces wider shifts in social order, political economy, and culture. During the last quarter of the twentieth century profound social changes occurred, suggesting a fundamental break in the trajectory of world development analogous in its scope to the rise of industrial capitalism some two centuries earlier. Whether or not this constitutes a new kind of social order with its own novel dynamic has been debated extensively (Callinicos 1989; Giddens 1994; Bauman 1997, 1998; Castells 1996–8; P. Hirst and Thompson 1999; Sparks 1997; Panitch and Leys 1999; Held *et al.* 1999; Giddens and Hutton 2000). The proliferation of labels for the new conjuncture indicates the problems in characterizing the society that is emerging: postmodernity, late modernity, post-Fordism, turbo-capitalism, risk society, globalization, information age, and so on. All connote undeniable aspects of current developments, but with different conceptions of their drivers, directions, and desirability. What is clear, however, is that several interrelated changes—technological, cultural, social, political/economic—coalesced during the 1970s to forge what is arguably a new political and social configuration, with profound implications for crime, order, and policing.

Many (mainly conservative) commentators have invoked the long historical process usually seen as the growth of 'permissiveness' to explain rising crime, disorder, and problems for policing. For example, at the May 2000 Police Federation annual conference, the Conservative Party leader, William Hague, spoke of a growing wave of lawlessness attributable to a supposedly dominant culture of liberalism. It is claimed that during the twentieth century there occurred a kind of democratization, a spread to the masses, of the values of Enlightenment liberalism such as individual autonomy, self-realization, and scepticism about claims of authority. The effect of this is said to have become precipitous since the 1960s, commonly seen as a critical watershed (Dennis 1998). The criminogenic consequence has been an undermining of the informal social controls and internalized inhibitions that once held deviant impulses in check. While not sharing the conservative negative evaluation of these trends, many liberal and radical analysts would agree that there has been a long-term progress towards greater individual autonomy and 'desubordination' (Miliband 1978; Dahrendorf 1985). This view is commonly found also in popular discourse and media representations, although with varying evaluations of whether it is desirable or not (Reiner, Livingstone, and Allen 2000*a, b*).

The legal and policy changes that are often referred to as promoting 'permissiveness', however, represented a restructuring rather simple weakening of social control (Newburn 1992). Furthermore, some areas of deviance exhibit quite opposite trends to increasing liberalization. A clear example is drugs policy, which has toughened into a 'war on drugs' despite growing consumption of illegal drugs indicating wider popular acceptance (South 1997*b*). In any event, while liberalization offers the potential for crime to rise if pressures or temptations increase, by itself it is no more an explanation of rising crime than failing brakes are of a car's forward motion. Changes in informal control and attitudes to authority make sense of increasing crime rates only in a context where other factors generate social strains and opportunities conducive to offending.

The inexorable rise in recorded crime that began in the late 1950s was kick-started by a number of consequences of the development of a mass consumerist 'affluent society'. This had several implications for the growth of property crime, which constitutes the bulk of offending. Perhaps the most obvious effect was the creation and proliferation of attractive and vulnerable criminal targets in the shape of new, widely available consumer goods. The car and its equipment, the most common 'victim' of an offence, proliferated. Mass-produced consumer durables were not only tempting to steal but relatively anonymous and untraceable and hence easier to dispose of without fear of identification. The proliferation of such consumer goods also heightened a sense of relative deprivation among those who were excluded from the new more materialistic and acquisitive culture.

The increases in recorded crime levels were accelerated further after the mid-1970s by the consequences of the fundamental shift in the political economy represented by the return of free-market economics, and the deregulation of increasingly globalized markets. A clear consequence has been a rapid increase in inequality and extreme socio-economic polarization (Hutton 1995; Levitas 1998). The share of national income of the bottom half of the British population fell from one-third to one-quarter between 1979 and the early 1990s (Commission on Social Justice 1994: 29). The proportion of children under eighteen living in households with incomes below the official poverty line increased from 10 per cent to one-third in the same period. The gap between the lowest- and the highest-paid is greater than at any time since records began in 1886 (I. Taylor 1999: 15). This amounts to a reversal of the long process, of more than two centuries' duration, of gradually increasing incorporation of all sections of society into a common status of citizenship, albeit with considerable—but diminishing—inequalities (T. Marshall 1950; Bulmer and Rees 1996).

The consequences for crime and social cohesion are enormous. In many parts of the world 'lawlessness and crime have so destroyed the social fabric that the State itself has withdrawn' (S. Cohen 1997b: 234). While not threatened by such extremes of social meltdown, Britain and other industrial societies are experiencing profound shifts in the modalities of crime, order and policing.

As social exclusion, economic insecurity, and inequality grow, so the motives and opportunities for crime multiply, and the restraining effects of both formal and informal social controls are eroded. The consequences for crime and order of this social earthquake are profound and intertwined (E. Currie, 1998a, b; Davies 1998; Young 1999; I. Taylor 1999). Growing exclusion and immiseration—and the perceived hopelessness of its reversal by legitimate means—not only increases pressures to offend, but also undermines the informal social controls of family, education, work, and community, and encourages a neo-Social Darwinist culture of survival of the fittest. The delegitimation of public expenditure and collective provision by the ethos of the market weakens the state's capacity to provide either the 'soft' controls of welfare provision or effective public policing. Inequalities in access to security widen, as a burgeoning private market in policing develops (Shearing and Stenning 1983, 1987; South 1988, 1997a; Johnston 1992, 2000; Michael 1997, 1999; Button 1998a, b, 1999; T. Jones and Newburn 1998; Forst and Manning 1999).

During the 1980s, the heyday of free-market triumphalism, recorded crime rates rocketed. Although recorded crime rates fell during most of the 1990s, this was largely a recording phenomenon. The British Crime Surveys show that victimization rates continued to rise until 1997. The fall in reporting and recording of crime was a paradoxical consequence of the high levels of offending. On the one hand, victims were deterred from reporting because of concern about their insurance policies. On the other hand, the police were under pressure to reduce the proportion of crimes they recorded because of the new 'businesslike' policing-by-numbers regime introduced to enhance their crime-fighting efficiency.

The architect of the 1993–4 reform package intended to achieve 'businesslike' policing in Britain, Conservative Home Secretary Kenneth Clarke, claimed that they amounted to the most profound reorganization since Sir Robert Peel's original establishment of the Metropolitan Police in 1829. Granted some political licence for this hyperbole, there can be no doubt that the police have experienced themselves as in deep crisis in recent years. They are facing great upheavals, only partly as a result of government pressure. I shall attempt to analyse their predicament, and hazard a glance at the future. Although I shall concentrate on the British police, the underlying pressures to which they are subject are clearly global phenomena, found in other jurisdictions too.

POLICING IN PERMANENT CRISIS

One interpretation of the particularity of the crisis in British policing is indeed that the police are undergoing a normalization process. Whereas in certain respects they used to be very different from other police forces, either in Europe or in the rest of the common law world (Bayley 1985; R. I. Mawby 1991, 1999; Brodeur, 1995, 1998; Marenin, 1996), there is now something of a convergence in organization and style, indicated by, for example, the almost universal fashionability of community- and problem-oriented policing at least at the level of lip-service. Facing similar domestic crime problems, and indeed confronting a common problem of growing international crime, police forces are adapting in similar ways, and this is facilitated by a direct diffusion of ideas and innovations through conferences, exchanges, and increasing collaboration (M. Anderson 1989; Dorn, Murji and South 1991; McLaughlin 1992; M. Anderson and den Boer 1992; N. Walker 1993; Sheptycki 1995, 1997, 1998a, b, 2000a; Hebenton and Thomas 1995; Anderson et al. 1995; Tupman and Tupman 1999; den Boer, 1999).

The modern British police were established during the first half of the nineteenth century against widespread opposition across the social and political spectrum, as shown in the first two chapters of this book. In order to overcome this, the architects of the British police tradition (Peel and the first two Metropolitan commissioners, Rowan and Mayne), strove to construct a distinctive organizational style and image for the police. They emphasized the idea of the police as an essentially civilian body, minimally armed, relying primarily on the same legal powers to deal with crime as all citizens shared, strictly subject to the rule of law, insulated from governmental control, and drawn from a representative range of working-class backgrounds to facilitate popular identification. This conception was succinctly summarized by an official inquiry conducted by the police staff associations: 'traditional British policing is relatively low in numbers, low on power, and high on accountability; ... it is undertaken with public consent.' (*Operational Policing Review* 1990: 4).

This image of British policing did not develop because of some peculiar affinity of British culture with civic values, as conservative historians suggest. In colonial situations (including Ireland) British policing developed on an overtly militaristic model (M. Brogden 1987). The pacific image of the British bobby was a myth deliberately constructed in order to defuse the virulent opposition to the very idea of police in early nineteenth-century Britain. Police legitimation owed at least as much to the more general long-term social process of greater social integration and consensus over the century between the 1850s and the 1950s as to any actions of the police themselves.

The sources of the English police image of impersonal and nonpartisan legal authority, reliance on minimal force, and cultivation of a service role—now encapsulated in the shibboleth of 'policing by consent'—lie not in social consensus but in conflict. During the first century and a quarter of the 'new police' there occurred a successful process of legitimation and depoliticization. It was the product of the police tactical tradition instituted in the early nineteenth century, together with a wider process of pacification and incorporation of the working class into the political and social order of growing liberaldemocratic capitalism.

During the 1970s a process of renewed politicization was manifested in growing debate about police malpractice, and an apparent change of overall tactics to a more coercive, 'fire brigade' style. This was commonly interpreted, especially on the Left, as a calculated shift in strategy. Anxiety about changing police practices prompted developing civil libertarian concern about limiting police powers and rendering the police more accountable. On the other hand, throughout the 1970s the police lobbied with increasing vociferousness for more powers to deal with 'the fight against crime', and to resist 'political' control.

If the reasoning behind the post-1964 trends in police tactics is examined, however, it becomes less plausible to see them as a coherent and deliberate strategy. Many changes, notably the development of 'fire brigade' policing out of the Unit Beat reorganization, were the unintended consequence of reforms aimed at achieving quite different results. Others, such as the use of more coercive tactics in crowd control and crime-fighting, were largely reactive, ad hoc, and unimaginative responses to pressing problems.

Both police and popular culture embody views of policing and its purposes that are at odds with the reality of police work. They exaggerate the extent to which policing is concerned with serious criminal offences, and overestimate the capacity of the police to deal with criminality by detection and deterrence. In practice most demands for police interventions are calls for the resolution of a diffuse range of minor conflicts, disorders and disputes—a 'peace-keeping' function. The police's legal powers (especially the capacity to use legitimate force) are the reasons for calling the police in an emergency, rather than, say, a priest, psychiatrist, or marriage guidance counsellor. There is scope for discussion about whether 'peace-keeping' interventions are adequately and fairly handled, especially in the case of violent domestic disputes. Concentration on the police's crime fighting image has distracted attention from exploration of how the craft of 'peace-keeping' can be cultivated by training and supervision. On the crime side of police work, research shows the central role of the public (as victims and witnesses) in uncovering and clearing up offences. Only in a relatively small number of atypical (although prominent) major cases does detective work have any resemblance to popular images.

During the 1970s and early 1980s, debate about police powers and accountability unfortunately became polarized between a 'law and order' and a civil libertarian lobby, both of which ignored the weaknesses of the 'rational deterrent' model (more sanctions = less offending) as a means of policing either crime or the police. The relationship between formal police powers and the extent of either ordinary crime or police malpractice is tenuous and uncertain.

The politicization of policing in the 1970s and 1980s stimulated a series of reform strategies. As new scandals arose they in turn prompted further soul-searching among police leaders and new policy initiatives. A repetitive dialectic seems to play itself out cyclically, with a thesis of tough 'law and order' prompting its antithesis in a renewed stress on the need for public consent. The culmination is usually a synthesis based on varying tactics chosen from the coercion–consent spectrum according to intelligence about the requirements of particular situations (the 1981 Scarman Report and the ACPO Tactical Options Manual are examples).

CYCLES OF REFORM

SCARMANIA TO NEWMANIA

The 1981 Scarman Report on the Brixton disorders became the focal point for a multifaceted reorientation of police thinking, which dominated police reform debates throughout the 1980s. The message of Scarman was far from entirely new. Indeed, he explicitly drew on Sir Richard Mayne's 1829 instructions to the New Metropolitan Police in his discussion of the 'two principles of policing' (paras. 4.55–4.60). Scarman adopted Mayne's definition of the functions of the police being 'the prevention of crime . . . the protection of life and property, the preservation of public tranquillity'. The nub of Scarman's approach was that he emphasized the priority of maintaining public tranquillity over law enforcement. Law enforcement must sometimes be sacrificed in the interest of public tranquillity. Skilful and judicious discretion—'the art of suiting action to particular circumstances'—may be the better part of valour.

Guided by these principles, Lord Scarman made several criticisms of the police as both background to and immediate precipitants of the Brixton disorders. Overall, he judged, 'the history of relations between the police and the people of Brixton during recent years has been a tale of failure' (para. 4.43). While not condoning the disorders or all police practices, Lord Scarman outlined how the deprivations, frustrations, and racial tensions of innercity life ensure that the 'recipe for a clash with the police is therefore ready-mixed' (para. 2.37). This had been aggravated by 'unimaginative and inflexible' police tactics, such as stop-and-search sweeps which antagonized the many innocent people who fell victim to them. These operations culminated in the notorious 'Swamp '81' which was the immediate trigger for the riots, a classic illustration of law enforcement at the expense of the maintenance of public tranquillity.

Lord Scarman made numerous recommendations for improving policing so as to prevent reoccurrences of the disorders. They incorporated many of the features that had contributed to improving relations between American police and black people after the 1960s ghetto riots in Watts (Los Angeles), Detroit, and elsewhere (Sherman 1983). There were several suggestions aimed at improving the calibre of individual officers, and making them less prejudiced (paras. 5.6–5.32). There were also recommendations for organizational reform: tightening discipline in relation to racially prejudiced or discriminatory behaviour (paras. 5.41–5.42), increasing consultation (paras. 5.55–5.71), increasing accountability through lay station visitors (paras. 7.7–7.10), more independent investigation of serious complaints (paras. 711–7.29), and narrowing the scope of highly discretionary powers (paras. 7.2–7.6).

The Scarman Report attracted anger from the Left for his denial that racism was 'institutionalised within police practice or in British society as a whole', a striking contrast with the central conclusion of the 1999 Macpherson Report on the Stephen Lawrence case. Scarman explicitly defined 'institutional racism' as discrimination which occurs 'knowingly, as a matter of policy' (para. 2.22). Critics argued that there was plentiful evidence of the discriminatory impact of official policies (of the police and other institutions), albeit often unwitting. While this may be a widely accepted usage (I used it myself in Chapter 4), it was not Lord Scarman's definition. There was indeed no evidence of institutional police racism in Scarman's specified sense of deliberately adopted policy. In the broader meaning of institutional racism as the unintended consequence of organizational policies, Scarman's analysis of the disastrous impact of such strategies as stop and search was eloquent testimony to his awareness of the problem. But Scarman was concerned that there might be a closing of ranks against change if he attacked the 'integrity and impartiality of the senior direction of the force' (para. 4.62). His proposals were intended to deal with both widespread rank-and-file racial prejudice *and* the unwitting discriminatory impact of policies like stop and search.

Scarman was the trigger for a reorientation of police thinking on a wide front. Indeed, by the late 1980s his ideas had become the predominant conception of policing philosophy among chief constables (Reiner 1991: Chap. 6). Scarman's principles first had practical impact through their influence on Sir Kenneth Newman's strategy for policing London, which he developed after becoming Metropolitan commissioner in October 1982. This was the prototype of similar programmes around the country over the following decade.

Newman's strategy was intended to be a fundamental reorientation of policy and organization, aimed at achieving the same success in legitimation as Rowan and Mayne's original formulation, but in the face of new problems. This momentous historical role was explicitly avowed. Newman himself described the changes as 'the most sweeping in the Met.'s more-than-150 years history'—a claim repeated a decade later by Kenneth Clarke when he launched a diametrically opposite package of police reforms!

Newman placed great emphasis on the idea of a 'notional social contract', based on the traditional notion of preventive policing. The vehicles for this were primarily the stimulation of greater public involvement, and the 'multi-agency' approach to social control. Among the key devices for public involvement were Scarman-style consultative committees (with lay station visitors reporting back to them), 'neighbourhood watch' ventures, crime prevention panels, victim support schemes, greater use of the Special Constabulary (and attempts to recruit more blacks into it). The 'multi-agency' approach involved police collaboration with other agencies, 'social, economic, cultural and educational', to develop solutions that 'address the root causes rather than the symptoms of crime' (*Commissioner's Report* 1983: 8). Newman's 'notional contract' also aimed at changes in police organization and culture. The key targets were more professional 'management by objectives', and the co-option of all ranks and sections into the overall strategy. Consideration was also given to the problem that has bedevilled all police managerial innovations: how to incorporate the rank and file. A new 'code of ethics' was formulated, and attempts were made to spread the ideas through the force. A 'corporate management' style of involving the rank and file in the formulation of objectives and the targeting of areas for priority attention was aimed at.

The strategy was undermined by the increasing social polarization due to the social and economic policies of the Thatcher government. The worst enemies of the police bid for legitimation were not their overt critics but their apparent benefactor—a 'law and order' government that was unconcerned about destroying the social preconditions of consensus policing and the virtues of the British police tradition. The Thatcher government's social and economic policies generated rapidly increasing inequality, long-term unemployment and political polarization. The vaunted return to 'Victorian values' was above all a return to the spectre of the 'two nations' invoked by Disraeli, and of levels of crime, violence, and disorder unprecedented since the nineteenth century. The policies that achieved police legitimation in the days of Queen Victoria had succeeded only because of the wider processes incorporating the working class into the social and political order. The last two decades of the twentieth century witnessed an accelerating de-incorporation of more and more layers of society. The young 'never-employed', especially concentrated among ethnic minorities, are swelling the ranks of the 'police property' groups who have always been the hard core of opposition to policing. The implications of deepening social divisions for policing problems were widely recognized by chief constables and the rank-and-file police themselves (Reiner 1991; Chap. 9; Rose 1996; Chap. 6).

The late 1980s and early 1990s were vintage years for police scandals, starting with the release of the Guildford Four by the court of appeal in 1989. This was closely followed by a succession of similar scandals—the cases of the Birmingham Six, the Maguires, Judith Ward, Winston Silcott and the other men convicted for the murder of PC Blakelock during the 1986 Broadwater Farm riots, the troubles of the West Midlands Serious Crimes Squad, and numerous other revelations and allegations of malpractice.

The scandals were reflected in a precipitous decline in the police's poll ratings after 1989. The contrast was sharpest with the postwar period, often regarded as a 'Golden Age' for the police. A Mori poll for *Newsnight* in 1989 found that only 43 per cent today had 'a great deal of respect' for the police, compared with 83 per cent of a national sample asked the same question in 1959 for the Royal Commission on the Police. Fourteen per cent had 'little respect', compared to only 1 per cent on 1959. Before this recent fall in generalized approval ratings, surveys had for several years provided particular pointers to an erosion of support for the police (Hough 1989). Those who tend to be at the receiving end of police powers—the young, male, and economically marginal in the inner cities—have been shown as generally critical of the police in survey after survey. Perhaps even more significantly, a harbinger of the early 1990s collapse of general support was growing opinion-poll evidence of an increasing perception of specific police abuses (such as corruption, excessive force, or racial discrimination) even among the 'respectable' majority of the population.

The other source of the decline in public confidence was the police's apparent failure to deliver effectively the protection that their own propaganda had promised. Recorded crime rates increased inexorably after the mid-1950s, and from the mid-1970s entered a phase justifiably described as 'hyper-crisis' (Kinsey, Lea, and Young 1986). Public confidence in the police was undermined by this combination of apparent police ineffectiveness and revelations of malpractice.

Newman's successors, Sir Peter Imbert and Sir Paul Condon, continued to pursue a strategy aimed at securing the re-legitimation of the police in the face of the many factors that had eroded it, as did police chiefs around the country. In essentials their strategies were similar to Newman's, and certainly incorporated the Scarman spirit.

This coincided with the advent of 'new realism' in the Labour Party under Neil Kinnock, and subsequently Tony Blair's 'tough on crime, tough on the causes of crime' slogan which aimed to recapture 'law and order' as a political issue. In the 1990s police leaders faced much less radical opposition, as the Labour position became only subtly distinct from that of the police elite (Sheerman 1991). The decline in public confidence in the police also bottomed-out in the 1990s, and appears to have remained stable since the nadir of 1991 (Mirrlees-Black and Budd 1997; Yeo and Budd 2000).

CONSUMERISM

Instead of the old Labour concern to rein in police power through enhanced accountability, the central theme of New Labour strategy for policing was effective crime reduction. There were of course still differences from either Tory or police versions of crime prevention. Local authorities, not the police themselves, were to be the primary agency coordinating crime prevention strategy (Loveday 1996b, 1997). Social crime prevention received as much emphasis as situational, target-hardening measures. But the police received their due weight as essential partners in crime prevention initiatives, and beat policing was accorded paramount importance. More familiar radical concerns were reflected in concern about racism and sexism within the force. However, these were equally emphasized in the statements of Sir Paul Condon and other police leaders. Accountability was seen as a matter of restoring the tripartite system enshrined in the 1964 Police Act, redressing the centralizing tendencies of the Tory years. At the same time, the need for effective national agencies for new forms of organized and international crime was recognized. So was the necessity for national oversight of policing standards by a beefed-up HM Inspectorate of Constabulary.

The new language of managerialism was prominent in Labour thinking, as it was in Conservative and police pronouncements. However, the clearest theme of police reform talk in the early 1990s was the rhetoric of consumerism. Both Conservative government (Citizen's Charter) and Labour opposition (the Quality Commission) offered their rival versions. The police elite themselves rapidly latched on to this new language as a way of founding a new ethic of service to revive their flagging status, circumventing more political forms of accountability.

This was evident in the first major national response by the police to the perceived crisis of public confidence. In 1990 there appeared the *Operational Policing Review* the report of a wide-ranging study of policing problems launched by an unprecedented collaboration between the three staff associations, the Police Federation, the Superintendents' Association, and the Association of Chief Police Officers (ACPO). The police assessment of the implications of their own study was that the priorities of police and public were out of kilter. The public expressed a preference for a community-oriented, service style of policing rather than an enforcement-based approach. The ensuing 'Statement of Common Purpose and Values' enshrined a philosophy of policing in which the watchword was service. It was amplified by a 'Strategic Policy Document on Quality of Service' endorsed by the three staff associations. The public were regularly spoken of as the 'customers'—even if they were prisoners!—with the paramount concern being to satisfy their requirements through 'a service culture' (Woodcock 1991: 82; Waters 1996; Squires 1998).

The early 1990s service-based, consumerist rhetoric was infinitely preferable to the tough 'law and order' promises and practices of the previous two decades, which been the initial police reaction to spiralling crime and disorder. Nevertheless, it could not restore the police to their former high in popular esteem, its avowed aim.

'BUSINESSLIKE' CRIMINAL-CATCHING

None of this self-engineered change proved sufficient to satisfy the government. As discussed in the Chapter 6, in 1993 the home secretary, Kenneth Clarke, launched a restructuring of police organization and accountability intended to make policing more 'businesslike' according to standards set by central government and its local appointees. This approach was embodied in the 1993 Report of the Sheehy Inquiry into Police Responsibilities and rewards, the 1993 White Paper on *Police Reform*, and the Home Office *Review of Police Core and Ancillary Tasks*. The last had been set up in 1993 to examine whether any police activities could be contracted-out, although in the end its 1995 report was able to suggest only escorting wide loads on highways as a possible candidate for privatization. The entire package was premised on an official definition of the police task as 'catching criminals' (specified in the White Paper), which reversed the notion of the priority of preserving public tranquillity as advocated by British police tradition from Peel to Scarman. The reforms were clearly directed at imposing the disciplines of the marketplace on policing, and the police felt under attack as never before.

All three staff associations strongly condemned the government's plans. At the annual conference of the Police Federation in May 1993 the ritual roasting of the home secretary contrasted strikingly with the enthusiastic reception for Labour's Tony Blair (*Police Review*, 28 May 1993: 12–13). The political alignments over policing appeared to have turned full circle from the days when law and order was seen as a clear Tory issue, and the police were the pets of the Thatcher government (Downes and Morgan 1997).

The political space for the Conservative government's confrontation with the police was created by the erosion of public support discussed above. The police were widely perceived as guilty of systematic malpractice as well as falling down on the job, despite generous treatment in terms of pay and conditions compared to other public services throughout the 1980s. This perception was largely exaggerated: malpractice had certainly been prevalent in the past as well, though more readily covered up. Although police resources have increased they have been outstripped by the growing demands placed upon the police, in terms of rising crime rates, greater disorder, heavier traffic volumes, and more emergency calls of all kinds. Whether justified or not, however, there has clearly been a decline in public confidence in the police, even though it remains robust compared to that in many other public institutions.

The 1993 Conservative package failed to be implemented as intended, because it aroused a storm of opposition, not only from the police, local government associations, and civil liberties groups, but from many members of the House of Lords including several former Conservative Home Secretaries, who objected to the centralizing thrust of the proposals. This wide phalanx of opposition succeeded in forcing several concessions and changes so that the eventual Police and Magistrates Courts Act 1994 is a much diluted version of the original vision. None the less, it does amount to a fundamental shift in police governance, towards a more 'businesslike' ethos under greater central government control.

NEW LABOUR AND POLICING

The new Labour government elected in 1997 substantially continued the policies on policing that it inherited from the Conservatives. The new governance structure embodied in the Police and Magistrates Courts Act 1994 remains intact, as does the quest for demonstrable value-for-money, quasi-market performance measurement and sanctions, and the prioritization of crime reduction objectives. However, there have been some important departures that would not have occurred under the Conservatives. These include the establishment of the Macpherson Inquiry into the mishandled investigation of Stephen Lawrence's murder, the Human Rights Act 1998 (due to become operational in the autumn of 2000), and the commitment to reform of the complaints system (discussed in Chapter 6). Above all, Labour has launched a new approach to crime reduction overall, which, while not downplaying the role of the police, places it in a broader context of policing, in partnership with local government and other agencies.

THE MACPHERSON REPORT AND STEPHEN LAWRENCE

The publication in late February 1999 of the Macpherson Report on the murder of Stephen Lawrence stimulated a flood of agonizing and analysis in all sections of the media. After all the stories, plays, and interviews, there can be few people left who are not aware of the basic facts about the horrific, unprovoked murder on 22 April 1993 of the eighteen-year-old black student by a gang of young racists.

(i)   The perfunctory reaction of many police officers who attended the murder scene, initially suspicious of the dying Stephen and of his friend, Duwayne Brooks.

(ii) The botched police investigation, and the abortive private prosecution of three of the prime suspects, which meant that whatever evidence came to light later they would be scot-free.

(iii) The boxing of the leadership of the Metropolitan Police into an unprecedented corner in which they were compelled to issue abject apologies for their numerous sins of commission and omission in the case.

(iv) The inspiring struggle of Stephen's parents to get at the truth of their son's death, culminating in their pyrrhic victory in the report, which concluded that the multiple failings of the police investigation, and the police's insufficiently sensitive handling of relationships with the Lawrence family and Duwayne Brooks, owed much to 'institutional racism'.

The public in general seemed understandably shocked and appalled at the catalogue of brutality, violent racism, and police incompetence and callousness that the media coverage revealed.

Yet in the light of the bitter experience of discrimination and violence against black people in this country over the last half-century perhaps the most frightening thing is this. The Lawrence case is unique in the political and public anxiety it has aroused. Sadly, it is far from unique as an example of either violent racism or discriminatory policing. There were at least three racist murders within the previous two years in the borough where Stephen Lawrence was killed (Cathcart 1999). In his definitive book on the subject, Ben Bowling (1999a) shows that since the murder in 1959 of Kelso Cochrane there have been at least ninety murders of black or Asian people which appear to be racially motivated. Such murders are only the tiny tip of a huge mass of cases of racial violence, intimidation, and harassment directed at all ethnic minorities (Bowling 1999a). Yet this is only a part of a broader picture of 'hate crimes' directed at other vulnerable minorities. In London in April 1999, bombs exploded in Brixton and Brick Lane, areas with a high proportion of ethnic-minority residents, and in the Admiral Duncan pub in Soho, a gay meeting-place, resulting in three deaths and many injuries; in June 2000 a neo-Nazi sympathizer was convicted of all three bombings. Most such cases, including many of the murders, are never cleared up by the police. This is partly because they are disproportionately 'stranger' attacks, which are harder to investigate than the more common examples of violence in which people are assaulted or killed by their supposed nearest and dearest.

What set the Lawrence case apart was not the brutality of the event itself, which had all too many counterparts, nor the police incompetence and racism that the inquiry uncovered. It was unique above all because of the character of the Lawrences themselves. Stephen Lawrence himself was the ideal-typical pure victim, a person of impeccable character suffering an entirely unprovoked attack. Even given this, however, the clinching factor was the perceptiveness and dedication of Stephen's parents in campaigning relentlessly to achieve a measure of truth, if not justice, for their son.

The Macpherson Report, which established all this, has transformed the terms of political debate about black people and criminal justice, and is a comparable landmark to the Scarman Report. Until it, attention had focused on the disproportionate rate of stops, arrests, convictions, and imprisonment of black people. Whether this was interpreted as evidence of racial discrimination in criminal justice, or of disproportionate black criminality, the primary concern was about black people as suspects. What had not featured in public awareness and political debate was the disproportionate rate at which black people suffered as victims of crime. Both sides of this issue reflect the social and geographical exclusion of black people in a discriminatory society. As discussed in Chapter 4 above, the differential involvement of black people with the criminal justice system was a recent historical development. Until the early 1970s official crime rates clearly showed that black people were relatively infrequently arrested. The growth of officially recorded higher black crime rates coincided with the disproportionate impact on young black men of the increasing economic and social divisions that developed after the early 1970s. This fed the vicious circle of police–black mistrust that was manifested once more in the Lawrence case.

It has become usual to compare the 1999 Macpherson Report favourably with the 1981 Scarman Report, because it grasped the nettle of institutional racism that Scarman had denied. Macpherson is undoubtedly more hard-hitting as a critique of police failure. It succeeded in gaining official acceptance of the existence of institutionalized racism, defined as the 'collective failure of an institution to provide an appropriate or professional service to people because of their colour, culture or ethnic origin'. Paradoxically, however, it was Scarman, for all his misplaced emphasis on individual police racism, who had the keener grasp of how police discrimination is intimately bound up with wider structures of racial and social inequality and disadvantage.

With the 20:20 vision of twenty years' more experience of police discrimination in relation to race, it has become clear that the Scarman Report failed to achieve any significant transformation. This was not because of its own failings, however, but because of the lack of political commitment to achieve the transformation of black people's social and economic circumstances, as well as the reforms of police organization and policy that it called for. What must be hoped is that the widespread anger and sorrow produced by the Lawrence tragedy may ultimately be the stimulus for some real breakthrough in the vexed relationship between black people and the police and criminal justice system.

CRIME REDUCTION AND PARTNERSHIP POLICING

The main thrust of New Labour's criminal justice policy, embodied in the Crime and Disorder Act 1998 and the Crime Reduction Programme, has been a departure from traditional Conservative or Labour policies. As many critics have pointed out, the Act contains provisions (notably the Anti-Social Behaviour Orders) which are potentially oppressive for human rights and counter-productive (Ashworth *et al.* 1998). Its main strategy, none the less, is novel and cannot be dismissed as either simply punitive or liberal. It is based on an intelligence-led, problem-solving approach, with systematic analysis and reflexive monitoring built into policy development. Its intellectual basis is a thorough review of the evidence concerning the effectiveness, costs, and benefits of the main strategies for dealing with offending: preventing the development of criminality by early childhood intervention and education, situational and community crime prevention, policing, sentencing, and alternative penal techniques (Nuttall, Goldblatt, and Lewis 1998).

The 1998 Crime and Disorder Act (s.6) requires local authorities and the police in partnership to audit local crime and disorder problems, identify their sources, and develop appropriate strategies for reducing them, with regular research evaluations of effectiveness. This is part of the 'evidence-led' Crime Reduction Programme, based on 'joined-up thinking', the realization that crime must be dealt with by wider-ranging policies than criminal justice alone (Nuttall, Goldblatt, and Lewis 1998). In principle this is tough on the causes of crime, not just (as the Tories were) tough on the few lottery losers of the criminal justice system who are convicted. The broad approach to policing, stressing problem-solving in conjunction with other agencies, including local government, acknowledges the research demonstrating the limits of the police's capacity to tackle crime alone. This echoes the analysis of Scarman and those police chiefs who were influenced by him, such as Newman and Imbert, which had been displaced by the emphasis solely on 'catching criminals' emanating from the Clarke–Howard reform package of 1993.

The problem with the Crime Reduction Programme, however, lies in its place within the overall strategy of New Labour, many other aspects of which threaten its possible success. Most obviously, the commitment to keep within Conservative spending plans undermines the capacity of the police, probation, education, and other social services to perform as intended, while exacerbating the pressures leading young people into crime, such as school exclusions and truancy (Downes 1998: 196–7). More generally the criminogenic consequences of failure to bring unemployment down by the New Deal and through macro-economic policy would vastly outweigh any crime-reducing effects of the Home Office programme. New Labour's commitment to old Tory economic policy is its new hostage to fortune in crime control policy. On the other hand, the intelligence-led approach to policing and crime reduction seems to be proving vulnerable to populist attacks from the Conservatives, led by William Hague and Ann Widdecombe. In May 2000 they launched an attack on Labour as 'soft' on crime, which appears to have influenced public opinion to turn towards them.

THE LIMITS OF POLICE REFORM

What remains missing from all these reform strategies is a fundamental sociological analysis of the role of the police, and of the sources of their present plight. Common to all the solutions considered is an unquestioned assumption that falling public confidence has been caused by a decline in police standards, manifested in which is both less effective and more prone to abuses of power.

Certainly there have been many scandals revealing serious police malpractice. But do these indicate that the standard of integrity of the British police force has fallen? The extent of police abuse at any time is unascertainable, and for obvious reasons there is likely to be a substantial dark figure of hidden police deviance. What we do know is that in the 'Golden Age' of the mid-twentieth century, when the police were symbols of national pride, there was extensive and routinized wrongdoing behind the scenes. This is clear from police memoirs (for example, the very revealing vignettes of life in the Manchester police in the 1930s and 1940s found in Mark 1978) and from oral histories of policing (such as M. Brogden 1991 and Weinberger 1995). It is also evident in the serious miscarriages of justice in that period that are now established beyond reasonable doubt (such as the cases of Timothy Evans and Derek Bentley; see Woffinden 1989).

What prevented these abuses from being revealed at the time was the much more deferential culture of the social strata at the receiving end of policing, and of the media and the educated middle class. Complaints were less likely to be made (rather than sullenly put up with as yet another unpleasant fact of life), and they were far less likely to be given credence by opinion-formers if they were expressed. It is plausible that what appears to be a growing amount of police malpractice is largely just a greater likelihood of it coming to light, due to a much more deep-seated cultural change: the progressive erosion of deference in the postwar period that has been described as a process of 'desubordination' (Miliband 1978).

Even if some of the increase in police scandals really is a reflection of more abuses of power by the police, it is too simplistic to see it as due to a unilateral decline of standards of legalism in the police. Police tactics have always constituted an array of more or less coercive methods, graduated according to the perceived scale of trouble they have to deal with (which the controversial ACPO Tactical Options Manual makes explicit but did not conjure up *ab initio*). As crime and disorder have grown, so the police have moved up the scale of coerciveness in their strategy.

The increase in crime and disorder problems confronting the police in recent years has profound social causes. Among them are growing social and economic divisions and deprivation, which have swelled the numbers of those who in Victorian times would have been called the 'dangerous classes' and today are referred to as the 'under-class' (Crowther 2000*a*, *b*). They have always constituted the prime business of the police, and have been aptly labelled 'police property'. As their 'property' and problems have increased, so the police have moved higher up the scale of coerciveness in their menu of tactics. This is liable to generate more malpractice, which in turn it is liable to reinforce tendencies to cynicism and authoritarianism in police culture. But these are symptoms of the problem, not its prime mover. Consequently, solutions aimed primarily at changing the police will miss the mark.

At the heart of the well-intentioned solutions considered above there is a systematic failure to confront the question of what policing really is. The consumerist approach, in particular, implies that the police can and should be whatever market surveys reveal consumer preferences to be. But what is the 'service' that the police have historically been organized to deliver? What is the 'service' that clients effectively demand when they call for the police? Research suggests that it is handling disorder or crime, inher-ently contentious situations, even though the police typically seek to resolve conflicts without recourse to their legal powers of coercion. The police are the specialist reposi-tory domestically of the state's monopoly of legitimate force, and the 'service' they are predominantly called upon to provide is 'the capacity for decisive action' (Bittner 1974: 35). As the title of one episode of the TV series *The Bill* put it succinctly: 'Force is Part of the Service'.

The police are thus inherently a 'dirty work' occupation, in Everett Hughes's term (E. Hughes1961). It is only in the most exceptional circumstances, such as the consensus climate of postwar Britain, that the police can be regarded widely as anything other than a regrettable necessity. This has always been the status of the police in even the most pacific and law-abiding countries. For the most part, the fashionable languages of managerialism, community and consumerism overlook the fact that policing is not about the delivery of an uncontentious service like any other. Their business is the inevitably messy and intractable one of regulating social conflict. They cannot control, but rather are buffeted by, the prevailing social currents.

The end product of reform cannot realistically be the restoration of the previous status of the police as beloved symbols of national pride. The pedestal on which they stood in the middle of the twentieth century was based on unique circumstances, in particular the consensus climate of Britain during and after the Second World War. PC George Dixon was not the norm for the British police, but their finest hour. In a postmodern society they cannot function as sacred totems of a collective conscience that has become dispersed and diversified. They will have to become a demystified, mundane institution of governmentality, competing and co-operating with other policing forms.

The prospects for reversing this decline by either the new 'businesslike' approach or Labour's Crime Reduction Programme suffer from the same problems as their earlier 'magic bullet' counterparts. All these strategies rest upon a fundamental misconception of policing, which while common has for many years been called into question by research, some of it conducted by the Home Office itself. The premise underlying current initiatives is that, if properly organized, policing can have a significant impact on crime levels, deterring crime in the first place by uniformed patrol, and detecting criminals efficiently after the event if crimes do occur.

There is, however, a substantial body of research evidence, much of it emanating from the Home Office Research and Planning Unit, suggesting that policing resources and tactics have at best a tenuous relationship to levels of crime or the clear-up rate. Innovative strategies may have some impact in particular situations but probably not much effect on overall levels of crime. The police function more or less adequately as managers of crime and keepers of the peace, but they are not realistically a vehicle for reducing crime substantially. Crime is the product of deeper social forces, largely beyond the ambit of any policing tactics, and the clear-up rate is a function of crime levels and other aspects of workload rather than police efficiency.

POLICING POSTMODERNITY

Underlying the many specific causes of controversy over policing, such as malpractice, militarization, or apparently declining effectiveness, there are the deeper and more fundamental changes in contemporary society that were pointed to earlier in this chapter. The rise of a specific organization specializing in policing functions coincided with the development of modern nation-states, and was an aspect of the process by which they sought to gain centralized control over a particular territory. This was particularly true of Britain, where bureaucratic police organizations came into being comparatively late by European standards and coincided with the historical trajectory towards greater social integration after the initial impact of the Industrial Revolution (Rawlings 1999). In all societies the police's symbolic functions are at least as important as their direct instrumental effectiveness in dealing with crime and disorder (N. Walker 1996; Manning 1997).

The position of the police as an organization symbolizing national unity and order is threatened fundamentally by the advent of those social changes often labelled as 'postmodernity', above all increasing fragmentation and pluralism. Postmodern culture lacks any central, commonly accepted reference point or conception of the good life (Bauman 1987, 1997, 1998; D. Harvey 1989; Jameson 1992). Consumerism has become the driving force of action, the 'pleasure principle' displacing the Puritan asceticism and discipline that were the cultural foundation of modern industrialism. The social structure of postmodernity follows the same dynamic of fragmentation, disorganisation, pluralism, and de-centring (Giddens 1990). Economic changes have transformed the economic and social framework, dispersing the centralized Fordist production systems of modern times, and polarizing the class structure into what is often referred to as the 'two thirds, one-third society' (Hutton 1995).

While the majority participate, albeit very unevenly and insecurely, in unprecedented levels of consumption, a substantial and growing 'underclass' is permanently and hopelessly excluded (Dahrendorf 1985: chap. 3; Galbraith 1992; Davies 1998; Crowther 2000a, b). Certainly with the political dominance of free-market economic policies there is no prospect at all of their incorporation into the general social order. In other words, the 'police property' group is far larger than ever before, and more fundamentally alienated. This economic fragmentation interacts with the long and complex process of cultural diversification, declining deference, erosion of moral absolutes, and growing 'anomia' (Dahrendorf 1985: chap. 2) to create a more turbulent, disorderly social world.

In this context, the British conception of the police as a body with an omnibus mandate, symbolizing order and harmony, becomes increasingly anachronistic (Reiner 1992b). The British police are moving towards the international pattern of specialist national units for serious crime, terrorism, public order, large-scale fraud, and other national or international problems. Local policing of particular communities remains, but with sharp differences between 'service'-style organizations in stable suburban areas, and 'watchman' bodies with the rump duties of the present police, keeping the lid on underclass symbolic locations.

For those in society who can afford it, provision of security is increasingly privatized, often in the 'mass private property' where more and more middle-class leisure and work takes place (Shearing and Stenning 1983, 1987; South 1988, 1997a; Rawlings 1991; Johnston 1991, 1992, 2000; Shearing 1992, 1996; T. Jones and Newburn 1998; Forst and Manning 1999). Specialized human policing in any form, however, is becoming a smaller part of an array of impersonal control processes built into the environment, technological control and surveillance devices, and the guarding and self-policing activities of ordinary citizens (M. Davis 1990, 1998; Norris and Armstrong 1999). *The* police are becoming part of a more varied assortment of bodies with policing functions, and a more diffuse array of policing processes, within and between nation-states (Sheptycki 2000a). Police officers can no longer be totems symbolizing a cohesive social order which no longer exists. They have to perform specific pragmatic functions of crime management and emergency peace-keeping in an effective and just way, or forfeit popular and political support.

THE LIMITS OF POLICING

Police and policing cannot deliver on the great expectations now placed on them in terms of crime control, whether by Conservative 'law and order' or New Labour intelligence-led crime reduction policies. 'Nothing works' was far too bleak and demoralizing a conclusion to draw from evaluation studies of criminal justice and police practice, as was frequently done in the 1970s. There are enough well-researched examples of targeted policing and crime prevention innovations, for example, to suggest that these can have a significant, if modest, effect on crime and fear (Sherman 1992a; Pease 1997; Ekblom 1998; Hope 1998; Jordan 1998). However, the burden placed on them by the Crime Reduction Programme is excessive. The kind of reductions that have been experienced or are envisaged—while welcome, and cost-effective compared to either more crime or mass imprisonment—would go nowhere near reversing the increases of the last quarter-century. For example, Home Office research suggests that targeting higher-risk areas (about one-tenth of households) with Safer Cities-style burglary prevention programmes would reduce national burglary rates by 5.5 per cent, and if this was extended to half the country's households the reduction would be just under one-eighth (Ekblom 1998: 35). Extensive delivery of crime- and criminality-reduction programmes to the most vulnerable, while justifiable even in cost-benefit terms, would involve significant public expenditure. This would affect fiscal policies, and amount to a significant redistribution of resources to the poorer sections of society.

A substantial return to earlier levels of crime is simply not possible without major changes in the conditions that generated the rise in the first place. The 'realist' exploration of what works more immediately is worthwhile, but at best can have modest results unless it becomes a wedge for broader reforms. It may be that the 'social' is indeed dead (N. Rose 1996), and that a return to Keynesian-style economic policies aimed at stabilization and solidarity are no longer feasible, because of global-ization and changes in popular values. But there is a price to be paid: living with a high-crime society permanently.

David Garland (1996) has cogently argued that states have already adjusted their policies and rhetoric in recognition of the limits to their sovereignty in terms of crime control. There has been a bifurcation between two levels of crime-control policy and discourse. On the one hand, there is promulgation of detailed policies to implement best practice in crime prevention—what Garland calls the 'criminologies of everyday life'—as in Labour's Crime Reduction Programme. Such discourses are largely stripped of moral condemnation, but treat crime pragmatically, as an actuarial risk to be calculated and minimized (Feeley and Simon 1994). On the other hand, there are regular moral panics about especially horrific crimes (such as the murder of Jamie Bulger or the Dunblane massacre), which become occasions for orgies of punitiveness and anguished Jeremiads about moral decline. The explosions of punitiveness prompted by the relatively rare, spectacular, exceptionally fear-provoking crimes symbolically assuage popular anxiety and frustration, while the 'criminologies of everyday life' are geared to provide as much limited pragmatic protection as possible against more mundane offences.

THE LONG GOOD-BYE

However, a continuation of high rates of routine crime, and the variety of security and control measures adopted to contain or reduce them, offers a highly dystopian image of the future. We are already getting accustomed to everyday routines geared to crime prevention, with varying tactics and success depending on social location. In essence there is a vicious circle of interdependence between social divisions and exclusion, crime, and crime-control strategy. Growing social divisions fuel rising crime, which in turn generates control strategies that accentuate social exclusion. In a variety of inter-locking ways crime and reactions to crime both exacerbate the social divisions that generated them.

The clearest example is the social bifurcation that produces and is in turn reinforced by the flourishing market in private security, aptly described as a 'new feudalism' (Shearing and Stenning 1983; I. Taylor 1999, chap. 7). The more privileged sections of society increasingly protect themselves from the burgeoning 'dangerous classes' of the socially excluded by a variety of environmental, spatial, architectural, and technological segregation devices such as the increasingly ubiquitous CCTV cam-eras. Together with private policing, these provide the 'moats' seeking to secure the castles of consumerism. The wealthy flit between 'security bubbles' in 'cities of quartz' guarded not so much by police (public or private) as by more or less subtle physical and social barriers (M. Davis 1990, 1998: chap. 7; Bottoms and Wiles 1997: 349–54). Inequalities in exposure to crime and disorder are exacerbated as policing and security increasingly become strategies of border control between the dreadful enclosures of the excluded and the gated denizens of the wealthy, between and within different countries.

Unable or unwilling to tackle the sources of rising crime, states and citizens react punitively on the hapless minority of criminals they encounter or apprehend. Tough new sentencing policies on the 'three strikes and out' model have swelled the prison populations of the USA, Britain, and other countries which have increasingly followed this example, to unprecedented levels (Morgan 1997; J. Young 1999: chap. 5). This is despite little evidence that it cuts crime to any substantial extent (Moxon 1998) None the less current policies will result in further huge growth of the penal empire, if only as an expression of impotent rage at the losers in the criminal justice lottery. An apparent rise in vigilante activity is the citizen counterpart of the increase in official punitiveness, striking at those suspected offenders who are at hand, as an expression of impotence in the face of crime and insecurity (Johnston 1996; Abrahams 1998).

This image of a society polarized between a gilded but insecure elite and a threatening, temporarily subjugated mass haunted dystopian visions of the future at the end of the nineteenth century, as in H. G. Wells's *The Time Machine*. They returned with a vengeance in the last quarter of the twentieth century not because of some inevitable *fin de siècle* phobia, but because of the rapid reversal of the slow march of social inclusion (Hobsbawm 1995; J. Young 1999). The proliferation of *Blade Runner*-style imaginings of the revolt of the repressed (M. Davis 1998: chaps. 6, 7) testify to a scarcely subconscious anxiety that the burgeoning array of sophisticated surveillance and control measures cannot indefinitely hold the lid down on the expanding excluded classes.

It is hard to see how order of any kind can be maintained if we head towards the '20:80' society of two-fifths excluded from legitimate work projected by some analysts of globalization (H.-P. Martin and Schumann 1997: chap. 1). There are, of course, already many parts of the world where functioning states and civil society have weakened to the extent that a 'new barbarism' prevails (Hobsbawm 1994: 53). In such places the tenuous modern distinction between crime and politics ceases to be useful as 'low intensity warfare runs into high intensity crime' (S. Cohen 1997*b*: 243). Up to the beginning of the twenty-first century, the new 'mixed economy' of control (South 1997*a*) has prevented such 'degree zero' collapses of order in most advanced industrial societies (Reiner 1999). However, given the huge increases in crime and disorder that have already occurred as a result of our current two-thirds/one-third societies, it is hard to be optimistic about the consequences of even more precipitous inequality and exclusion.

Whether this will be the shape of law and order in the twenty-first century is anyone's guess. But the prospects can be summed up by a paraphrase of Rosa Luxemburg. The choice is between some form of social democracy and at best, the barbarism of high crime-rates, and a fortified society. What is clear is that the police cannot protect us from increasing insecurity, not even if they are transformed into a more diverse array of 'pick 'n' mix' policing services.

In Chapter 1 I began my account of the rise of modern policing with a quote from Raymond Chandler's *The Long Good-Bye* and I shall conclude with another. In that classic 1953 private eye novel, Philip Marlowe made some prescient remarks about the prospects for policing and crime control: 'Crime isn't a disease, it's a symptom. Cops are like a doctor that gives you aspirin for a brain tumour, except that the cop would rather cure it with a blackjack' (Chandler 1977: 599). Blackjacks (tough 'law and order' policing) and aspirin (community policing) can be only temporary palliatives without more fundamental social surgery.

APPENDIX: CHRONOLOGY OF POLICE HISTORY

THE STRUGGLE OVER POLICE ESTABLISHMENT
1750–1829

1785	Gordon Riots and Pitt's abortive Police Bill
1786	Dublin Police Act
1792	Middlesex Justices Act
Late 18th century	Fieldings, Colquhoun, *et al.*, and the 'Science of Police'
1800	Thames River Police Act
1814	Peel's Irish 'Peace Preservation' Police
1819	Peterloo Massacre
1822	Parliamentary Committee on Police
1829	Metropolitan Police Act

DIFFUSION AND LEGITIMATION OF PEEL'S POLICE 1829–1919

1833	Coldbath Fields disorder
1835	Municipal Corporations Act
1839	County Police Act
1839	City of London Police Act
1842	Detective Dept. at Scotland Yard
1856	County and Borough Police Act
1886	Local Government Act

PROFESSIONALIZATION AND CONSTABULARY INDEPENDENCE 1919–1969

1918–19	Police strikes; Desborough Committee; Police Act
1929	Royal Commission on Police Powers and Procedure
1930	*Fisher v. Oldham*

1934	Hendon Police College
1936	Public Order Act
1948	Oaksey Committee; Police College (now at Bramshill)
1959–62	Royal Commission on Police
1964	Police Act 1964
1965–	Unit Beat reorganization; Met Special Patrol Group
1968	*R v. Metropolitan Police Commissioner, ex.p. Blackburn*

POLITICIZATION OF POLICING 1969–1986

1969–	Scotland Yard corruption scandals
1972	Saltley Gate
1972	Sir Robert Mark's Dimbleby Lecture
1975–9	Police Federation 'law and order' campaign
1976	Police Act 1976
1977	Fisher Report on Confait case
1979–81	Royal Commission on Criminal Procedure
1981	Urban disorders; Scarman Report; election of radical Labour metropolitan authorities
1984	Police and Criminal Evidence Act (PACE)
1984–5	Miners' strike
1985	Urban disorders (Handsworth, Brixton, Broadwater Farm)
1985	Local Government Act
1986	Public Order Act

'BUSINESSLIKE' POLICING: POSTMODERNITY: PRIVATIZATION AND PLURALIZATION 1986–?

1983	Home Office Circular 1983/114
1987	HMI Matrix of Police Performance Indicators
1988	Home Office Circular 1986/106
1989–91	'Guildford 4', 'Maguire 7', 'Birmingham 6' appeals
1990	Operational Policing Review and Statement of Common Purposes and Values
1990	Audit Commission Report *Footing the Bill: Financing Provincial Police Forces*
1992	National Criminal Intelligence Service
1992	Maastricht Treaty, 'Europol'
1991–3	Royal Commission on Criminal Justice

1993	Group 4 wins contract for prisoner transportation
1993	Sheehy Report; *Police Reform* White Paper; Posen Inquiry into Core and Ancillary Tasks
1993	Stephen Lawrence murdered
1994	Police and Magistrates Courts Act
1994	Criminal Justice and Public Order Act
1996	Police Act
1997	Police Act
1998	Crime and Disorder Act
1999	Report of the Macpherson Inquiry into the murder of Stephen Lawrence

REFERENCES AND BIBLIOGRAPHY

ABRAHAMS, R. (1998). *Vigilant Citizens.* Cambridge: Polity Press.

ADAMS, C. (1995). *'Balance' in Pre-Trial Criminal Justice: Suspects' Experiences in the Nick under the Revised PACE Code of Practice C.* Ph.D. thesis. London School of Economics.

ADAMS, C. (2000). 'Suspect Data: Arresting Research', in R. King and E. Wincup (eds.), *Research on Crime and Justice.* Oxford: Oxford University Press.

ADLAM, R. (1981). 'The Police Personality', in D. Pope and N. Weiner (eds.), *Modern Policing,* London: Croom Helm.

ADLAM, R. (1987). 'The Special Course'. *Policing,* 3/3: 185–95.

ALBROW, M. (1970). *Bureaucracy.* London: Macmillan.

ALBROW, M. (1996). *The Global Age.* Cambridge: Polity Press.

ALDERSON, J. (1979). *Policing Freedom.* Plymouth: Macdonald & Evans.

ALDERSON, J. (1984a). *Law and Disorder.* London: Hamish Hamilton.

ALDERSON, J. (1984b). *Human Rights and the Police.* Strasbourg: Council of Europe.

ALDERSON, J. (1998). *Principled Policing.* Winchester: Waterside Press.

ALEX, N. (1969). *Black in Blue.* New York: Appleton, Century, Crofts.

ALEX, N. (1976). *New York Cops Talk Back.* New York: Wiley.

ALLEN, J., LIVINGSTONE, S., and Reiner, R. (1998). 'True Lies: Changing Images of Crime in British Postwar Cinema'. *European Journal of Communication,* 13/1: 53–75.

ANDERSON, D. M., and KILLINGRAY, D. (eds.) (1991). *Policing the Empire: Government, Authority and Control, 1830–1940.* Manchester: Manchester University Press.

ANDERSON, D. M., and KILLINGRAY, D. (eds.) (1992). *Policing and Decolonisation: Politics, Nationalism and the Police, 1917–65.* Manchester: Manchester University Press.

ANDERSON, M. (1989). *Policing the World.* Oxford, Oxford University Press.

ANDERSON, M., and DEN BOER, M. (eds.) (1992). *European Police Co-operation.* Edinburgh: University of Edinburgh: Department of Politics.

ANDERSON, M., and DEN BOER, M. (eds.) (1994). *Policing across National Boundaries.* London: Pinter.

ANDERSON, M., DEN BOER, M., CULLEN, P., WILLMORE, W., RAAB, C., and WALKER, N. (1995). *Policing the European Union: Theory, Law and Practice.* Oxford: Oxford University Press.

ANDERSON, R., BROWN, J., and CAMPBELL, E. (1993). *Aspects of Sex Discrimination Within the Police Service in England and Wales.* London: Home Office Police Research Group.

ANTUNES, G., and SCOTT, E. S. (1981). 'Calling the Cops'. *Journal of Criminal Justice,* 9/2.

ASCOLI, D. (1979). *The Queen's Peace.* London: Hamish Hamilton.

ASHWORTH, A. (1998). *The Criminal Process* (2nd edn). Oxford: Oxford University Press.

ASHWORTH, A., GARDNER, J., MORGAN, R., SMITH, A. T. H., von HIRSCH, A., and WASIK, M. (1998). 'Neighbouring on the

Oppressive: the Government's 'Anti-Social Behaviour Order' Proposals'. *Criminal Justice*, 16: 7–14.

AUDIT COMMISSION (1990*a*). *Footing the Bill: Financing Provincial Police Forces.* London: HMSO.

AUDIT COMMISSION (1990*b*). *Effective Policing: Performance Review in Police Forces.* London: HMSO.

AUDIT COMMISSION (1993). *Helping with Enquiries: Tackling Crime Effectively.* London: HMSO.

AUDIT COMMISSION (1996). *Streetwise: Effective Police Patrol.* London: HMSO.

BACKMAN, J. (2000). 'The Hyperbola of Russian Crime and Police Culture', in A. Ledeneva and M. Kurkchiyan (eds.), *Economic Crime in Russia.* Deventer, Netherlands: Wolter Kluwer.

BAILEY, V. (1981*a*). *Policing and Punishment in the 19th Century.* London: Croom Helm.

BAILEY, V. (1981*b*). 'The Metropolitan Police, the Home Office and the Threat of Outcast London', in V. Bailey, *Policing and Punishment in the 19th Century.* London: Croom Helm.

BALDWIN, J., and McCONVILLE, M. (1977). *Negotiated Justice.* Oxford: Martin Robertson.

BALDWIN, J., and McCONVILLE, M. (1979). *Jury Trials.* Oxford: Oxford University Press.

BALDWIN, R. (1987). 'Why Accountability?'. *British Journal of Criminology*, 27/1: 97–105. (Reprinted in Reiner 1996*a*, ii.)

BALDWIN, R. (1989). 'Regulation and Policing by Code', in M. Weatheritt (ed.), *Police Research: Some Future Prospects.* Aldershot: Avebury.

BALDWIN, R., and KINSEY, R. (1982). *Police Powers and Politics.* London: Quartet Books.

BALL, J., CHESTER, L., and PERROTT, R. (1979). *Cops and Robbers.* Harmondsworth: Penguin Books.

BANTON, M. (1964). *The Policeman in the Community.* London: Tavistock.

BANTON, M. (1973). *Police—Community Relations.* London: Collins.

BANTON, M. (1983). 'Categorical and Statistical Discrimination'. *Ethnic and Racial Studies*, 6/3 (July).

BAUMAN, Z. (1987). *Legislators and Interpreters.* Cambridge: Polity Press.

BAUMAN, Z. (1997). *Postmodernity and Its Discontents.* Cambridge: Polity Press.

BAUMAN, Z. (1998). *Globalisation: The Human Consequences.* Cambridge: Polity Press.

BAXTER, J., and KOFFMAN, L. (1983). 'The Confait Inheritance-Forgotten Lessons?'. *Cambrian Law Review*, 14.

BAXTER, J., and KOFFMAN, L. (eds.) (1985). *Police: The Constitution and the Community.* Abingdon: Professional Books.

BAYLEY, D. (1983). 'Accountability and Control of Police: Some Lessons for Britain', in T. Bennett (ed.), *The Future of Policing.* Cambridge: Institute of Criminology. Cropwood Papers 15. (Reprinted in Reiner 1996*a*, ii.)

BAYLEY, D. (1985). *Patterns of Policing.* New Brunswick, NJ: Rutgers University Press.

BAYLEY, D. (1991). *Forces of Order: Police Behavior in Japan and the United States* (2nd edn). Berkeley, CA: University of California Press.

BAYLEY, D. (1992). 'Comparative Organization of the Police in English-Speaking Countries', in M. Tonry and N. Morris (eds.), *Modern Policing.* Chicago: Chicago University Press.

BAYLEY, D. (1994). *Police For the Future.* New York: Oxford University Press.

BAYLEY, D. (1996). 'What Do the Police

Do?', in W. Saulsbury, J. Mott, and T. Newburn (eds.), *Themes in Contemporary Policing*. London: Policy Studies Institute/Police Foundation.

BAYLEY, D. (ed.) (1998). *What Works in Policing?*. New York: Oxford University Press.

BAYLEY, D., and BITTNER, E. (1984). 'Learning the Skills of Policing'. *Law and Contemporary Problems*, 47: 35–60. (Reprinted in Reiner 1996*a*, ii.)

BAYLEY, D., and MENDELSOHN, H. (1968). *Minorities and the Police*. New York: Free Press.

BAYLEY, D., and SHEARING, C. (1996). 'The Future of Policing'. *Law and Society Review*, 30/3: 586–606.

BEAN, P., and NEMITZ, T. (1994). *Out of Depth and Out of Sight: Implementation of the Appropriate Adult Scheme*. Loughborough: Midlands Centre for Criminology, University of Loughborough. Final report for Mencap.

BECCARIA, C. (1963). *Of Crimes and Punishments* [first published as *Dei delitti e delle pene*, 1764]. Indiana: Bobbs-Merrill.

BECKER, H. (1963). *Outsiders*. New York: Free Press.

BECKER, H. (1967). 'Whose Side Are We On?'. *Social Problems*, 14/3: 239–47.

BEETHAM, D. (1991). *The Legitimation of Power*. London: Macmillan.

BENNETT, T. (1979). 'The Social Distribution of Criminal Labels'. *British Journal of Criminology*, 19: 134–45.

BENNETT, T. (ed.) (1983). *The Future of Policing*. Cambridge: Institute of Criminology. Cropwood Papers 15.

BENNETT, T. (1989). 'The Neighbourhood Watch Experiment', in R. Morgan and D. Smith (eds.), *Coming to Terms with Policing*. London: Routledge.

BENNETT, T. (1990). *Evaluating Neighbourhood Watch*. Aldershot: Gower.

BENNETT, T. (1991). 'The Effectiveness of a Police-initiated Fear-Reducing Strategy'. *British Journal of Criminology*, 31/1: 1–14.

BENNETT, T. (1994*a*). 'Recent Developments in Community Policing', in S. Becker and M. Stephens (eds.), *Police Force, Police Service*. London: Macmillan.

BENNETT, T. (1994*b*). 'Community Policing on the Ground: Developments in Britain', in D. P. Rosenbaum (ed.), *The Challenge of Community Policing: Testing the Premises*. Thousand Oaks, CA: Sage.

BENNETT, T. (1996). 'What's New in Evaluation Research?'. *British Journal of Criminology*, 36/4: 567–73.

BENNETT, T., and LUPTON, T. (1992*a*). 'A National Activity Survey of Police Work'. *Howard Journal of Criminal Justice*, 31/3: 200–23.

BENNETT, T., and LUPTON, R. (1992*b*). 'A Survey of the Use and Allocation of Community Constables in England and Wales'. *British Journal of Criminology*, 32/2: 167–82.

BENSTOCK, B. (ed.) (1983). *Essays on Detective Fiction*. London: Macmillan.

BENT, A. (1974). *The Politics of Law Enforcement*. Lexington, MA: D. C. Heath.

BENYON, J. (ed.) (1984). *Scarman and After*. Oxford: Pergamon.

BENYON, J., and BOURNE, C. (eds.) (1986). *The Police: Powers, Procedures and Proprieties*. Oxford: Pergamon.

BERNSTEIN, S., BIGELOW, B., COOPER, L., CURRIE, E., FRAPPIER, J., HARRING, S., KLARE, M., POYNER, P., RAY, G., SCHAUFFLER, R., SCRUGGS, J., STEIN, N., THAYER, M., and TRUJILLO, L. (1982). *The Iron Fist and the Velvet Glove: An Analysis of the US Police* (3rd edn). Berkeley, CA: Centre for Research on Criminal Justice.

BEVAN, V. T., and LIDSTONE, K. (1991). *The Investigation of Crime: A Guide To Police Powers*. London: Butterworth.

BILLINGSLEY, R., NEMITZ, T., and BEAN, P. (eds.) (2000). *Informers: Policing, Policy, Practice*. Cullompton, Devon: Willan.

BINDER, A., and SCHARF, P. (1982). 'Deadly Force in Law Enforcement'. *Crime and Delinquency*, 28.

BITTNER, E. (1967). 'The Police on Skid Row: A Study in Peacekeeping'. *American Sociological Review*, 32.

BITTNER, E. (1970). *The Functions of the Police in Modern Society*. Chevy Chase, MD: National Institute of Mental Health.

BITTNER, E. (1974). 'Florence Nightingale in Pursuit of Willie Sutton: A Theory of the Police', in H. Jacob (ed.), *The Potential for Reform of Criminal Justice*. Beverly Hills, CA: Sage.

BITTNER, E. (1983). 'Legality and Workmanship', in M. Punch (ed.), *Control in the Police Organization*. Cambridge, MA: MIT Press.

BLACK, D. (1970). 'Production of Crime Rates'. *American Sociological Review*, 35: 733–48. (Reprinted in Reiner 1996*a*, i.)

BLACK, D. (1971). 'The Social Organization of Arrest'. *Stanford Law Review*, 23: 1087–1111.

BLACK, D., and Reiss, A. J., Jr. (1970). 'Police Control of Juveniles'. *American Sociological Review*, 35: 63–77.

BLAIR, I. (1985). *Investigating Rape: A New Approach for Police*. London: Croom Helm.

BLOCH, P., and ANDERSON, D. (1974). *Policewomen on Patrol*. Washington, DC: Police Foundation.

BLOM-COOPER, L., and DRABBLE, R. (1982). 'Police Perception of Crime'. *British Journal of Criminology*, 22/1 (April): 184–7.

BOGOLMONY, R. (1976). 'Street Patrol: The Decision to Stop a Citizen'. *Criminal Law Bulletin*, 12/5.

BOOSTROM, R., and HENDERSON, J. (1983). 'Community Action and Crime Prevention'. *Crime and Social Justice*, 19 (summer).

BOTTOMLEY, A. K. (1973). *Decisions in the Penal Process*. Oxford: Martin Robertson.

BOTTOMLEY, A. K., and COLEMAN, C. (1981). *Understanding Crime Rates*. Farnborough: Gower.

BOTTOMS, A. E. (1990). 'Crime Prevention Facing the 1990s'. *Policing and Society*, 1/1: 3–22. (Reprinted in Reiner 1996*a*, i.)

BOTTOMS, A. E., and STEVENSON, S. (1990). 'The Politics of the Police 1958–1970', in R. Morgan (ed.), *Policing, Organised Crime and Crime Prevention*. Bristol: Bristol University, Centre for Criminal Justice. British Criminology Conference Papers 4.

BOTTOMS, A. E., and WILES, P. (1996). 'Crime and Policing in a Changing Social Context', in W. Saulsbury, J. Mott, and T. Newburn (eds.), *Themes in Contemporary Policing*. London: Policy Studies Institute/Police Foundation.

BOTTOMS, A. E., and WILES, P. (1997). 'Environmental Criminology', in M. Maguire, R. Morgan, and R. Reiner (eds.), *Oxford Handbook of Criminology* (2nd edn). Oxford: Oxford University Press.

BOWDEN, T. (1978). *Beyond the Limits of the Law*. Harmondsworth: Penguin Books.

BOWLING, B. (1996). 'Zero Tolerance: Cracking Down on Crime in New York City'. *Criminal Justice Matters*, 25.

BOWLING, B. (1999*a*). *Violent Racism*. Oxford: Oxford University Press.

BOWLING, B. (1999*b*). 'Arresting the Abuse of Police Power: Stop and Search in 'Post-Lawrence' London'. *Diversity-onLine*, www.diversity-onLine.org

BOWLING, B. (1999*c*). 'The Rise and Fall of New York Murder'. *British Journal of Criminology*, 39/4: 531–54.

BOWLING, B., and PHILLIPS, C. (2000*a*). *Racism, Crime and Justice*. London: Pearson Longman.

BOWLING, B., and PHILLIPS, C. (2000*b*). 'Racist Victimisation in England and Wales', in D. Hawkins (ed.), *The Nexus of Race, Class and Ethnicity*. Cambridge: Cambridge University Press.

BOX, S. (1983). *Power, Crime and Mystification*. London: Tavistock.

BOX, S. (1987). *Recession, Crime and Unemployment*. London: Macmillan.

BOX, S., and RUSSELL, K. (1975). 'The Politics of Discreditability'. *Sociological Review*, 23/2: 315–46. (Reprinted in Reiner 1996*a*, ii.)

BOYDSTUN, J. E. (1975). *San Diego Field Interrogation Study: Final Report*. Washington, DC: Police Foundation.

BRADLEY, D., WALKER, N., and WILKIE, R. (1986). *Managing the Police*. Brighton: Wheatsheaf.

BRAITHWAITE, J. (2000). 'The New Regulatory State and the Transformation of Criminology'. *British Journal of Criminology*, 40/2: 222–39.

BREWER, J., and STYLES, J. (eds.) (1980). *An Ungovernable People*. London: Hutchinson.

BREWER, J. D. (1991). 'Policing in Divided Societies'. *Policing and Society*, 1/3: 179–91.

BREWER, J. D., GUELKE, A., HUME, I., MOXON-BROWNE, E., and WILFORD, R. (1996). *The Police, Public Order and the State* (2nd edn). London: Macmillan.

BREWER, J. D., and MAGEE, K. (1990). *Inside the RUC*. Oxford: Oxford University Press.

BRIDGES, L. (1983a). 'Policing the Urban Wasteland'. *Race and Class*, autumn.

BRIDGES, L. (1983*b*). 'Extended Views: The British Left and Law and Order'. *Sage Race Relations Abstracts*, February.

BRODERICK, J. (1973). *Police in a Time of Change*. Morristown, NJ: General Learning.

BRODEUR, J.-P. (1983). 'High Policing and Low Policing: Remarks about the Policing of Political Activities'. *Social Problems*, 30/5 (June): 507–20. (Reprinted in Reiner 1996*a*, ii.)

BRODEUR, J.-P. (ed.) (1995). *Comparisons in Policing: An International Perspective*. Aldershot: Avebury.

BRODEUR, J.-P. (ed.) (1998). *How to Recognize Good Policing*. Thousand Oaks, CA: Sage.

BROGDEN, A. (1981). 'Sus is dead, but what about Sas?'. *New Community*, 9/1 (spring/summer).

BROGDEN, M. (1977). 'A Police Authority—The Denial of Conflict'. *Sociological Review*, 25/2: 325–49.

BROGDEN, M. (1981). 'All Police is Conning Bastards', in B. Fine, A. Hunt, D. McBarnet, and B. Moorhouse (eds.), *Law, State and Society*. London: Croom Helm.

BROGDEN, M. (1982). *The Police: Autonomy and Consent*. London and New York: Academic Press.

BROGDEN, M. (1983). 'The Myth of Policing by Consent', *Police Review*, 22 April: 760–1.

BROGDEN, M. (1987). 'The Emergence of the Police: The Colonial Dimension'. *British Journal of Criminology*, 27/1: 4–14. (Reprinted in Reiner 1996*a*, ii.)

BROGDEN, M. (1991). *On the Mersey Beat: An Oral History of Policing Liverpool Between the Wars*. Oxford: Oxford University Press.

BROGDEN, M. (1999). 'Community Policing as Cherry Pie', in R. Mawby (ed.), *Policing across the World*. London: UCL Press.

BROGDEN, M., and BROGDEN, A. (1983). 'From Henry VIII to Liverpool 8: The Complex Unity of Police Street Powers'. *International Journal of the Sociology of Law*, 12/1: 37–58. (Reprinted in Reiner 1996*a*, ii.)

BROGDEN, M., and GRAHAM, D. (1988). 'Police Education: The Hidden Curriculum', in R. Fieldhouse (ed.), *The Political Education of Servants of the State*. Manchester: Manchester University Press.

BROGDEN, M., JEFFERSON, T., and WALKLATE, S. (1988). *Introducing Policework*. London: Unwin.

BROGDEN, M., and SHEARING, C. (1993). *Policing for a New South Africa*. London: Routledge.

BROWN, D. (1987). *The Police Complaints Procedure: A Survey of Complainants' Views*. London: HMSO.

BROWN, D. (1989). *Detention at the Police Station under the Police and Criminal Evidence Act 1984*. London: HMSO.

BROWN, D. (1991). *Investigating Burglary: The Effect of PACE*. London: HMSO. Home Office Research Study 123.

BROWN, D. (1997). PACE Ten Years On: A Review of the Research. London: Home Office. Home Office Research Study 155.

BROWN, D., and ELLIS, T. (1994). *Policing Low-level Disorder: Police Use of Section 5 of the Public Order Act 1986*. London: PACE. Home Office Research Study 135.

BROWN, D., ELLIS, T., and LARCOMBE, K. (1992). *Changing the Code: Police Detention under the Revised PACE Codes of Practice*. London: HMSO.

BROWN, D., and ILES, S. (1985). *Community Constables: A Study of a Policing Initiative*. London: Home Office. Research and Planning Unit Paper 30.

BROWN, J. (1996). 'Police Research: Some Critical Issues', in F. Leishman, B. Loveday, and S. Savage (eds.), *Core Issues in Policing*. London: Longman.

BROWN, J. (1997). 'Equal Opportunities and the Police in England and Wales: Past, Present and Future Opportunities', in P. Francis, P. Davies, and V. Jupp (eds.), *Policing Futures*. London: Macmillan.

BROWN, J., HAZENBERG, A., and ORMISTON, C. (1999). 'Policewomen: An International Comparison', in R. Mawby (ed.) *Policing Across the World*. London: UCL Press.

BROWN, J., MAIDMENT, A., and BULL, R. (1993). 'Appropriate Skill–Task Matching or Gender Bias in Deployment of Male and Female Police Officers'. *Policing and Society*, 3/1: 121–36.

BROWN, J., and WATERS, I. (1993). 'Professional Police Research'. *Policing*, 9/3: 323–34.

BROWN, L. and WILLIS, A. (1985). 'Authoritarianism in British Police Recruits: Importation, Socialisation or Myth?'. *Journal of Occupational Psychology*, 58/1: 97–108.

BROWN, M. (1981). *Working the Street*. New York: Russell Sage.

BRYANT, L., DUNKERLEY, D., and KELLAND, G. (1985). 'One of the Boys'. *Policing*, 1/4: 236–44.

BUCKE, T. (1996). *Policing and the Police: Findings from the 1994 British Crime Survey*. London: Home Office. Research Findings 28.

BUCKE, T. (1997). *Ethnicity and Contacts With the Police: Latest Findings from the British Crime Survey*. London: Home Office Research, Development and Statistics Directorate. Research Findings 59.

BUCKE, T., and BROWN, D. (1997). *In Police Custody: Police Powers and Suspects' Rights under the Revised PACE Codes of Practice*. London: Home Office. Home Office Research Study 174.

BUCKE, T., and JAMES, Z. (1998). *Trespass and Protest: Policing under the Criminal Justice and Public Order Act 1994*. London: Home Office. Home Office Research Study 190.

BUCKE, T., STREET, R., and BROWN, D. (2000). *The Right of Silence: The Impact of the Criminal Justice and Public Order Act 1994*. London: Home Office. Home Office Research Study 199.

BULL, R., and HORNCASTLE, P. (1989). 'An Evaluation of Human Relations Training', in R. Morgan and D. Smith (eds.), *Coming to Terms with Policing*. London: Routledge.

BULMER, M., and REES, A. M. (eds.) (1996). *Citizenship Today: The Contemporary Relevance of T. H. Marshall*. London: UCL Press.

BUNYAN, T. (1977). *The Political Police in Britain*. London: Quartet Books.

BUNYAN, T. (1981). 'The Police against the People'. *Race and Class*, 23/2–3 (autumn–winter).

BUNYARD, R. (1978). *Police: Organisation and Command*. Plymouth: Macdonald and Evans.

BURKE, M. E. (1993). *Coming Out of the Blue*. London: Cassell.

BURKE, R. H. (ed.) (1998). *Zero Tolerance Policing*. Leicester: Perpetuity Press.

BURROWS, J., and LEWIS, H. (1988). *Directed Patrolwork: A Study of Uniformed Policing*. London: PACE.

BURROWS, J., and TARLING, R. (1982). *Clearing up Crime*, London: Home Office Research Unit.

BUTLER, A. J. (1982a). 'An Examination of the Influence of Training and Work Experience on the Attitudes and Perceptions of Police Officers'. MS. Bramshill, Hants: Police Staff College.

BUTLER, A. J. (1982b). 'Effectiveness, Accountability and Management: The Challenge of Contemporary Police Work', in C. Jones and J. Stevenson (eds.), *Yearbook of Social Policy in Britain 1980–1*. London: Routledge.

BUTLER, A. J. (1985). 'Objectives and Accountability'. *Policing*, 1/3: 174–86.

BUTLER, A. J. (1986). 'Purpose and Process'. *Policing*, 2/2: 160–6.

BUTLER, A. J. (1992). *Police Management* (2nd edn). Aldershot: Dartmouth

BUTTON, M. (1998a). *Under-researched, Under-utilised and Under-estimated: Private Security and Its Contribution to Policing*. Portsmouth: University of Portsmouth. Institute of Police and Criminal Justice Studies Paper 8.

BUTTON, M. (1998b). 'Beyond the Public Gaze: The Exclusion of Private Investigators from the British Debate over Regulating Private Security'. *International Journal of the Sociology of Law*, 26/1: 1–16.

BUTTON, M. (1999). 'An Unseen Force: The Powers of Private Security Officers'. Paper presented to the British Criminology Conference, John Moores University, Liverpool, July.

CAIN, M. (1973). *Society and the Policeman's Role*. London: Routledge & Kegan Paul.

CAIN, M. (1977). 'An Ironical Departure: The Dilemma of Contemporary Policing', in K. Jones (ed.), *Yearbook of Social Policy in Britain*. London: Routledge & Kegan Paul.

CAIN, M. (1979). 'Trends in the Sociology of Police Work'. *International Journal of Sociology of Law*, 7/2: 143–67.

CAIN, M., and SADIGH, S. (1982). 'Racism, the Police and Community Policing'. *Journal of Law and Society*, 9/1 (summer): 87–102.

CALLINICOS, A. (1989). *Against Postmodernism*. Cambridge: Polity Press.

CAMPBELL, B. (1993). *Goliath: Britain's Dangerous Places*. London: Methuen.

CAMPBELL, D. (1980). 'Society under Surveillance', in P. Hain (ed.), *Policing the Police 2*. London: Calder.

CARR-HILL, R., and STERN, N. (1979). *Crime, the Police and Criminal Statistics*. London and New York: Academic Press.

CARRIER, J. (1988). *The Campaign for the Employment of Women as Police Officers*. Aldershot: Avebury.

CARTER, A. (1982). 'The Wonderful World of Cops'. *New Society*, 23 September.

CASHMORE, E., and McLAUGHLIN, E. (1991). *Out of Order? Policing Black People*. London: Routledge.

CASTELLS, M. (1996–8). *The Information Age*, i–iii. Oxford: Blackwell.

CATHCART, B. (1999). *The Case of Stephen Lawrence*. London: Viking.

CAWELTI, J. G. (1976). *Adventure, Mystery and Romance*, Chicago: Chicago University Press.

CHAMBLISS, W., and MANKOFF, M. (eds.) (1975). *Whose Law, What Order?*. New York: Wiley.

CHAN, J. (1996). 'Changing Police Culture'. *British Journal of Criminology*, 36/1: 109–34.

CHAN, J. (1997). *Changing Police Culture: Policing in a Multicultural Society*. Cambridge: Cambridge University Press.

CHANDLER, R. (1944). 'The Simple Art of Murder'. *Atlantic Monthly*, December. (Reprinted in R. Chandler, *Pearls Are a Nuisance*, London: Penguin, 1964.)

CHANDLER, R. *The Long Good-Bye*. London: Heinemann. (Originally published 1953.)

CHAPMAN, B. (1970). *Police State*. London: Macmillan.

CHAPMAN, D. (1968). *Sociology and the Stereotype of the Criminal*. London: Tavistock.

CHATTERTON, M. (1976). 'Police in Social Control', in J. King (ed.), *Control Without Custody*. Cambridge: Institute of Criminology. Cropwood Papers No. 7.

CHATTERTON, M. (1979). 'The Supervision of Patrol Work under the Fixed Points System', in S. Holdaway (ed.), *The British Police*. London: Edward Arnold.

CHATTERTON, M. (1983). 'Police Work and Assault Charges', in M. Punch (ed.), *Control in the Police Organization*. Cambridge, MA: MIT Press.

CHATTERTON, M. (1987a). 'Assessing Police Effectiveness: Future Prospects'. *British Journal of Criminology*, 27/1: 80–6. (Reprinted in Reiner 1996a, i.)

CHATTERTON, M. (1987b). 'Front-line Supervision in the British Police Services', in G. Gaskell, and R. Benewick (eds.), *The Crowd in Contemporary Britain*. London: Sage.

CHATTERTON, M. (1989). 'Managing Paperwork', in M. Weatheritt (ed), *Police Research: Some Future Prospects*. Aldershot: Avebury.

CHATTERTON, M. (1995). 'The Cultural Craft of Policing – Its Past and Future Relevance', *Policing and Society*, 5/2: 97–108.

CHATTERTON, M., and ROGERS, M. (1989). 'Focused Policing', in R. Morgan and D. Smith (eds.), *Coming to Terms with Policing*. London: Routledge.

CHESSHYRE, R. (1989). *The Force*. London: Sidgwick & Jackson.

CHIBNALL, S. (1977). *Law and Order News*. London: Tavistock.

CHIBNALL, S. (1979). 'The Metropolitan Police and the News Media', in S. Holdaway (ed.), *The British Police*. London: Edward Arnold.

CHOO, A. (1989). 'Improperly Obtained Evidence: A Reconsideration'. *Legal Studies*, 9/3.

CHOONGH, S. (1997). *Policing as Social Discipline.* Oxford: Oxford University Press.

CHRISTENSEN, J., SCHMIDT, J., and HENDERSON, J. (1982). 'The Selling of the Police: Media, Ideology and Crime Control'. *Contemporary Crises*, 6.

CHRISTIAN, L. (1983). *Policing by Coercion.* London: GLC Police Committee and Pluto Press.

CHRISTOPHER, S. (1990). 'The Who and Why of Police Assaults'. *Police Review*, 98.

CLARENS, C. (1997). *Crime Movies.* New York: Da Capo.

CLARK, J. P. (1965). 'Isolation of the Police: A Comparison of the British and American Situations'. *Journal of Criminal Law, Criminology and Police Science*, 56/3: 307–19.

CLARKE, A. (1992). "You're Nicked!' TV Police Series and Fictional Representation of Law and Order', in D. Strinati and S. Wragg (eds.), *Come On Down – Popular Media Culture in Postwar Britain.* London: Routledge.

CLARKE, A., and TAYLOR, I. (1980). 'Vandals, Pickets, and Muggers'. *Screen Education*, 36 (autumn).

CLARKE, R., and HOUGH, M. (1980). *The Effectiveness of Policing.* Farnborough: Gower.

CLARKE, R., and HOUGH, M. (1984). *Crime and Police Effectiveness.* London: Home Office Research Unit.

CLARKE, R., and MAYHEW, P. (eds.) (1980). *Designing Out Crime.* London: Home Office Research Unit.

CLAYTON, R., and TOMLINSON, H. (1992). *Civil Actions against the Police* (2nd edn). London: Sweet & Maxwell.

COCHRANE, R., and BUTLER, A. J. (1980). 'The Values of Police Officers, Recruits and Civilians in England'. *Journal of Police Science and Administration*, 8: 205–11.

COHEN, P. (1979). 'Policing the Working Class City', in B. Fine, R. Kinsey, J. Lea, S. Picciotto, and J. Young (eds.), *Capitalism and the Rule of Law.* London: Hutchinson.

COHEN, S. (1972). *Folk Devils and Moral Panics.* London: Paladin (2nd edn, Oxford: Martin Robertson, 1980).

COHEN, S. (1979). 'The Punitive City'. *Contemporary Crises*, 3/4.

COHEN, S. (1985). *Visions of Social Control.* Cambridge: Polity Press.

COHEN, S. (1997a). 'The Revenge of the Null Hypothesis: Evaluating Crime Control Policies'. *Critical Criminologist*, 8: 21–5.

COHEN, S. (1997b). 'Crime and Politics: Spot the Difference', in R. Rawlings (ed.), *Law, Society and Economy.* Oxford: Oxford University Press.

COHEN, S., and SCULL. A. (eds.) (1983). *Social Control and the State.* Oxford: Martin Robertson.

COHEN, S., and YOUNG, J. (eds.) (1973). *The Manufacture of News.* London: Constable (2nd edn, 1981).

COLLINS, H. (1982). *Marxism and Law.* Oxford: Oxford University Press.

COLEMAN, C., and MOYNIHAN, J. (1996). *Understanding Crime Data.* Buckingham: Open University Press.

COLMAN, A., and GORMAN, L. (1982). 'Conservatism, Dogmatism and Authoritarianism in British Police Officers'. *Sociology*, 16/1: 1–11.

COLVIN, M., and NOORLANDER, P. (1998). *Under Surveillance: Covert Policing and Human Rights Standards.* London: Justice.

COLQUHOUN, P. (1795). *A Treatise on the Police of the Metropolis.* London: J. Mowman.

COLQUHOUN, P. (1800). *Treatise on the Commerce and Police of the River Thames.* London: J. Mowman.

COLQUHOUN, P. (1806). *Treatise on Indigence*. London: J. Mowman.

COLQUHOUN, P. *Treatise on the Wealth, Power and Resources of the British Empire*. London: J. Mowman.

COMMISSION ON SOCIAL JUSTICE (1994). *Social Justice: Strategies for National Renewal*. London: Vintage.

CORBETT, C. (1991). 'Complaints against the Police: The New Procedure of Informal Resolution'. *Policing and Society*, 2/1:47–60. (Reprinted in Reiner 1996a, ii.)

COUPE, T., and GRIFFITHS, M. (1996). *Solving Residential Burglary*. London: Home Office. Police Research Group Paper 77.

COX, B., SHIRLEY, J., and SHORT, M. (1977). *The Fall of Scotland Yard*. Harmondsworth: Penguin.

CRANDON, G. (1990). 'The Media View of the Police'. *Policing and Society*, 6/4: 578–81.

CRANDON, G., and DUNNE, S. (1997). 'Symbiosis or Vassalage? The Media and Law Enforcers'. *Policing and Society*, 8/1: 77–91.

CRANK, J. P. (1998). *Understanding Police Culture*. Cincinatti: Anderson Publishing.

CRAWFORD, A. (1997). *The Local Governance of Crime*. Oxford: Oxford University Press.

CRAWFORD, A. (1998). *Crime Prevention and Community Safety*. London: Longman.

CRAWFORD, A., JONES, T., WOODHOUSE, T., and YOUNG, J. (1990). *The Second Islington Crime Survey*. London: Middlesex Polytechnic Centre for Criminology.

CRAWSHAW, R., DEVLIN, B., and WILLIAMSON, T. (1998). *Human Rights and Policing*. The Hague: Kluwer.

CRAY, E. (1972). *The Enemy in the Streets*. New York: Anchor.

CRITCHER, C., and WADDINGTON, D. (eds.) (1996). *Policing Public Order: Theoretical and Practical Issues*. Aldershot: Avebury.

CRITCHLEY, T. A. (1970). *The Conquest of Violence*. London: Constable.

CRITCHLEY, T. A. (1978). *A History of Police in England and Wales* (2nd edn). London: Constable (1st edn 1967).

CROALL, H. (1992). *White Collar Crime*. Buckingham: Open University Press.

CROWTHER, C. (2000a). 'Thinking about the 'Underclass': Towards a Political Economy of Policing'. *Theoretical Criminology*, 4/2: 149–68.

CROWTHER, C. (2000b). *Policing Urban Poverty*. London: Macmillan.

CUMBERBATCH, G., WOODS, S., and MAGUIRE, A. (1995). *Crime in the News: Television, Radio and Newspapers*. Birmingham: Aston University Communications Research Group.

CUMMING, E., CUMMING, I., and EDELL, L. (1965). 'The Policeman as Philosopher, Guide and Friend'. *Social Problems*, 12/3: 276–86. (Reprinted in Reiner 1996a, ii.)

CURRIE, C. (1986). 'Divisional Command'. *Policing* 2/4: 318–24.

CURRIE, E. (1998a). *Crime and Punishment in America*. New York: Holt.

CURRIE, E. (1998b). 'Crime and Market Society: Lessons From the United States', in P. Walton and J. Young (eds.), *The New Criminology Revisited*. London: Macmillan.

DAHRENDORF, R. (1985). *Law and Order*. London: Sweet & Maxwell.

DAVEY, B. J. (1983). *Lawless and Immoral: Policing a Country Town 1838–57*. Leicester: Leicester University Press/New York: St Martin's Press.

DAVIES, N. (1998). *Dark Heart*. London: Verso.

DAVIES, N. (1999a). 'Getting Away With

Murder'. *The Guardian*, 11 January, 'Media' section: 4–5.

DAVIES, N. (1999*b*). 'Watching the Detectives: How the Police Cheat in the Fight against Crime'. *The Guardian*, 18 March: 12.

DAVIS, J. (1984). 'A Poor Man's System of Justice: The London Police Courts in the Second Half of the 19th Century'. *Historical Journal*, 27/2.

DAVIS, K. (1969). *Discretionary Justice*. Urbana, IL: University of Illinois.

DAVIS, K. (1975). *Police Discretion*. St Paul, MN: West Publishing.

DAVIS, M. (1990). *City of Quartz*. London: Vintage.

DAVIS, M. (1998). *Ecology of Fear*. New York: Metropolitan Books.

DAY, P., and KLEIN, R. (1987). *Accountabilities*. London: Tavistock.

DEAN, M. (1982). 'The Finger on the Policeman's Collar'. *Political Quarterly*, 53/2: 153–64.

DELLA PORTA, D., and DEN BOER, M. (eds.) (1998). *Policing Protest*. Minneapolis: University of Minnesota Press.

DEN BOER, M. (ed.) (1997). *Undercover Policing and Accountability from an International Perspective*. Maastricht: European Institute of Public Administration.

DEN BOER, M. (1999). 'Internationalisation: A Challenge to Police Organisations in Europe', in R. Mawby (ed.), *Policing Across the World: Issues for the Twenty-first Century*. London: UCL Press.

DENNIS, N. (ed.) (1998). *Zero Tolerance: Policing A Free Society* (2nd edn). London: Institute of Economic Affairs.

DITTON, J., and DUFFY, J. (1983). 'Bias in the Newspaper Reporting of Crime News'. *British Journal of Criminology*, 23/2 (April).

DIXON, B., and SMITH, G. (1998). 'Laying Down the Law: The Police, the Courts and Legal Accountability'. *International Journal of the Sociology of Law*, 26: 419–35.

DIXON, B., and STANKO, E. A. (1995). 'Sector Policing and Public Accountability'. *Policing and Society*, 5/2: 171–83.

DIXON, D. (1997). *Law in Policing*. Oxford: Oxford University Press.

DIXON, D., BOTTOMLEY, A. K., COLEMAN, C. A., GILL, M., and WALL, D. (1990). 'Safeguarding the Rights of Suspects in Police Custody'. *Policing and Society*, 1/2.

DIXON, D., COLEMAN, C., and BOTTOMLEY, K. (1990). 'Consent and the Legal Regulation of Policing'. *Journal of Law and Society*, 17/3: 345–62.

DIXON, W. (1999). *Popular Policing – Sector Policing and the Reinvention of Police Accountability*. Ph.D. thesis. Uxbridge: Brunel University.

DOBASH, R., and DOBASH, R. (1992). *Women, Violence and Social Change*. London: Routledge.

DOMINICK, J. (1978). 'Crime and Law Enforcement in the Mass Media', in C. Winick (ed.), *Deviance and Mass Media*. Beverly Hills, CA: Sage.

DONAJGRODSKI, A. P. (ed.) (1977*a*). *Social Control in Nineteenth Century Britain*. London: Croom Helm.

DONAJGRODSKI, A. P. (1977*b*). "Social Police' and the Bureaucratic Elite', in A. P. Donajgrodski (ed.), *Social Control in Nineteenth Century Britain*. London: Croom Helm.

DORN, N., MURJI, K., and SOUTH, N. (1991*a*). 'Mirroring the Market – Police Reorganisation and Effectiveness against Drug Trafficking', in R. Reiner and M. Cross (eds.), *Beyond Law and Order: Criminal Justice Policy and Politics into the 1990s*. London: Macmillan.

DORN, N., MURJI, K., and SOUTH, N. (1991b). *Traffickers: Drug Markets and Law Enforcement*. London: Routledge.

DOVE, G. (1982). *The Police Procedural*. Bowling Green, OH: Bowling Green University Popular Press.

DOVE, G., and BARGAINNIER, E. F. (eds.) (1986). *Cops and Constables: American and British Fictional Policemen*. Bowling Green, OH: Bowling Green Popular Press.

DOWNES, D. (1998). 'Toughing It Out: From Labour Opposition to Labour Government'. *Policy Studies*, 19/3–4: 191–8.

DOWNES, D., and MORGAN, R. (1997). 'Dumping the 'Hostages to Fortune' – The Politics of Law and Order in Post-War Britain', in M. Maguire, R. Morgan, and R. Reiner (eds.), *The Oxford Handbook of Criminology* (2nd edn). Oxford: Oxford University Press.

DOWNES, D., and WARD, T. (1986). *Democratic Policing*. London: Labour Campaign for Criminal Justice.

DUMMETT, M. (1980a). *Southall 23 April 1979*. London: National Council for Civil Liberties.

DUMMETT, M. (1980b). *The Death of Blair Peach*. London: National Council for Civil Liberties.

DUNHILL, C. (ed.) (1989). *The Boys in Blue: Women's Challenge to Policing*. London: Virago.

DUNNE, J. G. (1991). 'Law and Disorder in Los Angeles'. *New York Review of Books*, 38: 15, 17.

DUNNIGHAN, C., and Norris, C. (1999). 'The Detective, the Snout and the Audit Commission: The Real Cost of Using Informants'. *Howard Journal of Criminal Justice*, 38/1: 67–86.

EATON, M. (1995). 'A Fair Cop – Viewing the Effects of the Canteen Culture in *Prime Suspect* and *Between the Lines*', in

D. Kidd-Hewitt and R. Osborne (eds.), *Crime and the Media: the Post-Modern Spectacle*. London: Pluto.

EDWARDS, C. J. (1999). *Changing Policing Theories for 21st Century Societies*. Leichhardt, NSW: Federation Press.

EDWARDS, S. (1989). *Policing 'Domestic' Violence*. London: Sage.

EDWARDS, S. (1994). 'Domestic Violence and Sexual Assault', in S. Becker and M. Stephens (eds.), *Police Force, Police Service*. London: Macmillan.

EHRLICH, S. (1980). *Breaking and Entering: Police Women on Patrol*. Berkeley, CA: University of California Press.

EKBLOM, P. (1998). 'Situational Crime Prevention: Effectiveness of Local Initiatives', in C. Nuttall, P. Goldblatt, and C. Lewis (eds.), *Crime Reduction*. London: Home Office. Home Office Research Study 187.

EKBLOM, P., and HEAL, K. (1982). *The Police Response to Calls from the Public*. London: Home Office. Research and Planning Unit Paper 9.

EMSLEY, C. (1983). *Policing and Its Context 1750–1870*. London: Macmillan.

EMSLEY, C. (1987). *Crime and Society in England 1750–1900*. London: Longman.

EMSLEY, C. (1996). *The English Police: A Political and Social History* (2nd edn). London: Longman.

EMSLEY, C. (1997). 'The History of Crime and Crime Control Institutions', in M. Maguire, R. Morgan, and R. Reiner (eds.), *The Oxford Handbook of Criminology* (2nd edn). Oxford: Oxford University Press.

ERICSON, R. (1982). *Reproducing Order: A Study of Police Patrol Work*. Toronto: University of Toronto Press.

ERICSON, R. (1991). 'Mass Media, Crime, Law and Justice: An Institutional Approach'. *British Journal of Criminology*, 31/3: 219–49.

ERICSON, R. (1993). *Making Crime: A Study of Detective Work* (2nd edn). Toronto: University of Toronto Press.

ERICSON, R. (ed.) (1995). *Crime and the Media*. Aldershot: Dartmouth.

ERICSON, R., BARANEK, P., and CHAN, J. (1987). *Visualising Deviance: A Study of News Organisation*. Milton Keynes: Open University Press.

ERICSON, R., BARANEK, P., and CHAN, J. (1989). *Negotiating Control: A Study of News Sources*. Milton Keynes: Open University Press.

ERICSON, R., BARANEK, P., and CHAN, J. (1991). *Representing Crime: Crime, Law and Justice in the News Media*. Milton Keynes: Open University Press.

ERICSON, R., and HAGGERTY, K. (1997). *Policing Risk Society*. Oxford: Oxford University Press.

EVANS, P. (1974). *The Police Revolution*. London: Allen & Unwin.

EVANS, R. (1993). *The Conduct of Police Interviews with Juveniles*. London: HMSO. Royal Commission on Criminal Justice Research Study 8.

EVERSON, W. (1972). *The Detective in Film*. New York: Citadel.

FARRELL, A. (1992). *Crime, Class and Corruption: The Politics of the Police*. London: Bookmarks.

FARRINGTON, D., and DOWDS, E. (1985). 'Disentangling Criminal Behaviour and Police Reaction', in D. Farrington and J. Gunn (eds.), *Reactions to Crime: The Public, the Police, Courts and Prisons*. Winchester: Wiley.

FARRINGTON, D., GALLAGHER, B., MORLEY, L., ST. LEDGER, R. J., and WEST, D. J. (1986). 'Unemployment, School Leaving and Crime'. *British Journal of Criminology*, 26/4: 335–56.

FEELEY, M., and SIMON, J. (1994). 'Actuarial Justice: The Emerging New Criminal Law', in D. Nelken (ed.), *The Futures of Criminology*. London: Sage.

FELDMAN, D. (1990). 'Regulating Treatment of Suspects in Police Stations: Judicial Interpretations of Detention Provisions in the Police and Criminal Evidence Act 1984'. *Criminal Law Review*: 452–71.

FERDINAND, T., and LUCHTERHAND, E. (1970). 'Inner City Youths, the Police and Justice', *Social Problems*, 17 (spring).

FIELD, J. (1981). 'Police, Power and Community in a Provincial English Town: Portsmouth 1815–75', in V. Bailey (ed.), *Policing and Punishment in 19th Century Britain*. London: Croom Helm.

FIELD, S. (1990). *Trends in Crime and Their Interpretation: A Study of Recorded Crime in Post-War England and Wales*. London: HMSO. Home Office Research Study 119.

FIELD, S. (1999). *Trends in Crime Revisited*. London: Home Office. Home Office Research Study 195.

FIELD, S., and Southgate, P. (1982). *Public Disorder*. London: Home Office Research Unit.

FIELD, S., and THOMAS, P. (eds.) (1994). *Justice and Efficiency?*. Oxford: Blackwell.

FIELDING, N. (1981). 'The Credibility of Accountability', *Poly Law Review*, 6/2 (spring).

FIELDING, N. (1984). 'Police Socialisation and Police Competence'. *British Journal of Sociology*, 35/4: 568–90.

FIELDING, N. (1988). *Joining Forces*. London: Routledge.

FIELDING, N. (1989). 'Police Culture and Police Practice', in M. Weatheritt (ed), *Police Research: Some Future Prospects*. Aldershot: Avebury.

FIELDING, N. (1991). *The Police and Social Conflict*. London: Athlone.

FIELDING, N. (1994a). 'Cop Canteen Culture', in T. Newburn and E. A. Stanko (eds.), *Just Boys Doing Business: Men, Masculinity and Crime.* London: Routledge.

FIELDING, N. (1994b). 'The Organisational and Occupational Troubles of Community Police'. *Policing and Society*, 4/3: 305–22.

FIELDING, N. (1995). *Community Policing.* Oxford: Oxford University Press.

FIELDING, N. (1996). 'Enforcement, Service and Community Models of Policing', in W. Saulsbury, J. Mott, and T. Newburn (eds.), *Themes in Contemporary Policing.* London: Policy Studies Institute/Police Foundation.

FIELDING, N., and FIELDING, J. (1992). 'A Comparative Minority: Female Recruits to a British Constabulary Force', *Policing and Society*, 2/3: 205–18.

FIELDING, N., KEMP, C., and NORRIS, C. (1989). 'Constraints on the Practice of Community Policing', in R. Morgan and D. Smith (eds.), *Coming to Terms with Policing* London: Routledge.

FIJNAUT, C. and MARX, G. (eds.) (1996). *Undercover: Police Surveillance in Comparative Perspective.* The Hague: Kluwer.

FINE, B. and MILLAR, R. (eds.) (1985). *Policing the Miners' Strike.* London: Lawrence & Wishart.

FISHER, C., and MAWBY, R. (1982). 'Juvenile Delinquency and Police Discretion in an InnerCity area'. *British Journal of Criminology*, 22/1 (January): 141–63.

FISHER, SIR H. (1977). *The Confait Case: Report.* London: HMSO.

FISHMAN, M. (1978). 'Crime Waves as Ideology'. *Social Problems*, 25/4: 531–43.

FISHMAN, M., and CAVENDER, G. (1998). *Entertaining Crime: Television Reality Programmes.* Hawthorne, NY: Aldine de Gruyter.

FISKE, J., and HARTLEY, J. (1978). *Reading Television.* London: Methuen.

FITZGERALD, M. (1993). *Ethnic Minorities and the Criminal Justice System.* London: HMSO. Royal Commission on Criminal Justice Research Study 20.

FITZGERALD, M. (1999). *Report into Stop and Search.* London: Metropolitan Police.

FITZGERALD, M., and HALE, C. (1996). *Ethnic Minorities: Victimisation and Racial Harassment: Findings from the 1988 and 1992 British Crime Surveys.* London: Home Office. Home Office Research Study 154.

FOGELSON, R. (1977). *Big-City Police*, Cambridge, MA: Harvard University Press.

FORRESTER, D., CHATTERTON, M., and PEASE, K. (1988). *The Kirkholt Burglary Prevention Project.* London: Home Office. Crime Prevention Unit Paper 13.

FORST, B., and MANNING, P. (1999). *The Privatization of Policing.* Washington, DC: Georgetown University Press.

FOSTER, J. (1974). *Class Struggle in the Industrial Revolution.* London: Methuen.

FOSTER, J. (1989). 'Two Stations: An Ethnographic Study of Policing in the Inner City', in D. Downes (ed.), *Crime and the City.* London: Macmillan.

FOUCAULT, M. (1977). *Discipline and Punish.* Harmondsworth: Penguin/New York: Pantheon.

FRANCIS, P., DAVIES, P., and JUPP, V. (eds.) (1997). *Policing Futures: The Police, Law Enforcement and the Twenty-First Century.* London: Macmillan.

FREEMAN, M. (1984). 'Law and Order in 1984'. *Current Legal Problems 1984.*

FREEMAN, M. (1985). *The Police and Criminal Evidence Act 1984.* London: Sweet & Maxwell.

FRIEDMANN, R. (1992). *Community Policing: Comparative Perspectives and Prospects.*

Hemel Hempstead: Harvester Wheatsheaf.

FRIEDRICH, R. (1979). 'Racial Prejudice and Police Treatment of Blacks', in R. Baker and F. A. Meyer, Jr., (eds.), *Evaluating Alternative Law Enforcement Policies*. Lexington, MA: D. C. Heath.

FYFE, J. (1981). 'Race and Extreme Police–Citizen Violence', in R. McNeely and C. Pope (eds.), *Race, Crime and Criminal Justice*. Beverly Hills, CA: Sage.

FYFE, N. (1992). 'Towards Locally Sensitive Policing – Politics, Participation and Power in Community/Police Consultation', in D. J. Evans, N. R. Fyfe, and D. T. Herbert (eds.), *Crime, Policing and Place: Essays in Environmental Criminology*. London: Routledge.

GALBRAITH, J. K. (1992). *The Culture of Contentment*. London: Sinclair-Stevenson.

GARLAND, D. (1996). 'The Limits of the Sovereign State: Strategies of Crime Control in Contemporary Societies'. *British Journal of Criminology*, 36/4: 1–27.

GARLAND, D. (1997). '"Governmentality" and the Problem of Crime: Foucault, Criminology, and Sociology'. *Theoretical Criminology*, 1/2: 173–214.

GARLAND, D. (2000). 'The Culture of High Crime Societies: Some Preconditions of Recent 'Law and Order' Policies'. *British Journal of Criminology*, 40/3: 347–75.

GARLAND, D. (2001). *The New Culture of Crime Control*. Oxford: Oxford University Press (forthcoming).

GAROFALO, J. (1981). 'Crime and the Mass Media: A Selective Review of Research'. *Journal of Research in Crime and Delinquency*, 18/2 (July): 319–50.

GASH, N. (1961). *Mr Secretary Peel*. London: Longman.

GATRELL, V. (1980). 'The Decline of Theft and Violence in Victorian and Edwardian England', in V. Gatrell, B. Lenman, and G. Parker (eds.), *Crime and the Law*. London: Europa.

GATRELL, V. (1988). 'Crime, Authority and the Policeman-State 1750–1950', in F. M. Thompson (ed), *The Cambridge Social History of Britain*. Cambridge: Cambridge University Press.

GATRELL, V. (1994). *The Hanging Tree*. Oxford: Oxford University Press.

GATRELL, V., and HADDEN, T. (1972). 'Nineteenthcentury Criminal Statistics and Their Interpretation', in E. Wrigley (ed.), *Nineteenth-Century Society*. Cambridge: Cambridge University Press.

GEARY, R. (1985). *Policing Industrial Disputes*. Cambridge: Cambridge University Press.

GEHERIN, D. (1980). *Sons of Sam Spade*. New York: Ungar.

GELLER, W. (1983). 'Deadly Force: What We Know', in C. Klockars (ed.), *Thinking About Police*. New York: McGraw-Hill.

GELLER, W., and TOCH, H. (eds.) (1996). *Police Violence: Understanding and Controlling Police Abuse of Force*. New Haven: Yale University Press.

GIDDENS, A. (1990). *The Consequences of Modernity*. Cambridge: Polity Press.

GIDDENS, A. (1994). *Beyond Left and Right*. Cambridge: Polity Press.

GIDDENS, A., and HUTTON, W. (eds) (2000). *On the Edge*. London: Cape.

GIFFORD, LORD (1986). *The Broadwater Farm Inquiry*. London: Broadwater Farm Inquiry.

GILL, M., and MAWBY, R. I. (1990). *A Special Constable*. Aldershot: Avebury.

GILL, P. (1987). 'Clearing Up Crime: The Big 'Con''. *Journal of Law and Society*, 14/2: 254–65.

GILL, P. (1994). *Policing Politics: Security*

Intelligence and the Liberal Democratic State. London: Frank Cass.

GILL, P. (1997*a*). 'Making Sense of Police Intelligence – The Use of a Cybernetic Model in Analysing Information and Power in Police Intelligence Processes'. *Policing and Society,* 8/3: 289–314.

GILL, P. (1997*b*). 'Police Intelligence Processes: A Study of Criminal Intelligence Units in Canada'. *Policing and Society,* 8/4: 339–366.

GILLING, D. (1997). *Crime Prevention: Theory, Practice and Politics.* London: UCL Press.

GILROY, P. (1982). 'The Myth of Black Criminality', in *Socialist Register 1982.* London: Merlin.

GILROY, P. (1983). 'Police and Thieves', in Centre for Research on Contemporary Cultural Studies, *The Empire Strikes Back.* London: Hutchinson.

GOLDSMITH, A. (1990). 'Taking Police Culture Seriously: Police Discretion and the Limits of Law'. *Policing and Society,* 1/2: 91–114. (Reprinted in Reiner 1996*a,* ii.)

GOLDSMITH, A. (ed.) (1991). *Complaints against the Police: The Trend to External Review.* Oxford: Oxford University Press.

GOLDSTEIN, H. (1977). *Policing a Free Society.* Cambridge, MA: Ballinger.

GOLDSTEIN, H. (1979). 'Policing: A Problem-Oriented Approach'. *Crime and Delinquency,* 25/2: 236–58. (Reprinted in Reiner 1996*a,* i.)

GOLDSTEIN, H. (1990). *Problem-Oriented Policing.* New York: McGraw-Hill.

GOLDSTEIN, J. (1960). 'Police Discretion not to Invoke the Criminal Process: Lowvisibility Decisions in the Administration of Justice'. *Yale Law Journal,* 69: 543–94. (Reprinted in Reiner 1996*a,* ii.)

GOLDTHORPE, J., LLEWELLYN, C., and PAYNE, C. (1980). *Social Mobility and Class Struc-*

ture in Modern Britain. Oxford: Oxford University Press.

GORDON, P. (1983). *White Law.* London: Pluto Press.

GORDON, P. (1984). 'Community Policing: Towards the Local Police State'. *Critical Social Policy,* 10 (summer): 39–58.

GORER, G. (1955). *Exploring English Character.* London: Cresset.

GOULDNER, A. (1968). 'The Sociologist as Partisan'. *The American Sociologist,* May.

GRABER, D. A. (1980). *Crime News and the Public.* New York: Praeger.

GRAEF, R. (1989). *Talking Blues.* London: Collins.

GREEN, P. (1991). *The Enemy Without: Policing and Class Consciousness in the Miners' Strike.* Milton Keynes: Open University Press.

GREENBERG, D. (ed.) (1981). *Crime and Capitalism.* Palo Alto, CA: Mayfield.

GREENE, J. R., and MASTROFSKI, S. D. (eds.) (1988). *Community Policing: Rhetoric or Reality?.* New York: Praeger.

GREENWOOD, P., CHAIKEN, J., and PETERSILIA, J. (1977). *The Criminal Investigation Process.* Lexington, MA: D. C. Heath.

GREER, S. (1995*a*). *Supergrasses: A Study in Anti-Terrorist Law Enforcement in Northern Ireland.* Oxford: Oxford University Press.

GREER, S. (1995*b*). 'Towards a Sociological Model of the Police Informant'. *British Journal of Sociology,* 46/3: 509–29.

GREER, S., and MORGAN, R. (eds.) (1990) *The Right to Silence Debate.* Bristol: Bristol University Centre for Criminal Justice.

GREGORY, F. (1985). 'The British Police System', in J. Roach and J. Thomaneck (eds.), *Police and Public Order in Europe.* London: Croom Helm.

GREGORY, J., and LEES, S. (1999). *Policing Sexual Assault.* London: Routledge.

GRELLA, G. (1970). 'Murder and Manners: The Formal Detective Story'. *Novel*, 4/1.

GRIFFITH, J. (1997). *The Politics of the Judiciary* (5th edn). London: Fontana.

GRIGG, M. (1965). *The Challenor Case*. Harmondsworth: Penguin.

GRIMSHAW, R., and JEFFERSON, T. (1987). *Interpreting Policework*. London: Unwin.

GROSS, B. (1982). 'Some Anticrime Proposals for Progressives'. *Crime and Social Justice*, 17 (summer).

GUDJONNSON, G., CLARE, I., RUTTER, S., and PEARSE, J. (1993). *Persons at Risk during Interviews in Police Custody*. London: HMSO. Royal Commission on Criminal Justice Research Study 12.

HAIN, P. (ed.) (1979). *Policing the Police*. London: Calder.

HAIN, P. (ed.) (1980). *Policing the Police 2*. London: Calder.

HAIN, P. (1984). *Political Trials In Britain*. Harmondsworth: Penguin.

HALE, C. (1996). 'Fear of Crime: A Review of the Literature'. *International Review of Victimology*, 4/1: 79–150.

HALE, C. (1998). 'Crime and the Business Cycle in Post-War Britain Revisited'. *British Journal of Criminology*, 38/4: 681–98.

HALFORD, A. (1993). *No Way Up the Greasy Pole*. London: Constable.

HALL, P. T. (1998). 'Policing Order: Assessments of Effectiveness and Efficiency'. *Policing and Society*, 8/3: 225–52.

HALL, S. (1973). 'The Determination of News Photographs', in S. Cohen and Y. Young (eds.), *The Manufacture of News*. London: Constable.

HALL, S. (1979). *Drifting into a Law and Order Society*. London: Cobden Trust.

HALL, S., CRITCHER, C., JEFFERSON, T., CLARKE, J., and ROBERTS, B. (1978). *Policing the Crisis*. London, Macmillan.

HALLORAN, J., ELLIOTT, P., and MURDOCK, G. (1970). *Demonstrations and Communication*. Harmondsworth: Penguin.

HANMER, J., RADFORD, R., and STANKO, E. A. (eds.) (1989). *Women, Policing and Male Violence*. London: Routledge.

HARRING, S. (1983). *Policing a Class Society*. New Brunswick, NJ: Rutgers University Press.

HARRISON, J., and CRAGG, S. (1995). *Police Misconduct: Legal Remedies* (3rd edn). London: Legal Action Group.

HART, J. (1951). *The British Police*. London: Allen & Unwin.

HART, J. (1955). 'Reform of the Borough Police'. *English Historical Review*, 70: 411–27.

HART, J. (1956). 'The County and Borough Police Act 1835–56'. *Public Administration*, 34: 405–17.

HART, J. (1978). 'Police', in W. Cornish (ed.), *Crime and Law*. Dublin: Irish University Press.

HARVEY, D. (1989). *The Condition of Postmodernity*. Oxford: Blackwell.

HARVEY, L., GRIMSHAW, P., and PEASE, K. (1989). 'Crime Prevention Delivery: The Work of Crime Prevention Officers', in R. Morgan and D. Smith (eds.), *Coming to Terms with Policing*. London: Routledge.

HAUGE, R. (1965). 'Crime and the Press', in N. Christie (ed.), *Scandinavian Studies in Criminology 1*. London: Tavistock.

HAY, D. (ed.) (1975*a*). *Albion's Fatal Tree*. Harmondsworth: Penguin.

HAY, D. (1975*b*). 'Property, Authority and the Criminal Law', in D. Hay (ed.), *Albion's Fatal Tree*. Harmondsworth: Penguin.

HAY, D. (1980). 'Crime and Justice in 18th and 19th Century England', in N. Morris and M. Tonry (eds.), *Crime and Justice 2*. Chicago: Chicago University Press.

HAY, D., and SNYDER, F. (eds.) (1989). *Policing and Prosecution in Britain 1750–1850*. Oxford: Oxford University Press.

HAYCRAFT, H. (1941). *Murder for Pleasure*. New York: Appleton, Century.

HAYCRAFT, H. (ed.) (1946). *The Art of the Mystery Story*. New York: Grosset & Dunlap.

HEAL, K., TARLING, R., and BURROWS, J. (eds.) (1985). *Policing Today*. London: HMSO.

HEATON, R. (2000). 'The Prospects for Intelligence-Led Policing: Some Historical and Quantitative Considerations'. *Policing and Society*, 9/4: 337–56.

HEBENTON, B., and THOMAS, T. (1995). *Policing Europe: Co-operation, Conflict and Control*. London: Macmillan.

HEIDENSOHN, F. (1989). *Women in Policing in the USA*. London: Police Foundation.

HEIDENSOHN, F. (1992). *Women in Control – The Role of Women in Law Enforcement*. Oxford: Oxford University Press.

HEIDENSOHN, F. (1994). "We Can Handle It Out Here'. Women Police Officers in Britain and the USA and the Policing of Public Order'. *Policing and Society*, 4/4: 293–303.

HEIDENSOHN, F. (1996). *Women and Crime* (2nd edn). London: Macmillan.

HEIDENSOHN, F. (1997). 'Gender and Crime', in M. Maguire, R. Morgan, and R. Reiner (eds.), *The Oxford Handbook of Criminology* (2nd edn). Oxford: Oxford University Press.

HEIDENSOHN, F. (1998). 'Women in Policing'. *Criminal Justice Matters*, 32: 13–14.

HELD, D., McGREW, A., GOLDBLATT, D., and PERRATON, J. (1999). *Global Transformations*. Caambridge: Polity Press.

HERBERT, S. (1997). *Policing space: Territoriality and the Los Angeles Police Department*. Minneapolis: University of Minnesota Press.

HERBERT, S. (2000). 'Reassessing Police and Police Studies'. *Theoretical Criminology*, 4/1: 113–9.

HEWITT, P. (1982). *The Abuse of Power*. Oxford: Martin Robertson.

HILLYARD, P. (1981). 'From Belfast to Britain', in *Politics and Power 4: Law, Politics and Justice*. London: Routledge.

HILLYARD, P. (1982). 'The Media Coverage of Crime and Justice In Northern Ireland', in C. Sumner (ed.), *Crime, Justice and the Mass Media*. Cambridge: Institute of Criminology. Cropwood Papers 14.

HIRST, M. (1991). 'What Do We Mean By Quality?'. *Policing*, 7/3: 183–93.

HIRST, P. Q. (1975). 'Marx and Engels on Law, Crime and Morality', in I. Taylor, P. Walton, and J. Young (eds.), *Critical Criminology*. London: Routledge. (Reprinted from *Economy and Society*, 1973.)

HIRST, P. (2000). 'Statism, Pluralism and Social Control'. *British Journal of Criminology*, 40/2: 279–96.

HIRST, P., and Thompson, G. (1999). *Globalisation in Question* (2nd edn). Cambridge: Polity Press.

HOBBS, D. (1988). *Doing the Business: Entrepreneurship, the Working Class and Detectives in the East End of London*. Oxford: Oxford University Press.

HOBBS, D. (1995). *Bad Business*. Oxford: Oxford University Press.

HOBSBAWM, E. (1959). *Primitive Rebels*. Manchester: Manchester University Press.

HOBSBAWM, E. (1964). *Labouring Men*. London: Weidenfeld & Nicolson.

HOBSBAWM, E. (1968). *Industry and Empire*. London: Penguin.

HOBSBAWM, E. (1969). *Bandits*. London: Penguin.

HOBSBAWM, E. (1994). 'Barbarism: A User's Guide'. *New Left Review*, 206/1: 44–54.

HOBSBAWM, E. (1995). *The Age of Extremes*. London: Abacus.

HOBSBAWM, E., and RUDE, G. (1969). *Captain Swing*. London: Penguin.

HOFSTRA, B., and SHAPLAND, J. (1997). 'Who is in Control?'. *Policing and Society*, 6/4: 265–82.

HOLDAWAY, S. (1977). 'Changes in Urban Policing'. *British Journal of Sociology*, 28/2: 119–37. (Reprinted in Reiner 1996a, i.)

HOLDAWAY, S. (ed.) (1979). *The British Police*. London: Edward Arnold.

HOLDAWAY, S. (1983). *Inside the British Police*. Oxford: Basil Blackwell.

HOLDAWAY, S. (1986). 'The Holloway Incident'. *Policing*, 2/2: 101–13.

HOLDAWAY, S. (1989). 'Discovering Structure: Studies of the British Police Occupational Culture', in M. Weatheritt (ed), *Police Research: Some Future Prospects*. Aldershot: Avebury.

HOLDAWAY, S. (1991). *Recruiting a Multi-Ethnic Police Force*. London: HMSO.

HOLDAWAY, S. (1995). 'Culture, Race and Policy: Some Themes of the Sociology of the Police'. *Policing and Society*, 5/2: 109–21.

HOLDAWAY, S. (1996). *The Racialisation of British Policing*. London: Macmillan.

HOLDAWAY, S., and BARRON, A.-M. (1997). *Resigners – The Experience of Black and Asian Police Officers*. London: Macmillan.

HOLDAWAY, S., SPENCER, C., and WILSON, D. (1984). 'Black Police in the UK'. *Policing*, 1/1: 20–30.

HOLLWAY, W., and JEFFERSON, T. (1997). 'The Risk Society in an Age of Anxiety: Situating the Fear of Crime'. *British Journal of Sociology*, 48/2: 255–65.

HOME OFFICE (1981). *Racial Attacks: Report of a Home Office Study*. London: Home Office.

HOME OFFICE (1993). *Police Reform: A Police Service for the Twenty-First Century*. London: HMSO. White Paper Cm. 2281.

HOME OFFICE (1998). *Crime Reduction Programme Prospectus*. London: Home Office Research, Development and Statistics Directorate.

HOME OFFICE (1999). *Information on the Criminal Justice System in England and Wales: Digest 4*, ed. G. C. Barclay and C. Tavares. London: Home Office Research, Development and Statistics Directorate.

HOME OFFICE (2000a). *Recorded Crime Statistics, England and Wales*. London: Home Office Research, Development and Statistics Directorate. Statistical Bulletin 1/00.

HOME OFFICE (2000b). *Operation of Certain Police Powers Under PACE*. London: Home Office Research, Development and Statistics Directorate. Statistical Bulletin 9/00.

HOOGENBOOM, B. (1991). 'Grey Policing: A Theoretical Framework'. *Policing and Society*, 2/1: 17–30.

HOPE, T. (1998). 'Community Crime Prevention', in C. Nuttall, P. Goldblatt, and C. Lewis (eds.), *Crime Reduction*. London: Home Office. Home Office Research Study 187.

HOPE, T., and SPARKS, R. (eds.) (2000). *Crime, Risk and Insecurity*. London: Routledge (forthcoming).

HORTON, C. (1989). 'Good Practice and Evaluative Policing', in R. Morgan and D. Smith (eds.), *Coming to Terms with Policing*. London: Routledge.

HOUGH, M. (1980). *Uniformed Police Work and Management Technology*. London: Home Office Research Unit.

HOUGH, M. (1987). 'Thinking About Effectiveness'. *British Journal of Criminology*, 27/1: 70–79.

HOUGH, M. (1989). 'Demand for Policing and Police Performance: Progress and Pitfalls in Public Surveys', in M. Weatheritt (ed), *Police Research: Some Future Prospects*. Aldershot: Avebury.

HOUGH, M. (1996). 'The Police Patrol Function: What Research Can Tell Us', in W. Saulsbury J. Mott, and T. Newburn (eds.), *Themes in Contemporary Policing*. London: Policy Studies Institute/Police Foundation.

HOUGH, M., and MAYHEW, P. (1983). *The British Crime Survey*. London: Home Office Research Unit.

HOYLE, C. (1998). *Negotiating Domestic Violence: Police, Criminal Justice and Victims*. Oxford: Oxford University Press.

HUDSON, B. (1997). 'Social Control', in M. Maguire, R. Morgan, and R. Reiner (eds.), *The Oxford Handbook of Criminology* (2nd edn). Oxford: Oxford University Press.

HUGGINS, M. (1998). *Political Policing*. Durham, NC: Duke University Press.

HUGHES, E. C. (1961). 'Good People and Dirty Work'. *Social Problems*, 10/1.

HUGHES, G. (1994). 'Talking Cop Shop – A Case-study of Police Community Consultative Groups in Transition'. *Policing and Society*, 4: 253–70.

HUGHES, G. (1998). *Understanding Crime Prevention: Social Control, Risk and Late Modernity*. Buckingham: Open University Press.

HUMPHRY, D. (1979). 'The Complaints System', in P. Hain (ed.), *Policing the Police 1*. London: Calder.

HURD, G. (1979). 'The Television Presentation of the Police', in S. Holdaway (ed.), *The British Police*. London: Edward Arnold.

HUTTON, W. (1996). *The State We're In*. London: Vintage.

IANNI, E. R., and IANNI, R. (1983). 'Street Cops and Management Cops: The Two Cultures of Policing', in M. Punch (ed.), *Control in the Police Organization*. Cambridge, MA: MIT Press.

IGNATIEFF, M. (1978). *A Just Measure of Pain*. London: Macmillan.

IGNATIEFF, M. (1979). 'Police and People: The Birth of Mr. Peel's Blue Locusts'. *New Society*, 49.

IGNATIEFF, M. (1983). 'State, Civil Society and Total Institutions', in S. Cohen and A. Scull (eds.), *Social Control and the State*. Oxford: Martin Robertson. (Originally in M. Tonry and N. Morris (eds.), *Crime and Justice*, 3, Chicago University Press, 1981.)

INCIARDI, J., and DEE, J. L. (1987). 'From the Keystone Cops to Miami Vice: Images of Policing in American Popular Culture'. *Journal of Popular Culture*, 21/2: 84–102.

INNES, M. (1999*a*). '"An Iron Fist in an Iron Glove?' The Zero Tolerance Policing Debate'. *Howard Journal of Criminal Justice*, 38/4: 397–410.

INNES, M. (1999*b*). 'Policing Change and Changing Policing'. *Policing and Society*, 9/3: 287–308.

INNES, M. (1999*c*). 'The Media as an Investigative Response in Murder Enquiries'. *British Journal of Criminology*, 39/2: 268–85.

INNES, M. (1999*d*). *Investigating Murder: The Police Response to Criminal Homicide*. Ph.D. thesis. London: London School of Economics.

INNES, M. (2000). 'Professionalising the Role of the Police Informant: The British Experience'. *Policing and Society*, 9/4: 357–84.

IRVING, B., BIRD, C., HIBBERD, M., and WILLMORE, J. (1989). *Neighbourhood Policing: The Natural History of a Policing Experiment*. London: Police Foundation.

IRVING, B., and McKENZIE, I. (1989*a*). *Police Interrogation.* London: Police Foundation.

IRVING, B., and McKenzie, I. (1989*b*). 'Interrogating in a Legal Framework', in R. Morgan and D. Smith (eds.), *Coming to Terms with Policing.* London: Routledge.

IYENGAR, S. (1991). *Is Anyone Responsible? How Television Frames Political Issues.* Chicago: Chicago University Press.

JACOB, H., and RICH, M. (1980). 'The Effects of the Police on Crime: A Second Look'. *Law and Society Review*, 15/1: 109–22.

JACOB, H., and RICH, M. (1981). 'The Effects of the Police on Crime: A Rejoinder'. *Law and Society Review*, 16/1: 171–2.

JAMESON, F. (1992). *Postmodernism: Or the Cultural Logic of Late Capitalism?.* London: Verso.

JEFFERSON, T. (1987). 'Beyond Paramilitarism'. *British Journal of Criminology*, 27/1.

JEFFERSON, T. (1988). 'Race, Crime and Policing: Empirical, Theoretical and Methodological Issues'. *International Journal of the Sociology of Law*, 16/4: 521–39.

JEFFERSON, T. (1990). *The Case against Paramilitary Policing.* Milton Keynes: Open University Press.

JEFFERSON, T. (1993). 'The Racism of Criminalisation: Policing and the Reproduction of the Criminal Other', in L. Gelsthorpe and W. McWilliams (eds.), *Minority Ethnic Groups and the Criminal Justice System.* Cambridge: University of Cambridge, Institute of Criminology.

JEFFERSON, T., and Grimshaw, R. (1982). 'Law, Democracy and Justice', in D. Cowell, T. Jones, and J. Young (eds.), *Policing in Riots.* London: Junction Books.

JEFFERSON, T., and GRIMSHAW, R. (1984*a*). 'The Problem of Law Enforcement Policy in England and Wales: The Case of Community Policing and Racial Attacks'.

International Journal of Sociology of Law, 12 (May): 117–35.

JEFFERSON, T., and GRIMSHAW, R. (1984*b*). *Controlling the Constable: Police Accountability in England and Wales.* London: Muller.

JEFFERSON, T., McLAUGHLIN, E., and ROBERTSON, L. (1988). 'Monitoring the Monitors: Accountability, Democracy and Police Watching in Britain'. *Contemporary Crises*, 12/2.

JEFFERSON, T., and WALKER, M. A. (1992). 'Ethnic Minorities in the Criminal Justice System', *Criminal Law Review*: 83–95.

JEFFERSON, T., and WALKER, M. A. (1993). 'Attitudes to the Police of the Ethnic Minorities in a Provincial City'. *British Journal of Criminology*, 33/2: 251–66.

JEFFERSON, T., WALKER, M. A., and SENEVIRATNE, M. (1992). 'Ethnic Minorities, Crime and Criminal Justice: A Study in a Provincial City', in D. Downes (ed.), *Unravelling Criminal Justice.* London: Macmillan.

JEFFERY, K., and HENNESSY, P. (1983). *States of Emergency.* London: Routledge.

JOHNSON, B. (1976). 'Taking Care of Labour'. *Theory and Society*, 3/l.

JOHNSON, B. (1991). 'The Necessity for Real Change'. *Policing*, 7/3: 204–15.

JOHNSTON, L. (1988). 'Controlling Policework: Problems of Organisational Reform in Large Public Bureaucracies'. *Work, Employment and Society*, 2/1: 51–70.

JOHNSTON, L. (1991). 'Privatisation and the Police Function: From 'New Police' to 'New Policing'', in R. Reiner and M. Cross (eds.), *Beyond Law and Order: Criminal Justice Policy and Politics into the 1990s.* London: Macmillan.

JOHNSTON, L. (1992). *The Rebirth of Private Policing.* London: Routledge.

JOHNSTON, L. (1993). 'Privatisation and

Protection: Spatial and Sectoral Ideologies in British Policing and Crime Prevention'. *Modern Law Review*, 56/6: 771–92.

JOHNSTON, L. (1996). 'What Is Vigilantism?'. *British Journal of Criminology*, 36/2: 220–36.

JOHNSTON, L. (2000). *Policing Britain: Risk, Security and Governance*. London: Longman.

JONES, D. (1982). *Crime, Protest, Community and Police in Nineteenth-Century Britain*. London: Routledge.

JONES, D. (1983). 'The New Police, Crime and People in England and Wales 1829–88'. *Transactions of the Royal Historical Society*, 33.

JONES, D. (1996). *Crime and Policing in the Twentieth Century*. Cardiff: University of Wales Press.

JONES, M. (1980). *Organisational Aspects of Police Behaviour*. Farnborough: Gower.

JONES, P. (1981). 'Police Powers and Political Accountability', in *Politics and Power 4: Law, Politics and Justice*. London: Routledge.

JONES, S. (1983). 'Community Policing in Devon and Cornwall', in T. Bennett, (ed.), *The Future of Policing*. Cambridge: Institute of Criminology. Cropwood Papers 15.

JONES, S. (1986). 'Caught in the Act'. *Policing*, 2/2: 129–40.

JONES, S. (1987). *Policewomen and Equality*. London: Macmillan.

JONES, S., and LEVI, M. (1983). 'The Police and the Majority: The Neglect of the Obvious'. *Police Journal*, 56/4: 351–64.

JONES, T., MCLEAN, B., and YOUNG, J. (1986). *The Islington Crime Survey*. Aldershot: Gower.

JONES, T., NEWBURN, T., and SMITH, D. (1994). *Democracy and Policing*. London: Policy Studies Institute.

JONES, T., and NEWBURN, T. (1997). *Policing after the Act*. London: Policy Studies Institute.

JONES, T., and NEWBURN, T. (1998). *Private Security and Public Policing*. Oxford: Oxford University Press.

JORDAN, P. (1991). 'The Home Office Treasury Study: The Development of Police Management Information Systems'. London: Home Office. *Research Bulletin 31*.

JORDAN, P. (1998). 'Effective Policing Strategies For Reducing Crime' in C. Nuttall, P. Goldblatt, and C. Lewis (eds.), *Reducing Offending*. London: Home Office. Home Office Research Study 187.

JOSHUA, H., WALLACE, T., and BOOTH, H. (1983). *To Ride the Storm: The 1980 Bristol 'Riot' and the State*. London: Heinemann.

JUDGE, A. (1972). *A Man Apart*. London: Barker.

JUDGE, A. (1994). *The Force of Persuasion*. Surbiton: Police Federation.

KAHN, P., LEWIS, N., LIVOCK, P., and WILES, P. (1983). *Picketing*. London: Routledge.

KELLING, G. (1983). 'On the Accomplishments of the Police', in M. Punch (ed.), *Control in the Police Organization*. Cambridge, MA: MIT Press.

KELLING, G. *et al.* (1974). *The Kansas City Preventive Patrol Experiment*, Washington, DC: Police Foundation.

KELLING, G., and COLES, C. (1998). *Fixing Broken Windows: Restoring Order and Reducing Crime in Our Communities*. New York: Free Press.

KEMP, C., and MORGAN, R. (1989). *Behind the Front Counter: Lay Visitors to Police Stations*. Bristol: Bristol University, Centre for Criminal Justice.

KEMP, C., NORRIS, C., and FIELDING, N. (1992). *Negotiating Nothing: Police Decision-Making in Disputes*. Aldershot: Avebury.

KENT, J. (1986). *The English Village Constable 1580–1642*. Oxford: Oxford University Press.

KERR, P. (1981). 'Watching the Detectives'. *PrimeTime*, 1/1 (July).

KIDD-HEWITT, D., and OSBORNE, R. (1996). *Crime and the Media: The Post-Modern Spectacle*. London: Pluto Press.

KING, M., and BREARLEY, N. (1996). *Public Order Policing*, Leicester: Perpetuity Press.

KING, N. (1999). *Heroes in Hard Times: Cop Action Movies in the U.S.* Philadelphia: Temple University Press.

KING, P. (1984). 'Decision-makers and Decision-making in the English Criminal Law 1750–1800'. *Historical Journal*, 27:1.

KINSEY, R., and BALDWIN, R. (1982). *Police Powers and Politics*. London: Quartet.

KINSEY, R., LEA, J., and YOUNG, J. (1986). *Losing the Fight against Crime*. Oxford: Blackwell.

KLEINIG, J. (1996). *The Ethics of Policing*. Cambridge: Cambridge University Press.

KLOCKARS, C. (1980). 'The Dirty Harry Problem'. *The Annals*, 452 (November): 33–47.

KLOCKARS, C. (1985). *The Idea of Police*. Beverly Hills, CA: Sage.

KLOCKARS, C., and MASTROFSKI, S. (eds.) (1992). *Thinking About Police*. New York: McGraw-Hill.

KLUG, F. (1982). *Racist Attacks*. London: Runnymede Trust.

KNIGHT, S. (1980). *Form and Ideology in Crime Fiction*. London: Macmillan.

KNAFLA, L. A. (ed.) (1990). *Crime, Police and the Courts in British History*. London: Meckler.

KRASKA, P. and PAULSEN, D. (1997). 'Grounded Research into U.S. Paramilitary Policing: Forging the Iron Fist inside the Velvet Glove'. *Policing and Society*, 7/4: 253–70.

LACEY, N., and WELLS, C. (1998). *Reconstructing Criminal Law* (2nd edn). London: Butterworth.

LACEY, N., and ZEDNER, L. (1995). 'Discourse of Community in Criminal Justice'. *Journal of Law and Society*, 22/3: 301–25.

LA FAVE, W. (1962). 'The Police and Nonenforcement of the Law'. *Wisconsin Law Review*, January: 104–37, March: 179–239.

LA FAVE, W. (1965). *Arrest*. Boston: Little, Brown.

LAMBERT, J. (1970). *Crime, Police and Race Relations*. Oxford: Oxford University Press.

LAMBERT, J. (1986). *Police Powers and Accountability*. London: Croom Helm.

LANDAU, S. (1981). 'Juveniles and the Police'. *British Journal of Criminology*, 21/1 (January): 27–46.

LANDAU, S., and NATHAN, G. (1983). 'Selecting Delinquents for Cautioning in the London Metropolitan Area'. *British Journal of Criminology*, 23/2 (April): 128–49.

LANDAU, T. (1994). *Public Complaints against the Police*, Toronto: University of Toronto Centre of Criminology.

LANGBEIN, J. (1983). 'Albion's Fatal Flaws'. *Past and Present*, 98.

LARSON, R. (1976). 'What Happened to Patrol Operations in Kansas City?'. *Journal of Criminal Justice*, 3/4: 267–97.

LAURIE, P. (1970). *Scotland Yard*. London: Penguin.

LAYCOCK, G., and TILLEY, N. (1995). *Policing and Neighbourhood Watch: Strategic Issues*. London: Home Office. Police Research Group Paper 60.

LEA, J. (1986). 'Police Racism: Some Theories and Their Policy Implications', in R. Matthews and J. Young (eds.), *Confronting Crime* London: Sage.

LEA, J., and YOUNG, J. (1982). 'The Riots in Britain 1981', in D. Cowell, T. Jones, and J. Young, (eds.), *Policing the Riots*. London: Junction Books.

LEA, J., and YOUNG, J. (1984). *What Is To Be Done About Law and Order?*. Harmondsworth: Penguin.

LEE, J. A. (1981). 'Some Structural Aspects of Police Deviance in Relations with Minority Groups', in C. Shearing (ed.), *Organizational Police Deviance*. Toronto: Butterworth.

LEE, M. (1998). *Youth, Crime and Police Work*. London: Macmillan.

LEE, M. (1901). *A History of Police in England*. London: Methuen.

LEIGH, A., READ, T., and TILLEY, N. (1996). *Problem-Oriented Policing: Brit Pop*. London: Home Office. Police Research Group Paper 75.

LEIGH, L, (1977). 'The Police Act 1976'. *British Journal of Law and Society*, 4/1 (summer).

LEIGH, L. (1981). 'The Royal Commission on Criminal Procedure'. *Modern Law Review*, May.

LEIGH, L. (1986). 'Some Observations On the Parliamentary History of the Police and Criminal Evidence Act 1984', in C. Harlow (ed), *Public Law and Politics*. London: Sweet & Maxwell.

LEISHMAN, F. (1995). 'On Screen – Police On TV'. *Policing*, 11/2: 143–52.

LEISHMAN, F., Cope, S., and Starie, P. (1996). 'Reinventing and Restructuring: Towards A 'New Policing Order'', in F. Leishman, B. Loveday, and S. Savage (eds.), *Core Issues in Policing*. London: Longman.

LEISHMAN, F., Loveday, B., and Savage, S. (eds.) (1996). *Core Issues in Policing*. London: Longman.

LEMERT, E. (1967). *Human Deviance, Social Problems and Social Control*. New York: Prentice Hall.

LEON, C. (1989). 'The Special Constabulary'. *Policing* 5/4: 265–86.

LEON, C. (1990). 'The Special Constabulary: An Historical View'. *Journal of the Police History Society*, 5.

LEON, C. (1991). *A Study of the Special Constabulary*. Ph.D. thesis. Bath: Bath University, School of Humanities and Social Science.

LEVI, M. (1987). *Regulating Frand*. London: Tavistock.

LEVITAS, R. (1998). *The Inclusive Society?*. London: Macmillan.

LICHTER, R. S., LICHTER, L. S., and ROTHMAN, S. (1994). *Prime Time: How TV Portrays American Culture*. Washington, DC: Regnery Publishing.

LIDSTONE, K. (1984). 'Magistrates, the Police and Search Warrants'. *Criminal Law Review*, August.

LIDSTONE, K., and PALMER, C. (1996). *The Investigation of Crime – A Guide to Police Powers* (2nd edn). London: Butterworth.

LINEBAUGH, P. (1991). *The London Hanged: Crime and Civil Society in the Eighteenth Century*. London: Allen Lane.

LIPSET, S. M. (1969). 'Why Cops Hate Liberals, and Vice Versa'. *Atlantic Monthly*. (Reprinted in W. Bopp (ed.), *The Police Rebellion*. Springfield, IL: C. C. Thomas, 1971.)

LOADER, I. (1996). *Youth, Policing and Democracy*. London: Macmillan.

LOADER, I. (1997a). 'Private Security and the Demand for Protection in Contemporary Britain'. *Policing and Society*, 7/2: 143–62.

LOADER, I. (1997b). 'Policing and the Social: Questions of Symbolic Power'. *British Journal of Sociology*, 48/1: 1–18.

LOADER, I. (2000). 'Governing Policing in the 21st Century'. *Criminal Justice Matters*, 38: 9–10.

LOADER, I., and MULCAHY, A. (2000). 'The

Power of Legitimate Naming: Pt. I: Chief Constables as Social Commentators in Post-war England; Pt.II: Making Sense of the Elite Police Voice'. *British Journal of Criminology*, (forthcoming).

LOVEDAY, B. (1983). 'The Role of the Police Committee'. *Local Government Studies*, January–February: 39–53.

LOVEDAY, B. (1984). 'The Role of the Police Committee: Constitutional Arrangements and Social Realities, A Reply to Dr Waddington'. *Local Government Studies*, September–October.

LOVEDAY, B. (1985). *The Role and Effectiveness of the Merseyside Police Committee*. Liverpool: Merseyside Country Council.

LOVEDAY, B. (1987). 'The Joint Boards'. *Policing*, 3/3: 196–217.

LOVEDAY, B. (1988). 'Police Complaints in the USA'. *Policing*, 4/3: 172–93. (Reprinted in Reiner 1996a, ii.)

LOVEDAY, B. (1991). 'The New Police Authorities'. *Policing and Society*, 1/3: 193–212.

LOVEDAY, B. (1995a). 'Contemporary Challenges to Police Management in England and Wales: Developing for Effective Service Delivery'. *Policing and Society*, 5/4: 281–302.

LOVEDAY, B. (1995b). 'Reforming the Police: From Local Service to State Police?'. *Political Quarterly*, 66/2.

LOVEDAY, B. (1996a). 'Business As Usual? The New Police Authorities and the Police and Magistrates' Courts Act'. *Local Government Studies*, summer: 22–39.

LOVEDAY, B. (1996b). 'Crime at the Core?', in F. Leishman, B. Loveday, and S. Savage (eds.), *Core Issues in Policing*. London: Longman.

LOVEDAY, B. (1997). 'Crime, Policing and the Provision of Service', in P. Francis, P. Davies, and V. Jupp (eds.), *Policing Futures*. London: Macmillan.

LOVEDAY, B. (1999). 'Government and Accountability of the Police', in R. Mawby (ed.), *Policing across the World*. London: UCL Press.

LUNDMAN, R. (1974). 'Routine Police Arrest Practices'. *Social Problems*, 22. (Reprinted in R. Lundman (ed.), *Police Behaviour*. New York: Oxford University Press, 1980.)

LUNDMAN, R. (1979). 'Police Work with Traffic Law Violators'. *Criminology*, 17. (Reprinted in R. Lundman (ed.), *Police Behaviour*. New York: Oxford University Press, 1980.)

LUNDMAN, R. (ed.) (1980). *Police Behaviour*, New York: Oxford University Press.

LUNDMAN, R., SYKES, R., and CLARK, J. P. (1978). 'Police Control of Juveniles'. *Journal of Research in Crime and Delinquency*, 15. (Reprinted in R. Lundman (ed.), *Police Behaviour*. New York: Oxford University Press, 1980.)

LUSTGARTEN, L. (1982). 'Beyond Scarman: Police Accountability in Britain', in N. Glazer and K. Young (eds.), *Ethnic Pluralism and Public Policy*. London: Heinemann.

LUSTGARTEN, L. (1986). *The Governance of the Police*. London: Sweet & Maxwell.

McBARNET, D. (1976). 'Pretrial Procedures and the Construction of Conviction', in P. Carlen (ed.), *Sociological Review Monograph: The Sociology of Law*. Keele, Staffs: Keele University.

McBARNET, D. (1978a). 'The Police and the State', in G. Littlejohn, B. Smart, J. Wakeford, and N.Yuval-Davis (eds.), *Power and the State*. London: Croom Helm.

McBARNET, D. (1978b). 'False Dichotomies in Criminal Justice Research', in J. Baldwin and A. K. Bottomley (eds.), *Criminal Justice*. Oxford: Martin Robertson.

McBARNET, D. (1979). 'Arrest: The Legal Context of Policing', in S. Holdaway (ed.),

The British Police. London: Edward Arnold.

McBARNET, D. (1981). *Conviction.* London: Macmillan.

McBARNET, D. (1982). 'Legal Form and Legal Mystification'. *International Journal of the Sociology of Law,* 10: 409–17.

McCABE, S., and SUTCLIFFE, F. (1978). *Defining Crime.* Oxford: Basil Blackwell.

McCABE, S., WALLINGTON, P., ALDERSON, J., GOSTIN, L., and MASON, C. (1988). *The Police, Public Order and Civil Liberties.* London: Routledge.

McCARTHUR, C. (1972). *Underworld USA.* London: Secker & Warburg.

McCONVILLE, M., and BALDWIN, J. (1981). *Courts, Prosecution and Conviction.* Oxford: Oxford University Press.

McCONVILLE, M., and BRIDGES, L. (eds.) (1994). *Criminal Justice in Crisis.* Aldershot: Edward Elgar.

McCONVILLE, M., and HODGSON, J. (1993). *Custodial Legal Advice and the Right to Silence.* London: HMSO. Royal Commission on Criminal Justice Research Study 16.

McCONVILLE, M., HODGSON, J., BRIDGES, L., and PAVLOVIC, A. (1994). *Standing Accused.* Oxford: Oxford University Press.

McCONVILLE, M., SANDERS, A., and LENG, R. (1991). *The Case for the Prosecution: Police Suspects and the Construction of Criminality.* London: Routledge.

McCONVILLE, M., and SHEPHERD, D. (1992). *Watching Police, Watching Communities.* London: Routledge.

MacDONALD, I. (1973). 'The Creation of the British Police'. *Race Today,* 5/11 (December).

MacDONALD, L. (1976). *The Sociology of Law and Order.* London: Faber and Faber.

MACK, J. (1976). 'Full-time Major Criminals and the Courts'. *Modern Law Review,* 39.

McKENZIE, I. (1996). 'Violent Encounters: Force and Deadly Force in British Policing', in F. Leishman, B. Loveday, and S. Savage (eds.), *Core Issues in Policing.* London: Longman.

McKENZIE, I. (1998). 'Policing in England and Wales', in I. McKenzie (ed.), *Law, Power and Justice in England and Wales.* London: Praeger.

McKENZIE, I., and GALLAGHER, P. (1989). *Behind the Uniform.* Hemel Hempstead: Wheatsheaf.

McKENZIE, I., and IRVING, B. (1988). 'The Right to Silence'. *Policing,* 4/2: 88–105.

McKENZIE, I., MORGAN, R., and REINER, R. (1990). 'Helping the Police with Their Inquiries: The Necessity Principle and Voluntary Attendance at the Police Station'. *Criminal Law Review:* 22–33.

McLAUGHLIN, E. (1992). 'The Democratic Deficit: European Unity and the Accountability of the British Police'. *British Journal of Criminology,* 32/4: 473–87.

McLAUGHLIN, E. (1994). *Community, Policing and Accountability,* Aldershot: Avebury.

McLAUGHLIN, E., and MURJI, K. (1995). 'The End of Public Policing? Police Reform and the New Managerialism', in L. Noaks, M. Levi, and M. Maguire (eds.), *Issues in Contemporary Criminology.* Cardiff: University of Wales Press.

McLAUGHLIN, E., and MURJI, K. (1996). 'Times Change: New Formations and Representations of Police Accountability', in C. Critcher and D. Waddington (eds.), *Policing Public Order.* Aldershot: Avebury.

McLAUGHLIN, E. and MURJI, K. (1997). 'The Future Lasts a Long Time: Public Policework and the Managerialist Paradox', in P. Francis, P. Davies, and V. Jupp (eds.), *Policing Futures: The Police, Law Enforcement and the Twenty-First Century.* London: Macmillan.

McLaughlin, E., and Murji, K. (1998). 'Resistance Through Representation: 'Storylines', Advertising and Police Federation Campaigns'. *Policing and Society*, 8/4, 367–99.

McMullan, J. (1996). 'The New Improved Monied Police: Reform, Crime Control, and the Commodification of Policing in London'. *British Journal of Criminology*, 36/1: 85–108.

McMullan, J. (1998). 'Social Surveillance and the Rise of the 'Police Machine''. *Theoretical Criminology*, 2/1: 93–117.

McNee, D. (1979). 'The Queen's Police Keepeth the Peace'. *The Guardian*, 25 September: 25.

McNee, D. (1983). *McNee's Law*. London: Collins.

Macpherson, W. (1999). *The Stephen Lawrence Inquiry*. London: HMSO.

Maguire, M. (1988). 'Effects of the 'PACE' Provisions on Detention and Questioning'. *British Journal of Criminology*, 28/1: 19–43.

Maguire, M. (1991). 'Complaints against the Police: The British Experience', in A. Goldsmith (ed.), *Complaints against the Police: The Trend to External Review*. Oxford: Oxford University Press.

Maguire, M. (1997). 'Crime Statistics, Patterns and Trends: Changing Perceptions and Their Implications', in M. Maguire, R. Morgan, and R. Reiner (eds.), *The Oxford Handbook of Criminology* (2nd edn). Oxford: Oxford University Press.

Maguire, M. (1998a). 'Restraining Big Brother? The Regulation of Surveillance in England and Wales', in C. Norris, G. Armstrong, and J. Moran (eds.), *Surveillance, Closed Circuit Television and Social Control*. Aldershot: Ashgate.

Maguire, M. (1998b). 'POP, ILP and Partnership'. *Criminal Justice Matters*, 32: 21–2.

Maguire, M. (2000). 'Policing by Risks and Targets: Some Dimensions and Implications of Intelligence-Led Social Control'. *Policing and Society*, 9/4: 315–37.

Maguire, M., and Corbett, C. (1989). 'Patterns and Profiles of Complaints against the Police', in R. Morgan and D. Smith (eds.), *Coming to Terms with Policing*. London: Routledge.

Maguire, M., and Corbett, C. (1991). *A Study of the Police Complaints System*. London: PACE.

Maguire, M., and John, T. (1996a). *Intelligence, Surveillance and Informants: Integrated Approaches*. London: Home Office. Crime Detection and Prevention Series Paper 64.

Maguire, M., and John, T. (1996b). 'Covert and Deceptive Policing in England and Wales: Issues in regulation and Practice'. *European Journal of Crime, Criminal Law and Criminal Justice*, 4/3: 316–34.

Maguire, M., and Norris, C. (1992). *The Conduct and Supervision of Criminal Investigations*. London: HMSO. Royal Commission on Criminal Justice Research Report 5.

Maitland, R. (1885). *Justice and Police*. London: Macmillan.

Mandel, E. (1984). *Delightful Murder*. London: Pluto Press.

Manning, P. (1979). 'The Social Control of Police Work', in S. Holdaway (ed.), *The British Police*. London: Edward Arnold.

Manning, P. (1997). *Police Work* (2nd edn). Prospect Heights, IL: Waveland Press.

Manning, P., and Redlinger, J. (1977). 'Invitational Edges of Corruption', in P. Rock (ed.), *Politics and Drugs*. Rutgers, NJ: Dutton.

Manning, P., and Van Maanen, J. (eds.) (1978). *Policing: A View from the Street*. Santa Monica, CA: Goodyear.

MARENIN, O. (1983). 'Parking Tickets and Class Repression: The Concept of Policing in Critical Theories of Criminal Justice'. *Contemporary Crises*, 6/2: 241–66. (Reprinted in Reiner 1996*a*, i.)

MARENIN, O. (ed.) (1996). *Policing Change, Changing Police: International Perspectives*. New York: Garland.

MARK, R. (1977). *Policing a Perplexed Society*. London: Allen & Unwin.

MARK, R. (1978). *In the Office of Constable*. London: Collins.

MARSH, H. L. (1991). 'A Comparative Analysis of Crime Coverage in Newspapers in the United States and Other Countries from 1960–1989'. *Journal of Criminal Justice*, 19/1: 67–80.

MARSHALL, G. (1965). *Police and Government*. London: Methuen.

MARSHALL, G. (1978). 'Police Accountability Revisited', in D. Butler and A. H. Halsey (eds.), *Policy and Politics*. London: Macmillan.

MARSHALL, T. H. (1950). *Citizenship and Social Class*. Cambridge: Cambridge University Press.

MARTIN, C. (1996). 'The Impact of Equal Opportunities Policies on the Day-to-Day Experiences of Women Police Constables'. *British Journal of Criminology*, 36/4: 510–28.

MARTIN, H.-P., and SCHUMANN, H. (1997). *The Global Trap*. London: Zed Books.

MARTIN, J. P., and WILSON, G. (1969). *The Police: A Study in Manpower*. London: Heinemann.

MARTINSON, R., LIPTON, D., and WILKS, J. (1974). 'What Works? Questions and Answers about Prison Reform'. *Public Interest*, 35/1: 22–54.

MARX, G. (1988). *Undercover: Police Surveillance in America*. Berkeley, CA: University of California Press.

MARX, G. (1992). 'When the Guards Guard Themselves: Undercover Tactics Turned Inwards'. *Policing and Society*, 2/3: 151–72.

MASSING, M. (1998). 'The Blue Revolution', *New York Review of Books*, 19 November: 32–6.

MATZA, D. (1969). *Becoming Deviant*. New Jersey: Prentice Hall.

MAWBY, R. C. (1998*a*). 'Policing the Image'. *Criminal Justice Matters*, 32: 26–7.

MAWBY, R. C. (1998*b*). 'Managing the Image', in G. Berry, J. Izat, R. Mawby, L. Walley, and A. Wright (eds.), *Practical Police Management* (2nd edn). London: Police Review Publishing Group.

MAWBY, R. C. (1998*c*). 'The Changing Image of Policing in Television Drama 1956–96'. *Journal of the Police History Society*, 13: 39–44.

MAWBY, R. C. (1999). 'Visibility, Transparency, and Police–Media Relations'. *Policing and Society*, 9/3: 263–86.

MAWBY, R. I. (1979). *Policing the City*. Farnborough: Gower.

MAWBY, R. I. (1991). *Comparative Policing Issues*. London: Unwin.

MAWBY, R. I. (ed.) (1999). *Policing across the World: Issues for the Twenty-first Century*. London: UCL Press.

MAWBY, R. I., and BATTA, I. D. (1980). *Asians and Crime*. London: National Association for Asian Youth.

MAYHEW, P., and MIRRLEES-BLACK, C. (1993). *The 1992 British Crime Survey*. London: Home Office. Research Study 132.

MAZOWER, M. (ed.) (1997). *The Policing of Politics in the Twentieth Century*. Providence, RI: Berghahn Books.

MEYER, M. (1980). 'Police Shootings at Minorities: The Case of Los Angeles'. *The Annals*, 452 (November).

MEYERS, R. (1981). *TV Detectives.* San Diego, CA: Barnes.

MEYERS, R. (1989). *Murder on the Air.* New York: The Mysterious Press.

MICHAEL, D. (1997). 'The Private Police – Who Are They?'. Paper presented to the British Criminology Conference, Queen's University, Belfast, July.

MICHAEL, D. (1999). 'The Levels of Orientation Security Officers Have towards a Public Policing Function'. *Security Journal*, 12/4: 33–42.

MIDWINTER, E. (1968). *Law and Order in Early Victorian Lancashire.* York: St Anthony's Press.

MILIBAND, R. (1978). 'A State of Desubordination'. *British Journal of Sociology*, 29/4.

MILLER, D. A. (1981). 'The Novel and the Police'. *Glyph*, 8. (Reprinted in G. Most and W. Stowe (eds.), *The Poetics of Murder.* New York: Harcourt, Brace, Jovanovitch, 1983).

MILLER, W. (1999). *Cops and Bobbies* (2nd edn). Columbus, OH: Ohio State University Press.

MINTO, G. (1965). *The Thin Blue Line.* London: Hodder & Stoughton.

MIRRLEES-BLACK, C., and BUDD, T. (1997). *Policing and the Public: Findings from the 1996 British Crime Survey.* London: Home Office Research, Development and Statistics Directorate. Research Findings 60.

MITCHELL, B. (1984). 'The Role of the Public in Criminal Detection'. *Criminal Law Review*, August.

MIYAZAWA, S. (1992). *Policing in Japan: A Study in Making Crime.* Albany, NY: State University of New York Press.

MONKKONEN, E. (1981). *Police in Urban America 1860–1920.* Cambridge: Cambridge University Press.

MOORE, B., Jr. (1967). *The Social Origins of Dictatorship and Democracy.* London: Penguin/Boston, MA: Beacon.

MOORE, C., and BROWN, J. (1981). *Community versus Crime.* London: Bedford Square Press.

MOORE, M. (1992). 'Problem-Solving and Community Policing', in M. Tonry and N. Morris (eds.), *Modern Policing.* Chicago: Chicago University Press.

MOORE, M., and KELLING, G. (1983). '"To Serve and Protect': Learning from Police History'. *Public Interest*, 70 (winter):265–81.

MORGAN, J. (1987). *Conflict and Order: The Police and Labour Disputes in England and Wales 1900–1939.* Oxford: Oxford University Press.

MORGAN, R. (1989). 'Policing By Consent: Legitimating the Doctrine', in R. Morgan and D. Smith (eds.), *Coming to Terms with Policing.* London: Routledge.

MORGAN, R. (1992). 'Talking About Policing', in D. Downes (ed.), *Unravelling Criminal Justice.* London: Macmillan.

MORGAN, R. (1997). 'Imprisonment', in R. Maguire, R. Morgan, and R. Reiner (eds.), *The Oxford Handbook of Criminology* (2nd edn). Oxford: Oxford University Press.

MORGAN, R. (2000). 'The Utilitarian Justification of Torture'. *Punishment and Society*, 2/2: 181–96.

MORGAN, R., and MAGGS, C. (1984). *Following Scarman'.* Bath: Bath University. Social Policy Papers.

MORGAN, R., and MAGGS, C. (1985). *Setting the PACE.* Bath: Bath University. Social Policy Papers.

MORGAN, R., and NEWBURN, T. (1997). *The Future of Policing.* Oxford: Oxford University Press.

MORGAN, R., REINER, R., and McKENZIE, I.

(1990). *Police Powers and Policy: A Study of Custody Officers*. Final Report to the Economic and Social Research Council.

MORGAN, R., and SMITH, D. (eds.) (1989). *Coming to Terms with Policing*. London: Routledge.

MORGAN, R., and SWIFT, P. (1987). 'The Future of Police Authorities: Members' Views'. *Public Administration*, 65/3: 259–77.

MORRIS, A. (1987). *Women, Crime and Criminal Justice*. Oxford: Blackwell.

MORRIS, P., and HEAL, K. (1981). *Crime Control and the Police*. London: Home Office Research Unit.

MORRIS, T. (1985). 'The Case for a Riot Squad'. *New Society*, 29 November.

MORRISON, C. (1984). 'Why PC Plod Should Come off the Beat'. *The Guardian*, 30 July: 8.

MOST, G., and STOWE, W. (eds.) (1983). *The Poetics of Murder*. New York: Harcourt, Brace, Jovanovich.

MOXON, D. (1998). 'The Role of Sentencing Policy', in C. Nuttall, P. Goldblatt, and C. Lewis (eds.), *Reducing Offending*. London: Home Office. Home Office Research Study 187.

MUIR, K. W., JR. (1977). *Police: Streetcorner Politicians*. Chicago: Chicago University Press.

MULLIN, C. (1989). *Error of Judgement: The Truth about the Birmingham Bombings*. London: Chatto & Windus.

MURDOCK, G. (1982). 'Disorderly Images', in C. Sumner (ed.), *Crime, Justice and the Mass Media*. Cambridge: Institute of Criminology. Cropwood Papers 14.

MURJI, K. (1998). *Policing Drugs*. Aldershot: Ashgate.

NELKEN, D. (1997). 'White-Collar Crime', in M. Maguire, R. Morgan, and R. Reiner (eds.), *The Oxford Handbook of Crimin-ology* (2nd edn). Oxford: Oxford University Press.

NEOCLEOUS, M. (1998). 'Policing and Pin-Making: Adam Smith, Police and the State of Prosperity'. *Policing and Society*, 8/4: 425–49.

NEOCLEOUS, M. (2000), *The Fabrication of Social Order: A Critical Theory of Police Power*. London: Pluto Press.

NEWBURN, T. (1992). *Permissiveness and Regulation*. London: Routledge.

NEWBURN, T. (1997). 'Youth, Crime and Justice', in M. Maguire, R. Morgan, and R. Reiner (eds.), *The Oxford Handbook of Criminology* (2nd edn). Oxford: Oxford University Press.

NEWBURN, T. (1999). *Understanding and Preventing Police Corruption: Lessons from the Literature*, London: Home Office Policing and Reducing Crime Unit.

NEWBURN, T., BROWN, D., CRISP, D., and DEWHURST, P. (1991). 'Increasing Public Order'. *Policing*, 7/1.

NEWBURN, T., and JONES, T. (1996). 'Police Accountability', in W. Saulsbury, J. Mott, and T. Newburn (eds.), *Themes in Contemporary Policing*. London: Police Foundation/Policy Studies Institute.

NEWMAN, G. F. (1983). *Law and Order*. London: Granada.

NEWMAN, G. F. (1982). *Operation Bad Apple*. London: Methuen.

NIEDERHOFFER, A. (1967). *Behind the Shield*. New York: Doubleday.

NIEDERHOFFER, A., and BLUMBERG, A. (eds.) (1976). *The Ambivalent Force* (2nd edn). Hinsdale, IL: Dryden Press.

NOBLES, R., and SCHIFF, D. (2000). *Understanding Miscarriages of Justice*. Oxford: Oxford University Press.

NORRIS, C. (1989). 'Avoiding Trouble: The Police Officer's Perception of Encounters with the Public', in M. Weatheritt (ed),

Police Research: Some Future Prospects. Aldershot: Avebury.

NORRIS, C., and ARMSTRONG, G. (1999). *The Maximum Surveillance Society: The Rise of CCTV.* West Sussex: Berg.

NORRIS, C., and DUNNIGHAN, C. (2000). 'Subterranean Blues: Conflict as an Unintended Consequence of the Police Use of Informers'. *Policing and Society,* 9/4: 385–412.

NORRIS, C., FIELDING, N., KEMP, C., and FIELDING, J. (1992). 'Black and Blue: An Analysis of the Influence of Race on Being Stopped by the Police'. *British Journal of Sociology,* 43/3: 207–24.

NORRIS, C., and NORRIS, N. (1993). 'Defining Good Policing: The Instrumental and Moral in Approaches to Good Practice and Competence'. *Policing and Society,* 3/3: 205–22.

NORTHAM, G. (1988). *Shooting in the Dark.* London: Faber and Faber.

NUTTALL, C., GOLDBLATT, P., and LEWIS, C. (eds.) (1998). *Reducing Offending.* London: Home Office. Home Office Research Study 187.

OAKLEY, R. (1989). *Employment in Police Forces: A Survey of Police Forces.* London: Commission for Racial Equality.

OAKS, D. (1970). 'Studying the Exclusionary Rule in Search and Seizure'. *University of Chicago Law Review,* 37 (summer).

OLIVER, I. (1997). *Police, Government and Accountability* (2nd edn). London: Macmillan.

O'MALLEY, P., and PALMER, D. (1996). 'Post-Keynesian Policing'. *Economy and Society,* 25/2: 137–55.

OPERATIONAL POLICING REVIEW (1990). Joint Consultative Committee of the Police Staff Associations. Surbiton, Surrey: The Police Federation.

OSBORNE, D., and GAEBLER, T. (1992).

Reinventing Government. New York: Addison-Wesley.

OUSBY, I. (1976). *Bloodhounds of Heaven.* Cambridge, MA: Harvard University Press.

OUSBY, I. (1997). *The Crime and Mystery Book.* London: Thames and Hudson.

PACKER, H. (1968). *The Limits of the Criminal Sanction.* Stanford, CA: Stanford University Press and Oxford University Press.

PAINTER, K., Lea, J., Woodhouse, T., and Young, J. (1989). *Hammersmith and Fulham Crime and Police Survey 1988.* Enfield, Middx.: Middlesex University Centre for Criminology.

PALEY, R. (1989). 'An Imperfect, Inadequate and Wretched System'?: Policing London before Peel'. *Criminal Justice History,* 10: 95–130.

PALMER, J. (1976). 'Evils Merely Prohibited'. *British Journal of Law and Society,* 3/1 (summer).

PALMER, J. (1978). *Thrillers.* London: Edward Arnold.

PALMER, S. H. (1988). *Police and Protest in England and Ireland 1780–1850.* Cambridge: Cambridge University Press.

PANDIANI, J. (1978). 'Crime Time TV: If All We Knew Is What We Saw'. *Contemporary Crises,* 2: 437–58.

PANITCH, L., and LEYS, C. (eds.) (1999). *Global Capitalism Versus Democracy: Socialist Register 1999.* Rendlesham, Suffolk: Merlin Press.

PARISH, J. R., and PITTS, M. (1990*a*). *The Great Cop Pictures.* Metuchen, NJ: Scarecrow.

PARISH, J. R., and PITTS, M. (1990*b*). *The Great Detective Pictures.* Metuchen, NJ: Scarecrow.

PARK, W. (1978). 'The Police State'. *Journal of Popular Film,* 6/3: 229–38.

PASQUINO, P. (1991). 'Theatrum Politicum: The Genealogy of Capital – Police and the State of Prosperity', in G. Burchell, C. Gordon, and P. Miller (eds.), *The Foucault Effect: Studies in Governmentality*. Hemel Hempstead: Harvester Wheatsheaf. (Originally in *Ideology and Consciousness*, 4/1 (1978): 41–54.)

PATTEN, C. (1999). *A New Beginning: Policing Northern Ireland.* The Report of the Independent Commission on Policing for Northern Ireland. Norwich: HMSO Copyright Unit.

PAWSON, R., and TILLEY, N. (1994). 'What Works in Evaluation Research?'. *British Journal of Criminology*, 34/2: 291–306.

PEARSON, G. (1983). *Hooligan*. London: Macmillan.

PEARSON, G., SAMPSON, A., BLAGG, H., STUBBS, P., and SMITH, D. (1989). 'Policing Racism', in R. Morgan and D. Smith (eds.), *Coming to Terms with Policing*. London: Routledge.

PEASE, K. (1997). 'Crime Prevention', in M. Maguire, R. Morgan, and R. Reiner (eds.), *The Oxford Handbook of Criminology* (2nd edn). Oxford: Oxford University Press.

PERCY, A. (1998). *Ethnicity and Victimisation: Findings from the 1996 British Crime Survey*. London: Home Office. Home Office Statistical Bulletin 6/98.

PETROW, S. (1993). 'The Rise of the Detective in London, 1869–1914'. *Criminal Justice History*, 14: 91–108.

PHILIPS, C. (1982). 'Politics in the Making of the English Police', in *The Home Office*. London: Royal Institute of Public Administration (RIPA).

PHILIPS, D. (1977). *Crime and Authority in Victorian England*. London: Croom Helm.

PHILIPS, D. (1980). 'A New Engine of Power and Authority: The Institutionalisation of Law Enforcement in England 1780–1830', in V. Gatrell, B. Lenman, and G. Parker (eds.), *Crime and the Law*. London: Europa.

PHILIPS, D. (1983). 'A Just Measure of Crime, Authority, Hunters and Blue Locusts: The 'Revisionist' Social History of Crime and the Law in Britain 1780–1850', in S. Cohen and A. Scull (eds.), *Social Control and the State*. Oxford: Martin Robertson.

PHILIPS, D., and STORCH, R. (1999). *Policing Provincial England, 1829–1856*. Leicester: Leicester University Press.

PHILLIPS, C., and BROWN, D. (1998). *Entry into the Criminal Justice System: A Survey of Police Arrests and Their Outcomes*. London: Home Office. Home Office Research Study 185.

PIKE, M. (1985). *The Principles of Policing*. London: Macmillan.

PILIAVIN, I., and BRIAR, S. (1964). 'Police Encounters with Juveniles'. *American Journal of Sociology*, 70: 206–14. (Reprinted in Reiner 1996a, ii.)

POLANYI, K. (1944). *The Great Transformation*. Boston, MA: Beacon.

POLICE FOUNDATION/POLICY STUDIES INSTITUTE (1996). *The Role and Responsibilities of the Police: Report of an Independent Inquiry*. London: Police Foundation/ Policy Studies Institute.

POLICY STUDIES INSTITUTE (1983). *Police and People in London*; i, D. J. Smith, *A Survey of Londoners*; ii, S. Small, *A Group of Young Black People*; iii, D. J. Smith, *A Survey of Police Officers*; iv, D. J. Smith and J. Gray, *The Police in Action*. London: Policy Studies Institute.

PORTER, B. (1987). *The Origins of the Vigilante State*. London: Macmillan.

PORTER, D. (1981). *The Pursuit of Crime*. New Haven: Yale University Press.

POSEN, I. (1995). *Review of Police Core and Ancillary Tasks*. London: HMSO.

POTTER, C. B. (1998). *War on Crime: Bandits, G-Men, and the Politics of Mass Culture.* New Brunswick, NJ: Rutgers University Press.

POWER, A., and TUNSTALL, R. (1997). *Dangerous Disorder: Riots and Violent Disturbances in Thirteen Areas of Britain, 1991–2.* York: Joseph Rowntree Foundation.

POWERS, R. G. (1983). *GMen: Hoover's FBI in American Popular Culture.* Carbondale, IL: Southern Illinois University Press.

POWERS, S. P., ROTHMAN, D. J., and ROTHMAN, S. (1996). *Hollywood's America: Social and Political Themes in Motion Pictures.* Boulder, CO: Westview.

POWIS, D. (1977). *The Signs of Crime.* London: McGraw-Hill.

PRINCE, M. (1988). *God's Cop: The Biography of James Anderton.* London: Frederick Muller.

PUNCH, M. (1979*a*). *Policing the Inner City.* London: Macmillan.

PUNCH, M. (1979*b*). 'The Secret Social Service', in S. Holdaway (ed.). *The British Police.* London: Edward Arnold.

PUNCH, M. (ed.) (1983). *Control in the Police Organisation.* Cambridge, MA: MIT Press.

PUNCH, M, (1985). *Conduct Unbecoming: The Social Construction of Police Deviance and Control.* London: Tavistock.

PUNCH, M., and NAYLOR, T. (1973). 'The Police: A Social Service', *New Society,* 24: 358–61. (Reprinted in Reiner 1996*a*, i.)

RADZINOWICZ, L. (1948–86). *A History of the English Criminal Law and its Administration from 1750,* 5 vols. i: *The Movement for Reform* (1948); ii: *The Clash between Private Initiative and Public Interest in the Enforcement of the Law* (1956); iii: *Cross-Currents in the Movement for Reform of the Police* (1956); iv: *Grappling for Control* (1968); v: Radzinowicz, L., and Hood R.,

The Emergence of Penal Policy in Victorian and Edwardian England (1986). London: Stevens.

RAFTER, N. (2000). *Shots in the Mirror: Crime Films and Society.* New York: Oxford University Press.

RAWLINGS, P. (1991). 'Creeping Privatisation? The Police, the Conservative Government and Policing in the Late 1980s', in R. Reiner and M. Cross (eds.), *Beyond Law and Order: Criminal Justice Policy and Politics into the 1990s.* London: Macmillan.

RAWLINGS, P. (1995). 'The Idea of Policing: A History'. *Policing and Society,* 5/2: 129–49.

RAWLINGS, P. (1999). *Crime and Power: A History of Criminal Justice 1688–1998.* London: Longman.

REGAN, D. (1983). *Are the Police under Control?.* London: Social Affairs Unit. Research Reports Paper I.

REIMAN, J. (1997). *The Rich Get Rich and the Poor Get Prison: Ideology, Class and Criminal Justice.* Needham Heights, MD: Allyn and Bacon.

REINER, R. (1978). *The Blue-Coated Worker.* Cambridge: Cambridge University Press.

REINER, R. (1980). 'Fuzzy Thoughts: The Police and Law and Order Politics'. *Sociological Review,* 28/2 (March): 377–413. (Reprinted in Reiner 1996*a*, ii.)

REINER, R. (1981*a*). 'The Politics of Police Power', in *Politics and Power 4: Law, Politics and Justice.* London: Routledge.

REINER, R. (1981*b*). 'Keystone to Kojak: The Hollywood Cop', in P. Davies and B. Neve (eds.), *Politics, Society and Cinema in America.* Manchester: Manchester University Press.

REINER, R. (1984). 'Is Britain Turning into a Police State?'. *New Society,* 2 August.

REINER, R. (1988). 'British Criminology and the State'. *British Journal of Criminology*, 29/1: 138–58. (Reprinted in P. Rock (ed.), *The History of British Criminology*. Oxford: Oxford University Press, 1988.)

REINER, R. (1989a). 'Race and Criminal Justice'. *New Community*, 16/1: 5–22.

REINER, R. (1989b). 'The Politics of Police Research', in M. Weatheritt (ed), *Police Research: Some Future Prospects*. Aldershot: Avebury.

REINER, R. (1991). *Chief Constables*. Oxford: Oxford University Press.

REINER, R. (1992a). 'Police Research in the United Kingdom: A Critical Review', in N. Morris and M. Tonry (eds.), *Modern Policing*. Chicago: Chicago University Press.

REINER, R. (1992b). 'Policing a Postmodern Society'. *Modern Law Review*, 55/6: 761–81.

REINER, R. (1993). 'Race, Crime and Justice: Models of Interpretation', in L. Gelsthorpe and W. McWilliams (eds.), *Minority Ethnic Groups and the Criminal Justice System*. Cambridge: University of Cambridge Institute of Criminology.

REINER, R. (1994). 'The Dialectics of Dixon: The Changing Image of the TV Cop', in M. Stephens and S. Becker (eds.), Police Force, Police Service'. London: Macmillan.

REINER, R. (ed.) (1996a). *Policing*, i. *Cops, Crime and Control: Analysing the Police Function*; ii. *Controlling the Controllers: Police Discretion and Accountability*. Aldershot: Dartmouth.

REINER, R. (1996b). 'Have the Police Got a Future?', in C. Critcher and D. Waddington (eds.), *Policing Public Order*. Aldershot: Avebury.

REINER, R. (1996c). 'The Case of the Missing Crimes', in R. Levitas and W. Guy (eds.), *Interpreting Official Statistics*. London: Routledge.

REINER, R. (1997a). 'Media Made Criminality', in M. Maguire, R. Morgan, and R. Reiner (eds.), *The Oxford Handbook of Criminology* (2nd edn). Oxford: Oxford University Press.

REINER, R. (1997b). 'Policing and the Police', in M. Maguire, R. Morgan, and R. Reiner (eds.), *The Oxford Handbook of Criminology* (2nd edn). Oxford: Oxford University Press.

REINER, R. (1998). 'Process or Product? Problems of Assessing Individual Police Performance', in J.-P. Brodeur (ed.), *How to Recognise Good Policing*. Thousand Oaks, CA: Sage.

REINER, R. (1999). 'Order and Discipline', in I. Holliday, A. Gamble, and G. Parry (eds.), *Fundamentals in British Politics*. London: Macmillan.

REINER, R. (2000a). 'Police Research', in R. King and E. Wincup (eds.), *Doing Research on Crime and Justice*. Oxford: Oxford University Press.

REINER, R. (2000b). 'Crime and Control in Britain', *Sociology*, 34/1: 71–94.

REINER, R., and CROSS, M. (eds.) (1991). *Beyond Law and Order: Criminal Justice Policy and Politics into the 1990s*. London: Macmillan.

REINER, R., and LEIGH, L. (1992). 'Police Power', in G. Chambers and C. McCrudden (eds.), *Individual Rights in the UK since 1945*. Oxford: Oxford University Press/Law Society.

REINER, R., LIVINGSTONE, S., and ALLEN, J. (2000a). 'No More Happy Endings? The Media and Popular Concern about Crime since the Second World War', in T. Hope and R. Sparks (eds.), *Crime, Risk and Insecurity*. London: Routledge (forthcoming).

REINER, R., LIVINGSTONE, S., and ALLEN, J. (2000*b*). 'Casino Culture: The Media and Crime in a Winner–Loser Society', in K. Stenson and R. Sullivan (eds.), *Crime and Risk Society.* "Cullompton, Devon: Willan (forthcoming).

REINER, R., and SHAPLAND, J. (eds.) (1987). 'Why Police? Special Issue on Policing in Britain'. *British Journal of Criminology*, 27/1.

REINER, R., and SPENCER, S. (eds.) (1993). *Accountable Policing: Effectiveness, Empowerment and Equity.* London: Institute for Public Policy Research.

REISS, A. J., Jr. (1968). 'Police Brutality'. *Transaction*, 5. (Reprinted in R. Lundman (ed.), *Police Behaviour.* New York: Oxford University Press, 1980.)

REISS, A. J., Jr. (1971). *The Police and the Public.* New Haven: Yale University Press.

REITH, C. (1938). *The Police Idea.* Oxford: Oxford University Press.

REITH, C. (1940). *Police Principles and the Problem of War.* Oxford: Oxford University Press.

REITH, C. (1943). *British Police and the Democratic Ideal.* Oxford: Oxford University Press.

REITH, C. (1948). *A Short History of the Police.* Oxford: Oxford University Press.

REITH, C. (1952). *The Blind Eye of History.* London: Faber and Faber.

REITH, C. (1956). *A New Study of Police History.* London: Oliver & Boyd.

REYNOLDS, E. A. (1998). *Before the Bobbies.* London: Macmillan.

REYNOLDS, G., and Judge, A. (1968). *The Night the Police Went on Strike.* London: Weidenfeld.

ROBERTS, B. (1982). 'The Debate on 'Sus'', in E. Cashmore and B. Troyna (eds.), *Black Youth in Crisis.* London: Allen & Unwin.

ROBERTS, D. (1984). 'Taperecording the Questioning of Suspects'. *Criminal Law Review*, September.

ROBERTS, R. (1973). *The Classic Slum.* London: Penguin.

ROBINSON, C. (1978). 'The Deradicalisation of the Policeman'. *Crime and Delinquency*, 24/2: 129–51. (Reprinted in Reiner 1996*a*, ii.)

ROBINSON, C. (1979). 'Ideology as History'. *Police Studies*, 2/2 (summer): 35–49. (Reprinted in Reiner 1996*a*, i.)

ROBINSON, C., and SCAGLION, R. (1987). 'The Origins and Evolution of the Police Function in Society: Notes Towards A Theory'. *Law and Society Review*, 21/l: 109–53.

ROBINSON, C., SCAGLION, R., and OLIVERO, J. M. (1994). *Police in Contradiction: The Evolution of the Police Function in Society.* Westport, CT: Greenwood.

ROCK, P. (1973). 'News as Eternal Recurrence', in S. Cohen and J. Young (eds.), *The Manufacture of News.* London: Constable.

ROCK, P. (1977). 'Law, Order and Power in Late Seventeenth and Early Eighteenth-century England'. *International Annals of Criminology*, 16. (Reprinted in S. Cohen and A. Scull (eds.), *Social Control and the State.* Oxford: Martin Robertson, 1983.)

ROLPH, C. H. (ed.) (1962). *The Police and the Public.* London: Heinemann.

ROSE, D. (1992). *A Climate of Fear: The Murder of PC Blakelock and the Case of the Tottenham Three.* London: Bloomsbury.

ROSE, D. (1996). *In the Name of the Law: The Collapse of Criminal Justice.* London: Jonathan Cape.

ROSE, N. (1996). 'The Death of the Social? Refiguring the Territory of Government'. *Economy and Society*, 25/3: 321–56.

ROSE, N. (2000). 'Government and Control'.

British Journal of Criminology, 40/2: 321–39.

ROSENBAUM, D. (ed.) (1994). *The Challenge of Community Policing: Testing the Promise*. Thousand Oaks, CA: Sage.

ROSHIER, R. (1973). 'The Selection of Crime News by the Press', in S. Cohen and J. Young (eds.), *The Manufacture of News*. London: Constable.

ROSHIER, R. (1989). *Controlling Crime*. Milton Keynes: Open University Press.

ROSOW, E. (1978). *Born to Lose*. New York: Oxford University Press.

ROYAL COMMISSION ON CRIMINAL JUSTICE (1993). *Report*. London: HMSO. Cm. 2263.

ROYAL COMMISSION ON CRIMINAL PROCEDURE (1981). *Report and Law and Procedure*. London: HMSO. Cmnd 8092.

ROYAL COMMISSION on the POLICE (1962). *Final Report*. London: HMSO. Cmnd 1728.

RUBIN, M. (1999). *Thrillers*. Cambridge: Cambridge University Press.

RUBINSTEIN, J. (1973). *City Police*. New York: Ballantine.

RUCHELMAN, L. (1974). *Police Politics*. Cambridge, MA: Ballinger.

RUDE, G. (1964). *The Crowd in History*. New York: Wiley.

RUDE, G. (1970). *Paris and London in the 18th Century*. London: Collins.

RUEHLMAN, W. (1974). *Saint with a Gun*. New York: New York University Press.

ST. JOHNSTON, E. (1978). *One Policeman's Story*. Chichester: Barry Rose.

SACCO, V. F. (1995). 'Media Constructions of Crime'. *Annals of the American Academy of Political and Social Science*, 539: 141–54.

SANDERS, A. (1988). 'Rights, Remedies and the Police and Criminal Evidence Act'. *Criminal Law Review*, 802–12.

SANDERS, A. (1997). 'From Suspect to Trial', in M. Maguire, R. Morgan, and R. Reiner (eds.), *The Oxford Handbook of Criminology* (2nd edn). Oxford: Oxford University Press.

SANDERS, A., and Bridges, L. (1990). 'Access to Legal Advice and Police Malpractice'. *Criminal Law Review*, 494–509.

SANDERS, A., and YOUNG, R. (1994). *Criminal Justice*. London: Butterworth.

SANDERS, W. (1977). *Detective Work*. Glencoe, MN: Free Press.

SAULSBURY, W., and BOWLING, B. (1991). *The Multi-Agency Approach in Practice: The North Plaistow Racial Harassment Project*. London: Home Office. Home Office Research Study 64.

SAULSBURY, W., MOTT, J., and NEWBURN, T. (eds.) (1996). *Themes in Contemporary Policing*. London: Police Foundation/Policy Studies Institute.

SAVAGE, S. (1984). 'Political Control or Community Liaison?'. *Political Quarterly*, 55/1 (January–March): 48–59.

SAVAGE, S. (1998). 'The Shape of the Future'. *Criminal Justice Matters*, 32: 4–6.

SAVAGE, S., and CHARMAN, S. (1996). 'Managing Change', in F. Leishman, B. Loveday, and S. Savage (eds.), *Core Issues in Policing*. London: Longman.

SAVAGE, S., and WILSON, C. (1987). 'Ask a Policeman: Community Consultations in Practice'. *Social Policy and Administration*, 21/3.

SAVAGE, S., CHARMAN, S., and COPE, S. (1996). 'Police Governance: The Association of Chief Police Officers and Constitutional Change'. *Public Policy and Administration*, 11/2: 92–106.

SAYERS, D. L. (ed.) (1928). *Tales of Detection*. London: Everyman.

SCARMAN, LORD (1981). *The Scarman Report: The Brixton Disorders*. London: HMSO. Cmnd 8427. (Reprinted London: Penguin, 1982.)

SCHLESINGER, P., and TUMBER, H. (1992). 'Crime and Criminal Justice in the Media', in D. Downes (ed.), *Unravelling Criminal Justice*. London: Macmillan.

SCHLESINGER, P., and TUMBER, H. (1993). 'Fighting the War Against Crime: Television, Police and Audience'. *British Journal of Criminology*, 33/1: 19–32.

SCHLESINGER, P., and TUMBER, H. (1994). *Reporting Crime*. Oxford: Oxford University Press.

SCHLESINGER, P., TUMBER, H., and MURDOCK, G. (1991). 'The Media Politics of Crime and Criminal Justice'. *British Journal of Sociology*, 442/3: 397–420.

SCHWARTZ, R. D., and MILLER, J. C. (1964). 'Legal Evolution and Societal Complexity'. *American Journal of Sociology*, 70/1: 159–69.

SCRATON, P. (1985). *The State of the Police*. London: Pluto.

SCRATON, P. (ed.) (1987). *Law, Order and the Authoritarian State*. Milton Keynes: Open University Press.

SCRIPTURE, A. (1997). 'The Sources of Police Culture: Demographic or Environmental Variables?'. *Policing and Society*, 7/3: 163–76.

SHADOIAN, J. (1977). *Dreams and Dead Ends*. Cambridge, MA: MIT Press.

SHAPLAND, J., and HOBBS, D. (1989). 'Policing on the Ground', in R. Morgan and D. Smith (eds.), *Coming to Terms with Policing*. London: Routledge.

SHAPLAND, J., and VAGG, J. (1987). 'Using the Police'. *British Journal of Criminology* 27/1: 54–63. (Reprinted in Reiner 1996a, i.)

SHAPLAND, J., and VAGG, J. (1988). *Policing by the Public*. London: Routledge.

SHAW, M., and WILLIAMSON, W. (1972). 'Public Attitudes to the Police'. *Criminologist*, 7/26.

SHEARING, C. (1981a). 'Subterranean Processes in the Maintenance of Power'. *Canadian Review of Sociology and Anthropology*, 18/3: 283–98.

SHEARING, C. (ed.) (1981b). *Organisational Police Deviance*. Toronto: Butterworth.

SHEARING, C. (1981c). 'Deviance and Conformity in the Reproduction of Order', in C. Shearing (ed.), *Organisational Police Deviance*. Toronto: Butterworth.

SHEARING, C. (1992). 'The Relation between Public and Private Policing', in M. Tonry and N. Morris (eds.), *Modern Policing*. Chicago: Chicago University Press.

SHEARING, C. (1996). 'Reinventing Policing: Policing as Governance', in O. Marenin (ed.), *Policing Change, Changing Police*. New York: Garland.

SHEARING, C., and ERICSON, R. (1991). 'Culture As Figurative Action'. *British Journal of Sociology*, 42/4: 481–506.

SHEARING, C., and LEON, J. (1978). 'Reconsidering the Police Role: A Challenge to a Challenge of a Popular Conception'. *Canadian Journal of Criminology and Corrections*, 19.

SHEARING, C., and STENNING, P. (1983). Private Security: Implications for Social Control'. *Social Problems*, 30/5: 493–506. (Reprinted in Reiner 1996a, i.)

SHEARING, C., and STENNING, P. (eds.) (1987). *Private Policing*. Beverly Hills, CA: Sage.

SHEEHY, P. (1993). *Report of the Inquiry into Police Responsibilities and Rewards*, 2 vols. London: HMSO. Cm. 2280.

SHEERMAN, B. (1991). 'What Labour Wants'. *Policing*, 7/3: 194–203.

SHEPTYCKI, J. (1991). 'Innovations in the Policing of Domestic Violence in London, England'. *Policing and Society*, 2/2: 117–37.

SHEPTYCKI, J. (1993). *Innovations in Policing Domestic Violence*. Aldershot: Avebury.

SHEPTYCKI, J. (1995). 'Transnational Policing and the Makings of a Postmodern State'. *British Journal of Criminology*, 35/4: 613–35.

SHEPTYCKI, J. (1997). 'Insecurity, Risk Suppression, and Segregation: Some Reflections on Policing in the Transnational Age'. *Theoretical Criminology*, 1/3: 303–15.

SHEPTYCKI, J. (1998a). 'Policing, Postmodernism and Transnationalisation'. *British Journal of Criminology*, 38/3: 485–503.

SHEPTYCKI, J. (1998b). 'The Global Cops Cometh'. *British Journal of Sociology*, 49/1: 57–74.

SHEPTYCKI, J. (ed.) (2000a). *Issues in Transnational Policing*. London: Routledge.

SHEPTYCKI, J. (2000b). 'Surveillance, Closed Circuit Television and Social Control'. *Policing and Society*, 9/4: 429–34.

SHEPTYCKI, J. (2000c). 'Policing and Human Rights: An Introduction'. *Policing and Society*, 10/1: 1–10.

SHERMAN, L. (1978). *Scandal and Reform: Controlling Police Corruption*. Berkeley, CA: University of California Press.

SHERMAN, L. (1980). 'Causes of Police Behaviour: The Current State of Quantitative Research'. *Journal of Research in Crime and Delinquency*, 17/1: 69–99. (Reprinted in Reiner 1996a, ii.)

SHERMAN, L. (1983). 'After the Riots: Police and Minorities in the US 1970–1980', in N. Glazer and K. Young (eds.), *Ethnic Pluralism and Public Policy*. London: Heinemann.

SHERMAN, L. (1992a). 'Attacking Crime: Police and Crime Control', in M. Tonry and N. Morris (eds.), *Modern Policing*. Chicago: Chicago University Press.

SHERMAN, L. (1992b). *Policing Domestic Violence*. New York: Free Press.

SHERMAN, L. (1993). 'Why Crime Control Is Not Reactionary', in D. Weisburd, C. Uchida, and L. Green (eds.), *Police Innovation and Control of Police*. New York: Springer-Verlag.

SHERMAN, L., and BERK, R. (1984). 'The Specific Deterrent Effects of Arrest for Domestic Assault'. *American Sociological Review*, 49 (April): 261–72.

SHERMAN, L., MILTON, C., and KELLEY, T. (1983). *Team Policing*. Washington, DC: Police Foundation.

SHERR, A. (1989). *Freedom of Protest, Public Order and the Law*. Oxford: Basil Blackwell.

SICHEL, J. (1978). *Women on Patrol*. Washington, DC: US Department of Justice.

SIEGHART, P. (1985). 'Sanctions against Abuse of Police Powers'. *Public Law*, autumn.

SILBERMAN, C. (1978). *Criminal Violence, Criminal Justice*. New York: Vintage.

SILVER, A. (1967). 'The Demand for Order in Civil Society', in D. Bordua (ed.), *The Police*. New York: Wiley.

SILVER, A. (1971). 'Social and Ideological Bases of British Elite Reactions to Domestic Crises 1829–1832', *Politics and Society*, 1 (February).

SILVERMAN, E. (1999). *NYPD Battles Crime: Innovative Strategies in Policing*. Boston, MA: Northeastern University Press.

SIM, J. (1982). 'Scarman: The Police Counterattack', in *Socialist Register 1982*. London: Merlin.

SKOGAN, W. (1990a). *The Police and Public in England and Wales: A British Crime Survey Report*. London: HMSO.

SKOGAN, W. (1990b). *Disorder and Decline*. New York: Free Press.

SKOGAN, W. (1994). *Contacts between Police and Public: Findings from the 1992 British*

Crime Survey. London: HMSO. Home Office Research Study 134.

SKOGAN, W. (1996). 'Public Opinion and the Police', in W. Saulsbury, J. Mott, and T. Newburn (eds.), *Themes in Contemporary Policing*. London: Policy Studies Institute/ Police Foundation.

SKOGAN, W., and HARTNETT, S. (1997). *Community Policing, Chicago Style*. New York: Oxford University Press.

SKOLNICK, J. (1966). *Justice without Trial*. New York: Wiley.

SKOLNICK, J. (1969). *The Politics of Protest*. New York: Bantam.

SKOLNICK, J. (1972). 'Changing Conceptions of the Police', in *Great Ideas Today*. Chicago: Encyclopaedia Britannica.

SKOLNICK, J., and BAYLEY, D. B. (1986). *The New Blue Line*. New York: Free Press.

SKOLNICK, J., and BAYLEY, D. B. (1988). *Community Policing: Issues and Practices around the World*. Washington, DC: National Institute of Justice.

SKOLNICK, J., and FYFE, J. (1993). *Above the Law: Police and the Excessive Use of Force*. New York: Free Press.

SLAPPER, G., and TOMBS, S. (1999). *Corporate Crime*. London: Longman.

SMITH, A. T. H. (1987). *Offences against Public Order*. London: Sweet & Maxwell.

SMITH, D. A., and KLEIN, J. R. (1984). 'Police Control of Interpersonal Disputes'. *Social Problems*, 31/4 (April).

SMITH, D. A., and VISHER, C. A. (1981). 'Streetlevel Justice: Situational Determinants of Police Arrest Decisions'. *Social Problems*, 29/2 (December).

SMITH, D. J. (1997). 'Ethnic Origins, Crime, and Criminal Justice', in M. Maguire, R. Morgan, and R. Reiner (eds.), *The Oxford Handbook of Criminology* (2nd edn). Oxford: Oxford University Press.

SMITH, G. (1997a). *Police Crime: A Consti-* *tutional Perspective*. Ph.D. thesis. London: University College.

SMITH, G. (1997b). 'The DPP and Prosecutions of Police Officers'. *New Law Journal*, 147/6804: 1180.

SMITH, G. (1999). 'Double Trouble'. *New Law Journal*, 149/6900: 1223.

SMITH, G. (2000). 'Managing Police Misconduct: Reform of the Discipline Process and Unresolved Accountability Issues'. Paper presented to European Group for the Study of Deviance and Social Control Conference, University of Wales, Bangor, 25–27 April.

SMITH, P. THURMOND. (1985). *Policing Victorian London*. Westport, CT: Greenwood Press.

SOUTH, N. (1988). *Policing for Profit*. London: Sage.

SOUTH, N. (1997a). 'Control, Crime and 'End of Century' Criminology', in P. Francis, P. Davies, and V. Jupp, (eds.), *Policing Futures*. London: Macmillan.

SOUTH, N. (1997b). 'Drugs: Use, Crime, and Control', in M. Maguire, R. Morgan, and R. Reiner (eds.), *The Oxford Handbook of Criminology* (2nd edn). Oxford: Oxford University Press.

SOUTH, N. (2000). 'Late-Modern Tensions not Post-modern Transformations'. *Criminal Justice Matters*, 38: 5–6.

SOUTHGATE, P. (1982). *Police Probationer Training in Race Relations*. London: Home Office Research Unit.

SOUTHGATE, P. (ed.) (1988). *New Directions in Police Training*. London: HMSO.

SOUTHGATE, P., and EKBLOM, P. (1984). *Contacts between Police and Public*. London: Home Office Research Unit.

SOUTHGATE, P., and EKBLOM, P. (1986). *Police–Public Encounters*. London: HMSO. Home Office Research Study 90.

SPARKS, R. (1992). *Television and the Drama*

of Crime. Milton Keynes: Open University Press.

SPARKS, R. (1993). 'Inspector Morse', in G. Brandt (ed.), *British Television Drama in the 1980s.* Cambridge: Cambridge University Press.

SPARKS, R. (1997). 'Recent Social Theory and the Study of Crime and Punishment', in M. Maguire, R. Morgan, and R. Reiner (eds.), *The Oxford Handbook of Criminology* (2nd edn). Oxford: Oxford University Press.

SPARKS, R., GENN, H., and DODD, D. (1977). *Surveying Victims.* London: Wiley.

SPITZER, S. (1987). 'Security and Control in Capitalist Societies: The Fetishism of Security and the Secret Thereof', in J. Lowman, R. J. Menzies, and T. S. Palys (eds.), *Transcarceration: Essays in the Theory of Social Control.* Aldershot: Gower.

SPITZER, S., and SCULL, A. (1977*a*). 'Privatisation and Social Control'. *Social Problems*, 25.

SPITZER, S., and SCULL, A. (1977*b*). 'Social Control in Historical Perspective', in D. Greenberg (ed.), *Corrections and Punishment.* Beverly Hills, CA: Sage.

SQUIRES, P. (1998). 'Cops and Customers?: Consumerism and the Demand for Police Services'. *Policing and Society*, 8/2: 169–88.

SQUIRES, P. (2000*a*). 'Firearms and Policing: Driven to It?'. *Criminal Justice Matters*, 38: 18–19.

SQUIRES, P. (2000*b*). *Gun Culture or Gun Control? Firearms, Violence and Social Order*, London: Routledge (forthcoming).

STALKER, J. (1988). *Stalker.* London: Harrap.

STALLION, M., and WALL, D. (1999). *The British Police: Police Forces and Chief Officers 1829–2000.* Bramshill, Hants: Police History Society.

STANKO, E. (1984). *Intimate Intrusions.* London: Routledge.

STEAD, P. (ed.) (1977). *Pioneers in Policing.* Montclair, NJ: Patterson Smith.

STEAD, P. (1985). *The Police of Britain.* New York: Macmillan.

STEEDMAN, C. (1984). *Policing the Victorian Community.* London: Routledge.

STEER, D. (1980). *Uncovering Crime.* London: HMSO. Royal Commission on Criminal Procedure Research Study 7.

STENNING, P. (ed.) (1995). *Accountability in Criminal Justice.* Toronto: University of Toronto Press.

STENNING, P., and Shearing, C. (1984). 'Corporate Justice'. *Australian and New Zealand Journal of Criminology*, 17 (June).

STENSON, K. (1993). 'Community Policing as a Governmental Technology'. *Economy and Society*, 22/3: 373–89.

STENSON, K. (2000). 'Someday Our Prince Will Come: Zero Tolerance Policing and Liberal Government', in T. Hope and R. Sparks (eds.), *Crime, Risk and Insecurity.* London: Routledge (forthcoming).

STENSON, K., and SULLIVAN, R. (eds.) (2000). *Crime in Risk Society.* Cullompton, Devon: Willan (forthcoming).

STEPHENS, M. (1988). *Policing: The Critical Issues.* Hemel Hempstead: Wheatsheaf.

STEPHENS, M., and BECKER, S. (1994). *Police Force, Police Service.* London: Macmillan.

STEVENS, P., and WILLIS, C. (1979). *Race, Crime and Arrests.* London: Home Office Research Unit.

STEVENS, P., and WILLIS, C. (1981). *Ethnic Minorities and Complaints against the Police.* London: Home Office Research Unit.

STEVENSON, J. (1977). 'Social Control and the Prevention of Riots in England 1789–1829', in A. P. Donajgrodski (ed.), *Social Control in Nineteenth-Century Britain.* London: Croom Helm.

STEVENSON, J., and COOK, C. (1977). *The Slump.* London: Jonathan Cape.

STINCHCOMBE, A. (1963). 'Institutions of Privacy in the Determination of Police Administrative Practice'. *American Journal of Sociology*, 69/2: 150–60. (Reprinted in Reiner 1996a, ii.)

STODDARD, E. R. (1968). 'The Informal Code of Police Deviancy: A Group Approach to Bluecoat Crime'. *Journal of Criminal Law, Criminology, and Police Science*, 59/2: 201–13.

STORCH, R. (1975). 'The Plague of Blue Locusts: Police Reform and Popular Resistance in Northern England 1840–57'. *International Review of Social History*, 20: 61–90.

STORCH, R. (1976). 'The Policeman as Domestic Missionary'. *Journal of Social History*, 9/4 (summer): 481–509. (Reprinted in Reiner 1996a, ii.)

STORCH, R. (1989). 'Policing Rural Southern England before the Police: Opinion and Practice 1830–1856', in D. Hay and F. Snyder (eds.), *Policing and Prosecution in Britain 1750–1850*. Oxford: Oxford University Press.

STYLES, J. (1977). 'Criminal Records'. *Historical Journal*, 20/4.

STYLES, J. (l982). 'An 18thcentury Magistrate as Detective'. *Bradford Antiquary* new series, 47.

STYLES, J. (1983). 'Sir John Fielding and the Problem of Criminal Investigation in 18thcentury England'. *Transactions of the Royal Historical Society*, 33.

STYLES, J. (1987). 'The Emergence of the Police: Explaining Police Reform in Eighteenth- and Nineteenth-Century England'. *British Journal of Criminology* 27/1: 15–22.

SULLIVAN, R. (1998). 'The Politics of British Policing in the Thatcher/Major State'. *Howard Journal of Criminal Justice*, 37/3: 306–18.

SUMNER, C. (ed.). (1982a). *Crime, Justice and the Mass Media*. Cambridge: Institute of Criminology. Cropwood Papers 14.

SUMNER, C. (1982b). "Political Hooliganism' and 'Rampaging Rioters': The National Press Coverage of the Toxteth 'Riots", in C. Sumner (ed.), *Crime, Justice and the Mass Media*. Cambridge: Institute of Criminology. Cropwood Papers 14.

SUMNER, C. (1997). 'Social Control: The History and Politics of a Central Concept in Anglo-American Sociology', in R. Bergalli and C. Sumner (eds.), *Social Control and Political Order*. London: Sage.

SUMSER, J. (1996). *Morality and Social Order in Television Crime Drama*. Jefferson, NC: McFarland.

SURETTE, R. (1998). *Media, Crime and Criminal Justice* (2nd edn). Belmont, CA: Wadsworth.

SYKES, R., and CLARK, J. (1975). 'A Theory of Deference Exchange in Police–Civilian Encounters'. *American Journal of Sociology*, 81: 584–600.

SYKES, R., FOX, J., and CLARK, J. (1976). 'A Sociolegal Theory of Police Discretion', in A. Niederhoffer and A. Blumberg (eds.), *The Ambivalent Force* (2nd edn). Hinsdale, IL: Dryden Press.

SYMONS, J. (1972). *Bloody Murder*. London: Penguin.

TAKAGI, P. (1974). 'A Garrison State in 'Democratic' Society'. *Crime and Social Justice*, spring–summer.

TARLING, R. (1988). *Police Work and Manpower Allocation*. London: Home Office. Research and Planning Unit Paper 47.

TARLING, R., and BURROWS, J. (1985). 'The Work of Detectives', in K. Heal, R. Tarling, and J. Burrows (eds.), *Policing Today*. London: HMSO.

TAYLOR, D. (1997). *The New Police in Nineteenth-Century England: Crime, Conflict and Control*. Manchester: Manchester University Press.

TAYLOR, D. (1998). *Crime, Policing and Punishment in England, 1750–1914*. London: Macmillan.

TAYLOR, H. (1998a). 'The Politics of the Rising Crime Statistics of England and Wales 1914–1960'. *Crime, History and Societies*, 2/1: 5–28.

TAYLOR, H. (1998b). 'Rising Crime: The Political Economy of Criminal Statistics since the 1850s'. *Economic History Review*, 51: 569–90.

TAYLOR, H. (1999). 'Forging the Job: A Crisis of 'Modernisation' or Redundancy for the Police in England and Wales 1900–39'. *British Journal of Criminology*, 39/1: 113–35.

TAYLOR, I. (1980). 'The Law and Order Issue in the British General Election and Canadian Federal Election of 1979'. *Canadian Journal of Sociology*, 5/3 (summer).

TAYLOR, I. (1981). *Law and Order: Arguments for Socialism*. London: Macmillan.

TAYLOR, I. (1996). 'Fear of Crime, Urban Fortunes and Suburban Social Movements'. *Sociology*, 30/3: 317–37.

TAYLOR, I. (1997a). 'Crime, Anxiety and Locality: Responding to the 'Condition of England' Question at the End of the Century'. *Theoretical Criminology*, 1/1: 53–76.

TAYLOR, I. (1997b). 'The Political Economy of Crime', in M. Maguire, R. Morgan, and R. Reiner (eds.), *The Oxford Handbook of Criminology* (2nd edn). Oxford: Oxford University Press.

TAYLOR, I. (1998a). 'Crime, Market-Liberalism and the European Idea', in V. Ruggiero, N. South, and I. Taylor (eds.), *The New European Criminology*. London: Routledge.

TAYLOR, I. (1998b). 'Free Markets and the Cost of Crime: An Audit for England and Wales', in P. Walton and J. Young (eds.), *The New Criminology Revisited*. London: Macmillan.

TAYLOR, I. (1999). *Crime in Context: A Critical Criminology of Market Societies*. Cambridge: Polity Press.

TAYLOR, L. (1984). *In the Underworld*. Oxford: Basil Blackwell.

TAYLOR, P. (1983). 'How Hendon Police Cadets are Wooed away from Racialism'. *Police*, August.

TEMKIN, J. (1987). *Rape and the Legal Process*. London: Sweet & Maxwell.

THOMAS, T. (1988). 'The Police and Criminal Evidence Act 1984: The Social Work Role'. *Howard Journal of Criminal Justice*, 27/4.

THOMAS, T. (1994). *The Police and Social Workers*. Aldershot: Arena.

THOMPSON, E. P. (1968). *The Making of the English Working Class*. London: Penguin.

THOMPSON, E. P. (1971). 'The Moral Economy of the English Crowd'. *Past and Present*, 50.

THOMPSON, E. P. (1975). *Whigs and Hunters*. London: Penguin.

THOMPSON, E. P. (1980). *Writing by Candlelight*. London: Merlin.

THOMPSON, E. P. (1992). *Customs in Common*. London: Merlin.

TIERNEY, J. (1989). 'Graduating in Criminal Justice'. *Policing* 5/3.

TILLEY, N. (1993). *After Kirkholt: Theory, Methods and Results of Replication Evaluations*. London: Home Office. Crime Prevention Unit Paper 47.

TOBIAS, J. (1967). *Crime and Society in the Nineteenth Century*. London: Penguin.

TROJANOWICZ, R., and BUCQUEROUX, B. (1990). *Community Policing*. Cincinnati: Anderson Publishing Co.

TUCK, M. (1989). *Drinking and Disorder: A Study of Non-Metropolitan Violence*. London: HMSO. Home Office Research and Planning Unit Study 108.

TUCK, M., and SOUTHGATE, P. (1981). *Ethnic

Minorities, Crime and Policing. London: Home Office Research Unit.

TULLETT, T. (1981). *Murder Squad.* London: Granada.

TUMBER, H. (1982). *Television and the Riots.* London: British Film Institute.

TUPMAN, B., and TUPMAN, A. (1999). *Policing in Europe: Uniformity in Diversity.* Exeter: Intellect Books.

TURK, A. (1982*a*). *Political Criminality.* Beverly Hills, CA: Sage.

TURK, A. (1982*b*). 'Policing in Political Context', in R. Donelan (ed.), *The Maintenance of Order in Society.* Ottawa: Canadian Police College.

TUSKA, J. (1978). *The Detective in Hollywood.* New York: Doubleday.

UGLOW, S. (1988). *Policing Liberal Society.* Oxford: Oxford University Press.

VAN MAANEN, J. (1973). 'Observations on the Making of Policemen'. *Human Organisation,* 32.

VAN MAANEN, J. (1974). 'Working the Street', in H. Jacob (ed.), *The Potential for Reform of Criminal Justice.* Beverly Hills, CA: Sage.

VAN MAANEN, J. (1978). 'Watching the Watchers', in P. K. Manning and J. Van Maanen (eds.), *Policing.* Santa Monica, CA: Goodyear.

VAN MAANEN, J. (1983). 'The Boss', in M. Punch (ed.), *Control in the Police Organization.* Cambridge, MA: MIT Press.

VENNARD, J. (1984). 'Disputes within Trials over the Admissibility and Accuracy of Incriminating Statements'. *Criminal Law Review,*

VICK, C. (1981). 'Police Pessimism', in D. Pope and N. Weiner (eds.), *Modern Policing.* London: Croom Helm.

VOGLER, R. (1991). *Reading the Riot Act.* Milton Keynes: Open University Press.

WADDINGTON, D. (1992). *Contemporary Issues in Public Disorder.* London: Routledge.

WADDINGTON, D., JONES, K., and CRITCHER, C. (1989). *Flashpoints: Studies in Public Disorder.* London: Routledge.

WADDINGTON, P. A. J. (1982*a*). 'Why the 'Opinionmakers' No Longer Support the Police'. *Police,* December.

WADDINGTON, P. A. J. (1982*b*). 'Conservatism, Dogmatism ad Authoritarianism in the Police: A Comment'. *Sociology,* November: 592–4.

WADDINGTON, P. A. J. (1983*a*). 'Beware the Community Trap'. *Police,* March: 34.

WADDINGTON, P. A. J.(1983*b*). *Are the Police Fair?.* London: Social Affairs Unit. Research Paper 2.

WADDINGTON, P. A. J. (1984*a*). 'Black Crime, the 'Racist' Police and Fashionable Compassion', in D. Anderson (ed.), *The Kindness that Kills.* London: Society for Promoting Christian Knowledge.

WADDINGTON, P. A. J. (1984*b*). 'The Role of the Police Committee: Constitutional Arrangements and Social Realities'. *Local Government Studies,* September–October: 27–49.

WADDINGTON, P. A. J. (1986*a*). *The Effects of Manpower Depletion during the NUM Strike 1984–5.* London: Police Foundation.

WADDINGTON, P. A. J. (1986*b*). 'Mugging as a Moral Panic: A Question of Proportion'. *British Journal of Sociology,* 2/2: 245–59.

WADDINGTON, P. A. J. (1987). 'Towards Paramilitarism: Dilemmas in Policing Civil Disorder'. *British Journal of Criminology,* 27/1: 37–46. (Reprinted in Reiner 1996*a*, i.)

WADDINGTON, P. A. J. (1991). *The Strong Arm of the Law.* Oxford, Oxford University Press.

WADDINGTON, P. A. J. (1993a). *Calling the Police.* Aldershot: Avebury.

WADDINGTON, P. A. J. (1993b). "The Case Against Paramilitary Policing' Considered'. *British Journal of Criminology,* 33/3: 14–16.

WADDINGTON, P. A. J. (1994). *Liberty and Order: Public Order Policing in a Capital City.* London: UCL Press.

WADDINGTON, P. A. J. (1999a). *Policing Citizens.* London: UCL Press.

WADDINGTON, P. A. J. (1999b). 'Police (Canteen). Sub-Culture: An Appreciation'. *British Journal of Criminology,* 39/2: 286–308.

WADDINGTON, P. A. J., and BRADDOCK, Q. (1991). "Guardians' or 'Bullies'?: Perceptions of the Police amongst Adolescent Black, White and Asian Boys'. *Policing and Society,* 2/1: 31–45.

WALDEN, J. (1982). *Visions of Order.* Toronto: Butterworth.

WALKER, C., and STARMER, K. (eds.) (1999). *Miscarriages of Justice* (2nd edn). London: Blackstone.

WALKER, M. (1992). 'Do We Need a Clear Up Rate?'. *Policing and Society* 2/4.

WALKER, M. (1995). *Interpreting Crime Statistics.* Oxford: Oxford University Press.

WALKER, N. (1993). 'The International Dimension', in R. Reiner and S. Spencer (eds.), *Accountable Policing: Effectiveness, Empowerment and Equity.* London: Institute for Public Policy Research.

WALKER, N. (1996). 'Defining Core Police Tasks: The Neglect of the Symbolic Dimension'. *Policing and Society,* 6/1: 53–71.

WALKER, S. (1977). *A Critical History of Police Reform.* Lexington, MA: D. C. Heath.

WALKER, S. (1980). *Popular Justice.* New York: Oxford University Press.

WALKER, S. (1983). *Police in America.* New York: McGraw-Hill.

WALKER, S. (1993). *Taming the System: The Control of Discretion in Criminal Justice 1950–1990.* New York: Oxford University Press.

WALKLATE, S. (1992). 'Jack and Jill Join Up at Sun Hill: Public Images of Police Officers'. *Policing and Society,* 2/3: 219–32.

WALKLATE, S. (1996). 'Equal Opportunities and the Future of Policing', in F. Leishman, B. Loveday, and Savage, S. (eds.), *Core Issues in Policing.* London: Longman.

WALKLATE, S. (1997). 'Risk and Criminal Victimisation: A Modernist Dilemma'. *British Journal of Criminology,* 37/1: 35–46.

WALKLATE, S. (1998). 'Excavating the Fear of Crime'. *Theoretical Criminology,* 2/4: 403–18.

WALKLATE, S. (2000). 'Reflections on 'New Labour' or 'Back to the Future'?'. *Criminal Justice Matters,* 38: 7–8.

WALKLATE, S., and EVANS, K. (1999). *Zero Tolerance or Community Tolerance? Managing Crime in High Crime Areas.* Aldershot: Ashgate.

WALL, D. (1997). 'Policing the Virtual Community: The Internet, Cyberspace and Cybercrime', in P. Francis, P. Davies, and V. Jupp (eds.), *Policing Futures.* London: Macmillan.

WALL, D. (1998). *The Chief Constables of England and Wales.* Aldershot: Avebury.

WALSH, J. L. (1977). 'Career Styles and Police Behaviour', in D. H. Bayley (ed.), *Police and Society.* Beverly Hills, CA: Sage.

WAMBAUGH, J. (1971). *The New Centurions.* London: Sphere/New York: Dell.

WAMBAUGH, J. (1973). *The Blue Knight.* London: Sphere/New York: Dell.

WAMBAUGH, J. (1973). *The Onion Field.* London: Sphere/New York: Dell.

WAMBAUGH, J. (1976). *The Choir-Boys.* London: Futura/New York: Dell.

WARD, T. (1986). *Death and Disorder.* London: Inquest.

WATERS, I. (1996). 'Quality of Service: Politics or Paradigm Shift?', in F. Leishman, B. Loveday, and S. Savage (eds.), *Core Issues in Policing.* London: Longman.

WATSON, C. (1971). *Snobbery with Violence.* London: Eyre & Spottiswoode.

WATTS-MILLER, W. (1987). 'Party Politics, Class Interest and Reform of the Police 1829–56'. *Police Studies,* 10/1: 42–60. (Reprinted in Reiner 1996*a*, i.)

WEATHERITT, M. (1983). 'Community Policing: Does it Work and How Do We Know? A Review of Research', in T. Bennett (ed.), *The Future of Policing.* Cambridge: Institute of Criminology. Cropwood Papers 15.

WEATHERITT, M. (1986). *Innovations in Policing.* London: Croom Helm.

WEATHERITT, M. (ed.) (1989). *Police Research: Some Future Prospects.* Aldershot: Avebury.

WEATHERITT, M. (1993). 'Measuring Police Performance: Accounting or Accountability?', in R. Reiner and S. Spencer (eds.), *Accountable Policing: Empowerment, Effectiveness and Equity.* London: Institute for Public Policy Research.

WEATHERITT, M. (ed.) (1998). *Zero Tolerance.* London: Police Foundation.

WEAVER, M. (1994). 'The New Science of Policing: Crime and the Birmingham Police Force, 1839–1842'. *Albion,* 26: 289–308.

WEBB, J. (1959). *The Badge: The Inside Story of the Los Angeles Police Department.* London: W. H. Allen/New York: Prentice-Hall.

WEBER, M. (1964). *The Theory of Social and Economic Organization.* Glencoe, MN: Free Press. Originally translated 1947.

WEINBERGER, B. (1981). 'The Police and the Public in Mid19thcentury Warwickshire', in V. Bailey (ed.), *Policing and Punishment in 19thCentury Britain.* London: Croom Helm.

WEINBERGER, B. (1991). *Keeping the Peace? Policing Strikes in Britain 1906–1926.* Oxford: Berg.

WEINBERGER, B. (1995). *The Best Police in the World.* London: Scolar Press.

WEINBERGER, B., and REINKE, H. (1991). 'A Diminishing Function? A Comparative Historical Account of Policing in the City'. *Policing and Society,* 1/3.

WEINER, A. (1973). 'Crime Wave: The TV Cops'. *New Society,* 12 December.

WEISBURD, D., UCHIDA, C., and GREEN, L. (eds.) (1993). *Police Innovation and Control of Police.* New York: Springer-Verlag.

WELLS, R. (1991). 'Implementation and Non-Implementation of the 1839–40 Policing Acts in East and West Sussex'. *Policing and Society* 1/4.

WERTHMAN, C., and PILIAVIN, I. (1967). 'Gang Members and the Police', in D. Bordua (ed.), *The Police.* New York: Wiley.

WESTLEY, W. (1970). *Violence and the Police.* Cambridge, MA: MIT Press.

WHITAKER, B. (1964). *The Police.* London: Penguin.

WHITAKER, B. (1979). *The Police in Society.* London: Eyre Methuen.

WHITE, J. (1986). *The Worst Street in North London.* London: Routledge.

WILBANKS, W. (1987). *The Myth of a Racist Criminal Justice System.* Monterey, CA: Brooks/Cole.

WILLIAMS, P., and DICKINSON, J. (1993). 'Fear of Crime: Read All About It? The Relationship between Newspaper Crime

Reporting and Fear of Crime'. *British Journal of Criminology*, 33/1: 33–56.

WILLIAMSON, T. (1996). 'Police Investigation: The Changing Criminal Justice Context', in F. Leishman, B. Loveday, and S. Savage (eds.), *Core Issues in Policing*. London: Longman.

WILLIAMSON, T., and MOSTON, S. (1990). 'The Extent of Silence in Police Interviews', in S. Greer and R. Morgan (eds.), *The Right to Silence Debate*. Bristol: Bristol University Centre for Criminal Justice.

WILLIS, C. (1983). *The Use, Effectiveness and Impact of Police Stop and Search Powers*. London: Home Office Research Unit.

WILLIS, C., MACLEOD, J., and NAISH, P. (1988). *The Tape-Recording of Police Interviews with Suspects*. London: HMSO. Home Office Research Study 97.

WILSON, C. (1993). 'Police', in W. Outhwaite, T. Bottomore, E. Gellner, R. Nisbet, and A. Touraine (eds.), *The Blackwell Dictionary of Twentieth-Century Social Thought*. Oxford: Blackwell.

WILSON, C. P. (2000). *Cop Knowledge: Police Power and Cultural Narrative in Twentieth Century America*. Chicago: Chicago University Press.

WILSON, I. (1981). 'Political Awareness in Policing', in D. Pope and N. Weiner (eds.), *Modern Policing*. London: Croom Helm.

WILSON, J. Q. (1968). *Varieties of Police Behavior*. Cambridge, MA: Harvard University Press.

WILSON, J. Q. (1975). *Thinking about Crime*. New York: Vintage.

WILSON, J. Q., and BOLAND, B. (1978). 'The Effects of the Police on Crime'. *Law and Society Review*, 12/3: 367–90.

WILSON, J. Q., and BOLAND, B. (1981). 'The Effects of the Police on Crime: A Response to Jacob and Rich'. *Law and Society Review*, 16/1.

WILSON, J. Q., and KELLING, G. (1982). 'Broken Windows'. *Atlantic Monthly*, March: 29–38. (Reprinted in Reiner 1996a, i.)

WINICK, C. (ed.) (1978). *Deviance and Mass Media*. Beverly Hills, CA: Sage.

WITT, R., CLARKE, A., and FIELDING, N. (1999). 'Crime and Economic Activity: A Panel Data Approach'. *British Journal of Criminology*, 39/3: 391–401.

WOFFINDEN, B. (1989). *Miscarriages of Justice*. London: Coronet.

WOODCOCK, J. (1991). 'Overturning Police Culture'. *Policing*, 7/3: 172–82.

WOOLF, LORD JUSTICE (1991). *Prison Disturbances April 1990*. London: HMSO. Cmnd. 1456.

WREN–LEWIS, J. (1981–2). 'TV Coverage of the Riots'. *Screen Education*, 40 (autumn–winter): 15–33.

WRIGHT, M. (1982). *Making Good*. London: Burnett.

YEO, H., and BUDD, T. (2000). *Policing and the Public: Findings from the 1988 British Crime Survey*. London: Home Office Research, Development and Statistics Directorate. Research Findings 113.

YOUNG, J. (1971). 'The Role of the Police as Amplifiers of Deviancy', in S. Cohen (ed.), *Images of Deviance*. London: Penguin.

YOUNG, J. (1994). *Policing the Streets: Stop and Search in North London*. Enfield, Middx.: Middlesex University Centre for Criminology.

YOUNG, J. (1997). 'Left Realist Criminology', in M. Maguire, R. Morgan, and R. Reiner (eds.), *The Oxford Handbook of Criminology* (2nd edn). Oxford: Oxford University Press.

YOUNG, J. (1998). 'From Inclusive to Exclusive Society: Nightmares in the European Dream', in V. Ruggiero,

N. South, and I. Taylor (eds.), *The New European Criminology*. London: Routledge.

YOUNG, J. (1999). *The Exclusive Society*. London: Sage.

YOUNG, M. (1991). *An Inside Job: Policing and Police Culture in Britain*. Oxford: Oxford University Press.

YOUNG, M. (1993). *In the Sticks: An Anthropologist in a Shire Force*. Oxford: Oxford University Press.

YOUNG, M. (1995). 'Black Humour – Making Light of Death'. *Policing and Society*, 5/2: 151–68.

ZANDER, M. (1974). 'Are Too Many Professional Criminals Avoiding Conviction?: A Study of Britain's Two Busiest Courts'. *Modern Law Review*, 37.

ZANDER, M. (1979). 'The Investigation of Crime: A Study of Cases Tried at the Old Bailey'. *Criminal Law Review*, 203–19.

ZANDER, M. (1982). 'Police Powers'. *Political Quarterly*, 53/2 (April–June): 128–43.

ZANDER, M. (1995). *The Police and Criminal Evidence Act 1984* (3rd edn). London: Sweet & Maxwell.

ZANDER, M., and HENDERSON, P. (1993). *Crown Court Study*. London: HMSO. Royal Commission on Criminal Justice Research Study 19.

ZEDNER, L. (1993). 'Social Control', in W. Outhwaite, T. Bottomore, E. Gellner, R. Nisbet, and A. Touraine (eds.), *The Blackwell Dictionary of Twentieth-Century Social Thought*. Oxford: Blackwell.

ZEDNER, L. (1997). 'Victims', in M. Maguire, R. Morgan, and R. Reiner (eds.), *The Oxford Handbook of Criminology* (2nd edn). Oxford: Oxford University Press.

ZUCKERMAN, A. A. S. (1987). 'Illegally Obtained Evidence: Discretion as a Guardian of Legitimacy', in *Current Legal Problems 1987*. London: Stevens.

INDEX